Legal Rights

The Amherst Series in Law, Jurisprudence, and Social Thought

Each work included in The Amherst Series in Law, Jurisprudence, and Social Thought explores a theme crucial to an understanding of law as it confronts the changing social and intellectual currents of the late twentieth century.

Legal Rights

Historical and Philosophical Perspectives

Edited by Austin Sarat and
Thomas R. Kearns

Ann Arbor
THE UNIVERSITY OF MICHIGAN PRESS

Copyright © by the University of Michigan 1996
All rights reserved
Published in the United States of America by
The University of Michigan Press
Manufactured in the United States of America
⊚ Printed on acid-free paper

1999   1998   1997   1996   4   3   2   1

A CIP catalog record for this book is available from the British Library.

Library of Congress Cataloging-in-Publication Data

Legal rights : historical and philosophical perspectives / edited by
   Austin Sarat and Thomas R. Kearns.
      p.   cm. — (The Amherst series in law, jurisprudence, and
social thought)
   Includes bibliographical references and index.
   ISBN 0-472-10633-3 (hc : alk. paper)
   1. Civil rights—History.   2. Civil rights—Philosophy.   3. Human
rights—History.   4. Human rights—Philosophy.   I. Sarat, Austin.
II. Kearns, Thomas R.   III. Series.
JC571.L378 1995
340'.112—dc20   95-34539
                                             CIP

Contents

Part 1. Imagining Rights and the Rights Tradition

**Part 2. The Foundations of Rights or Rights
without Foundations**

Acknowledgments

Legal Rights: Philosophical and Historical Perspectives seeks to combine two disciplinary traditions—philosophy and history—that are often kept apart. It does so to illuminate a familiar subject in jurisprudence and, in so doing, to claim it as an object for interdisciplinary legal study of the kind fostered in Amherst College's Department of Law, Jurisprudence, and Social Thought. The essays collected in this volume were first presented at a conference entitled "The Paradoxes of Rights," which was held at Amherst in November 1992. We are grateful to the participants in that conference and to the Keck and Arthur Vining Davis foundations as well as the Massachusetts Foundation for the Humanities for their financial support.

Editorial Introduction

Austin Sarat and Thomas R. Kearns

The language and practices of legal rights have, for a long time, had particular resonance in this culture, and never more so than today.[1] Recently, that language and those practices have been internationalized, and the idea of rights now enjoys nearly universal appeal.[2] Yet despite its current prominence, neither the meaning nor the significance of legal rights is well understood. Because of this, the subject of rights compels attention; sooner or later, every discussion of law in contemporary society seems to turn to the subject of rights.[3]

In *Legal Rights: Historical and Philosophical Perspectives,* we take up that subject.[4] We seek to advance understanding by bringing together two genres of scholarship on rights—the historical and the philosophical—that are usually kept apart. While many volumes have been written exploring the moral or epistemological groundings of legal rights,[5] or arguing about the place of rights in American

1. See Lawrence Friedman, *Total Justice* (New York: Russell Sage Foundation, 1985), 5: "There has developed in this country what I call a *general expectation of justice, and a general expectation of recompense for injuries and loss.* Together, these make up a demand for what will be called 'total justice' " (emphasis in the original).

2. See Abdullahi Ahmed An-Na'im, ed., *Human Rights in Cross-Cultural Perspective: A Quest for Consensus* (Philadelphia: University of Pennsylvania Press, 1992).

3. Alexis de Tocqueville, *Democracy in America,* vol. 1, trans. Francis Bowen (Boston: John Allyn, 1876), 311. But as Marry Ann Glendon claims, "law-talk in Tocqueville's day was not nearly so saturated with rights talk as it has been since the end of World War II" (*Rights Talk: The Impoverishment of Political Discourse* [New York: The Free Press, 1991], 3).

4. This is a volume in the Amherst Series in Law, Jurisprudence, and Social Thought. Previous volumes include *The Fate of Law, Law's Violence, Law in Everyday Life, The Rhetoric of Law,* and *Identities, Politics, and Rights.*

5. For examples, see L. W. Summer, *The Moral Foundation of Rights* (Oxford: Clarendon Press, 1987), and Lloyd Weinreb, *Natural Law and Justice* (Cambridge: Harvard University Press, 1987).

history,[6] these two kinds of writings about rights typically have been pursued in isolation. As a result, rights scholarship has suffered from an unfortunate schizophrenia in which abstract, normative treatments of rights have been divorced from analyses of the way rights are shaped by, and emerge from, particular social and cultural contexts.[7]

Locating legal rights in history, and locating the history of rights in a broad philosophical context, represents, we believe, an important advance in scholarship; it resists both the impulse to take rights for granted and the impulse to treat them as self-evident.[8] Attending to the history of our subject reveals that the twentieth century is, in one sense, "the century of rights."[9] Or, as Louis Henkin puts it, "Ours is the age of rights."[10] During this century, the meaning and reach of traditionally recognized rights have been dramatically expanded;[11] new rights have been recognized;[12] and rights have been extended to previously marginalized groups.[13] Yet today, at the very time rights and rights talk seem to be thriving, criticism of rights has dramatically escalated. As Henkin notes, "The bill of particulars against the idea of

---

6. See Morton Horwitz, *The Transformation of American Law, 1870–1960: The Crisis of Legal Orthodoxy* (New York: Oxford University Press, 1992). Also Lawrence Friedman, *The Republic of Choice: Law, Authority, and Culture* (Cambridge: Harvard University Press, 1990).

7. See Paul Brest, "The Fundamental Rights Controversy: The Essential Contradictions of Normative Constitutional Scholarship," *Yale Law Journal* 90 (1981): 1063.

8. Louis Henkin, *The Age of Rights* (New York: Columbia University Press, 1990). Henkin argues, "To Americans the idea of individual rights seems axiomatic, a 'truth,' 'self-evident,' Jefferson said. In fact, we know, the idea is modern and its wide acceptance only contemporary, since the Second World War" (181).

9. "There is no more telling indicator of the extent to which legal notions have penetrated both popular and political discourse than our increasing tendency to speak of what is most important to us in terms of rights. . . . The high season of rights came upon the land only rather recently, propelled by, and itself promoting, a gradual evolution in the role of courts." See Glendon, *Rights Talk,* 4. Also Friedman, *The Republic of Choice,* 97.

10. Henkin, *The Age of Rights,* ix.

11. See David Kirp, "Proceduralism and Bureaucracy: Due Process in the School Setting," *Stanford Law Review* 28 (1976): 841.

12. See David Engel, "Law, Culture, and Children with Disabilities: Educational Rights and the Construction of Difference," *Duke Law Journal* (1991): 166.

13. As Lawrence Friedman argues, "more and more is heard about the rights of mental patients, the elderly, the young—just about everybody. . . . Special rights for the handicapped are the product of another recent and startling development" (*Total Justice* [New York: Russell Sage Foundation, 1985], 87–88).

rights is long and weighty."[14] At the very moment when nations and peoples around the world, from Argentina and Brazil to Russia and Eastern Europe, are embracing rights, here in the United States rights are under attack. At the very moment of their ascendancy, rights are subject to intense scrutiny.

This scrutiny has been prompted, in large part, by the development of postmodernism in legal scholarship.[15] Postmodern legal scholars have questioned the grounding or foundation of rights and have been skeptical about the coherence and integrity of rights talk and the legal rights that give rise to it.[16] Rights, so the skeptics contend, cannot escape history; they cannot be grounded successfully in a universalized, objective ethics.[17] This is the case because legal rights involve just another language game which, in particular historical contexts, assumes particular rhetorical force.[18] Yet whenever such language is invoked, whenever someone says, "I have a right to something," as Thomas Haskell notes,

> whether it is to exercise dominion over a possession, or enjoy equal employment opportunities, or express controversial opinions in public—I am not merely saying that I want to do it and hope others will let me; I am saying that they ought to let me, have a duty to let me, and will be guilty of an injustice, a transgression against established moral standards, if they fail to do so.[19]

---

14. Henkin, *The Age of Rights*, 182.

15. See, for example, Peter Fitzpatrick, ed., *Dangerous Supplements: Resistance and Renewal in Jurisprudence* (London: Pluto Press, 1991), and Gillian Rose, *The Dialectics of Nihilism: Post-Structuralism and Law* (New York: Basil Blackwell, 1984).

16. See C. B. Macpherson, "Natural Rights in Hobbes and Locke," in *Political Theory and the Rights of Men*, ed. D. Raphael (Bloomington: Indiana University Press, 1967). MacPherson claims that "Human rights can only be asserted as a species of natural right . . ." (14).

17. Mark Tushnet, "An Essay on Rights," *Texas Law Review* 62 (1984): 1363.

18. Stanley Fish, *Doing What Comes Naturally: Change, Rhetoric, and the Practice of Theory in Literary and Legal Studies* (Durham: Duke University Press, 1989), chap. 6.

19. Thomas Haskell, "The Curious Persistence of Rights Talk in the 'Age of Interpretation,'" *Journal of American History* 74 (1987), 984. Ronald Dworkin argues, "Individual rights are political trumps held by individuals. Individuals have rights when, for some reason, a collective goal is not a sufficient justification for denying them what they wish, as individuals, to have or to do, or not a sufficient justification for imposing some loss or injury upon them" (*Taking Rights Seriously* [Cambridge: Harvard University Press, 1977], xi). Also Jeremy Waldron, "A Right-Based Critique of Constitutional Rights," *Oxford Journal of Legal Studies* 13 (1993): 30.

The language of rights would seem to demand a grounding or foundation in something timeless and universal, something that establishes the transcultural and transhistorical basis of ethics and duty. Yet today, many criticize the search for the timeless, the universal, and the transcendent; at the same time, they seek to hold onto the language of rights.[20] Can they have it both ways? Can we have rights without foundations, and if so, at what price to rights themselves? As Jeremy Waldron argues,

> Talk of individual rights is often supposed to be a way of registering fairly basic objections to the arcane computations of the utilitarian calculus. . . . The theorist of rights . . . is supposed to be the one who can produce the trump card, the preemptory argument stopper. . . . The idea of rights has often been seized on precisely as a way of avoiding the casuistry of trade-offs and complex moral calculations. . . . The sad fact is, however, that this simplicity and moral certainty is simply unavailable. No one now believes that the truth about rights is self-evident or that, if two people disagree about rights, one of them at least must be either corrupt or morally blind.[21]

In addition to these philosophical criticisms of rights, the subject of rights raises difficult questions of historical interpretation. What are the historical sources of rights? When, and in what conditions, are new rights imagined, and through what struggles are they brought into being? Once brought into being, what are their limits? How can one reliably decide whether a rights claim can and should be honored?

These questions are, of course, not new. Contemporary criticism of rights echoes Marx's warning that "the so-called rights of man . . . are simply the rights of a member of civil society, that is, of egoistic man, of man separated from other men and from the community . . . of man regarded as an isolated monad, withdrawn into

---

20. See Martha Minow, "Interpreting Rights: An Essay for Robert Cover," *Yale Law Journal* 96 (1987): 1680.

21. See Waldron, "A Rights-Based Critique," 29. Also see Dworkin, *Taking Rights Seriously*, xiv: "It is no part of my theory that any mechanical procedure exists for demonstrating what political rights, either background or legal, a particular individual has. . . . [T]here are hard cases, both in politics and at law, in which reasonable lawyers will disagree about rights, and neither will have available any argument that must necessarily convince the other."

himself."[22] Alternatively, it draws on Burke's denigration of abstract, sterile theorizing about "natural" or "universal" rights.[23] Echoing perhaps Marx or Burke, contemporary critics insist that rights cannot transcend the history of their creation and the interests and contexts out of which they develop. They suggest that scholarly attention must be directed to particular rights claims in particular places at particular times.

Yet despite the trenchant and restless philosophical criticism of rights, rights talk persists, as Thomas Haskell has usefully reminded us.[24] Haskell argues that philosophical debates about the moral grounding of rights talk have little salience to the actual historical practice of legal rights. Skepticism about the objectivity or rational grounding of rights has not undermined their political significance. "Rights," Haskell argues,

> not only survive but flourish after more than a century of skepticism about their timelessness and universality. The plainest meaning of the paradoxical persistence of rights in an "age of interpretation" is that . . . neither rights nor the practice they authorize need foundations sunk deep into the heart of nature. This is evidently a set of practices so amply supported by the prevailing form of life that our inability to formulate an entirely satisfying theoretical justification for it has no bearing on its staying power.[25]

Rights, so it seems, can be many things at once. On the one hand, they speak in a universal, timeless language, yet on the other hand, they have, in every culture where rights are taken seriously, a

---

22. See Karl Marx, "On the Jewish Question," in *The Marx-Engels Reader,* ed. Robert Tucker (New York: Norton, 1972), 42.

23. Burke himself contrasted such rights with what he called the "real rights of men." Men, Burke argued,

> have a right to the fruits of their industry and to the means of making their industry fruitful. They have a right to the acquisitions of their parents, to the nourishment and improvement of their offspring, to instruction in life, and to consolation in death. Whatever each man can separately do, without trespassing upon others, he has a right to do for himself; and he has a right to a fair portion of all which society, with all its combinations of skill and force, can do in his favour.

See Edmund Burke, *Reflections on the Revolution in France,* ed. J. G. A. Pocock (Indianapolis: Hackett Publishing, 1987), 51.

24. Haskell, "The Curious Persistence."

25. Ibid., 29.

distinct and often distinctive history. Because they speak in a universal, timeless language, they are said to need grounding in an objective, transhistorical, moral vocabulary, yet rights persist at a time of deep skepticism about such moral claims. In the age of power/knowledge, they seem disposable, yet all the more indispensable.[26] More and more, we hear claims about the universality of rights, and yet the voices of local resistance grow stronger and more articulate. More and more, careful historical analysis can learn from well-argued philosophical inquiry, just as philosophers of legal rights can learn from historians. Nonetheless, in contemporary scholarship, they seldom are brought together.

It is the work of *Legal Rights: Historical and Philosophical Perspectives* to bridge that gap, to draw historical analysis and philosophical inquiry into productive dialogue and, in so doing, explore the many-sidedness of rights and rights talk. In this book we inquire into the history that gives rise to legal rights as well as the meaning of the rights that are generated. In the first part of this book, "Imagining Rights and the Rights Tradition," we explore the history of rights and rights talk and the distinctive ways new rights are imagined. The essays collected under this theme ask where new rights come from, and they alert us to the particularity and contingency of all rights talk.

The first of those essays, Annabel Patterson's "Very Good Memories: Self-Defense and the Imagination of Legal Rights in Early Modern England," examines two treason trials, the trial of Sir Nicholas Throckmorton in 1555 and the trial of John Lilburne approximately one hundred years later. Patterson analyzes those trials for what they tell us about the emergence of hitherto unrecognized rights. In both trials the defendants successfully argued in favor of the principle of jury nullification in a context where both were denied counsel and the right to call witnesses for the defense.

Patterson argues that the recognition of rights, like the right to counsel in the American Bill of Rights, depended on their articulation in earlier periods. Here, the universality of rights is grounded, paradoxically, in the particulars of history and context. Rights, which are claimed to be natural and unalienable, do not spring fully formed at

---

26. For an argument about the dispensability of rights and rights talk, see Michael Perry, "Taking Neither Rights-Talk nor the 'Critique of Rights' Too Seriously," *Texas Law Review* 62 (1984): 1405.

the conclusion of some philosophical argument or analysis; instead, they take a long time to be realized and instantiated.

Both the Throckmorton and Lilburne cases provide, for Patterson, vivid examples of the imagination of rights as people, in particular historical contexts, reason from the experience of felt injustice to articulate new principles of fairness. The rights tradition unfolds gradually as new rights are extrapolated from practices already present in the culture in which rights claimants find themselves. Imagination and cultural bricolage, rather than philosophical reflection, Patterson suggests, provide the key resources for the articulation and recognition of new rights.

Like Patterson, Morton J. Horwitz writes against what he sees as the stereotypical ways in which Americans usually invoke natural law in the rights tradition. He argues that, in the United States, appeals to natural law are not characterized by an ahistorical, abstract universalism. Indeed, Horwitz contends that reference here should be to multiple traditions since, he suggests, natural law has meant different things depending on the historical contexts in which it has been articulated. Horwitz juxtaposes the "communitarian, organicist, and hierarchical character of traditional natural law" against the "individualistic ideas of natural rights" found in seventeenth-century social contract theory. He shows how these ideas were skillfully intermixed with other notions of natural law and natural right by Jefferson. Yet he contends that, in spite of Jefferson's skill, "[f]or most of American legal history since 1798, the issue of higher law has been a marginal issue." When natural rights have been the subject of legal thought, discussion has usually turned on the question of what is "natural" and whether legal reasoning itself was "natural" or "artificial."

Horwitz goes on to review the natural law–positive law debate in jurisprudence and to show that "the uses and meanings of natural law and natural rights have varied enormously in modern Western culture . . ." He urges students of rights to "address the multiple meanings of natural law in its varied historical contexts . . ." Like Patterson, Horwitz seeks to remind us that what now seems self-evident is often the product of a contested history. He shows the indeterminacy of traditionally recognized natural rights and, in so doing, suggests that appeals to them cannot resolve controversies at the level of positive rights.

Historicizing the imagination of rights and the rights tradition is also the work of William E. Cain's "Lincoln, Slavery, and Rights." By putting Lincoln's attitude toward black slavery in its historical context, Cain highlights the paradoxical quality of Lincoln's attachment to the idea of equal rights. This quality is exemplified in Lincoln's belief that, while the rights to work freely and to rise economically were keys to American exceptionalism, black and white workers could not enjoy those rights in common and live together in a single union. Thus, in Cain's view, Lincoln's embrace of emancipation was, at best, ambivalent. He wanted to preserve the Union more than to extend equal rights to blacks. He insisted that the rights of man applied to everyone, regardless of race, yet he was deeply skeptical of the capacity of blacks to exercise those rights equally.

Lincoln did not doubt that blacks were included in the guarantees of the Declaration of Independence and the Constitution. At the same time, Lincoln was uncertain about the extent of their rights and about the setting in which those rights should be exercised. Lincoln's view of rights was, Cain contends, a product of a profound moral vision which was, in turn, tempered by the political context of mid-nineteenth-century America. Thus, Lincoln's own understanding of the logic of rights and imagining of new rights for blacks was deeply paradoxical. He worked to let loose a logic of emancipation and equality that he "then sought to restrain." In the end, Cain warns against a contemporary criticism of Lincoln's ambivalence, which would detach "rights from the historical situation in which he [Lincoln] understood and explicated them and in which he sought to make them more capacious than they had been."

Jeremy Waldron concludes Part 1 on "Imagining Rights and the Rights Tradition" by attending to a present-day controversy about the adequacy of rights and their utility for disadvantaged groups. In his essay "Rights and Needs: The Myth of Disjunction," he seeks to imagine a new way of thinking and talking about rights that would free them from an apparently paradoxical relation to needs. Waldron's imagining begins with a rejection of the traditional disjunction between rights and needs. He defends rights by showing their adaptability, and he sees that adaptability as key to their continued vibrancy and utility. Thus, he provides a vivid contemporary example of one way in which the rights tradition is periodically renewed and refreshed.

As against other theorists who, in his view, uncritically accept the conventional separation of rights and needs, Waldron believes that rejecting rights in favor of needs as a way of attending to the position of the socially disadvantaged is both strategically unwise and conceptually flawed. Needs, he argues, are no more determinate or politically compelling than rights, and they are "every bit as querulous, individualistic, and self-absorbed as rights talk . . ." Rights, in turn, can, when correctly understood, be used to do the work often assigned to needs, namely, to express demands and justification for assistance and positive action.

At the heart of Waldron's imagining is the belief that both rights and needs are strengthened when they are seen as mutually constitutive. Rights talk, he suggests, "provides an indispensable *framework* in which talk of needs can be related to ideas about personhood, self-assertion, and dignity." Needs, in turn, solve one of the problems of rights by focusing "attention on the network of duties and responsibilities that individual needs are supposed to give rise to." In the end, Waldron argues that linking rights and needs requires us to create "new structures of thought about personhood, citizenship, universality, community, and equality."

Part 2 of *Legal Rights: Historical and Philosophical Perspectives* is entitled "The Foundations of Rights or Rights without Foundations." Among the questions addressed in this part of the book are: What is the proper grounding of rights? Can we have rights if we are unable or unwilling to commit to an ethical discourse that separates values from preferences? What happens to rights under the gaze of postmodernism?

Thomas L. Haskell attempts to answer this last question in the context of a discussion of academic freedom. He sees a deep paradox in the postmodern insistence that all knowledge is contingent and political and in postmodernists' strident insistence that their right to advance such arguments is protected by academic freedom. "Justifying the Rights of Academic Freedom in the Era of 'Power/Knowledge'" argues that the politicization and demystification of rights that typically accompanies a postmodern epistemology undermines the very values that make academic freedom and other rights possible.

Haskell grounds his philosophical discussion in a careful examination of the history of academic freedom and pays particular attention to the early-twentieth-century origins of the modern university. He asserts that the history of academic freedom is intimately connected to particular epistemological assumptions and particular assumptions about the relationship between power and knowledge that are rejected in a postmodern conception of power/knowledge. "[T]he whole point of academic freedom," Haskell contends, "was to expand the spheres of disinterested knowledge and fence it off from power."

Can a right to academic freedom survive at the same time that many suggest that no knowledge can be disinterested and that neither knowledge nor rights can be separated from the play of power? Haskell is worried that it cannot. He sees postmodernism as deeply antithetical to the premises of academic freedom. Academic freedom is, and depends upon, a defense of authority, in particular the authority of "communities of competence" represented by academic disciplines. Haskell suggests that the antirealist epistemologies of postmodernism erode the basis on which academics can argue for deference to the judgment of such "communities of competence," and he concludes that we need a new grounding for that right "in which both we and the educated public can believe."

In his essay "The New Jural Mind: Rights without Grounds, without Truths, and without Things That Are Truly Rightful," Hadley Arkes shares Haskell's skepticism about the tenability of a postmodern conception of rights and about the tenability of rights without foundations. Arkes makes this case by noting the paradoxical position of liberal defenders of civil rights for African-Americans when they confront pro-life arguments in favor of civil rights for the unborn. Arkes illustrates this paradox by asking whether or not Congress may legislate to expand the scope of rights and/or the scope of beings protected by already recognized rights. He notes the inconsistency that afflicts the arguments of liberals who would defend the right of Congress to do so in the cause of civil rights for African-Americans, but would refrain from doing so when Congress seeks to protect the rights of the unborn through the human life bill.

For Arkes, however, the problem of rights goes beyond the allegedly perverse attachment of liberals to abortion. The problem, as Arkes sees it, is that both liberals and conservatives have rejected natural law as a basis for the articulation of rights and uncritically embraced legal positivism. Positivism, in his view, can provide no secure grounding for rights because it encourages "a tendency, widespread among lawyers, to . . . back away from the claims of reason" on which rights are properly based.

There has been an unfortunate erosion among lawyers of the belief that "there are genuine moral truths, which can supply the substance of moral reasoning" and provide the foundation for rights. The nature and limits of our rights, Arkes contends, depend on identifying the "grounds" on which we can distinguish "between the restrictions of freedom that are justified or unjustified, reasonable or unreasonable." Without such a grounding, " 'rights' cease to name things that are 'truly rightful' " and are "reduced mainly to a set of conventions."

Michael J. Perry's "Is the Idea of Human Rights Ineliminably Religious?" is another effort to identify the foundations or grounding of rights, in this case international human rights. For him the central question that every theory of human rights must confront is the question of justification, of how to explain to those who do not respect human rights why they *must*. He reminds us that many to whom human rights claims are addressed have no articulated moral point of view. They adopt an uncritical tribal or national perspective. Through a careful analysis of the jurisprudential writing of Ronald Dworkin, Perry attempts to show that no secular response can explain adequately why "every human being is sacred" and why therefore every human being should be accorded human rights. The fact that we can love others without being religious does not, in Perry's view, respond to the question of justification when that question arises.

If one is to be able to respond to that question, one must inevitably turn to religion. Only a religious commitment can explain why all human beings are sacred or why human beings have " 'inherent dignity' " and should be treated as ends in themselves. To say that human rights depend on religious belief is not to favor any particular theology; a religious vision of human rights is, according to Perry, "a vision of final and radical reconciliation, a set of beliefs about how one is or can be bound or connected to the world—to the 'other' and to 'nature'—and above all, to Ultimate Reality in a profoundly intimate way."

Pierre Schlag's "Rights in the Postmodern Condition" concludes this book by contending that the efforts of scholars such as Arkes and Perry to provide a stable grounding for rights and a compelling justification for rights claims inevitably must fail. As Schlag argues, rights are "floating signifier(s) into which each subject projects his or her own . . . fears or hopes." As a result, Schlag argues, "there is no serious articulate account of a generally recognized robust ontology for rights." This fact defeats various philosophical efforts to identify the foundations of rights or to provide an objective grounding of rights.

Schlag notes that the proliferation of rights and what he labels the "hypertrophic legalism" of the late modern age paradoxically are occurring at precisely the *historical* moment when the grounding of rights is unraveling. Law and rights, Schlag argues, are turning out to be, in very important senses, the productions of certain stylized aesthetics. In turn, these aesthetics and the rhetorics they enact have turned out to be "lacking in intellectual credibility."

Schlag calls the aesthetics that have been used to try to ground rights "analytic" and "instrumental." The analytic aesthetic, which was dominant in the late nineteenth century, treats law and rights as a field to be mapped, in which different domains of rights could be analytically separated. In this aesthetic, rights were thought of in relation to particular external objects (e.g., property), which they were thought to control. Rights could be owned by persons who through such ownership control things in the world.

The analytic aesthetic depended on the conception of free-willed subjects who, in and through rights, could pursue their own self-determined will. It was quite appealing because it brought a sense of order and clarity to rights talk, and it remains powerful in organizing the arguments of both the critics and the defenders of rights. However, the instrumentalist aesthetic provides, on Schlag's account, a more prevalent grounding for rights in the late twentieth century.

The instrumentalist aesthetic, in contrast to the analytic, is not oriented toward order and clarity; instead, it is associated with change, reform, and progress. It substitutes motion for space as the metaphorical basis of rights. In this conception, rights are seen as sources, instruments, or ends of change. Rights become subordinated to various jurisprudential and social projects. Law is given a mission, and rights become instruments in the fulfillment of that mission. But just as the analytic aesthetic was destabilized by the recognition of the anomic character of radical individualism, the instrumentalist aesthetic is destabilized by the recognition of the bureaucratic regimentation that it promotes.

In the postmodern condition, both aesthetics operate with the result that rights exist in "increasingly intricate legal mazes." Both aesthetics unravel even as rights proliferate. As they unravel, Schlag claims, "we encounter all the other . . . problematics of the postmodern condition—the referent of 'rights' disappearing . . . , the signifier of 'rights' invoking multiple, sometimes dissonant identities, the identities of 'rights' performing simultaneously in many different modalities . . ." What this means is that despite current efforts to identify the foundations of rights, there is "no distinct aesthetic that would allow us in any determinate way to make sense (or nonsense) of rights."

From Patterson's historical analysis of the way legal rights are imagined to Schlag's careful philosophical inquiry into the grounding of rights in the late twentieth century, each of the essays in *Legal Rights: Historical and Philosophical Perspectives* highlights the richness and complexity of the subject of rights. Taken together, these essays alert us both to the particularities of rights and their general appeal. They alert us to the ways legal rights take on meaning in different contexts and the ways those contexts complicate efforts to provide a firm philosophical grounding for rights. And when history and philosophy are brought together, abstract debates come alive in the struggles of real people to cope with, and improve, the real conditions under which they live. Here, then, the significance of legal rights can be measured not just in terms of a set of philosophical categories or a collection of dead histories, but as a set of lived yet reflective experiences.

Part 1
Imagining Rights and
the Rights Tradition

Very Good Memories: Self-Defense and the Imagination of Legal Rights in Early Modern England

Annabel Patterson

> K. must remember that the proceedings were not public; they could certainly, if the Court considered it necessary, become public, but the Law did not prescribe that they must be made public. Naturally, therefore, the legal records of the case, and above all the actual charge-sheets, were inaccessible to the accused and his counsel, consequently one did not know in general, or at least did not know with any precision, what charges to meet in the first plea . . . One could draw up genuinely effective and convincing pleas . . . only later on, when the separate charges and the evidence on which they were based emerged more definitely or could be guessed at from the interrogations . . . Strictly speaking, none of the counsels for the Defense was recognized by the Court. [Counsel] was not allowed to be present during the examination, consequently he had to cross-question the accused immediately after an interrogation, . . . and piece together from the usually confused reports he got anything that might be of use to the Defense.[1]

This alarming account of trial procedure will no doubt be recognized as an excerpt from Franz Kafka's surreal novel *The Trial*, and one

---

1. Franz Kafka, *The Trial*, trans. Willa and Edwin Muir (New York: Schocken Books, 1968), 115, 117.

might easily be tempted to exclude it, as not merely fiction but absurd-
ist fiction to boot, from a serious discussion of rights. Yet it has been
argued that Kafka's nightmare vision was only an exaggeration of
certain features of the Austro-Hungarian code at the end of the nineteenth century[2] and, more to our point, that the juridical practice of
early modern England was even more outrageous if judged by standards now taken for granted, at least in principle, in the United
States. One does not need, therefore, to *imagine* a world like Kafka's.
One need merely remember its existence and the directly causal connection between that world and our own.

It was, after all, precisely those clauses in the original Bill of Rights
that deal with trial procedure and what leads up to it—the requirement
of a search warrant (Fourth Amendment), the provision that no one
shall be compelled in a criminal case to be a witness against himself
(Fifth Amendment), the right to a speedy and public trial, to be informed of the nature and cause of the accusations, to confront the
witnesses for the prosecution and to be able to obtain witnesses in his
favor (Sixth Amendment), the right of trial by jury (Seventh Amendment), and the embargo against excessive bail, excessive fines, and
"cruel and unusual punishment" (Eighth Amendment)—exactly five
out of the first ten "new commandments"—that were deemed necessary in 1791 because English common law practice gave no secure or
comprehensive protection in these areas even at the end of the eighteenth century. When Thomas Salmon brought out the first edition of
the great collection of *State Trials* in 1719, documents clearly designed to
support a "Whig" agenda, he compared Scots civil law procedures
favorably to what still pertained in England. "It must be admitted, that
the Party accused has in Scotland all the fair play imaginable: he has
what Counsel he thinks fit; he has a Copy of his Charge in his own
language; his Counsel are permitted to inspect the very Depositions
against him before he is brought to Trial; and they are in so little haste to
dispatch a State-Prisoner, that the Trial often lasts some months."[3] It is

2. See Martha Robinson, "The Law of the State in Kafka's *The Trial*," *ASLA Forum*
6 (1982): 127–48.

3. *A Complete Collection of State Trials*, 4 vols., ed. Thomas Salmon (London: Timothy Goodwin, 1719), 1:2. For an account of the various editions of *State Trials* and the
agendas they served, see Donald Thomas, *State Trials*, 4 vols. (London and Boston:
Routledge and Kegan Paul, 1972), 1:4–8. Salmon's preface in 1719 spoke directly to
rights theory: "that Learning which shews how life, honour, and innocence are to be
defended, when they shall happen to be injuriously attack'd, will not . . . be thought
inferior to that, which instructs us how to defend our less important rights."

clearly to be inferred from Salmon's "in Scotland" that none of these
protections existed in England at the time.

This chapter will examine two treason trials of early modern England, in which the accused was *not* allowed counsel for the defense, a rule that persisted in treason cases until altered by a statute of William III in 1696, and in all other capital cases until well into the eighteenth century.[4] The practice was archaic in the sense that the accused was required to speak for himself, in the full expectation that he *would* incriminate himself; in other words, self-defense was expected to serve, in the traditions of the residually magic political rituals of the day, as a form of confession. Although in 1362 Parliament had decreed that all legal proceedings had to be carried on in English, the formal indictment was still written in Latin.

In the first case, the trial of Sir Nicholas Throckmorton, most of the evidence for the prosecution consisted of depositions of conversations the accused was supposed to have had, with men who were not brought in to confront him. Despite the fact that the treason law then in force required two witnesses for the prosecution, only one appeared in person, and he was known to be bargaining for his life by turning state's evidence; whereas a witness for the defense who was already in court was not allowed to testify. The case turned on some precise wording in treason legislation, which had for the previous two decades been in a state of constant and contradictory revision; but when Throckmorton asked that the relevant statutes be read aloud to the members of the jury, his request was denied. Nevertheless, he managed to conduct his defense with such a mixture of legal sophistication and moral superiority, spiced with wit and the common touch, that the jury acquitted him. Its members were thereupon themselves thrown into prison and fined so exorbitantly that the case became something of a skeleton in the cupboard of British legal historians.[5]

In the different cupboard of libertarian thought, this case became, conversely, an inspiration—at least for the person who features as my second exhibit, John Lilburne, who was tried for treason almost exactly

---

4. See Thomas Andrew Green, *Verdict According to Conscience: Perspectives on the English Criminal Trial Jury 1200–1800* (Chicago: University of Chicago Press, 1985), 135.

5. Modern historians of the jury trial have downplayed the case, treating it as an exception to a system that worked (within its own legal terms) with reasonable integrity. Compare Green, *Verdict According to Conscience*, 141, where Throckmorton's case appears in a single footnote; J. S. Cockburn, *History of English Assizes: 1558–1714* (Cambridge: Cambridge University Press, 1972, reprint, 1986), where, again, Throckmorton's case appears in a single footnote (123).

a century later, ironically by those very parliamentarians who had established themselves as the defenders of "liberty" against monarchical prerogative. Lilburne was the intellectual leader of the Levellers, the group of religious activists partly based on the army, who attemped to push the midcentury revolution further in the direction of social reorganization than its leaders had ever intended. Lilburne had published pamphlets disputing the legality of the Long Parliament in highly insulting terms. In fact, he called its members tyrants, weasels, and polecats. This would not in itself, one would have thought, been a capital crime, especially in a revolutionary period when political rhetoric was excited. But Lilburne's life was indeed in danger, and, as we shall see, he had informed himself of Throckmorton's case as a precedent, in strategic terms, for his own. Lilburne, too, defended himself so ably that the jury aquitted him, to the enormous enthusiasm of the London citizenry.

My reason for resurrecting these cases from the British past is to reinflect contemporary rights theory in the United States with the politicolegal history of early modern England, part of my larger agenda to keep the latter from being sloughed off as irrelevant to a nation, and an educational system, struggling with seemingly more pressing issues of identity and multiculturalism. In the first instance, this reprise is to remind us of the obvious, that what are sometimes referred to as natural or inalienable rights took a very long time to claim, and even longer to instantiate. It is even more important to remember that their successful instantiation in the United States depended on, in the causal sense, their having been claimed, and *claimed unsuccessfully*, in England, where for at least three centuries before the American Bill of Rights was articulated, the evidence of what new rights were necessary was painfully established by those who, unlike Throckmorton and Lilburne, were not agile enough to outwit the system. The fact that these two *were* successful in their challenge, however, entitles them to a special eminence in a story that otherwise features repeated defeat; for where the repetitive story of injustice has its own accumulative cathexis in the schedule of reform, it never hurts to be able to point to occasions where the right arguments, though made at the wrong time for major historical change, nevertheless created a peephole into the future.

The 1791 amendments to the Constitution were not only necessary (and intended) to distinguish the American juridical system from the British as a sign of the republic's more general emancipation, but inarguable signs of *change*. This chapter, therefore, also intends a contribution to the theoretical problem that besets all kinds of history: How do we get change? How do people imagine the existence of rights they or others currently do not have, that are nowhere recognized within the legal and political structures into which they are born? How is it possible to arrive at a situation where legal rights that never previously existed can come, just a few centuries later, to be called "fundamental"?

Contemporary Rights Theory

Today this problem has been posed as whether there can be, constitutionally, "unenumerated rights." As debated, for example, between Ronald Dworkin and Richard Posner, the question is stated as one that theory alone can solve.[6] That is to say, it is framed as a dispute over whether the level of generality or abstraction in the Bill of Rights and subsequent amendments permits us to take the widest view, or requires us to take the narrowest, as to what those documents mean by such terms as *liberty* and *equality*. But few would dispute that when those documents were framed, the meaning of their abstractions carried for the framers a particular historical imperative: the need to mark the separation from England by the construction of markedly different legal and sociopolitical norms. While "liberty" and "equality" themselves had been around almost from time immemorial as ideological vessels, the American Amendments Four through Eight signified their break with the past by grounding both abstractions in certain specific provisions—all of which illustrated equality in the abstract by concrete provisions for improving equality before the law.

The changes embodied in the 1791 Bill of Rights were, moreover, enacting a set of "rights" or protections of the individual against the state that had been imagined, and articulated, centuries earlier. But how, then, were those earlier claims formulated? How far back can we push the search for the origins of rights talk? Must all ideas have precedents in other ideas? The question runs parallel to

---

6. See Ronald Dworkin, "Unenumerated Rights: Whether and How *Roe* should be Overruled," *University of Chicago Law Review* 59 (1992): 381–432; Richard Posner, "Legal Reasoning from the Top Down and from the Bottom Up: The Question of Unenumerated Constitutional Rights," *University of Chicago Law Review* 59 (1992): 433–50.

current debates in the history of political thought, as to whether the American Revolution owed more, conceptually, to the rationalist tradition attributed to Hobbes and Locke (with their emphasis not only on contract theory but on "essentialism") or to classical republicanism (a chain of ideas, literally derived from classical Greece and especially Rome, refigured in the Renaissance in the context of early modern state formation) or to what we might modestly call "circumstances" (a complex blend of political contingency with a strong economic edge and its more or less conscious rationalization). Joyce Appleby, who provides a trenchant contribution to these debates, would seem to adopt the third alternative, though not without a certain nostalgia for the ideal of the "disinterested citizen" implied in the second.[7] She gives too little credit to the power of inherited ideas as proposed by John Pocock and Quentin Skinner, perhaps because her/their idea of tradition is limited to intellectual history. And she is surely mistaken in asserting that "minimizing the importance of Hobbes and Locke has had the effect of nearly eliminating what was distinctively English about early modern political thought and . . . represents the ultimate rejection of Whig historiography."[8] The assertion depends on setting cardinal English influences much too late in the early modern period. By assuming that "liberalism," a vexed term, derives from Hobbes and Locke (whom a *political* historian would see as on opposite sides of the political divide), Appleby not only stacks the definition of liberalism in favor of possessive individualism; she also ignores earlier figures (such as St. German, Goodman, Coke, Milton) whose different contributions to libertarianism may legitimately be thought of as part of liberalism's story. My plan here is to add Throckmorton and Lilburne to that list.

My own theory of how people reason toward rights they do not possess would appear to be a mixture of all three sources of political thought—the rationalist-essentialist, the historical-traditional, and the experiential-determinist. Working backward from three to one, I suggest that people reason from experience of felt injustice to principles of fairness: finding oneself in a legal predicament (such as one's own trial for treason) where the cards are stacked against one throws the justice of the system into question. When such thoughts pass

    7. Joyce Appleby, *Liberalism and Republicanism in the Historical Imagination* (Cambridge: Harvard University Press, 1992), esp. 1–33, 124–39.
    8. Ibid., 133.

from the intuitive stage to the analytical, people will turn for assistance to whatever models of protest or imagined alternatives their society contains in its repertoire. This repertoire includes, along with the high-intellectual tradition of politicolegal and utopian critique over time, both the folkloric or popular cultural tradition with its victim-heroes, engaging the hindsight of complaint and the foresight of millenarianism, and (somewhere between the high and the low traditions) the testimony of "history" as the written story of the society in question.

At the third (rationalist-esssentialist) stage of analysis, what has happened to oneself and what has happened to others can be merged with ideas of what should and should not happen to anyone—that is to say, the discovery of principles. I suggest, moreover, that people can reason from rights *already* established in their system to broader principles underlying them, which in turn are then asked to authorize new ("unenumerated") rights. This is reasoning from the bottom up, what Dworkin calls "the best conceptions" and which Frank Easterbrook complains of as "boosting the level of generality."[9] Thus, in early modern England the long-established right to trial by a jury of one's peers was capable of rational extension, and Throckmorton and Lilburne so extended it, to the principle that the jury should be entitled, as themselves rational if unexpert persons, to *interpret* the law, discern injustice, and protect the isolated citizen against the power of the monarch and her administration. It is important to grasp, however, especially when one goes back into the past, that neither these "levels" of discovery nor the categories I identified within the cultural repertoire can be clearly kept apart. In particular, as the cases of Throckmorton and Lilburne will show, persons and books tend to merge, as in cultural history persons can only survive as written records, though they animate and validate those records as ideas alone can never do.

The Role of the Historian

It is much to my point about records and remembering that our only detailed knowledge of the trial of Sir Nicholas Throckmorton depends

---

9. Frank Easterbrook, "Abstraction and Authority," *University of Chicago Law Review* 59 (1992): 349–80, esp. 355.

on the principles—historiographical and other—of the most important of the sixteenth-century chronicles, the huge work we continue to identify by the name of Raphael Holinshed.[10] Holinshed's principles were articulated early in his history of England as a network of beliefs we now, thanks to John Pocock, refer to as "ancient constitutionalism,"[11] but which Holinshed inflected also with his own interest in jurisprudence and economic justice. In describing the Norman Conquest of England by William I, Holinshed focused on the new legal code that the Conqueror established, and its disadvantages for the subject nation:

> . . . abrogating in maner all the ancient lawes used in times past, and instituted by the former kings for the good order and quietnes of the people, he made new, *nothing so equall* or easie to be kept, which neverthelesse those that came after (not without their great harme) were constreined to observe: as though it had beene an high offense against God to abolish those evill lawes, which king William (a prince nothing friendly to the English nation) had first ordeined, and to bring in other and more tollerable. (2:13; italics added)

And, Holinshed continued:

> Here by the waie I give you to note a great absurditie; namelie, that those lawes which touched all, and ought to be knowne of all, were notwithstanding written in the Norman toong, which the Englishmen understood not; so that even at the beginning you should have great numbers, partly by the iniquitie of the lawes, and partlie by ignorance in misconstruing the same, to be wrongfully condemned. (4:31)

These themes, of the skepticism that changes in the law can produce, that rulers do not necessarily have the interests of their subjects in

---

10. Raphael Holinshed, *Chronicles of England, Scotland, and Ireland,* 3 vols. (1577, 1587; reprint, six vols., London: J. Johnson et al., 1808; New York: AMS Press, 1965). I shall cite from the nineteenth-century edition. After Holinshed's death, the second edition was produced by a group of five antiquaries, with Abraham Fleming as chief editor.

11. J. G. A. Pocock, *The Ancient Constitution and the Feudal Law* (Cambridge: Cambridge University Press, 1957; reprint, with a "Retrospect," 1987).

mind when the laws are established, that there will be ideological pressure (inflected with religion) against reform, and that the "lawes ought to be knowne of all," constituted Holinshed's brand of ancient constitutionalism, in which, it is no coincidence, the idea of "equall" law is paramount.

These principles were undoubtedly retained in the mind of Elizabethan readers when, hundreds of pages later, they came across what appeared to be a complete transcript of Throckmorton's trial,[12] with the following introduction:

> But now for as much as a copy of the order of Sir Nicholas Throckmorton's arreignment hathe come into my hands, and that the same may give light to the history of that dangerous rebellion I have thought it *not impertinent* to insert the same: not wishing that it should be offensive to anie, sith it is in every mans libertie to weie his words uttered in his owne defense, and likewise the dooings of the quest [jury] in acquitting him, as maie seeme good to their discretions, sith I have delivered the same as I have it, without prejudicing anie mans opinion, to thinke thereof otherwise than as the cause maie move him. (4:31; italics added)

The Trial of Sir Nicholas Throckmorton (1554)

The "dangerous rebellion" that Holinshed mentioned as the context (though not, I think, the real motive) for his "not impertinent" introduction of the Throckmorton trial was the uprising led by Sir Thomas Wyatt the younger against Mary Tudor, who had just assumed the throne in defiance of the rival Protestant faction that asserted the claims to the succession of Lady Jane Grey. The motives for the rebellion combined religion and politics, in that Mary was not only herself a Roman Catholic, for some an unwelcome change back from the Edwardian Reformation, but planned to marry Philip II of Spain, which portended foreign domination. Throckmorton was accused of

---

12. For a detailed argument as to how far this "transcript" can be taken as representing what was actually said during the trial, see my " 'For Words Only': From Treason Trial to Liberal Legend in Early Modern England," *Yale Journal of Law and the Humanities* 5, no 2 (1993): 389–416.

complicity in the rebellion, though nothing, as I have said, could be
brought in evidence against him except certain conversations.

Throckmorton had had a career that balanced court service under
Edward VI, who had knighted him and given him a post in the privy
chamber, with considerable parliamentary experience. He seems to
have survived the chaotic transition to the new reign by ingratiating
himself with both factions. His signature appears on the letters patent
of June 7, 1553, which limited the succession to the Protestant Lady
Jane Grey; but on the day of the king's death, he sent Mary a warning
to protect against the Grey faction led by Northumberland. In other
words, Throckmorton, who sported a bright red beard, was one of
nature's foxes. Nevertheless, on February 20, 1554, he was sent to the
Tower of London, on the testimony of one of Wyatt's lieutenants,
Cuthbert Vaughan, that he and Throckmorton had discussed the
plans for the uprising. Throckmorton admitted that he had talked to
Sir Peter Carew and Wyatt himself about the potential for a rebellion,
but he utterly denied any further complicity. Especially he denied that
words alone, without any overt act and given the legislation then in
force, were sufficient for a charge of treason. But by words alone, one
might say, he accomplished his own deliverance. And when Holinshed inserted this long report of the trial, which is many pages
longer than accounts of the trials of the principals, Lady Jane, Northumberland, and Wyatt himself, the reader might well wonder why
such emphasis was to be placed on this conveniently "found" text,
and put more than two and two together. Indeed, the readers of the
Chronicles were really being invited to themselves take on the responsibility of jury duty, along with the injunction to independent judgment
that the role ideally implies.

Reading the report ourselves (which is presented in dialogue or
dramatic form, with speech prefixes), it is clear from the start that
Throckmorton planned his trial as an appeal to broader principles that
might be thought to inhere in the trial by jury as it had evolved since
the Norman Conquest, principles that included impartiality and access to the necessary information to reach an impartial verdict. A large
part of Throckmorton's strategy in the opening moments of the trial
consisted in a struggle for control over procedure, implying that the
accepted rules of procedure were stacked against the defendant and
including the suggestion that "due process" meant taking enough
time: "My lords I praie you," he said, when his judges expressed

impatience, "Make not too much hast with me, neither thinke not long for your dinner, for my case requireth leasure, and you have well dined when you have doone justice trulie. Christ said, Blessed are they that hunger and thirst for righteousnesse."

When the clerk asked him, "How wilt thou be tried?" the only proper answer was "By God and the Countrie." But the only proper answer was not forthcoming:

Throckmorton: Shall I be tried as I would, or as I should?
Bromley: You shall be tried as the law will, and therefore you must saie
　　by God and the countrie.
Throckmorton: Is that your law for me? It is not as I would, but sith you
　　will have it so, I am pleased with it, and doo desire to be tried by
　　faithfull just men, which more feare God than the world. (4:32)[13]

[margin handwriting: knows it's not a fair trial]

The choices those jurors will face are, therefore, already established, before any evidence has been heard, in the simple contrasts between "tried as I should, or as I would," between procedural formalism and fairness, and between those who answer to God and those who answer to some other master.

Concordant with this strategy was a set of guidelines that Throckmorton conveyed to the jury about what to expect in the realm of legal hermeneutics, which came in the form of a hortatory appeal to the commissioners who were about to try him:

I praie you remember I am not alienate from you, but that I am your christian brother; neither you so charged, but you ought to consider equitie; nor yet so privileged, but that you have a dutie of God appointed you how you shall doo your office; which if you exceed, will be greevouslie required at your hands. It is lawfull for you to use your gifts which I know God hath largelie given you, as your learning, art, and eloquence, so as thereby you doo not seduce the minds of the simple and unlearned jurie, to credit matters

---

13. Compare John Bellamy, *The Tudor Law of Treason* (London: Routledge and Kegan Paul, 1979), 140: "When the indicted traitor had been asked how he would plead and had given the answer 'not guilty,' it was further demanded of him how he would be tried. To this the only proper response was "by God and the country," "country" meaning a petty jury or, if the accused was of noble blood, "by God and my peers." Evidently, Throckmorton's response to this question was both impertinent and deliberately resistant to legal formalism.

otherwise than they be. For master sergeant, I know how by per-
suasions, inforcements, presumptions, applieng, implieng, inferring, conjecturing, deducing of argument, wresting and exceeding
the law, the circumstances, the depositions and confessions, that
unlearned men may be inchanted to thinke and judge those that be
things indifferent, or at the woorst but oversights to be great treasons; such power orators have, and such ignorance the unlearned
have. Almightie God by the mouth of his prophet dooth conclude
such advocates be curssed, speaking these words: Curssed be he
that dooth his office craftilie, corruptlie, and maliciously. And consider also, that my bloud shall be required at your hands, and
punished in you and yours, to the third and fourth generation.
Notwithstanding, you and the justices excuse alwaies such er-
ronious dooings, when they be after called in question, by the
verdict of the twelve men: but I assure you, the purgation serveth
you as it did Pilat, and you wash your hands of the bloudshed, as
Pilat did of Christs. (4:33–34)

Athough this speech was formally addressed to the commissioners,
its true intended audience was the jury of "the twelve men," who
were thereby instructed in the hermeneutics of suspicion, in the *style*
of the early modern treason trial ("applieng, implieng, inferring, conjecturing . . . wresting and exceeding the law"), and warned to be on
their guard against them.

Tudor Treason Law

To understand what Throckmorton meant by "wresting and exceeding the law," however, we need to go beyond the hermeneutics of
suspicion to the survey of Tudor treason law provided by John Bellamy, who has shown incontrovertibly that from Henry VIII through
Elizabeth I the law changed its mind dramatically several times as to
what could count as treason.[14] What we mean by the law changing its
mind, of course, is the instability introduced by political or religious
agendas or, in the case of Henry VIII, sexual agendas. The Henrician
Treason Act of November 1534 (*Statutes of the Realm*, 26 Hen. 8, c. 13),
which was produced in the inflammatory circumstances of Henry's

---

14. Bellamy, *Tudor Law of Treason*, 9–35.

divorce from Katherine of Aragon to marry Anne Boleyn and the break from Rome that these actions appeared to necessitate, was clearly designed to suppress all criticism of the monarch. To that end, it calmly introduced three brand-new treasons, including treasonable words that were merely spoken. It was now treason to call the king, even in speech, a heretic, a schismatic, a tyrant, or an infidel, any of which terms might have reasonably been used by a devout Roman Catholic at the time. In 1547 the king's heir, now Edward VI, openly repudiated this definition in a new treason statute (*Statutes of the Realm*, 1 Edw. 6, c. 12), which opened by describing the 1534 act as "verie streighte, sore, extreme and terrible." Edward's act claimed to be a return to the ancient definition of the medieval Edward III's treason statute of 1352 (*Statutes of the Realm*, 25 Edw. 3, st. 5., c. 2), which required "overt act," but in fact retained certain provisions of the 1534 act, with respect to challenging the royal supremacy over the church. When Mary came to the throne, the rival defeated faction was tried under the treason acts of *both* Edward III and Edward VI; but before Throckmorton was indicted, she had produced a treason act of her own, whose preamble recorded her abhorrence of the fact that under her predecessors men had "many times, for woordes onelye without other facte or dede doone or perpetrated," been convicted for treason and executed.

Bellamy determined that the indictment against Throckmorton was drawn illegally in terms of the then-applicable statutes; it claimed that Throckmorton and ten other gentlemen, conspiring with certain traitors, "had *compassed* to deprive the queen of her crown," which had been made treason in 1534 and again in 1547, but repealed in 1553, and that he had also "compassed" to levy war against her, which (as distinct, of course, from actually levying it) was not treason by any act. Bellamy inferred that those lawyers who drew up the indictment against Throckmorton "did so without having the recent amendments to the treason laws in mind," perhaps because they worked from the indictments of Northumberland and his adherents, which had preceded the Marian statute of repeal. In fact, a charge of imagining the queen's death should have been both illegal under the statute of 1352 and sufficient (leaving aside the question of its truthfulness) to incriminate Throckmorton as merely one of a group of conspirators, regardless of whether he had subsequently supported the "imaginings" by overt act; but by drawing the indictment incorrectly the Crown's lawyers made, from their perspective, a fatal mistake.[15]

Aware that these recent changes in the law should work in his favor, Throckmorton requested a courtroom reading of both the Marian statute, which repealed all previous treason laws except that of Edward III, and that ancient Edwardian statute itself. This request was refused; "No sir, there shall be no bookes brought at your desire, we doo all know the law sufficientlie without booke," said Sir Thomas Bromley, the lord chief justice (4:45); whereupon, despite the fact that he had earlier made much of his ignorance of the law, Throckmorton produced from his memory the precise *wording* of the relevant statutes. "Now I praie you of my jurie which have my life in triall," he continued, "note well what things *at this daie* be treasons, and how these treasons must be tried and decerned; that is to say, by open deed, which the lawes dooth at some time terme (Overt act.)" (4:46; italics added). The surprise that he had sprung on the queen's lawyers is dramatically indicated in Bromley's irate question: "Why doo not you of the queenes learned councell answer him? Me thinke, Throckmorton, you need not have the statutes, for you have them meetlie perfectlie."

In addition, Throckmorton deftly applied his experience as a member of Parliament, where he had recently served alongside the very men who were now serving as commissioners in his trial. He reminded them sharply of their own role in constructing Mary's new treason act, with its preamble declaring that the laws of her father and brother had been unjust:

> To what purpose serveth the statute of repeale the last parlement, where I heard some of you here present, and diverse other of the queenes learned councell, grievouslie inveie against the cruell and bloudie lawes of King Henrie the eight, and against some lawes made in my late sovereigne lord and masters time, king Edward the sixt. Some termed them Dracos lawes, which were written in bloud: some said they were more intollerable than anie laws that Dionysius or anie other tyrant made. In conclusion, as manie men, so manie bitter tearmes and names those lawes had. And moreover, the preface of the same [Marian] statute doth

---

15. Bellamy, *Tudor Law of Treason*, 55.

recite, that for words onelie, manie great personages, and other of good behaviour, have beene most cruellie cast awaie by these former sanguinolent thirstie lawes, with manie other suggestions for the repeale of the same. (4:52)

He thereby managed to cast his judges in the role of time servers who now choose to forget their own reformist statements of the very recent past. And, turning to the jury, he concluded: "honest men which are to trie my life, consider these opinions of my life, judges be rather agreable to the time, than to the truth: for their judgements be repugnant to their own principle, repugnant to their godlie and best learned predecessors opinions, repugnant I saie to the proviso in the statute of repeale made in the last parlement." His final appeal was both to religion and to the civil society: "And in that you all be citizens, I will take my leave of you with St. Paules farewell to the Ephesians, citizens also you be" (4:53). It was a masterly blend of my three categories of reasoning, rationalist-essentialist (the appeal to principles), historical-traditional (the appeal to "learned predecessors"), and experiential-determinist (it was *his* life that, being in such danger, had sharpened Throckmorton's wits and his memory). Especially his memory. As commissioner Southwell put it, with grudging admiration, "You have a very good memorie" (4:49). If the law is to justify itself by its long memory, it would be well, Holinshed's record implies, if we all had memories as good as Throckmorton's.

The Defiance of Throckmorton's Jury

It took the jury about three hours to bring in a verdict of not guilty, to the fury and embarrassment of the commissioners and also Queen Mary. As Holinshed had stated in his own preamble to the trial, "with which verdict the judges and councillors there present were so much offended, that they bound the jurie in the summe of five hundred pounds apeece," to appear before the Star Chamber. On April 21, they appeared before the Star Chamber judges, "from whense after certeine questioning, they were committed to prison, Emanuell Lucar and master Whetston to the tower, and the other[s] to the Fleet" (4:31). Four of them, under this pressure, submitted and confessed they had erred in their verdict. Many pages later, Holinshed had carefully recorded some information he had found in John Foxe's *Acts and Monuments* (1563), as to the fate of eight of "those honest men that had beene of Throckmortons quest," who refused, though imprisoned, to admit their verdict was wrong. They were called back to the court of Star Chamber, where Lucar "said openlie before all the lords that they had doone in the matter like honest men, and true and faithfull subjects." Not surprisingly, the Star Chamber judges "taking their words in marvellous evill part, judged them worthie to paie excessive fines" (4:64). Five of them were sentenced to pay 1,000 marks apiece, and the intransigent Whetston and Lucar £2,000 apiece. Still later, Holinshed recorded that, just before Christmas 1555, these fines were commuted to more realistic amounts, £220 in some cases and £60 in others, thereby confirming the ritual or intimidatory function (*in terrorem*) of the original penalties.[16]

Throckmorton himself, though acquitted, was not released, but was sent back to the Tower of London, where he remained, attending clemency, for a year. On January 18, 1556, all the members of the Privy Council went together to the tower and released all the political prisoners who had been accused of complicity with Wyatt. Throckmorton went on to have a successful career as a diplomat under Elizabeth I.

From Throckmorton to Lilburne (1649)

There exists a remarkable verse biography of Throckmorton, which may have been written by a member of his family.[17] Francis Peck, its Whig editor in the eighteenth century, remarked in his preface that "the trials of Sir Nicholas Throckmorton & John Lilburn, are (for the prisoners excellent defence of themselves) the two most remarkable, I

---

16. In Elizabeth's reign, Sir Thomas Smith clearly alluded to Throckmorton's trial without mentioning it by name. In his *De Republica Anglorum*, Smith wrote that he had seen in his time (carefully adding in parentheses "not in the reigne of the Queene nowe") "an enquest for pronouncing one not guiltie of treason contrarie to such evidence as was brought in . . . not onely imprisoned for a space but an houge fine set upon their heads, which they were faine to pay"; and he further recorded the public response to this episode: "those doinges were even then of many accounted verie violent, and tyrannical, and contrarie to the libertie and custome of the realme of England." Sir Thomas Smith, *De Republica Anglorum*, ed. Mary Dewar (Cambridge: Cambridge University Press, 1982), 121.

17. Among many other things, this poem explains how it was that he was able to make himself into the early modern equivalent of the gaolhouse lawyer. The poem refers to "the mann who lent mee lawe of late, / To save my life, and putt himselfe in danger." See *The Legend*, ed. J. G. Nichols (London: The Roxburgh Club, 1874), 30.

think, of any we have yet extant."[18] The pairing was intelligent, for it turns out that Lilburne had access to Holinshed's record of the Throckmorton trial and applied it to very good effect.

An equally detailed, apparently verbatim account of Lilburne's trial was published in London[19] almost instantly after his acquittal. The agent-editor of this pamphlet was "Theodorus Verax," which was the pseudonym of the radical Clement Walker, who was himself engaged in a publishing campaign against the Long Parliament.[20] Halfway through the pamphlet, Lilburne himself made an allusion to

> Throgmorton, in queen Mary's time, who was impeached of higher Treason than now I am; and that in the days of the commonly accounted bloodiest and cruellest prince that this many hundred of years hath reigned in England: . . . Throgmorton was in this place arraigned as a Traitor, and enjoyed as much, if not more [procedural] favour, than I have now enjoyed, although his then judges and prosecutor were bent to take away his life.[21]

And Walker's pamphlet carried at this point a telling marginal annotation: "Whose remarkable and excellent Defence you may at large read in Hollingshead's Chronicle, in the Life of Queen Mary, *which discourse is excellently well worth the speedily reprinting, especially seeing men are made traitors for words*" (21; italics added). That men were indeed still being made traitors for words in 1649 is demonstrated by Walker's own fate. Thanks to the appearance of the second part of his *History of Independency*, and also, no doubt, to his determination to enter

---

18. Francis Peck, ed., *The Legend of Sir Nicholas Throckmorton, Kt.Chief Butler of England & Chamberlain of the Exchecquer; who died of Poison, A.D. 1570, an Historical Poem: By (his Nephew) Sir Thomas Throckmorton of Littleton* . . . (London: 1736), 32.

19. Theodorus Verax [Clement Walker], *The Triall of Lieut. Collonel J. Lilburne* . . . *Unto which is annexed a necessary Appendix. Published by Theodorus Verax.* ([London:] printed by Hen-Hills in Southwark, 1949)

20. Clement Walker is best known as the author of *Anarchia Anglicana, or, The history of Independency. The second part* (1649), which is hostile to the Independents. Although at the beginning of the civil war he joined the parliamentary side, by 1647 he was suspected of being one of the instigators of the London riots, and in 1648 he voted in favor of an agreement with Charles I and was consequently expelled from the House of Commons in Pride's Purge. Like Lilburne himself, Walker was an indefatigable publicist, and from 1643 to 1651 he used the press to promote and defend his opinions.

21. I cite from *A Complete Collection of State Trials*, 21 vols, ed. T. B. Howell (London: R. Bagshaw, 1816), 4:1288.

Lilburne's trial in the public record, on November 13, 1649, he himself was arraigned on a charge of treason, and placed in the Tower of London, where he died, never having come to trial, in 1651.

Many of the tricks that Lilburne used in his own self-defense he clearly learned from Throckmorton: namely, his constant procedural challenges, especially in the important opening moves,[22] challenges which Lilburne himself presented as part of a larger argument that legal formalism is designed to confuse the ordinary defendant (4:1294–95); his insistence on the importance of two witnesses; and his sense of the value of humor in winning over the jury. There is a particularly comedic moment, when Lilburne declared he could proceed no further without access to a chamber pot, which was brought into the courtroom and filled accordingly. Whether or not Lilburne intended it, this episode, presented as if by a stage direction ["Whilst it was fetching, Mr. Lilburne followeth his papers and books close; and when the pot came, he made water, and gave it to the foreman."][23] is, as it were, the essence of the common touch.

The most certain proof of what Lilburne learned from Throckmorton must, however, be his strategic appeal to the preamble of the Marian statute as evidence that even the arbitrary monarchs of previous generations "abhorred and detested the making of words or writing to be treason; which is such a bondage and snare, that no man knows how to say or do, or behave himself" (4:1401). By implication, therefore, he anticipated the U.S. First Amendment. And another unenumerated right articulated in both these trials is the layperson's right of access to the law, which is obviously connected to but exceeds the right to legal counsel. It had been Throckmorton's strategy to pretend ignorance of the law, all the better to surprise his judges with his memory of it when his request for a reading of the statutes was refused. But the effect of this strategy was that he was able to stage, for the jury's

22. Lilburne in fact managed to squeeze in a long speech at the beginning, craving "no more but that which is properly and singly the liberty of every free-born Englishman, viz. The benefit of the Laws and Liberties thereof, which by my birth-right and inheritance is due unto me." He challenged the legality of a commission of oyer and terminer, which he failed to find authorized in the Petition of Right and Magna Carta, he refused to hold up his hand to identify himself, and he demanded counsel, of course unsuccessfully, all this before adding his own gloss, like Throckmorton, to the formal question, "By whom wilt thou be tried?" Lilburne answered, "By the known laws of England, I mean, by the liberties and privileges of the laws of England, and a jury of my equals legally chosen," (Ibid., 4:1270–71, 1275, 1294).

23. Ibid., 4:1379.

corruption of justice (handwritten annotation)

benefit, an encounter with his judges over the *public's* access to the law
in more general terms, by emphasizing the importance of the published statutes, which being in English, were in theory legible by all
citizens. On the judges' part it was made very clear that knowledge of
the law by laypeople was undesirable altogether, a dangerous im-
propriety. "You know it were indifferent [fair]," Throckmorton had
declared, "that I should know and heare the law whereby I am ad-
judged, and forasmuch as the statute is in English, men of meaner
learning than the justices can understand it, or else how should we
know when we offend." "What would you doo with the statute
booke?" said Hare, "The jurie doth not require it, they have heard the
evidence, and they must upon their conscience trie whether you be
guiltie or no, so as the booke needeth not," (4:45–46).

(handwritten margin note: idea of being judged via conscience)

Lilburne grasped both the tactical and theoretical advantages of
this position. Throughout his two-day trial, he explicitly thematized
the problem of the layman's access to the law. He constantly referred
to his own reading of such "good old English laws" as were written in
English. In accordance with his charge that the Long Parliamentarians
are a reincarnation of the Norman Yoke, Lilburne complained: "you
come to ensnare and entrap me with unknown niceties and formali-
ties that are locked up in the French and Latin tongue, and cannot be
read in English books, they being not expressed in any law of the
kingdom, published in our own English tongue: it is not fair play
according to the Law of England, plainly in English expressed in the
Petition of Right, and other the good old statute laws of the land,"
(4:1294). Lilburne was evidently not possessed of Throckmorton's
mnemonic powers, and he was in this respect treated with greater
latitude, for he was allowed to bring with him into the court bundles
of notes, a copy of Coke's *Institutes*, and a statute book, from which he
read to the jury the statutes of Edward VI on the need for two witnesses. "Here is the statute-book, let the Jury hear it read," cried
Lilburne (4:1396). In contrast, the attorney general warned the rest of
the commissioners that to grant Lilburne's demand for legal counsel
and for a copy of the indictment in English "would be a precedent for
all future times; by means of which there would never be an end of
trials in criminal cases" (4:1309).

(handwritten margin note: not in English)

(handwritten margin note, left side: access to law)

Behind this strategy, which Lilburne had learned from Throckmorton, lay the following ideas: that branch of ancient constitutionalism which had always called for the law to be conducted in English;

proto-Enlightenment theories of the individual's educability and responsibility for himself; and a democratization of the law, which stood for a larger idea of democratization. But Lilburne rendered their connection visible—by his constant references to Magna Carta and the Petition of Right of 1628 and by his claim that "due process" was as much "the common right of all or any of the people of England, as well as parliament men" (4:1393). In his summation of his defense, he reiterated his claim that denial of counsel and of witnesses for the defense meant that his judges "go about to murder" him, "without law and against law." And therefore he commended himself to the protection of his "honest jury and fellow-citizens," who "are the conservators and sole judges of my life, having in them alone the judicial power of the law, as well as fact"; whereas his judges, he extravagantly asserted, were "but cyphers to pronounce the sentence," as well as "the Norman Conqueror's intruders" (4:1395). And, according to Clement Walker, "The People with a loud voice cried, *Amen, Amen,* and gave an extraordinary great hum," causing such unease in the Guildhall that the attending military officer sent for "more fresh companies of foot-soldiers." Huge demonstrations of joy were to follow the verdict of "not Guilty"; "And yet for all his acquittal by the law, his adversaries kept him afterwards so long in prison, that the people wondered, and began to grumble that he was not discharged" (4:1405).

Back to the Future

In 1648 the Leveller *Agreement of the People* had included law reforms in its utopian constitution, including access to the law in English, the right of the accused to call witnesses on his own behalf and to avoid self-incrimination, and the restriction of capital punishment to cases of murder or violent insurrection.[24] Yet the section that contains these provisions is bracketed as somewhat futuristic: "These following Particulars were offered to be inserted in the Agreement, but judged fit, as the most eminent grievances, to be redressed by the next Representative." We are back where we started, with the 1791 Amendments to the American Constitution and the long century and a half between these proposals and their acceptance on the other side of the Atlantic.

---

24. See *Leveller Manifestoes of the Puritan Revolution,* ed. D. M. Wolfe (London & New York: T. Nelson, 1944), 301–2.

It is possible, however, that these two trials contributed to making that lag no longer than it was. Lilburne, as I have shown, learned from Throckmorton (thanks to Holinshed's *Chronicles*). Exactly the same case has been made by Olivia Smith for the exemplary function that Lilburne's trial played for William Hone, defending himself against the charge of blasphemous libel in 1817. Hone had encountered Lilburne's trial by accident, in the form of a single sheet from the 1710 reprint of Walker's pamphlet, which he had found being used for wrapping paper, and tracked to its source. In Hone's three trials, Smith shows, he modeled his strategy, his language, and his articulation of principles on what he found in Lilburne, including the class difference between himself and his judges and the claim to be speaking "on behalf of the whole people of England."[25] And, like Throckmorton, Hone had a very good memory indeed.[26]

It will perhaps make these exemplary cases all the more compelling (and my representation of them less vulnerable to the charge of naive "liberalism") if I close the argumentative frame that began with Kafka's *The Trial* by returning to that somber and sardonic text. One of Kafka's darkest points was that the closer one's acquaintance with the law, the less likely one would be to risk suggesting that justice could be advanced by change:

> For although the pettiest lawyer might be to some extent capable of analyzing the state of things in the Court, it never occurred to the lawyers that they should suggest or insist on any improvements in the system, while . . . almost every accused man, even quite simple people among them, discovered from the earliest stages a passion for suggesting reforms which often wasted time and energy that could have been better employed in other directions . . . One must lie low, no matter how much it went against the grain, and try to understand that this great organization remained, so to speak, in a state of delicate balance, and that if someone took it upon himself to alter the disposition of things around him, he ran the risk of losing his footing and falling to destruction, while the organization would simply right itself by some compensating reaction in another part of its machinery. (121)

---

25. Olivia Smith, *The Politics of Language 1791–1819* (Oxford: Oxford University Press, 1984), 196–201.

26. See Louis James, *Print and the People, 1819–1851* (London: Allen Lane, 1976), 71.

Natural Law and Natural Rights

Morton J. Horwitz

Unless we first see how it is that certain questions enter jurisprudential controversy, we reproduce all the pathologies of abstraction and reification that have been hallmarks of Anglo-American jurisprudence.

The debate over natural law/rights in American history has arisen in widely varying contexts and drawn on disparate strands in the discourse of "higher law."[1] Our recent intense interest in the question derives from contemporary struggle over the scope and meaning of the rights legacy of the Warren court and the fear that various rights, most particularly the right to an abortion articulated in *Roe v. Wade*,[2] were in jeopardy. The legacy of the Warren Court, in turn, is often measured in relation to debates over the meaning of the *Lochner* era. In the still dominant Progressive rendition of constitutional history, the *Lochner* era Supreme Court illegitimately appealed to higher law principles in order to extend the Constitution to cover "substantive" as well as "procedural" due process.[3] For Progressive historians bent on delegitimating the *Lochner* Court, "The Revival of Natural Law Concepts" was among the most important accusations hurled at the Court.[4]

---

1. M. Horwitz, "Rights," *Harvard Civil Rights, Civil Liberties Law Review* 23 (1988): 393, 393–94 n. 2–13.

2. Roe v. Wade, 410 U.S. 113 (1973).

3. See M. Horwitz, *Transformation of American Law 1870–1960* (1992): 156 n. 77; (hereafter cited as *TAL*); C. Haines, *The Revival of Natural Law Concepts* (Cambridge: Harvard University Press, 1930); E. Corwin, *The "Higher Law" Background of American Constitutional Law* (Great Seal Books, 1955) [originally published in *Harvard Law Review* 42 (1928–29): 149, 365]; B. Wright, *American Interpretations of Natural Law* (Cambridge: Harvard University Press, 1931).

4. See S. Fine, *Laissez Faire and the General-Welfare State* (Ann Arbor: University of Michigan Press, 1956), 126–64; C. Jacobs, *Law Writers and the Courts* (Berkeley: Univer-

In American constitutional history, Justice Samuel Chase formulated the debate in the early case of *Calder v. Bull* (1798),[5] around
whether it was legitimate to appeal over and above the specific provisions of the Constitution to "the *great first principles* of the *social com-
pact.*" In fact, few American jurists were willing to accept Chase's
formulation. Two of the most prominent jurists of the *Lochner* era,
Christopher G. Tiedeman[6] and Thomas M. Cooley,[7] expressly rejected
it. More generally, as Robert M. Cover has shown in his discussion of
the influence of higher law ideas on antislavery judges before the
Civil War, natural law/rights conceptions did not usually operate as
principles that alone could determine the validity or invalidity of positive law.[8] Instead, as I would put it, these ideas were usually imbed-
ded in standard legal discourse. In a typical expression, one of these
antislavery judges declared in 1845:

> Slavery is wrong, inflicted by force and supported alone by the
> municipal power of the state or territory wherein it exists. It is
> opposed to the principles of natural justice and right, and is a
> mere creature of positive law. Hence, it being my duty to
> declare the law, not to make it, the question is not, what
> conforms to the great principles of natural right and universal

sity of California Press, 1954), 85–93; A. Paul, *Conservative Crisis and the Rule of Law:
Attitudes of Bar and Bench, 1887–1895* (Ithaca, N.Y.: Cornell University Press, 1960), 209–
21; B. Twiss, *Lawyers and the Constitution* (Princeton: Princeton University Press, 1942).

5. Calder v. Bull, 3 U.S. (3 Dall.) 386 (1798). See T. Grey, "Do We Have an Unwrit-
ten Constitution?" *Stanford Law Review* 27 (1975): 703.

6. C. Tiedeman, *A Treatise on the Limitations of the Police Power in the United States*
(St. Louis: F. H. Thomas, 1886). See also sources in note 4.

7. Thomas Cooley, *A Treatise on the Constitutional Limitations Which Rest Upon the
Legislative Power of the States of the American Union*, 7th ed. (Boston: Little Brown, 1903),
232–33.

8. In *Justice Accused: Antislavery and the Judicial Process* (New Haven: Yale University Press, 1975), Robert M. Cover showed how antebellum judges who believed slavery was contrary to natural right nevertheless did not go behind positive law to follow
their beliefs. They preserved a distinction between positive law and political philosophy. Stanley N. Katz made a similar argument about a different property relation in
Republicanism and the Law of Inheritance in the Revolutionary Era, Michigan Law Review 76
(1977): 1,6. He emphasized "the mainstream . . . tradition clearly marked by the positivist spirit of Blackstone and the theorists of legislative sovereignty" that made Nunne-
macher v. State, 129 Wis. 190 202–203, 108 N.W. 627, 630 (1906), "an isolated moment in
the history of American jurisprudence." In that case, the Wisconsin Supreme Court
held that "the right to demand that property pass by inheritance or will is an inherent
right subject only to reasonable regulation by the Legislature."

freedom—but what do the positive laws and institutions command and direct.[9]

As Cover indicates, this statement captures the place of higher law doctrines in the structure of antebellum constitutional discourse. He writes:

[T]he courts uniformly recognized a hierarchy of sources of law . . . in which "natural law" was subordinate to constitutions, statutes, and well-settled precedent. This hierarchy was clearly established and unambiguously articulated by the courts. The reason for natural law's subordinate place was a thoroughgoing positivism concerning the origin of "law." Law was perceived as operative and valid because of a human constituent process and by virtue of valid lawmaking processes in pursuance of that Constitution. It was the will of men that gave law its force. But men took to various sources for the content of their law. And one very important kind of source is that which declares what is right and just. Most of the jurists of this period feel comfortable designating this tradition as "natural law" and finding it in books and maxims that were self-styled statements of the law of nature. This body of principles and rules was conceived as "existing," though without authority, apart from its incorporation, by virtue of men's wills, in the "law" of a particular state. Natural law was, indeed, a subject for study by the lawyer or law student because it was helpful in understanding the principles underlying so much of a rational legal system. It was also one potential source for formulating new rules or modifying old ones.[10]

Much of the confusion over the role of higher law in American history derives from lack of clarity about how nineteenth-century judges and lawyers thought about the question.[11] At the time of the drafting of the Declaration of Independence, there was confusion

9. Cover, *Justice Accused*, 120–21, quoting State v. Hoppess, 2 W.L.J. 279, 285 (Ohio 1845), reprinted in 10 Ohio Dec. Reprint 105, 110–111 (1896).

10. Ibid., 34.

11. Horwitz, *TAL*, 156.

over at least four different conceptions of higher law.[12] The first was medieval Thomistic natural law, with its premise that any positive law that violated natural law was void.[13] While this view had never been as influential in England as it was on the Continent, by the late eighteenth century it had been largely marginalized by English jurists.[14]

The communitarian, organicist, and hierarchical character of traditional natural law also began to be transformed by the emergence of individualistic ideas of natural rights in seventeenth-century social contract theories. Emphasizing the primacy of prepolitical rights in nature, the liberal social contract thinkers believed that positive law, especially laws dealing with property, should reflect or mirror those natural rights that individuals retained when they agreed to enter into civil society.[15]

In the period leading up to the American Revolution, these two very different versions of higher law were perhaps overshadowed in English and American constitutional thought by the seventeenth-century Whig notion of fundamental law, which usually referred to the "immemorial rights of Englishmen" or some other version of immemorial custom.[16] Jefferson's great accomplishment was in managing to weave all these different strands of higher-law thinking into the Declaration, adding a fourth variation as traditional natural law ideas were slowly reformulated into a Newtonian (and then Kantian) vision of universal (moral) laws.[17] By the time the Deist Jefferson appealed to those "self evident . . . truths" deriving from the "laws of nature" and "nature's god," " 'Nature,' " in Carl Becker's words, ". . . as never before . . . had stepped in between man and God; so there was

---

12. See Carl Becker, *The Declaration of Independence* (New York: Harcourt, Brace, 1922), 24–79.

13. See O. Gierke, *Natural Law and the Theory of Society*, 2 vols., trans. E. Barker (Cambridge: Cambridge University Press, 1934); A. P. d'Entreves, *Natural Law* (London, New York: Hutchinson's University Library, 1951).

14. See J. Gough, *Fundamental Law in English Constitutional History* (Oxford: Clarendon Press, 1955).

15. See I. Shapiro, *The Evolution of Rights in Liberal Theory* (Cambridge: Cambridge University Press, 1986); J. Finnis, *Natural Law and Natural Rights* (Oxford: Oxford University Press, 1980); C. B. MacPherson, *The Political Theory of Possessive Individualism* (Oxford: Oxford University Press, 1962); M. Kammen, *A Machine That Would Go of Itself: The Constitution in American Culture* (New York: Knoph, 1986).

16. See B. Bailyn, *Ideological Origins of the American Revolution* (Cambridge: Harvard University Press, 1967), 175–98.

17. See G. Wills, *Inventing America* (Garden City, N.Y.: Doubleday, 1978), 93–110.

no longer any way to know God's will except by discovering the 'laws' of Nature . . ." During the nineteenth century an increasingly secularized natural rights discourse was as often concerned with determing what was natural as it was with defining what was right. Social thinkers became increasingly more comfortable with simply describing the inevitable unfolding of progress or of Anglo-Saxon custom or, indeed, of the survival of the fittest, while becoming correspondingly less comfortable with the normative and the prescriptive, especially as it was embodied in the still dominant discourse of religious culture. Under the influence of Darwinism, discovering what was natural increasingly became the dominant medium for prescribing what was right.[18] Nature thus became the focus for inquiries into what is desirable.

What is Natural in Natural Law/Rights

For most of American legal history since 1789, the issue of higher law has been a marginal issue. Few legal writers have believed that it was appropriate for higher law directly to trump positive law, and the Constitution has been more or less consistently understood as a form of superpositive law enacted by the sovereign people. Instead, the central question for nineteenth-century legal thinkers was whether judges "discover" or "make" law; "nature" has played a prominent role in efforts to demonstrate that judges simply find the law. Two sets of issues have generated most of the battles over natural law/rights. The first has concerned starting points and background assumptions, what Cass Sunstein has called "baselines." Many of these questions have turned on definitions of what is "natural."

For example, the privileging of "omissions" over "acts," and negative freedom over positive freedom, has derived from state-of-nature premises. Likewise, the nineteenth century's privileging of contract over tort (allowing contracting out of tort obligations), of private law over public law, and of common law over statutory law ("statutes in derogation of the common law are to be strictly construed") were all similarly structured by state-of-nature background assumptions.

The natural–nonnatural distinction was central to late-nineteenth-century efforts at legal classification: for example, natural versus

18. See Horwitz, *TAL*, 140–42, 210, and chap. 4.

artificial uses of water resources and land as in *Rylands v. Fletcher*;[19] whether the corporation was a natural or artificial entity;[20] whether causation was objective and arranged in a "natural sequence";[21] whether there was a prepolitical natural right to property[22] and to contract in the future.[23] In all of these conceptualizations, the basic model of the common law was that it mirrored what had existed in a prior state of nature. By discovering what was natural, judges could find the law. During the late nineteenth century, a will theory of contract[24] was embedded in a conception of a neutral and self-executing market. Laissez-faire premises expressed the view that the natural starting point for legal analysis was the private law of contract, which reflected the voluntary agreements people would arrive at in a state of nature.[25]

Eventually, Progressives and legal realists from 1905 to 1940 attacked the notion that property is a natural right and instead insisted, in Holmes's words, that property is "a creation of law."[26] In general, they declared that judges make, not find, the law, and that state-of-nature assumptions should not be regarded as the starting point for legal analysis.[27]

A second set of issues also derived from controversies over what was natural. They dealt with whether legal reasoning was "natural" or "artificial"[28] and whether law was to be derived from power and will or from reason and nature. So, for example, the question of whether analogical reasoning was neutral or political,[29] whether there were natural categories that make it possible to say that one case was

19. Rylands v. Fletcher, L.R. 3 H.L. 330 (1868); see generally F. Bohlen, "The Rule in Rylands v. Fletcher," *University of Pennsylvania Law Review* 59 (1911): 293, 373; Horwitz, *TAL*, 104–5.

20. Horwitz, *TAL*, 67–68.

21. Horwitz, *TAL*, 51–52.

22. Horwitz, *TAL*, 147–49, 151–52.

23. See Ogden v. Saunders, 25 U.S. (12 Wheat.) 213, 344–45 (1827).

24. Horwitz, *TAL*, 34–36.

25. Horwitz, *TAL*, 151 n. 36.

26. International News Service v. Associated Press, 248 U.S. 215, 246 (1918) (Holmes, J.).

27. See sources in notes 3–4; Compare Cohen, "Property and Sovereignty," *Cornell Law Quarterly* 13 (1927): 8 (applying a natural rights theory to assert that it is just for the state to limit or take private property without compensation for the benefit of the public.

28. Horwitz, *TAL*, 157, 200–203, 205.

29. Horwitz, *TAL* 201–205. See also D. Kennedy and F. Michelman, "Are Property and Contract Efficient," *Hofstra Law Review* 8 (1980): 711, 751.

"like" another or, instead, whether the construction of all legal categories and classifications ultimately depended on the social function the
categories were meant to serve[30]—these questions were all debated
within a natural rights framework.

The most prominent question that became the focal point for
many of the debates about legal reasoning involved the legitimate
scope of legal implication. The question of how much it is legitimate
to "imply" from a provision in a contract, statute, or constitution has
been a perennial issue in legal theory.[31] From John Marshall's effort to
"imply" from the commerce and necessary and proper clauses a
power to charter a federal bank in *McCulloch v. Maryland*[32] to the
success of late-nineteenth-century legal thinkers in creating "implied
limitations" deriving from the separation of powers between legislature and judiciary to the debate over "implied" contracts[33] in classical
legal thought, jurists struggled over the scope of legal reasoning. The
debate over whether the scope of implication should be narrow or
broad has ultimately turned on whether there is some neutral and
natural mode of legal reasoning or whether the scope of implication is
not inevitably dependent upon prior starting points. Likewise, all
questions of interpretation have turned on debates over theories of
language and whether language is natural or conventional, that is,
whether it too is a "mirror of nature" or, instead, socially created.
Thus, all arguments over whether categories or meanings have a
"core" and a "periphery" are arguments about whether meanings
reflect natural essences or are socially constructed.[34]

With the emergence of abolitionist thought in the two decades
before the Civil War, there was immediate division over whether
antislavery principles could be derived from the Constitution or
whether the "slave Constitution" itself needed to be subordinated to
higher law principles.[35] The Garrisonian "higher law" challenge to
slavery was matched by Frederick Douglass's insistence that the Constitution, "construed in the light of well established rules of legal
interpretation, might be made consistent . . . with the noble pur-

---

30. Horwitz, *TAL*, 18.
31. See Horwitz, *TAL*, chap. 2.
32. McCulloch v. Maryland, 17 U.S. (4 Wheat.) 316 (1819).
33. Horwitz, *TAL*, 36–39.
34. See Shapiro, *Evolution of Rights*; and Horwitz, *TAL*, 18.
35. See S. Touster, "In Search of Holmes from Within," *Vanderbilt Law Review* 18
(1965): 437; and Horwitz, *TAL*, chap. 4.

poses avowed in its preamble." He believed that the document could "be wielded in behalf of emancipation."[36] But as the *Dred Scott* case[37] demonstrated, natural rights principles could as easily be invoked to justify slavery as part of the right to property.

Law and Morals

The controversy over natural law is most familiar to the American constitutional lawyer or historian in the "higher law/substantive due process" version that the Progressive critique of the *Lochner* court made famous;[38] among philosophers and students of jurisprudence, however, the question has usually been framed as one of the relation between law and morals (natural law/rights versus legal positivism) or, occasionally, between facts and values (natural law/rights versus ethical positivism).

What I wish briefly to do is to outline the very different circumstances under which questions about the relation between law and morals have been raised. My intellectual strategy, as above, is to catalog the widely varying versions of natural law/rights discourse and to insist that only through disaggregation and contextualization of the debates can we see the vastly different political and historical circumstances that have given rise to questions about natural law.

In our own time, the debates between H. L. A. Hart and Lon Fuller[39] and between Hart and Ronald Dworkin[40] have had that air of abstraction, that inattention to context and history, that has marked Anglo-American jurisprudence since Bentham. Rarely is there any reference to the fundamentally different legal starting points or to the strikingly different legal cultures of England and America. From the time of the first written state constitutions enacted after the American Revolution, Americans became aware that they were developing a fundamentally different picture of law and lawmaking than they had inherited from an English system of parliamentary sovereignty lacking

---

36. W. S. McFeely, *Frederick Douglass* (Touchstone, 1991), 169.

37. Dred Scott v. Sandford, 60 U.S. 393 (1857) (holding that "the negro might justly and lawfully be reduced to slavery for [the white man's] benefit" [407]).

38. Horwitz, *TAL*, 33–36.

39. See H. L. A. Hart, "Positivism and the Separation of Law and Morals," *Harvard Law Review* 71 (1958): 593; and L. Fuller, *Positivism and Fidelity to Law—A Reply to Professor Hart, Harvard Law Review* 71 (1958): 630.

40. See R. Dworkin, *Taking Rights Seriously* (Cambridge: Harvard University Press, 1977), chaps. 1–3.

a written constitution and judicial review. For Americans, the strict theories of precedent that nineteenth-century English courts seemed to "derive" from principles of parliamentary supremacy were never favored. American courts were usually more willing to ignore a precedent if it meant adhering to some more general "principle." Even in the age of classical legal thought, American courts were less formalistic and more explicitly "policy oriented" than the highly professionalized English judiciary. In America, natural law/rights ideas entered into the everyday process of judicial interpretation in ways that their English counterparts would have denounced as judicial legislation.

Let us now examine the intellectual history of the law-morality dichotomy in Anglo-American jurisprudence. It was the "founder" of English jurisprudence, John Austin, who made the separation between law and morality the fundamental starting point of English jurisprudence.[41] What was at stake in this distinction?

On the Continent, the emergence of Comptean positivism reintroduced the conflict between religion and science that had been muted before the French Revolution in Diderot's great *Encyclopedia*. For European liberals of the nineteenth century, positivism stood for the overthrow of religious superstition and an all-powerful church. A sharp separation between facts and values and between law and morals expressed their desire to allow science, not religion, to offer objective truth about the world. In law, the liberal agenda focused on the reform-oriented lawmaking functions of popularly elected parliaments in which law was the "command" of a sovereign people.[42] In all European countries, nineteenth-century liberals were legal positivists who insisted that the separation between law and morality meant that those decentralized medieval lawmaking institutions of church, guild, and manor should be subordinated to parliamentary supremacy and the triumph of science over religion.

In England, Bentham was the underlying inspiration for Austin's positivism. But the English case stood institutionally midway between the two poles established by the post-Revolutionary American and

---

41. Horwitz, *TAL*, 154.

42. J. S. Mill defined positivism in a letter to Comte as "the substitution of the scientific for the religious point of view. . . ." Roger Soltau, *French Political Thought in the Nineteenth Century* (New York: Russell & Russell, 1959) 205. See F. Neumann, *The Democratic and the Authoritarian State* (Glencoe, Ill.: Free Press, 1957); and A. P. d'Entreves, *Natural Law: An Introduction to Legal Philosophy* (London: Hutchinson of London, 1970), as cited in Horwitz, *Rights*, 399 n. 39.

continental European legal orders. Like the Europeans, by 1789 the English had accepted the principle of parliamentary (if not popular) sovereignty. If, after the Glorious Revolution of 1689, parliamentary supremacy had become the established political reality, during the course of the eighteenth century it had also become the established constitutional reality. As seventeenth-century Whig fundamental law ideas withered, by 1765 Blackstone could proclaim the constitutional understanding that fundamental law could not control an act of parliament.[43]

If the English were more like the Europeans in dispensing with a higher-law tradition, they were more like the Americans in continuing to justify the common law power of judges in terms that were inconsistent with parliamentary supremacy. Bentham's vigorous attack on Blackstone and the common law in 1776 illustrates this point.[44]

Bentham understood that, due to the triumph of parliamentary supremacy, Blackstone's glorification of the common law as a "mysterious science" constituted a reactionary effort to entrench a conception of an autonomous common law within English legal culture.[45] Unlike post-revolutionary European judges, common law judges thus continued to insist that law was not "made" but "discovered." Why did Bentham challenge Blackstone on this point?

Blackstone's contemporary, the poet Alexander Pope, captured the underlying worldview of Blackstone's *Commentaries*. Let us look to Nature, Pope declared.

> All are but parts of one stupendous whole,
> Whose body Nature is, and God the soul; . . .
> All Nature is but art, unknown to thee;
> All chance, direction, which thou canst not see;
> All discord, harmony not understood;
> All partial evil, universal good:
> And, spite of pride, in erring reason's spite,
> One truth is clear, whatever is, is RIGHT.
>
> (from "An Essay on Man," 1733)

---

43. See J. W. Gough, *Fundamental Law in English Constitutional History* (Oxford: Clarendon Press, 1955), cited in Horwitz, *Rights,* 396 n. 22, 399 n. 39.

44. See J. Bentham, *A Comment on the Commentaries and A Fragment on Government,* ed. J. Burns and H. Hart (London: University of London Athlone Press/Atlantic Highlands, N.J.: Humanities Press, 1977). See also Horwitz, *TAL,* 121.

45. Horwitz, *TAL,* 121, 153.

For Bentham, the common law represented not the slow unfolding of Reason or the reflection of Nature but the survival of feudal conceptions that amounted to a barbarous and unjust system.[46] He rebelled against Blackstone's effort to represent the incoherent principles of English law as "one stupendous whole . . . which thou canst not see," because its "discord" and "partial evil" were actually "harmony not understood" and "universal good." For Bentham, Blackstone had invoked natural law/natural rights ideas in order to conclude that "whatever is, is right."

If, in the United States, both constitutional and common law theory introduced questions about higher or fundamental law, in England the triumph of parliamentary supremacy forced these questions into a common law structure. On the Continent, by contrast, both legislating and judging were brought within a common structure of parliamentary (or popular) sovereignty.

Bentham's advocacy of codification (along the lines of the Napoleonic Code) was his way of encouraging reform by subordinating the common law to both parliamentary supremacy and principles of utility.[47] But if codification was logically consistent with parliamentary sovereignty, its association with the French Revolution and principles of popular sovereignty made it deeply suspect both in England and in the United States. During the slow emergence of popular sovereignty after the English Reform Bills of 1832 and 1867 and the elimination of the House of Lords veto in the constitutional revolution of 1911, a conception of an autonomous common law system (in which custom and natural law merged) was developed as one of the important alternatives to democratic legitimacy.

What was the significance of Austin's attempt to establish a sharp separation between law and morals? As on the Continent, the distinction between law and morals stood for the separation between secular and religious sources of law, which was the basis for being able to claim that law was a "science." But for Austin, as for Bentham, the law-morals distinction also paralleled the separation between law and custom.[48]

---

46. See Bentham, *Comment on the Commentaries.*

47. See J. King, *Utilitarian Jurisprudence in America: The Influence of Bentham and Austin on American Legal Thought in the Nineteenth Century* (New York: Garland, 1986), chap. 5; E. Halevy, *The Growth of Philosophic Radicalism* (New York: Macmillan, 1928), 76–81.

48. Horwitz, *TAL,* 121–23.

Bentham's attack on Blackstone was precisely such an effort to delegitimate customary law as the product of feudal barbarism and the superstition of kings and popes. The first question asked by all followers of Austin was how to distinguish between law and custom.

By seeking to break the connection between the common law and custom, Austin thus sought not only to subordinate the common law to parliamentary supremacy but also to subordinate feudal customary law to the more general "common" law. If his analysis did not result in legislative codification (which since the French Revolution was increasingly feared as the expression of popular rule), it would nevertheless derive all judge-made rules from the underlying principles of parliamentary legislation. Law was no longer discovered; it was made.

Since Austin, the debate within English jurisprudence has been over whether principles of judging must be derived from parliamentary sovereignty or whether there are autonomous common law principles that in some loose sense are to be derived from natural or fundamental law. The Austinian distinction between law and morals has been used both to completely subordinate the common law to parliamentary will and to create an autonomous "science" of law that remains resistant to the encroachments of parliamentary (and popular) sovereignty.

Conclusion

I have sought to show that the uses and meanings of natural law and natural rights have varied enormously in modern Western culture and that it is not useful to address the question with the unhistorical and abstract universalism that has become characteristic of Anglo-American jurisprudence since Bentham and Austin. How natural law and natural rights have entered into legal discourse has varied widely depending on the particular context of the problems that the discourse was called upon to address. Whether natural law/rights ideas represent "higher law" located "outside" prevailing legal discourse or instead simply constitute the unavoidable baselines and background assumptions that inevitably exist "inside" all legal discourse has not received enough attention. Similarly, multiple versions of natural law have arisen because they have served widely different functions. For example, natural law has taken different

forms depending on whether it has been used to justify or criticize
authority or property or slavery. It has varied depending on whether
or not it has arisen in the context of a written constitution with
judicial review; and on whether it has been invoked to defend or
restrict parliamentary or popular sovereignty; and on whether it has
represented religion or science in the great modern struggles over
legitimation. Unless we can address the multiple meanings of natural law in its varied historical contexts, we will continue to stereo-
type the question of the role of natural law ideas in the modern
United States.

Lincoln, Slavery, and Rights

William E. Cain

Abraham Lincoln possessed a powerful sense of persons at work, fulfilling and improving themselves and building the new American nation, and in the process serving as a source of enlightenment and encouragement to the benighted world. The United States was special, he stated repeatedly, because it accorded its people the right to work freely and rise economically.[1] Lincoln expressed this faith during a period of xenophobia, religious intolerance, and, above all, slavery.[2] He affirmed it yet again, with fratricidal war under way, in his December 3, 1861, Message to Congress:

> The prudent, penniless beginner in the world, labors for wages awhile, saves a surplus with which to buy tools or land for himself; then labors on his own account another while, and at length hires another new beginner to help him. This is the just, and generous, and prosperous system, which opens the way to all— gives hope to all, and consequent energy, and progress, and improvement of condition to all.[3]

Scholars have been inclined, however, to challenge Lincoln's vision in passages like this one, noting that in the decades before the Civil War, and during the war itself, industrialization eroded the promise

---

1. On this point, see Stephen B. Oates, *Abraham Lincoln: The Man Behind the Myths* (New York: New American Library, 1985), 59.

2. See J. R. Pole, *Paths to the American Past* (New York: Oxford University Press, 1979), 126.

3. Abraham Lincoln, *Speeches and Writings*, 2 vols. (New York: Library of America, 1989), 2:297. Further references will be given in the text.

that an individual could rise through earnest, independent work. As Eric Foner has said, Lincoln was attempting to preserve a "premodern" society—"the world of the small shop, the independent farm, and the village artisan."[4]

Even more, scholars have argued that Lincoln was unwilling to extend to blacks the same scale of rights that he described for whites. Lincoln hated slavery—a "monstrous injustice," he termed it in an October 16, 1854, speech on the Kansas-Nebraska Act (1:315)—and he judged that the black man should receive wages, maintaining in a July 17, 1858, speech that "in the right to put into his mouth the bread that his own hands have earned," he "is the equal of every other man, white or black" (1:478). But Lincoln nevertheless seems to have been unable to imagine America as a land in which white and black workers could enjoy full social and political rights in common and live together in a single Union. In his August 21, 1858, debate with Stephen Douglas in Ottawa, Illinois, Lincoln reckoned that blacks should be accorded "natural rights" but never be raised to "perfect equality" with whites (1:512).

Yet the passage in which Lincoln makes this statement is complicated. It begins firmly, but then mutes, even as it continues to propound, the claim for inequality:

> I have no purpose to introduce political and social equality between the white and the black races. There is a physical difference between the two, which in my judgment will probably forever forbid their living together upon the footing of perfect equality, and inasmuch as it becomes a necessity that there must be a difference, I, as well, as Judge Douglas, am in favor of the race to which I belong, having the superior position. I have never said anything to the contrary, but I hold that notwithstanding all this, there is no reason in the world why the Negro is not entitled to all the natural rights enumerated in the Declaration of Independence, the right to life, liberty and the pursuit of happiness. [Loud cheers.] I hold that he is as much entitled to these as the white man. I agree with Judge Douglas he is not my equal in many respects—certainly not in color, perhaps not in moral

---

4. Eric Foner, *Politics and Ideology in the Age of the Civil War* (New York: Oxford University Press, 1980), 32.

or intellectual endowment. But in the right to eat the bread, without leave of anybody else, which his own hand earns, *he is my equal and the equal of Judge Douglas, and the equal of every living man.* [Great applause.] (1:512)

It would be interesting to know whether the audience was applauding Lincoln's affirmation of rights for blacks or, instead, commending him for recognizing that blacks should be sealed in a zone of inequality. The German-born journalist Henry Villard, who covered the Ottawa debate and favored Douglas, observed that Lincoln seemed "inspired by sound convictions in consonance with the true spirit of American institutions."[5] But what did this "true spirit" signify? Lincoln's central assertion is that "the Negro," too, participates in the guarantees of the Declaration of Independence; but he couples it with comforting words to whites that he does not mean blacks are thereby equal to them.

Still, Lincoln's insistence on inequality is hedged, more than it needed to be. The physical difference "probably" will keep blacks and whites apart for all time. "Probably forever" is a canny locution, forthright and yet seeded with a doubt. The kind of inequality to which Lincoln refers with confidence is only the most obvious one—*color*; as for moral and intellectual endowment, he will go only as far as "perhaps." The deliberate looseness of Lincoln's phrasing suggests that the whole matter of racial difference is arbitrary. It is serious and must be addressed; but it can be gotten past with a simple acknowledgment of the weight of "necessity." If there must be a difference, then of course, Lincoln as a white man wants his race to be "superior"—the intimation being that blacks could tender a similar claim for themselves, in favor of the race to which they belong.

But isn't there a further development of Lincoln's argument from "necessity"? What about Lincoln's longtime interest in, and support for, emigration and colonization? Wasn't this his blunt answer to the problem of black rights and to the prospect of a society that would precariously mix unequals, the "inferior" blacks and the "superior" whites? The historian John Hope Franklin has in fact said that one can nearly always measure Lincoln's "approach to emancipation by

---

5. Henry Villard, *Memoirs*, 2 vols. (Boston: Houghton, Mifflin, 1904), 1:93.

studying the increasing intensity of his efforts to formulate a feasible program of colonization."[6] Lincoln, it appears, was a moderate on racial differences but ultimately could conceive of emancipation for blacks only if they would agree to reside outside the United States, taking their rights with them.

This notion represents an unattractive legacy of Kentucky senator Henry Clay, whom Lincoln admired ("my beau ideal of a statesman" [1:526]) for his sense of the importance of national unity and sectional interdependence as well as for his stands against slavery and in favor of colonization.[7] Lincoln carried a book of Clay's speeches, quoting from it to dramatize Clay's contempt for slavery. But, like Clay, Lincoln believed that calls for the abolition of slavery, as opposed to arguments for limiting it, would endanger the Union and its prosperity. So, too, would the sheer presence of blacks, slave or free—which is why Lincoln was drawn to the idea that blacks could be relocated in Liberia, Central America, or Haiti.[8]

Colonization was not only Lincoln's and Clay's goal, however, but Thomas Jefferson's and James Madison's as well. Jefferson attacked slavery and the slave trade in, for example, *A Summary View of the Rights of British America* (1774), in the draft version of the Declaration of Independence (1776), and in *Notes on the State of Virginia* (1787), where he closed Query VIII by naming slavery as a "great political and moral evil." But he favored emancipation *and* colonization, detailing at length in Query XIV of *Notes* the many "political, physical, and moral objections" to the idea that blacks might be "incorporated" into the American nation.[9] Like Jefferson, Madison believed, as he stated in 1819, that "to be consistent with existing and probably unalterable prejudices in the United States, the freed blacks ought to be permanently removed beyond the region occupied by, or allotted to, a white

---

6. John Hope Franklin, *The Emancipation Proclamation* (1963; reprint, New York: Anchor, 1965), 31. See also Benjamin Quarles, *The Negro in the Civil War* (1953; reprint, Boston: Little, Brown, 1969), 145–57.

7. In *Henry Clay: Statesman for the Union* (New York: Norton, 1991), Robert V. Remini notes Clay's significant influence on Lincoln (8, 447, 643–44, 786). See also Lincoln's July 6, 1852, eulogy on Clay (1:271).

8. Relevant studies include Warren A. Beck, "Lincoln and Negro Colonization in Central America," *Abraham Lincoln Quarterly* 6 (1950): 162–83; and Paul J. Scheips, "Lincoln and the Chiriqui Colonization Project," *Journal of Negro History* 37 (1952): 418–53.

9. Thomas Jefferson, *Writings* (New York: Library of America, 1984), 22, 115, 214, 264.

population. The objections to a thorough incorporation of the two people are, with most of the whites insuperable; and are admitted by all of them to be very powerful."[10] Most Americans, Madison concluded, were harshly prejudiced against blacks and would not tolerate living among them. Madison's desire to be true to the principles of the American Revolution led him in one direction, while his dependence on slavery and distaste for black people led him in another.[11]

Jefferson, Madison, and Clay recognized that blacks should be granted natural rights—or, to shift the point slightly, that blacks could not legitimately be denied such rights. But slavery, freedom, and natural rights were always linked for these statesmen to the impossibility of a biracial society. Neither experience nor education could lift blacks to the point where white Americans would tolerate them: this was the vision of the future that Jefferson, Madison, and Clay shared. Racial prejudice, they believed, was "ineradicable" and would remain in force even if slavery were abolished.[12] For Madison, and for Lincoln as well, racism was irrational and regrettable, but above all it was insurmountable.[13] Clay declared that colonization was a blessing because it reaffirmed that blacks and whites could not live together: "the God of nature, by the differences in color and physical constitution, has decreed against it."[14]

Following Jefferson, Madison, and Clay, Lincoln insisted that while blacks were covered by the terms of the Declaration of Independence, they could not permanently dwell in the nation that this inaugural document defined and thus were barred from rising through

---

10. James Madison, *The Mind of the Founder: Sources of the Political Thought of James Madison*, ed. Marvin Meyers (Indianapolis: Bobbs-Merrill, 1973),' 399–400, 422–27. See also Matthew T. Mellon, *Early American Views on Negro Slavery* (1934; new ed. New York: New American Library, 1969), 133.

11. See Adrienne Koch, *Madison's "Advice to My Country"* (Princeton: Princeton University Press, 1966), 142–44; Ralph Ketcham, *James Madison: A Biography* (1971; reprint, Charlottesville: University of Virginia Press, 1990), 625–26; and Staughton Lynd, *Class Conflict, Slavery, and the United States Constitution: Ten Essays* (Indianapolis: Bobbs-Merrill, 1967), 180.

12. See Thomas Brown, *Politics and Statesmanship: Essays on the American Whig Party* (New York: Columbia University Press, 1985), 139; and Robert Middlekauf, *The Glorious Cause: The American Revolution, 1763–1789* (New York: Oxford University Press, 1982), 331–32.

13. Drew McCoy, *The Last of the Fathers: James Madison and the Republican Legacy* (New York: Cambridge University Press, 1989), 278.

14. Henry Clay, cited in Clement Eaton, *Henry Clay and the Art of American Politics* (Boston: Little, Brown, 1957), 133.

America's "just, and generous, and prosperous" economic system. Given his doubts about blacks ever becoming full-fledged U.S. citizens, it does appear that Lincoln was "a pessimist on the subject of the possibility of an interracial, egalitarian society."[15]

Toward the end of Reconstruction, Frederick Douglass made a version of just this point with punishing clarity. In a speech delivered on April 14, 1876, Douglass said that Lincoln

> was preeminently the white man's President, entirely devoted to the welfare of white men. He was ready and willing at any time during the first years of his administration to deny, postpone, and sacrifice the rights of humanity in the colored people to promote the welfare of the white people of this country. In all his education and feeling he was an American of the Americans.[16]

While much evidence points to Lincoln's uneasiness about extending complete rights to blacks, much of this same evidence, when examined closely, is mixed and ambiguous. It is often difficult to identify how Lincoln really understood the rights of black persons, and the degree to which he concluded these should be permanently limited. This difficulty can be discerned not only in the speech in which Lincoln rebutted Stephen Douglas in Ottawa in August 1858, with its curious verbal details, but in countless other speeches, letters, and documents.

One of the best examples that emblematizes Lincoln's paradoxes, tactical silences, and forceful yet equivocal affirmations, is his well-known August 22, 1862, letter to Horace Greeley, Republican party champion and editor of the New York *Tribune*. In his August 20 "Prayer of Twenty Millions," Greeley had beseeched Lincoln to grant freedom to slaves who crossed into Union lines. Lincoln responded almost immediately, and, as it happens, did so one week after he had given a well-publicized address to a "Committee of Colored Men" in which he accented racial differences and the benefits of colonization

---

15. Harry V. Jaffa, *Crisis of the House Divided: An Interpretation of the Lincoln-Douglas Debates* (1959; reprint, Seattle: University of Washington Press, 1973), 384; and "Abraham Lincoln," in *American Political Thought: The Philosophic Dimension of American Statesmanship*, 2d ed., ed. Morton J. Frisch and Richard G. Stevens (Itasca: Peacock, 1983), 201.

16. Frederick Douglass, *The Life and Writings of Frederick Douglass*, ed. Philip S. Foner, 5 vols. (New York: International, 1950–1975), 4:312.

for blacks and upbraided them in advance for "extreme selfishness" if they recoiled at leaving the United States (2:353–57).

Lincoln told Greeley:

> I would save the Union. I would save it the shortest way under the Constitution. The sooner the national authority can be restored; the nearer the Union will be "the Union as it was." If there be those who would not save the Union, unless at the same time they could *save* slavery, I do not agree with them. If there be those who would not save the Union unless they could at the same time *destroy* slavery, I do not agree with them. My paramount object in this struggle *is* to save the Union, and it is *not* either to save or to destroy slavery. If I could save the Union without freeing *any* slave I would do it, and if I could save it by freeing *all* the slaves, I would do it; and if I could save it by freeing some and leaving others alone I would also do that. What I do about slavery, and the colored race, I do because I believe it helps to save the Union; and what I forbear, I forbear because I do *not* believe it would help to save the Union. I shall do *less* whenever I shall believe what I am doing hurts the cause, and I shall do *more* whenever I shall believe doing more will help the cause. I shall try to correct errors when shown to be errors; and I shall adopt new views so fast as they appear to be true views. (2:358)

This letter has typically been interpreted to prove that Lincoln loved the Union more than he hated slavery. The Indiana Republican George Julian recalled years later that this letter angered "anti-slavery critics of the President" who "insisted that in thus dealing with slavery as a matter of total indifference he likened himself to Douglas, who had declared that he didn't care whether slavery was voted up or voted down in the Territories."[17]

Yet does this letter illuminate Lincoln's views or mask them? When he wrote to Greeley and earlier when he met with the Committee of Colored Men, Lincoln had already drafted his Emancipation Proclamation.[18] He had first mentioned "the subject of emancipating

---

17. George W. Julian, *Political Recollections, 1840–1872* (1884; reprint, New York: Negro Universities Press, 1969), 221.

18. Glyndon G. Van Deusen, *Horace Greeley: Nineteenth-Century Crusader* (Philadelphia: University of Pennsylvania Press, 1953), 283–88.

the slaves by proclamation" to Gideon Welles and William Seward on July 13, 1862, indicating to them privately that "it was a military necessity absolutely essential for the salvation of the Union": "we must free the slaves or be ourselves subdued." According to Welles, Lincoln and the members of his cabinet had always judged that in line with the Constitution, slavery should be left to the states; but the extent of the rebellion, and the labor provided by slaves in sustaining it, "impelled the Administration to adopt extraordinary measures to preserve the national existence."[19]

Lincoln thus had chosen and told his cabinet about a course of action for which he was preparing the way in public by highlighting the separation of the races and the primacy of the Union's survival. His words to Greeley were more popular than the deed he was about to perform, and he needed to utter them—invested in them a lot or a little himself—in order to equip the majority of Northerners to concur with the proclamation of freedom for slaves he was going to announce. It would not have been possible for Lincoln to gain approval for emancipation unless he made known that American Union required any sacrifice, including either preserving or ending slavery.

It is this second possibility—that the life of the Union might demand the death of slavery—that makes the letter to Greeley more potent than at first it might appear. In it Lincoln acknowledges that he would free the slaves to save the Union, and, again, he had *already* taken this step, as the public learned in September 1862 when Lincoln said he would emancipate the slaves in the rebellious states. To maintain, then, as does the historian Kenneth Stampp, that the letter to Greeley shows Lincoln's "public posture of indifference" to slavery is misleading.[20] Lincoln's indifference to slavery was blended with the determination to destroy it if necessary.

Scholars often assume that Lincoln's letter was published in the *Tribune*, and indeed it was, in the August 25 issue. But Lincoln chose to publish it first, on August 23, in the Washington, D.C., *National Intelligencer*, a paper that was mixed in its response to Lincoln and

19. Gideon Welles, *Diary*, 3 vols., ed. John T. Morse Jr. (Boston: Houghton Mifflin, 1911), 1:70, 71, 142–44.

20. Kenneth Stampp, "One Alone? The United States and National Self-Determination," in *Lincoln, the War President*, ed. Gabor S. Borrit (New York: Oxford University Press, 1992), 141.

sympathetic to the plight of the South.[21] Greeley himself later said that Lincoln's letter was so careful and well reasoned that he suspected it had been written before Greeley's own letter appeared. He also noted that Lincoln had not really addressed the main thrust of the "Prayer," which was that Lincoln should employ the Confiscation Act, already on the books, to the case of slaves escaping from the rebels. In his reply, Lincoln treated the general issue of abolition, whereas Greeley simply wanted the president to execute the existing law of the land for the purpose of emancipation. Both because Lincoln did not take up Greeley's proposal, and because his tone appeared balanced and cautious, many blacks and abolitionists found the letter to Greeley extremely disappointing.[22] But in their regret that Lincoln failed to say that he *would* destroy slavery, they did not see that he was *willing* to destroy it if he had to.

But there is still another point to be made about the letter to Greeley. Lincoln says he would agree to the continuation of slavery. But he does not say he would agree to the *extension* of slavery. At one time, Lincoln was prepared to accept extension if it was the only means through which to save the Union. He conceded in the Kansas-Nebraska speech of 1854 that "much as I hate slavery, I would consent to the extension of it rather than see the Union dissolved, just as I would consent to any GREAT evil, to avoid a GREATER one" (1:333). But by the later 1850s and early 1860s, Lincoln had altered his position, and his letter to Greeley is consistent with it: slavery could remain where it was but could not expand anywhere else. He said this often, as in a December 10, 1860, letter to Lyman Trumbull, a lawyer, jurist, and Republican senator from Illinois: "Let there be no compromise on the question of *extending* slavery. If there be, all our labor is lost, and, ere long, must be done again" (2:190; see also 2:191).[23]

Lincoln possessed a keen sense of "calculation," of gauging when

21. Robert S. Harper, *Lincoln and the Press* (New York: McGraw-Hill, 1951), 173; and *Abraham Lincoln: A Press Portrait*, ed. Herbert Mitgang (Chicago: Quadrangle, 1971), 300–302.

22. Benjamin Quarles, *Lincoln and the Negro* (1962; reprint, New York: Da Capo, 1990), 129.

23. Lincoln underscored this principle on February 23, 1861, when he talked with delegates to a peace conference who hoped to resolve the secession crisis. See *Lincoln on Democracy*, ed. Mario M. Cuomo and Harold Holzer (New York: Harper Collins, 1990), 200.

to act and what to say, particularly on the perilous question of rights for blacks.[24] It is temptingly easy to affirm rights in the abstract and, with Frederick Douglass, to rebuke Lincoln for representing white America and for failing to blazon that blacks are equal to whites in every respect and should therefore enjoy identical rights from top to bottom. But the problem with such an indictment of Lincoln is that it detaches rights from the historical situation in which he understood and explicated them and in which he sought to make them more capacious than they had been.[25]

With a background in the Whig party of Clay and Daniel Webster, both of whom had opposed extension, Lincoln was a "free soiler" and a leading Republican in the 1850s: he held fast to "the principles of free labor, self-help, social mobility, and economic independence."[26] The Free Soil party itself, which included members of the abolitionist Liberty party and antislavery Democrats and Whigs, devised a platform in 1848 that was antiexpansion. It proposed "no interference by Congress with Slavery within the limits of any State" even as it also insisted, "No more Slave States and no more Slave Territory."[27] Lincoln's own "free soil" attitudes, marked by his votes in Congress for the Wilmot Proviso in the 1840s, combined resistance to slavery expansion with acceptance of it where it existed.[28] This position had wide appeal in the North, because it enabled people to define "free soil" at the expense of black rights. It meant (or was taken to mean) "free soil" for whites only, who thereby would not compete in the marketplace

---

24. Shelby Foote, in Geoffrey C. Ward, with Ric Burns and Ken Burns, *The Civil War: An Illustrated History* (New York: Knopf, 1990), 270.

25. Another dimension of Lincoln and the issue of "rights" involves the limits he placed on civil liberties during the war. See Frank L. Klement, *The Limits of Dissent: Clement L. Vallandigham and the Civil War* (Lexington: University Press of Kentucky, 1970); and Mark E. Neely Jr., *The Fate of Liberty: Abraham Lincoln and Civil Liberties* (New York: Oxford University Press, 1991).

26. Stephen B. Oates, "Abraham Lincoln: Republican in the White House," in *Abraham Lincoln and the American Political Tradition,* ed. John L. Thomas (Amherst: University of Massachusetts Press, 1986), 101.

27. Free Soil party platform, reprinted in Frederick J. Blue, *The Free Soilers: Third Party Politics, 1848–1854* (Urbana: University of Illinois Press, 1973), 294–95.

28. In August 1846, David Wilmot, an antislavery Democrat from Pennsylvania, introduced a measure in the House of Representatives (the so-called "Wilmot Proviso") that would have prohibited slavery in any territory acquired during the Mexican war. This measure was debated for years but never received full Congressional approval. See Chaplain W. Morrison, *Democratic Politics and Sectionalism: The Wilmot Proviso Controversy* (Chapel Hill: University of North Carolina Press, 1967).

with slaves and would not suffer the shame of laboring amid inferior, degraded "colored" men and women.

Lincoln, then, was not unusual in distinguishing antislavery from the "immediate abolition" that William Lloyd Garrison and the American Anti-Slavery Society had advocated since the 1830s. Politically, this was the only practical course—condemning slavery and cordoning it off while, for the sake of the Union, leaving it alone where it endured. Salmon P. Chase, Republican governor and senator from Ohio and later Lincoln's secretary of the treasury, always insisted he was "an antislavery man," not an abolitionist. He proposed to cripple slavery by preventing its spread; he would not attack it directly in the states where it existed and enjoyed constitutional protection. Chase wanted to "denationalize" slavery.[29] As he stated in a speech in March 1850, "we have no power to legislate on the subject of slavery in the States. We have power to prevent its extension, and to prohibit its existence within the sphere of the exclusive jurisdiction of the general government."[30]

Chase made his own position hinge on the Constitution, but others in the broad antiexpansionist movement concentrated on race, on the racial imperative to rid the nation of slavery so that whites would be rescued from the contamination of blacks. James Watson Webb, the editor of the New York City *Courier and Enquirer* and a virulent antiabolitionist in the 1830s, became a free soiler by the 1850s. He still found nothing intrinsically wrong with black slavery and despised abolitionists. But he judged that slavery cursed white workers, endangered Northern states and territories, and demoralized the nation. By the outbreak of the Civil War, Webb was clamoring that the "Slave Power" should be crushed, slavery annihilated, and—the next necessary step for him—free blacks deported.[31] Deportation, different from colonization, meant sending blacks out of the country whether they wanted to go or not.

Lincoln made use of the appeal to whites of "free soil" doctrine. In the Kansas-Nebraska speech cited earlier, he praised Jefferson as the

---

29. Albert Bushnell Hart, *Salmon P. Chase* (1899; reprint, New York: Chelsea, 1980), 54–55. See also Henry S. Foote, *Casket of Reminiscences* (1874; reprint, New York: Negro Universities Press, 1968), 133–34.

30. Cited in Hart, *Salmon P. Chase*, 125.

31. See Leonard L. Richards, *"Gentlemen of Property and Standing": Anti-Abolition Mobs in Jacksonian America* (1970; reprint, New York: Oxford University Press, 1973), 31–32.

prolocutor for the Ordinance of 1787, which prohibited slavery in the northwest territory: "It is now what Jefferson foresaw and intended— the happy home of teeming millions of free, white, prosperous people, and no slave amongst them" (1:309). He stated that "the best use" of "new territories" was in the national interest: "We want them for the homes of free white people" (1:331).

But in this same speech, Lincoln aligned himself with the Declaration of Independence, asserting that slavery profanes its ideals and the principles of self-government upon which the future of the nation rested:

> No man is good enough to govern another man *without that man's consent.* I say this is the leading principle—the sheet anchor of American republicanism. . . . According to our ancient faith, the just powers of governments are derived from the consent of the governed. Now the relation of masters and slaves is, PRO TANTO, a total violation of this principle. (1:328; see also 1:416)

But no sooner did Lincoln make this point than he backed away from what it implied: "Let it not be said I am contending for the establishment of political and social equality between the whites and blacks" (1:329). He embraced the Declaration of Independence; he attacked the concept of master and slave; and he affirmed that *all* men, governing themselves, must have an equal voice in the national government. Blacks had rights, but not all rights.

Here, the effect is the opposite of the one that I described earlier, and it is harder to fathom. In the reply to Douglas at Ottawa in 1858, Lincoln thrust forward a strong case for racial difference even as he qualified it. In the 1854 speech, Lincoln made the logical and moral case against slavery and on behalf of the right of all persons to self-government but attached to it reservations that his own logic could not sustain.

The absorbing, maybe unanswerable, question is how much to weigh the words of qualification. One possibility is that between 1854 and 1858 Lincoln changed, becoming through the years more willing to tone down or prudently retract the racial distinctions that audiences expected to hear confirmed. A second possibility—close but not identical to the first—is that Lincoln knew what had to be said. He perceived that rights in the United States were growing more inclu-

sive yet were very unevenly accepted: the idea of full rights for everybody had to be ingrained into the national consciousness with painstaking caution.

It was not simply that Lincoln was pragmatic, though he was, but
that he worked within and created conditions for more inclusive
rights. He adjusted and shaped these conditions so that he could then
labor for the rights of all men and women within them. Lincoln was a
man of the moment, but, at the same time, he was always looking
backward to 1776—"I have never had a feeling politically that did not
spring from the sentiments embodied in the Declaration of Independence" (2:213)—*and* he was glancing ahead, even as he never quite
identified just how far ahead he was willing to see. To do *that*, after
all, might mean asking Americans to envision something they were
not ready for. Lincoln was an eloquent speaker and writer, but at key
junctures he was shrewdly silent.

Much of the fascination of Lincoln lies in the complex verbal
performances through which he addressed and piloted the nation. He
advocated and stood behind the declaration's promises of natural
rights, which he deemed applicable to *all*, even as he emphasized that,
of course, these could not be wholly fulfilled for persons with dark
skin. To put it another way: he upheld the principle of self-government
for everybody, including blacks, but then denied to blacks its implications. His manner of resolving, or at least maneuvering around, this
inconsistency demanded political acumen of the highest order and
adroit literary artistry. It was an inconsistency in his thinking, and in
the consciousness of the country, and Lincoln had no choice but to
accept it as his starting point. Lincoln accepted and yet, ultimately,
moved beyond the dominant belief in the North that blacks should
never be accorded equal rights and did not belong in the United
States. He succeeded in performing this feat precisely because he
could feel in himself the resistances to blacks that existed among
whites everywhere.

The more one ponders the details of Lincoln's career and administration, the more complicated does his perception, as well as his
articulation, of rights become. Lincoln's positions on slavery, equality, and rights did turn more radical—if always artfully managed—in
the 1850s. This change was largely the result of Lincoln's horror at
the Kansas-Nebraska Act, which suspended debate over the morality of slavery in order—via Stephen Douglas's doctrine of "popular

sovereignty"—to allow settlers in the territories to decide for themselves whether they would countenance it.[32] But the term *radical*
does not so much connote a basic change in Lincoln's views in the
aftermath of Kansas-Nebraska as it does his more tenacious alle-
giance to free soil/Republican party ideology, with its acceptance of
slavery where it already existed and opposition to it where it had not
reached.

Lincoln adhered to this tenet until the last possible moment. On
the eve of the Civil War, in December 1860, he stated that he was willing
to endorse a constitutional amendment proposed by Senator John J.
Crittenden of Kentucky that would have permanently guaranteed slavery in the Southern states. The amendment might have passed if
Crittenden had not hooked another one to it that would have extended
the old Missouri Compromise line from east to west across the territories to the Pacific, permitting slavery below that line.[33] Lincoln could
not accede to this: his hatred of slavery was abiding, and he was determined to thwart its growth. Yet he would not risk dismantling the
Union by attacking slavery in the South. He was late, it seems, in
divining the connection between a slavery system that was determined
to expand—the South viewed restriction as an abridgment of its
rights—and the sectional discord that was tearing the Union apart.

Lincoln was also late, or again so it appears, in perceiving the
connection between the actual prosecution of the war and the institution of slavery. Greeley, Garrison, and Wendell Phillips pleaded that
slavery had to be smashed if the war was to be won. Not only was it
evil in itself, but it also gave the South a force of laborers for its
armies. Yet, as Douglass, George Julian, Cassius M. Clay of Kentucky,
and other pro-Union, antislavery, and abolitionist speakers reported,
Lincoln was wary about transforming the war against sectional rebellion into a campaign to exterminate slavery: he did not think the

32. Richard N. Current, *The Lincoln Nobody Knows* (New York: McGraw-Hill,
1958), 214–36; and Robert W. Johannsen, *Lincoln, the South, and Slavery* (Baton Rouge:
Louisiana State University Press, 1991), 8. See also Johannsen, *The Frontier, the Union,
and Stephen A. Douglas* (Urbana: University of Illinois Press, 1989).

33. On the importance of the Crittenden proposal, see Richard N. Current, *Speak-
ing of Abraham Lincoln: The Man and His Meaning for Our Times* (Urbana: University of
Illinois Press, 1983), 95; Merton L. Dillon, *The Abolitionists: The Growth of a Dissenting
Minority* (1974; reprint, New York: Norton, 1979), 248; and Kenneth M. Stampp, *And the
War Came: The North and the Secession Crisis, 1860–61* (1950; reprint, Chicago: University
of Chicago Press, 1965), 123–58.

people would back him.[34] In this sense, Lincoln was not an abolitionist but a solid antislavery Republican. He aimed to keep slavery *out* of
the territories and keep the southern states *in* the Union, even with
their four million slaves and "total violation" of self-government. As
Garrison explained in February 1862, "neither [Lincoln], nor the party
by whom he was chosen, had any more thought or intention of interfering with the 'peculiar institution' of the South, than of annexing
the United States to Great Britain or Austria."[35]

In another sense, however, Lincoln *was* a type of abolitionist, for
he was sure, as he said numerous times, that the Founding Fathers
had placed slavery on the road to "ultimate extinction" (e.g., 2:38). He
could afford to forestall the demands of the Garrisonians because he
was confident that slavery would one day be abolished: history was
against it, progress would overrule it.

Slavery would die, Lincoln knew, and he believed that this lesson
was taught by the Founding Fathers and inscribed by them in the
Constitution, in Article 1, Section 9, which allowed for the banning of
the slave trade after 1808. The Quaker poet and abolitionist John Greenleaf Whittier noted in a January 31, 1861, article on the secession crisis
that, as far as expansion of slavery was concerned, "Lincoln stands
exactly where George Washington, James Madison, and Thomas Jefferson did."[36] But to the South, Lincoln's lack of regret over the prospect
of slavery's demise meant that he scorned their rights and was disloyal
to their inviolable system. "Ultimate extinction," to the Southern
states, "meant ultimate emancipation."[37]

For Lincoln, the issue of slavery expansion boiled down to the
choice between keeping slavery on the path to extinction or putting
freedom on this path instead.[38] He was certain about the choice he
had to make; it was tied to his "compelling sense of responsibility to
history."[39] Slavery must remain headed for extinction; as Lincoln

---

34. See the collection edited by Allen Thorndike Rice, *Reminiscences of Abraham
Lincoln By Distinguished Men of His Time* (New York: Published by *The North American
Review*, 1888), 62–63, 189, 303–4, 531.

35. William Lloyd Garrison, *Letters*, 6 vols., ed. Walter M. Merrill and Louis
Ruchames (Cambridge: Harvard University Press, 1971–81), 5:68.

36. John Greenleaf Whittier, *Letters*, 3 vols., ed. John B. Pickard (Cambridge:
Harvard University Press, 1975), 3:8.

37. Johannsen, *Lincoln*, 67.

38. Jaffa, *Crisis*, 371.

39. Pole, *Paths*, 151.

stated in his February 27, 1860, speech at Cooper Union, he would fasten as a true conservative to "the old policy of the fathers" and resist the "revolutionary innovations" of the South (2:122).

Lincoln explained that the South had nothing to fear from him, since he did not intend to touch slavery where it existed. In this respect, Lincoln was correct to paint himself as a conservative or, as one scholar has said, an "extreme moderate" fixed on preserving a Union that would tolerate slavery but not its expansion.[40] On election day, November 6, 1860, before the returns were in, the Garrisonian abolitionist Samuel May remarked that the Republican party's "issues with the slave power are the fewest possible, and its controlling purpose anything but that of extirpating slavery from the land." May added that if Lincoln were elected, "it is greatly feared he will make unmanly and cowardly concessions" to the South.[41]

The political facts lent substance both to May's fear and to Lincoln's view that he was no threat to the South's zealously guarded property rights. The thirty-seventh Congress, elected with Lincoln, included 108 Republicans in the House, with 129 in the opposition, and 29 Republicans in the Senate, compared to the other side's 37. Congress would not be able to pass legislation outlawing slavery in the federal territories or in the District of Columbia—both of which Congress *did* enact once the war began and the South surrendered its seats.

President Buchanan emphasized the split in congressional representation in December 1860, saying that the South should remember, whatever its anger at the abolitionists and the "antislavery party," that "no single act has ever passed Congress, unless we may possibly except the Missouri compromise, impairing in the slightest degree the rights of the South to their property in slaves; and it may also be observed, judging from present indications, that no probability exists of the passage of such an act by a majority of both Houses, either in the present or in the next Congress."[42]

But, on the other hand, the newly elected Lincoln had the veto and could deter the admission of any new slave states to the Union: all

---

40. Quarles, *Lincoln and the Negro*, 82.

41. Samuel May, in *British and American Abolitionists: An Episode in Transatlantic Understanding*, ed. Clare Taylor (Edinburgh: Edinburgh University Press, 1974), 449.

42. James Buchanan, in *A Compilation of Messages and Papers of the Presidents*, 11 vols., ed. James D. Richardson (1897; reprint, n.p.: Bureau of National Literature, 1911), 5:3159. See also Don E. Fehrenbacher, *The South and Three Sectional Crises* (Baton Rouge: Louisiana State University Press, 1980), 46.

that lay ahead for the South was the spectacle of appalling isolation, as one free state after another entered the Union.[43]

Lincoln was unable to see the image he had created for himself in the South as "an infuriatingly patient and persistent executioner of slavery."[44] As early as October 1845, in a letter to a fellow Whig from Illinois, Lincoln had declared that while he would never interfere with slavery where it was, "I hold it to be equally clear, that we should never knowingly lend ourselves directly or indirectly, to prevent that slavery from dying a natural death—to find new places for it to live in, when it can no longer exist in the old."[45] His feelings about slavery were a matter of public record, and these undermined his assertions that he was friendly to the South's interests.

In an important March 1, 1859, speech in Chicago, Lincoln reaffirmed that the Constitution protected Southern slavery. But he added that "the Republican principle, the profound central truth, [is] that slavery is wrong and ought to be dealt with as a wrong." When slavery moved to expand, "we should in every way resist it as a wrong, treating it as a wrong, with the fixed idea that it must and will come to an end" (2:15, 17).

Lincoln assumed that slavery where it was could (and should) be tolerated because he knew that it would expire and had no constitutional right to new sources of life. Again, Lincoln thought this policy would reassure the South that he would not harm it, but it cut against the South's sense of what slavery, their fundamental institution, required. That is why an editorial in the *Southern Literary Messenger* in 1860 said that the South should not be misled by Lincoln's apparent friendliness; he was at heart an enemy of Southern rights, "and the danger to the South will be in exact proportion to his goodness."[46]

---

43. Harry V. Jaffa, "The Emancipation Proclamation," in *One Hundred Years of Emancipation*, ed. Robert A. Goldwin (1964; reprint, Chicago: Rand McNally, 1966), 12. See also John Witherspoon DuBose, *The Life and Times of William Lowndes Yancey* (Birmingham: Roberts and Son, 1892), 549–51.

44. William Appleman Williams, *The Contours of American History* (1961; reprint, Chicago: Quadrangle, 1966), 297.

45. *Lincoln On Democracy*, 31.

46. Cited in Rembert W. Patrick, *Jefferson Davis and His Cabinet* (Baton Rouge: Louisiana University Press, 1944), 5. For additional background, see Emerson Fite, *The Presidential Campaign of 1860, with Party Platforms and Campaign Speeches* (New York: Macmillan, 1911); John McCardell, *The Idea of a Southern Nation: Southern Nationalists and Southern Nationalism, 1830–1860* (New York: Norton, 1979); and Betty L. Mitchell, *Edmund Ruffin: A Biography* (Bloomington: Indiana University Press, 1981).

One wonders how Lincoln envisioned that slavery would finally end. He said slavery was monstrously evil; the South said it was a positive good. How would Lincoln keep from violating the Southern rights that he claimed he would protect, even as he made certain that the right of the black person to himself or herself was granted? What kind of action was he prepared to take?

Possibly Lincoln shared the program sketched by Gamaliel Bailey, the editor of *The National Era* (which published Harriet Beecher Stowe's *Uncle Tom's Cabin*) and an influence on the Liberty, Free Soil, Free Democratic, and Republican parties. Like Lincoln, Bailey judged that the federal government could not terminate slavery in the Southern states. But he stated that it could halt Southern control of the government by repealing proslavery tax structures, the system of representation that favored the South, fugitive slave laws, and all support for slavery expansion. Bailey trusted that once the national buttressing of slavery crumbled, the Southern states would themselves eliminate their peculiar institution.[47]

Lincoln was careful, however, never to say anything that specific. As the slavery crisis intensified in the mid- to late 1850s, and as his campaign for the presidential nomination proceeded in 1860, Lincoln stated that he was firmly against slavery expansion *and* that he would never endorse political and social equality for blacks. Lincoln was a "good party man," and this was sound Republican teaching that he promulgated.[48] As Lyman Trumbull announced in 1859: "We, the Republican party, are the white man's party. We are for the free white man, and for making white labor acceptable and honorable, which it can never be when negro slave labor is brought into competition with it."[49] Such sentiments clarify why Garrison and the abolitionists were dismayed by the Republicans, who seemed content only to limit slavery, not extirpate it, and who were continually telling voters that they would restrict rights for blacks—even to the extent, finally, of encouraging deportation or colonization.[50]

47. Stanley Harrold, *Gamaliel Bailey and Antislavery Union* (Kent, Ohio: Kent State University Press, 1986), 104.

48. Richard Hofstadter, *The Idea of a Party System: The Rise of Legitimate Opposition in the United States, 1780–1840* (Berkeley: University of California Press, 1969), 270.

49. Lyman Trumbull, cited in Eugene H. Berwanger, *The Frontier Against Slavery: Western Anti-Negro Prejudice and the Slavery Extension Controversy* (1967; reprint, Urbana: University of Illinois Press, 1971), 133. See also Bernard Mandel, *Labor: Free and Slave* (New York: Associated, 1955), 149–50.

50. Garrison, *Letters*, 4:408–10.

Black abolitionists hence found Lincoln and the Republicans un-
sympathetic to them, concerned only with white Americans, white
rights. William J. Watkins noted in a September 5, 1859, essay in the
Weekly Anglo-African that "with a few exceptions, its leaders [i.e., of
the Republican party] are not disposed to take the broad, consistent,
and righteous ground of opposition to the *existence* of slavery. They
prefer to harp upon the popular and palatable doctrine of its non-
extension to the Territories of the Republic, and appear exceedingly
afraid of the imputation of Abolitionism." Thomas Hamilton, in a
March 17, 1860, editorial in the same paper, put the matter starkly:
"Their opposition to slavery means opposition to the black man—
nothing else."[51]

But it was Frederick Douglass who made the case against Lincoln
and the Republicans with special force and eloquence in a commentary on the election he published in December 1860. He remarked that
he was heartened that someone with at least an "anti-slavery reputation" had been elected president. Yet he emphasized—reiterating Lincoln's point about himself—that the new president posed no threat to
the South: "With the single exception of the question of slavery extension, Mr. Lincoln proposes no measure which can bring him into
antagonistic collision with the traffickers of human flesh, either in the
States or the District of Columbia. . . . Slavery will be as safe, and
safer, in the Union under such a President, than it can be under any
President of a Southern Confederacy."[52]

But it was in fact difficult, if not impossible, for Lincoln to both
invoke and curtail the right of self-government. This right was a crucial feature of American political discourse, and it indicates why slavery was not safe under Lincoln, who believed in it so strongly. "A
government of our own is our natural right," said Thomas Paine in
Common Sense (1776) when he called for American independence.[53]
And antislavery writers and speakers had long capitalized upon the
sacred principle that many besides Paine had expressed. "It was the
glory of the American people," reflected the eminent Unitarian divine
William Ellery Channing in his influential book *Slavery* (1835), "that,

<hr />

51. For Watkins and Hamilton, see *The Black Abolitionist Papers*, 5 vols., ed. C.
Peter Ripley et al. (Chapel Hill: University of North Carolina Press, 1985–92), 5:31–
32, 72.
    52. Douglass, *Life and Writings*, 2:527.
    53. Thomas Paine, *Complete Writings*, 2 vols., ed. Philip S. Foner (New York:
Citadel, 1945), 1:29.

in their Declaration of Independence, they took the ground of the indestructible rights of every human being. They declared all men to be essentially equal, and each born to be free."[54]

Lincoln would have concurred with Paine and Channing that independence signified freedom, equality, self-government, and national self-rule. Furthermore, when he praised the declaration, exalted the Revolution, and foregrounded the right of all persons to govern themselves and take part in the government of the land, as he did in the Kansas-Nebraska speech, he intimated that slaves and masters, blacks and whites, should be placed on an equal footing. He averred that this was not what he meant, yet the resonances of his language told otherwise and focused a logic that Lincoln let loose and then sought to restrain. If black rights were authorized and legitimated by the Declaration of Independence, then slavery was wrong *and* rights for blacks should no longer be nullified: this was the unmistakable destination of Lincoln's logic. It explains why the black abolitionist Martin R. Delany judged that whether Lincoln intended it or not, his policies would surely lead to emancipation, and more.[55]

This was a point that a number of observers stressed. Writing from England on the eve of the 1860 election, Frederick Milnes Edge, for example, stated that "the issue pending between the Free and the Slave States is not one of the abolition, but of the extension or non-extension of slavery." He cited lengthy passages from Seward, Chase, and Lincoln to substantiate this view, saying that the basic division in American politics, between "Slavery extensionists and Slavery prohibitionists," had been formed at the time of the Missouri Compromise debates of 1819–20. But, he added, the "logical consequence" of the Republicans' antislavery position was "the eventual freedom of the slave": "*Slavery restriction involves Slavery abolition,* as the greater circle includes the less."[56]

In a noteworthy essay for *Fraser's* magazine, "The Contest in America," published in February 1862 and soon reprinted as a pamphlet in Boston, the Utilitarian reformer John Stuart Mill, like Delany

54. William Ellery Channing, *Works* (Boston: American Unitarian Association, 1888), 702.

55. Victor Ullman, *Martin R. Delany: The Beginnings of Black Nationalism* (Boston: Beacon, 1971), 263.

56. Frederick Milnes Edge, *Slavery Doomed: or, The Contest Between Free and Slave Labour* (1860; reprint, New York: Negro Universities Press, 1969), 3, 69, 93.

and Edge, sliced through the distinction that Lincoln and the Republicans upheld: "If they have not taken arms against slavery, they have against its extension. And they know, as we may know if we please, that this amounts to the same thing. The day when slavery can no longer extend itself, is the day of its doom."[57]

Lincoln never declared in his correspondence or speeches—as radicals in his own party did—that the eventual target would indeed be slavery in the states.[58] But Delany, Edge, and Mill saw that Lincoln was an abolitionist in the drift of the arguments he had made. It was true that he honored views and values that he could not impel himself to put into practice immediately. He clung to (and claimed to represent) the principles of the Declaration of Independence, yet attached codicils to them—unequal equal rights and colonization. But once you start with the Declaration of Independence as Lincoln did, then these limiting conditions have to fall away: neither logic nor morality nor the progress of American history and an ever expanding field of rights could bear them.

Lincoln insisted on equality, yet also on inequality, on the necessary subordination of blacks to whites. He said that he would not allow blacks to intermarry with whites, would not permit them to serve as jurors or to hold office, and would not grant them citizenship in the state of Illinois or the right to vote.[59] He thus was in favor of self-government for blacks in the sense of self-ownership and wages for labor, but no more than that. This, however, is where his own argument against slavery, and his fidelity to the Declaration of Independence, could be hurled against him. His own faith in it, finally, was deep enough to overcome his doubts and fears about its consequences.

The heart of Lincoln's argument against slavery was that any defense of black bondage could also be used to defend white bondage: no white person's freedom would be secure. In a fragment on

57. John Stuart Mill, in *Union Pamphlets of the Civil War*, 2 vols., ed. Frank Freidel (Cambridge: Harvard University Press, 1967), 1:334. See also Daniel R. Goodwin, *Southern Slavery in Its Present Aspects* (1864; reprint, New York: Negro Universities Press, 1969), 322–23.

58. George Sinkler, *The Racial Attitudes of American Presidents from Abraham Lincoln to Theodore Roosevelt* (Garden City: Doubleday, 1971), 32; and Laura White, "Charles Sumner and the Crisis of 1860–61," in *Essays in Honor of William E. Dodd*, ed. Avery Craven (Chicago: University of Chicago Press, 1935), 138.

59. David M. Potter, *The Impending Crisis, 1848–1861,* completed and edited by Don E. Fehrenbacher (New York: Harper and Row, 1976), 344–45.

slavery, probably written in July 1854, Lincoln said: "If A. can prove, however conclusively, that he may, of right, enslave B.—why may not B. snatch the same argument, and prove equally, that he may enslave A.?" (1:303). No one could really risk making an argument that sanctioned slavery, Lincoln concluded, because this same argument, whatever its basis (skin color, intellect, or interest), could be deployed to justify enslaving the person making it.[60]

This argument was clearly articulated, but it was even more serviceable than Lincoln at first imagined. It could function to demonstrate the egregious evil and manifest folly of slavery, and, propelled further, it could disclose the defect in the claim that all men were created equal but that blacks were not equal to whites: If A can prove, however conclusively, that he may, of right, claim greater equality than B—why may not B snatch the same argument, and prove that he is more equal than A?

In a speech in Chicago on July 10, 1858, Lincoln repeated his logical, moral, and political critique of slavery:

> Turn in whatever way you will—whether it come from the mouth of a King, an excuse for enslaving the people of his country, or from the mouth of men of one race as a reason for enslaving the men of another race, it is all the same old serpent, and I hold if that course of argumentation that is made for the purpose of convincing the public mind that we should not care about this, should be granted, it does not stop with the negro. I should like to know if taking this old Declaration of Independence, which declares that all men are equal upon principle and making exceptions to it, where will it stop. If one man says it does not mean a negro, why not another say it does not mean some other man? If that declaration is not the truth, let us get out the Statute book, in which we find it and tear it out! Who is so bold as to do it! (1:457)

The enslavement felt by the revolutionaries of 1776 and the Founding Fathers pervaded their rhetoric.[61] It formed a crucial part of

---

60. Glen E. Thurow, *Abraham Lincoln and American Political Religion* (Albany: State University of Albany Press, 1976), 44–52.

61. See, among many examples, John Adams, "A Dissertation on the Canon and Feudal Law" (1765); John Dickinson, *Letters from a Farmer in Pennsylvania* (1767); Thomas Jefferson, *A Summary View of the Rights of British America* (1774); and Thomas Paine, *American Crisis* papers (1776–83). As Bernard Bailyn has said, for the generation of 1776,

their testament, as Lincoln keenly understood. In his speech in Chicago, he implied that if Americans truly cherished the declaration, then they had no choice but to believe that slavery must end. If they refused to extend the promise of equality to the enslaved, then they would be traitors to their own history, forsaking the ideals that Revolutionary heroes had been willing to die for.

As Forrest McDonald has pointed out, the doctrines espoused in the Declaration of Independence were not widely shared before July 1776, but "once the Declaration was made, it became not only immoral but virtually unthinkable to hold any other position": all men were endowed with the right to life, liberty, and the pursuit of happiness.[62] Yet the signers of the declaration evaded the double meaning of slavery, acknowledging it as evil for themselves while seeking to control and sidestep it as an evil for black persons, as Lincoln later would aim himself to master and two-tone the meanings of equality. "The identification between the cause of the colonies and the cause of the Negroes bound in chattel slavery—an identification built into the very language of politics—became inescapable," Bernard Bailyn has observed, and yet it was not faced.[63]

The leaders of the Revolution could not accept the consequence to which their fight for their freedom and rights led—freedom and rights for blacks. Instead, they stressed the right of slaveholders to their human property—a right that could not be tampered with.[64] Patrick Henry, George Washington, Jefferson, and other slaveholders concluded that the social complexities of emancipation were too daunting for them to resolve, and the immediate liberation of their own slaves, the loss of this property, too costly to endure.

Liberation would be the work of later generations, and this was the arduous task that the persons who enlisted in abolitionism and antislavery performed, as they lamented America's failure to be loyal to the declaration and called attention to the need at last to confer equality on all the enslaved. When William Ellery Channing commented on the slaves who had revolted aboard the slave ship *Creole* in

---

the term *slavery* connoted "the absolute political evil." See *The Ideological Origins of the American Revolution* (1967; reprint, Cambridge: Harvard University Press, 1980), 232.

62. Forrest McDonald, *E Pluribus Unum: The Formation of the American Republic, 1776–1790*, 2d ed. (Indianapolis: Liberty, 1979), 18.

63. Bailyn, *Ideological Origins*, 235.

64. Robert William Fogel, *Without Consent or Contract: The Rise and Fall of American Slavery* (1989; reprint, New York: Norton, 1991), 243.

1841, he conceded that they had "shed blood." But, he asked, "Does a republic, whose heroic age was the revolution of 1776, and whose illustrious men earned their glory in a sanguinary conflict for rights, find no mitigation of this bloodshed in the greater wrongs to which the slave is subjected?"[65] Lincoln would not have condoned slave revolt and rebellion, and, again, he professed that he would enforce the fugitive slave laws and the Dred Scott decision. He would not abolish slavery. But he would make certain that slavery stayed on the route to ultimate extinction, as he was convinced the Founding Fathers had wished.

Lincoln knew his case was effective to many in the Northeast and West: the aura of the Revolution was present everywhere in American society and culture, and it served particularly well to illuminate and revivify the abolitionist and antislavery causes. But centered in the verbal guarantee of equality, Lincoln's case went only so far: at some point the racism of white America had to be grappled with or, at a minimum, accepted as a menacing reality. What would equality actually mean, and which rights would blacks be accorded once they became free?

White antislavery reformers and politicians, as well as ardent abolitionists, often referred passionately to the Declaration of Independence, and it energized and justified their campaigns. Yet it was an ambivalent legacy. The fact was that most white Americans, including many who were hostile to slavery, could not conceive of blacks as citizens. Lincoln could not, or said that he could not, either. The "prevailing ideology" of the antebellum period proclaimed that "it was the African Americans' incapacity for freedom and responsible citizenship" that stood as the "major roadblock" to their emancipation.[66] Before the war and during its early phases, Lincoln anticipated the eventual death of slavery but *not* emancipation: he wanted slavery to die but could not visualize free black citizens, millions of them. The declaration bore witness that blacks deserved freedom and equality, not the right to be free and equal Americans.

During his debates with Lincoln in the United States Senate race of 1858, Stephen Douglas catcalled that "Mr. Lincoln and the Black Republican Party" were "in favor of the citizenship of the negro,"

---

65. Channing, *Works*, 868.
66. David Brion Davis, "The American Dilemma," *New York Review of Books*, July 16, 1992: 14.

adding that he was himself "opposed to negro citizenship in any and every form."[67] Lincoln replied: "anything that argues me into his [Douglas's] idea of perfect social and political equality with the negro is but a specious and fantastic arrangement of words, by which a man can prove a horse chestnut to be a chestnut horse" (1:511).

For Lincoln, slavery was a moral issue entwined with politics and prejudice, his own and the nation's. In 1860, New York voted for Lincoln even as it overwhelmingly defeated a proposal on the ballot for equal suffrage for blacks—a proposal that voters continued to defeat through 1869, until the ratification of the Fifteenth Amendment in March 1870. One Republican from New York City said with pride that of the 32,000 who cast votes for Lincoln in 1860, only 1,600 voted for the suffrage proposal.[68] During the 1850s, Ohio and Indiana denied the vote to blacks as part of their state constitutions; and Michigan (1850), Iowa (1857), and Wisconsin (1857) by popular referenda turned back proposals to give voting rights to blacks. As of 1861, none of the seven midwestern states allowed blacks to vote or serve in the militia, and all included a range of restrictive policies and practices in education, law, marriage, and other areas of everyday life.[69]

Northerners loathed the prospect of amalgamation, integration, and economic competition between white and black workers. As Leon Litwack has shown, Northerners favored "voluntary colonization, forced expulsion, or legal and social prescription."[70] Lincoln's home state of Illinois incorporated a provision in its constitution in 1848 that barred the immigration of blacks; and Indiana (1851), Iowa (1851), and Oregon (1857) did the same. In Illinois, the vote passed by a more than two-to-one margin. A number of states (Ohio, Indiana, Illinois, Iowa, Michigan, and Oregon) also obliged blacks traveling

67. Stephen Douglas, in Lincoln, *Speeches and Writings*, 1:504.
68. Leon F. Litwack, *North of Slavery: The Negro in the Free States, 1790–1860* (1961; reprint, Chicago: University of Chicago Press, 1971), 271.
69. V. Jacque Voegeli, *Free But Not Equal: The Midwest and the Negro During the Civil War* (1967; reprint, Chicago: University of Chicago Press, 1970), 2. See also Theodore Clarke Smith, *The Liberty and Free Soil Parties of the Northwest* (New York: Longmans, 1897), 332–37; and Chilton Williamson, *American Suffrage: From Property to Democracy, 1760–1860* (Princeton: Princeton University Press, 1960), 277–78.
70. Litwack, *North of Slavery*, 64. See also Paul Simon, *Lincoln's Preparation for Greatness: The Illinois Legislative Years* (1965; reprint, Urbana: University of Illinois Press, 1971), 121–37; and Paul Kleppner, *The Cross of Culture: A Social Analysis of Midwestern Politics, 1850–1900* (New York: Free Press, 1970), 91.

into the state to post bonds, ranging from $500 to $1000, to guarantee their good behavior and self-support.[71]

As political democracy expanded in the first half of the nineteenth century, its possibilities were at the same time withheld from blacks. By 1840, approximately 93 percent of the free black population in the North lived in states that completely or practically excluded them from the vote. Blacks in 1840 could vote on an equal basis with whites only in Massachusetts, New Hampshire, Vermont, and Maine. From 1819, when Maine was admitted to the Union, until 1865, every new state granted the right to vote to whites only. Since the time the Republic was founded, not a single state, North or South, as of 1865, had expanded the political rights of blacks.[72]

Being a citizen meant having the right to vote: "The central innovation of nineteenth-century democratic political theory was the equation of citizenship with suffrage."[73] Voting entailed participation in the electoral process, representation, and involvement in political parties. By 1860, twenty-one of the thirty-three states practiced manhood suffrage without the old property or tax-paying requirements—but for whites only.

This situation indicates what Lincoln confronted when he ran for the senate and the presidency and when he occupied the chief executive's office from 1861 to 1865. The Democratic opposition painted him and the Republican party as proponents of racial equality and amalgamation, with all the social and economic and political horrors such policies would unleash. White labor would be undercut; white settlements would be curtailed or rendered impossible as blacks from the South flooded the Northern states and territories; and the differences between the races would be erased as intermarriage became rampant and created a population of "white Negroes."[74]

---

71. Eugene H. Berwanger, "Negrophobia in Northern Proslavery and Antislavery Thought," *Phylon* 33 (1972): 267.

72. Litwack, *North of Slavery*, 74–75, 79. See George M. Fredrickson, *The Black Image in the White Mind: The Debate on Afro-American Character and Destiny, 1817–1914* (1971; reprint, New York: Harper and Row, 1972), 91; Ronald T. Takaki, *Iron Cages: Race and Culture in 19th-Century America* (New York: Knopf, 1979), 111; and Eric Foner, *Reconstruction: America's Unfinished Revolution, 1863–1877* (New York: Harper and Row, 1988), 184.

73. Stow Persons, *American Minds: A History of Ideas* (New York: Henry Holt, 1958), 149.

74. See Dwight Lowell Dumond, *Antislavery: The Crusade for Freedom in America* (1961; reprint, New York: Norton, 1966), 350–56.

Throughout the entire antebellum period, no charge was more common than that emancipation meant amalgamation; and it had been at the center of some of the worst antiabolitionist rioting and mobbing.[75] If the races were not kept separate—and slavery was the best means for doing so, rivaled only by freedom linked to deportation or colonization—then the white race would be made impure, debased, and corrupted as the black race blended with it, so the argument went. Douglas, before, during, and after the debates, announced that Lincoln was not only an advocate of black citizenship but also an amalgamationist. Lincoln retorted in a June 26, 1857, speech on the Dred Scott decision:

> There is a natural disgust in the minds of nearly all white people, to the idea of an indiscriminate amalgamation of the white and black races. . . . He [Douglas] finds the Republicans insisting that the Declaration of Independence includes ALL men, black as well as white; and forthwith he boldly denies that it includes negroes at all, and proceeds to argue gravely that all who contend it does, do so only because they want to vote, and eat, and sleep, and marry with negroes! He will have it that they cannot be consistent else. (1:397)

Douglas was consistent: he stated that blacks were not included in the Declaration of Independence, which chartered only the rights of whites. Lincoln disagreed but then tried to define a consistent position of his own that somehow would gloss over its internal inconsistency—equality but not the same equality, rights but not the same rights, freedom for all persons but not full freedom for persons of different skin colors.

Lincoln's career reveals an uncanny interplay between his own tense, skillful engagement with his era's harsh racism and his vocalizing of the racism that he felt himself. What was in him was real and powerful, and many have regretted its presence; yet it was largely *in* Lincoln because he saw it in the nation he addressed and eventually came to lead. He believed in limiting rights for blacks because most of the nation did, and he mirrored the white majority's views about "the Negro" while softening this majority's disdain. In the North, as David

---

75. Richards, *"Gentlemen,"* 43.

W. Blight has noted, "free blacks lived circumscribed lives; they worked primarily as menial laborers and in most states were denied all political and legal rights."[76] Lincoln intimated that this was wrong even as he appeared willing to abide by it. But his critique of slavery did have the capacity to upset arguments and policies that designated blacks as both equal and unequal to whites. Lincoln distinguished between natural rights and perfect equality, yet was hindered by the knowledge that this distinction failed.

In closing his July 10, 1858, speech in Chicago, Lincoln said:

> In relation to the principle that all men are created equal, let it be as nearly reached as we can. . . . Let us discard all this quibbling about this man and the other man—this race and that race and the other race being inferior, and therefore they must be placed in an inferior position—discarding our standard that we have left us. (1:458)

Lincoln was impatient with vain efforts to set fussy, futile, immoral boundaries between one race and another; and the Declaration of Independence was a formidable weapon for him to wield against slavery as a system and against Southern moves to extend its dictatorial domain of rights denied. Lincoln cited the declaration as the "stumbling block" that the Founding Fathers had built as a means to prevent tyrants and despots from seizing power: it would get in their way, obstructing their ambitions (1:399). But the same declaration also got in Lincoln's way as he allotted more equality, more rights, to whites than to blacks.

Lincoln's thinking about race relations was limited by the citizenry he led and by his own temperament. It chafed against a logic in favor of full equality that he could not, or preferred not to, pursue. Probably Lincoln did believe sincerely in colonization as the best solution to the "Negro problem"; but he also touted it because it was what the vast majority of voters demanded and because his own party rallied behind it. He thought seriously about colonization, but on "two levels of consciousness."[77] He wondered whether it might in-

76. David W. Blight, *Frederick Douglass's Civil War: Keeping Faith in Jubilee* (Baton Rouge: Louisiana State University Press, 1989), 150.
77. Gabor S. Boritt, *Lincoln and the Economics of the American Dream* (Memphis: Memphis State University Press, 1978), 258.

deed work, yet he also perceived that while it probably would not work, it had to be engaged, discussed, even supported, because it spoke to the desire of whites that blacks not live in the same country with them. Lincoln had to deal with a situation in which most of the North, certainly the West, hankered after free soil, feared the encroachments of the "Slave Power," and hated "Negroes," picturing emancipation as both right and barbaric—barbaric in its implications for whites.

If Lincoln had said more than he did, or something other than he did, he would not have been elected in 1860. Nor could he have governed effectively. He included blacks within the terms of the Declaration of Independence but not completely, and he insisted they should be granted legal protections while also stressing that they should not vote, sit on juries, or testify in cases that involved whites. He never urged states in the North to extend the right to vote to blacks, nor did he speak against the Black Laws and segregationist and exclusionist policies of the North. Even this was not enough, however, to ward off the attacks by Democrats and the fears of Northern voters.[78]

In 1858, the year of Lincoln's losing battle against Douglas for the Illinois U.S. Senate seat, Republicans from the House and Senate advised the party to promote colonization in South or Central America as the best remedy for the aggrieved, mistreated members of an unfortunate race—a race that was, it was added, suited to the warmer climate of the tropics anyway. Colonization would also make plain to voters that the Republicans harbored no plan to mingle blacks with whites. Whites and blacks could not live together: this was fate, destiny, Providence. Sealed by the divine will, it was a "higher law" than any formulated by men and implemented in government.[79]

Colonization soothed the fears of many whites in the North, and for this reason it was extremely helpful to Lincoln and to the Republicans. When the Civil War began, and during its first two difficult years, "Negro colonization" was official policy of the Republican party.[80] He treated it favorably in his meeting with the Committee of Colored Men on August 14, 1862, and again in his Preliminary Emancipation Procla-

---

78. Philip S. Foner, *History of the Labor Movement in the United States*, vol. 1 (1947; reprint, New York: International, 1962), 293–96.

79. Voegeli, *Free But Not Equal*, 27–28.

80. Ibid., 22; and Blight, *Civil War*, 122–47.

mation in September and in the December 3 Message to Congress. Yet in this message, even as he said, "I strongly favor colonization," he mentioned that whites should not worry that free blacks would displace them as laborers. After all, the amount of labor that needed to be done would remain the same: "logically, there is neither more nor less of it" (2:412). In the final Emancipation Proclamation of January 1, 1863, Lincoln deleted the reference to colonization; and the proclamation also stated that blacks freed from slavery "will be received into the armed service of the United States to garrison forts, positions, stations, and other places, and to man vessels of all sorts in said service" (2:425).[81] The recruitment of black regiments was in fact already under way: it had begun in August 1862, the same month in which Lincoln met with the Committee of Colored Men, when Lincoln's secretary of war Edwin M. Stanton had announced plans for it, and by the end of that year several regiments had been organized.

Lincoln came to this decision slowly, reluctantly. In his diary entry of July 21, 1862, Salmon P. Chase noted that he, Stanton, and Seward favored the enlistment of black troops but that Lincoln "expressed himself as averse to arming negroes."[82] But what lay ahead, Lincoln eventually saw, was not emancipated black men leaving the United States for "bright prospects" abroad. It was, rather, black men wearing the uniform of the Union army and fighting for their and the nation's freedom. Winning the war meant emancipation and—the next stage in the sequence—black men serving in the Union army; and once they served, how could they be denied residence in the United States, as though they did not belong to the nation they had protected? H. Ford Douglas, a black soldier in the 95th Illinois infantry, wrote in a February 1863 article in *Frederick Douglass's Monthly* that "this war will educate Mr. Lincoln out of his idea of the deportation of the Negro. . . . National duties and responsibilities are not to be colonized, they must be heroically met and religiously performed."[83] By

81. I cannot deal in detail here with the Emancipation Proclamation itself. The best recent discussion is Mark E. Neely Jr., *The Last Best Hope of Earth: Abraham Lincoln and the Promise of America* (Cambridge: Harvard University Press, 1993), 95–122.

82. Salmon P. Chase, *Inside Lincoln's Cabinet: The Civil War Diaries of Salmon P. Chase*, ed. David Donald (New York: Longmans, 1954), 96. See also J. W. Schuckers, *The Life and Public Services of Salmon Portland Chase* (New York: Appleton, 1874), 420.

83. H. Ford Douglas, *A Grand Army of Black Men: Letters from African-American Soldiers in the Union Army, 1861–1865*, ed. Edwin S. Redkey (New York: Cambridge University Press, 1992), 25.

the end of the war, 180,000 black men had served in the Union army—more than 20 percent of the black male population of the United States between the ages of eighteen and forty-five.[84]

There is one more disconcerting twist to record, however. On December 31, 1862, Lincoln signed a government contract with a business entrepreneur named Bernard Kock, who agreed to "colonize five thousand persons of African descent" on the Haitian island of A' Vache, at the price of fifty dollars apiece. Kock was in fact an unscrupulous adventurer, and, launched with a few hundred black settlers who intended to raise cotton, the colony was a failure. By the end of 1863 the colonists made known their desire to return to the United States—and the government of Haiti stated that it would be glad to see them leave. The secretary of the interior, John Palmer Usher, ordered a ship to pick up the dispirited colonists, and they returned on March 20, 1864, their ship anchoring in the Potomac River, opposite Alexandria, Virginia. This effort at colonization was poorly planned and pathetically executed; and Lincoln never tried colonization again. Perhaps he was only half-serious about it to begin with, caring more about the symbolism than about the reality. Yet he was slow to shake its appeal. On July 2, 1864, Congress voted to repeal the appropriation for funds for other ventures of that kind.[85]

The nation not only was divided North and South, but also white and black, as the allure of colonization schemes to white politicians and statesmen exhibited. Lincoln tried, contradictorily, to bridge racial differences that he knew had to be maintained if perpetual union ever was to occur. His leadership in dealing with race and racism was extraordinary in many respects—so much so that Garry Wills has professed that at Gettysburg in November 1863, Lincoln "recontracted" American society "on the basis of the Declaration as our

---

84. Studies of African-American soldiers in the Civil War include: Blight, *Civil War*, 148–74; Quarles, *Lincoln and the Negro*, 183–213; Forrest G. Wood, *Black Scare: The Racist Response to Emancipation and Reconstruction* (1968; reprint, Berkeley: University of California Press, 1970), 40–52; and Philip S. Paludan, *"A People's Contest": The Union and the Civil War, 1861–1865* (New York: Harper and Row, 1988), 208–14.

85. On this incident, see John G. Nicolay and John Hay, *Abraham Lincoln: A History*, 10 vols. (New York: Century, 1890), 6:353–67; and P. J. Staudenraus, *The African Colonization Movement, 1816–1865* (New York: Columbia University Press, 1961), 247. On John Palmer Usher's role in promoting colonization schemes, see *The Abraham Lincoln Encyclopedia*, ed. Mark E. Neely Jr. (1982; reprint, New York: Da Capo, n.d.), 316–17.

fundamental charter."[86] As Wills sees it, Lincoln wrote the declaration *into* the Constitution and thereby "corrected the Constitution without overthrowing it."[87] But such claims obscure the fact that Lincoln's engagement with the declaration had been under way for decades before the Gettysburg Address: Lincoln's statement in the first lines of the speech—that the "new nation, conceived in liberty, was dedicated to the proposition that all men are created equal" (2:536)—was one that he had articulated, and then qualified, countless times before.

The claim that the Constitution had been based on the tenets of the Declaration of Independence was, after all, a staple of much abolitionist and antislavery rhetoric among Americans and their supporters abroad. The Irish radical Daniel O'Connell, one of Garrison's heroes, contended in an October 11, 1843, speech in Dublin that no one could claim the Constitution prevented the abolition of slavery, because "the Constitution of America is founded" on "the self-evident truths of the Declaration."[88] William Goodell made the identical point in *Views of American Constitutional Law* (1844); the declaration, he said, with its guarantee of "self-evident truths," stood as "the *fundamental basis and ground work of* AMERICAN CONSTITUTIONAL LAW."[89]

What mattered at Gettysburg in November 1863 was the noble economy and elegance of the address and its rightness for the occasion, not anything that Lincoln was saying for the first time. The issue for Lincoln, in his role as president, was not whether blacks were included in the declaration or the Constitution, but the extent of their rights and the setting in which these should be exercised. He sought to imagine how blacks could be absorbed into a Union from which most white Americans, and Lincoln at times, too, hoped they could be ejected.

---

86. Garry Wills, *Inventing America: Jefferson's Declaration of Independence* (1978; reprint, New York: Vintage, 1979), xiv.

87. Garry Wills, "The Words That Remade America: Lincoln at Gettysburg," *The Atlantic Monthly*, June 1992: 79; and *Lincoln at Gettysburg: The Words That Remade America* (New York: Simon and Schuster, 1992). See also Yehoshua Arieli, *Individualism and Nationalism in American Ideology* (1964; reprint, Baltimore: Penguin, 1966), 293–318; and Cushing Strout, *The New Heavens and New Earth: Political Religion in America* (New York: Harper and Row, 1974), 194–95.

88. Daniel O'Connell, "Address," October 11, 1843. Loyal National Repeal Association. Tract no. 2:2.

89. William Goodell, *Views of American Constitutional Law, In Its Bearing Upon American Slavery* (Utica: Jackson and Chaplin, 1844), 136.

In the Gettysburg Address, Lincoln used the word *proposition*—
"the *proposition* [emphasis added] that all men are created equal"
(2:536). This was a key word, as Charles Eliot Norton noted in October 1865:

> The proposition that *all* men are created equal,—equal that is in
> certain inalienable rights, among which are life, liberty, the pur-
> suit of happiness,—equal as moral and responsible beings,—has
> sunk deep into the very hearts of this people, and is moulding
> them in accordance with the conclusions that proceed from it. It
> is the inspiration and the explanation of our progress and our
> content. To embody it, continually and more completely in our
> institutions of government and of society is the conscious or un-
> conscious desire and effort of all good men among us.[90]

But a proposition is a theory that remains to be demonstrated,
that has not yet been proven.[91] Lincoln realized that America was
permanently propositional: its people were (and always would be)
making distinctions among equalities, wishing they could rescind or
temper or adjust the rights that they affirmed, and warring with the
Declaration of Independence that they revered. Lincoln knew that the
nation's future success would be tied, probably forever, to its failure.
But "failure" is, for Lincoln, both the right and an inadequate term.
In his December 1860 message to Congress, President Buchanan had
stressed that no act of Congress had impaired the South's system of
slavery and, further, that none was probable. By Lincoln's second inaugural, March 4, 1865, the nation had divided in two, endured a horrific
war that cost 618,000 lives, and witnessed the destruction of slavery.[92]
It is no wonder that Lincoln described the results of the war as "fundamental and astounding" (2:686). Before it, even as he condemned slav-

---

90. Charles Eliot Norton, *Letters,* 2 vols., ed. Sara Norton and M. A. DeWolfe
Howe (Boston: Houghton Mifflin, 1913), 1:285–86.
91. See the historian Ray Basler, cited in Pole, *Paths,* 157–58.
92. The total number of casualties was 1 million, in a country whose population
was 31 million. The breakdown of the death toll of 618,000 was 360,000 North, 258,000
South. See Maris A. Vinovskis, "Have Social Historians Lost the Civil War?: Some
Preliminary Demographic Speculations," in *Toward a Social History of the Civil War:
Exploratory Essays,* ed. Maris A. Vinovskis (New York: Cambridge University Press,
1990), 5–9; and T. Harry Williams, *Selected Essays* (Baton Rouge: Louisiana State University Press, 1983), 32–33.

ery, he had stood against equal rights for black people, but in March 1864 and again in April 1865 he recommended, moderately but pointedly, that at least some black men should be accorded the franchise (2:579, 699–700). It was a right that earlier he had not been prepared to grant them.

In one of his best, basic insights, Lincoln realized that rights do not exist in the abstract: they exist in practice, in historical *practices*, contexts, conditions. Rights, he saw in the late 1850s and 1860s, could not be enacted perfectly for all persons immediately—not in the United States, where, when the war began, slavery was legal in the South and racism embedded in law and custom in the North as well as in the South. Through his leadership, Lincoln made the nation perceive that slavery had to end, or else the Union would not survive and the right of white Americans to rise in the world and prosper would be lost forever. He knew that the rights of so many white Americans—penniless beginners—were implicated in the rights that had been denied to blacks, and he brought the nation to the same knowledge, destroying slavery, winning the war, and placing the United States on the verge of reunion and reconstruction. It is fitting and inevitable that we will always wonder how the history of rights in America would have unfolded had Lincoln lived beyond 1865.

Rights and Needs:
The Myth of Disjunction

Jeremy Waldron

What is the relation between the language of *rights* and the language of *needs*? Are they alternatives—the "disjunction" I refer to in the title—so that the choice of one rather than the other amounts to a significant political statement? Or are they complementary, so that it is possible for us to talk about the role played by needs in the construction of an adequate theory of rights?

The first of these positions—that we face a genuine choice between the language of rights and the language of needs—has been put forward by critical legal studies (CLS) scholar Mark Tushnet. Responding to a statement by Judge Posner that "the concept of liberty in the Fourteenth Amendment does not include a right to basic services" such as education, housing, and welfare assistance,[1] Tushnet wrote as follows:

> One can argue that the party of humanity ought to struggle to reformulate the rhetoric of rights so that Judge Posner's description would no longer seem natural and perhaps would even seem strained. I cannot pretend to have an argument against that course and would not want to weaken my comrades' efforts to build a society that guarantees positive as well as negative rights. But there do seem to be substantial pragmatic reasons to think that abandoning the rhetoric of rights would be the better course to pursue for now. People need food

1. Jackson v. City of Joliet, 715 F.2d 1200, 1204 (7th Cir. 1983).

and shelter right now, and demanding that those needs be satisfied—whether or not satisfying them can today persuasively be characterized as enforcing a right—strikes me as more likely to succeed than claiming that existing rights to food and shelter must be enforced.[2]

This chapter will be largely an exploration of various reasons for *not* following Tushnet's suggestion.

I take it his idea is not that poverty law advocates should go into federal courtrooms armed only with claims about the *needs* of their clients. Surely Tushnet does not think that strategy is more likely to yield results in litigation than one that couches the claims of the poor in the language of constitutional rights.

Perhaps he thinks the latter strategy is unlikely to succeed anyway; he may be arguing that activists should eschew constitutional litigation and pursue claims of need more directly in the political forum. I have no quarrel with that, nor with any attack on rights that is calculated to reverse the American practice of using courts and lawyers to confront issues that should be dealt with through ordinary representative institutions.[3]

The fact is, however, that the language of rights has now become the normal currency (or at least *a* normal currency) of ordinary political discussion. It is commonly used without prejudice to the question of whether views expressed in these terms should be embodied in a constitution, or made justiciable at the hands of courts empowered to strike down legislation. People use the language of rights to express their vision of the good society or their conception of the respect we owe each other. They use it in conversation, in legislatures, in pressure groups, in academic seminars, in democratic deliberations of all sorts. Perhaps, as Mary Ann Glendon and others have argued, they use it too much and too stridently;[4] but it has long ceased to be a

---

2. Mark Tushnet, "An Essay on Rights," *Texas Law Review* 62 (1984): 1394.

3. See the excellent account of the impact of this practice in William E. Forbath, "The Shaping of the American Labor Movement," *Harvard Law Review* 102 (1989): 1109–1256.

4. See Mary Ann Glendon, *Rights Talk: The Impoverishment of Political Discourse* (New York: Free Press, 1991).

language specific to (the threat of) legal proceedings. Maybe this is an instance of de Tocqueville's claim about Americans feeling obliged to borrow the language of litigation for their ordinary political debates.[5] If so, the borrowing has continued for so long, and the idioms have taken on such a life of their own, that the currency has lost whatever juridical shine it originally possessed. It is now just part of the normal language of politics—which is not to say it should necessarily remain as such, but only that its allegedly litigious connotations are no longer a reason for abandoning it.

Indeed, it is arguably a mistake to regard rights talk[6] as an instance of de Tocqueville's observation. The claim that "right is the child of law," understood as an imputation on the legitimacy of "*natural* rights," "*moral* rights," or "*human* rights," is perhaps no older than Jeremy Bentham's polemic against the French *Declaration of the Rights of Man and the Citizen* in 1789.[7] In seventeenth-century theories of natural rights, the term was used whenever one wanted to draw attention to duties imposed by God, nature, or reason for the benefit of human individuals.[8] It is true that rights were associated with natural *law*, so the concept remained juridical to that extent. But natural law simply comprised the most fundamental standards that reason could deploy: there *were* no basic principles that were non-"legal" in that sense. The point is that the role of rights in early modern theory conveyed nothing about the appropriateness of using human courts to vindicate them. The remedy with which they were associated was

---

5. Alexis de Tocqueville, *Democracy in America*, trans. H. Reeve (New Rochelle, N.Y.: Arlington House, n.d.), vol. 1, chap. 16, 270: "Scarcely any question arises in the United States which does not become, sooner or later, a subject of judicial debate; hence all parties are obliged to borrow the ideas, and even the language usual in judicial proceedings, in their daily controversies." Lawrence Friedman expresses something similar when he observes that life in modern America has become "a vast, diffuse school of law": Lawrence Friedman, "Law, Lawyers and Popular Culture," *Yale Law Journal* 98 (1989): 1598, quoted in Glendon, *Rights Talk*, 3.

6. I adapt this phrase from Glendon's title, *Rights Talk*.

7. See, for example, Jeremy Bentham, "Supply Without Burthen," in Jeremy Waldron, *Nonsense Upon Stilts: Bentham, Burke and Marx on the Rights of Man* (London: Methuen, 1987), 72–73: "What a legal right is I know. I know how it was made. . . . Right is with me the child of law: from different operations of law result different sorts of rights. A natural right is a son that never had a father."

8. See Richard Tuck, *Natural Rights Theories: Their Origin and Development* (Cambridge: Cambridge University Press, 1979) for an account of the different forms that this term took.

more often revolution than litigation.[9] When constitution writing became fashionable in the late eighteenth century, the use of rights to
express constraints on legislatures was more a matter of constitutional
lawyers borrowing from political morality than the other way around.

Nor have there been any particularly litigious overtones to the
prominence of rights talk in modern Anglo-American philosophy.
The explosion of books and articles on rights since the early 1970s
amounts largely to an attempt to articulate alternatives to utilitarianism as a basis for political morality. Following John Rawls's lead,
theorists turned to rights as a way of expressing individual-oriented
moral standards, thinking that only principles of this sort "take seriously the distinction between persons."[10] The idea of rights that are
moral rather than legal has posed little difficulty for these discussions.
It has been assumed for the most part—and I think correctly—that
Bentham was just wrong to say that rights could not operate outside a
legal context. The concept of moral duty is reasonably well understood, and it is clear that Hohfeldian analytics can be used to define a
logical relation between moral duty and moral right just as easily as
between legal duty and legal right.[11] Rights can therefore be part of a
structured moral *theory* every bit as articulate as the theory of general
utility. I shouldn't imply that this has been a bloodless victory, that
utilitarians have put up no resistance, or that there is a consensus
among rights theorists about what such a theory should look like. But
in all these debates, the issue has been how to express our general
moral concerns. Are rights trumps? Can indirect utilitarianism sustain
a theory of rights? What is the relation between rights and social
justice? Can rights be balanced against each other or do they express
agent-relative side constraints? Can groups have rights? These are
questions about the structure of morality. They have little or nothing
to do with constitutional law.

Today it is natural to resort to rights talk whenever one is advanc-

---

9. See John Locke, *Two Treatises of Government*, ed. P. Laslett (Cambridge: Cambridge University Press, 1988), vol. 2, sects. 222 ff.

10. John Rawls, *A Theory of Justice* (Oxford: Oxford University Press, 1971), 27.

11. See H. L. A. Hart, "Natural Rights: Bentham and John Stuart Mill," in his
collection *Essays on Bentham: Jurisprudence and Political Theory* (Oxford: Oxford University
Press, 1982), 79–90. See also Carl Wellman, *A Theory of Human Rights: Persons Under
Laws, Institutions, and Morals* (New York: Rowman and Allenheld, 1985), chap. 5, and
Jeremy Waldron, "Introduction," in *Theories of Rights,* ed. Jeremy Waldron (Oxford:
Oxford University Press, 1984), 5.

ing or opposing a political claim. There may be limits on the claims that are expressible in this idiom: maybe rights are limited to individualistic claims, or deontological claims, or claims associated with liberty. These are matters of controversy. Few think that individual rights define the whole of morality.[12] But even fewer believe that rights talk is limited to constitutional litigation. So the broader question raised by Tushnet's critique is just this: should we persevere with this language in political discussion generally or should we press for its replacement—again, in the normal currency of critical conversation—by the language of need?

The question assumes, of course, that it is somehow *up to us* what sort of language gets used in politics. It is easy for theorists to exaggerate the extent to which this is under our control. But it is *partly* under our control: we can certainly affect the way we talk to one another. For example, followers of the CLS movement have succeeded—even more than Republican political strategists—in discrediting the term *liberal* among legal scholars, and indeed in largely discrediting any explicit appeal to the heritage of liberal philosophy. Something similar happened with the idea of "*natural* rights," though the roots of that critique are much older: no one now uses the phrase except in a disparaging sense. It is not inconceivable that the term *rights* itself will go the way of *natural rights* and *liberalism,* and that sustained scholarly critique may so harass rights talk that it becomes the property of a small rump of unreconstructed philosophers who defy professional embarrassment to use it furtively or defensively in expounding their "old-fashioned" theories. That, I take it—or that *at least*—is what Tushnet and others are hoping for.

What, then, is the case against "rights"? And how would "needs" improve matters? The second question is as important as the first. Unless one looks forward to a general decline in political articulacy, the idea is to replace one type of talk with another on the grounds that the new discourse would better serve the purposes for which we engage in political conversation.

At least one basis for Tushnet's suggestion falls at this first hurdle. Rights, he says, are indeterminate and essentially contestable. No one

---

12. For an excellent argument, see Joseph Raz, "Right-Based Moralities," in *Theories of Rights*, ed. Jeremy Waldron (Oxford: Oxford University Press, 1984), 182–200.

agrees what rights we have, and even when they do agree—usually to some spectacularly abstract formulation such as "Equal concern and respect"—no one can agree about what, in detail, it commits us to.[13]

But claims about needs are *at least* as indeterminate as claims about rights, probably more so. The term "need" is used in two ways in political argument. Sometimes "P needs X" is followed by "in order to Y," and other times the way it is used expresses a sense that no such supplement is called for. I shall call the first the *instrumental* sense of "need," and the second the *categorical* sense of the term.

The instrumental sense of "need"—"P needs X in order to Y"—is relatively straightforward: it states that X is a necessary condition for Y; and once the truth of that is granted, debate will center obviously enough on whether Y is an appropriate matter for political concern. Need in this sense is relatively determinate, as determinate as the idea of instrumentality. The cost, however, is a complete *in*determinacy in the specification of the Y term. I can say "Tom needs food in order to live" or "Dick needs a Weimar pfennig in order to complete his coin collection" or "Harry needs spray paint in order to scrawl racist graffiti." The concept of one thing being needed for another or, more generally, the concept of a necessary condition, places no limits on that.[14]

If we turn to the categorical sense of the word, we find need presenting itself as a much narrower concept. To say "P needs X" [*period*] is to say something like—and this is very much a ballpark formulation— "X is necessary as a minimum condition for P to have a bearable human life." I call this a ballpark formulation, because the most it does is capture the flavor of the many competing analyses that have been suggested in the literature. Others include: "P will suffer (serious) harm if P lacks X,"[15] "X is what P would want if P were choosing freely and without false consciousness,"[16] and "P must have X in order to survive,

13. Tushnet, "An Essay on Rights," 1375.

14. Brian Barry believes, I think mistakenly, that this instrumental sense of "need" is the only sense. He says: "Whenever someone says 'X is needed' it always makes sense (though it may be pedantic in some contexts) to ask what purpose it is needed for." From this assertion he concludes that political philosophers need not concern themselves particularly with the concept of need as such, "for it is . . . derivative and the only interesting questions arise in connection with the ends" (*Political Argument* [London: Routledge, 1965], 48–49).

15. David Miller, *Social Justice* (Oxford: Clarendon Press, 1976), 130. See also David Wiggins, "Claims of Need," in *Morality and Objectivity,* ed. Ted Honderich (London: Routledge, 1985), 153–59.

16. Herbert Marcuse, *One Dimensional Man* (Boston: Beacon Press, 1991), 21–23.

be healthy, and function properly."[17] The concept is evidently a contestable one; and contestable not just between these different analyses, but also in our understanding of the abstract terms in which each is couched: "bearable," "human," "harm," "serious," "freely," "false consciousness," "healthy," "function properly," and so on.

Occasionally it is suggested that we should pin down the concept to *survival*, so that we count something as a need only if a person will die without it. But this remains ambiguous. How likely must death be, and how imminent? What does the formulation assume about normal life expectancy and mortality patterns?[18] Anyway, theorists of need are unanimous that such a concept would be an impoverished one. We want a philosophy of *human* need, not just biological need.[19] Certainly, no such minimalist theory could do anything like the work rights have done in political debate—signaling concerns about threats to self-respect, religious convictions, free expression, control of body and sexuality, choice of career, cultural and political participation, and so forth.

Tushnet is dreaming, therefore, if he thinks that needs talk would be any more determinate than rights talk. The point of this observation is not to *discredit* the concept of needs (or the concept of rights, for that matter). Political concepts simply *are* indeterminate and contestable: that follows from the fact that they are a dialectical response among a diverse and quarrelsome community of thinkers to the complexity of human life and its problems. The task is to understand and take advantage of all that, not embark on a futile search for definitional determinacy.[20]

----

17. James Griffin, *Well-Being: Its Meaning, Measurement and Moral Importance* (Oxford: Clarendon Press, 1986), 42.

18. As Amartya Sen points out, "People have been known to survive with incredibly little nutrition, and there seems to be a cumulative improvement of life expectation as dietary limits are raised. In fact, physical opulence seems to go on increasing with nutrition over a very wide range; Americans, Europeans, and Japanese have been growing measurably in stature as their diets have continued to improve. There is difficulty in drawing a line somewhere, and the so-called 'minimum nutritional requirements' have an inherent arbitrariness that goes well beyond variations between groups and regions" (*Poverty and Famines* [Oxford: Clarendon Press, 1981], 12.)

19. Cf. "*Lear*: 'O, reason not the need! Our basest beggars / Are in the poorest thing superfluous. / Allow not nature more than nature needs, / Man's life is cheap as beast's.' " Shakespeare, *King Lear*, act 2, scene 4, lines 264–67.

20. CLS discussions of these matters show little awareness of the extensive literature in modern philosophy and political theory reflecting on conceptual indeterminacy. See: W. B. Gallie, "Essentially Contested Concepts," *Proceedings of the Aristotlean Society* 56

Even if it is no less contestable, might not talk of needs be politically more compelling than rights talk? This too seems unlikely.

There is, first, an analytic point. To acknowledge that P has a *right* to X is to acknowledge that someone, possibly the person doing the acknowledging, has a *duty* or *responsibility* to secure it for P. That's what saying "P has a right" means. Nothing analogous is true (or straightforwardly or uncontroversially true) of the language of needs. As David Wiggins points out, there is no contradiction in saying, "This patient needs a blood transfusion, but she ought not to be given one."[21] I don't mean that the language of need is purely descriptive and value neutral, with no emotive overtones. On the contrary, it combines an evaluative with an essentially plaintive illocutionary force. But it is not straightforwardly *pre*scriptive in the way that rights talk is.

This language may make it harder to get someone to accept a rights statement than a needs statement, inasmuch as the former contains an implicit commitment to action. But then the comparative ease of getting the needs statement accepted is a hollow victory anyway, because one *still* has to get the statement acted upon.

In general, we should remember the exchange between L'Abbe Guyot Desfontaines and the minister of state, the Comte D'Argenson, who was questioning him about a dangerously satirical piece he had written. I write for a living, protested the unhappy author, "Il faut que je vive!" ("I need to live!") "Je n'en vois pas la nécessité," ("I do not see the necessity.") responded the minister. The experience of our century too has not shown that officials (or societies) are galvanized to action by the discovery that somebody needs something, even to survive. Those who found themselves falling back upon the elemental claim that simply because one is human, one deserves to live, have had to discover, in Michael Ignatieff's words, that this is sometimes the weakest, not the strongest, claim that people can make to one other.[22]

(1955–56); Alasdair Macintyre, "The Essential Contestability of Some Social Concepts," *Ethics* 84 (1973); Hanna Pitkin, *Wittgenstein and Justice* (Berkeley: University of California Press, 1972); W. E. Connolly, *The Terms of Political Discourse* (Oxford: Martin Robertson, 1983); Ronald Dworkin, *Law's Empire* (Cambridge: Harvard University Press), 31–113.

21. Wiggins, "Claims of Need," 188–89.

22. Michael Ignatieff, *The Needs of Strangers* (London: Chatto and Windus, 1984), 51. See also Hannah Arendt, *The Origins of Totalitarianism*, 2d ed. (New York: Meridian Books, 1958), 299: "The world found nothing sacred in the abstract nakedness of being human." (I should point out, however, that in context, Arendt's remark is an attack also on the idea of rights grounded simply in human nature.)

All this discussion is relevant to Tushnet's proposal. Patricia Williams observes that statements like Tushnet's "about the relative utility of needs over rights discourse overlook that blacks have been describing their needs for generations. They overlook a long history of legislation *against* the self-described needs of black people." She continues,

> For blacks, describing needs has been a dismal failure as a political activity. It has succeeded only as a literary achievement. The history of our need is certainly moving enough to have been called poetry, oratory, epic entertainment—but it has never been treated by white institutions as the statement of a political priority. . . . Some of our greatest politicians have been forced to become ministers or blues singers. Even white descriptions of "the blues" tend to remove the daily hunger and hurt from need and abstract it into a mood. And whoever would legislate against depression? Particularly something as rich, soulful, and sonorously productive as black depression.[23]

For blacks, she says, "the battle is not deconstructing rights, in a world of no rights; nor of constructing statements of need, in a world of abundantly apparent need." It is not the luxury of choosing from a menu of discourses. Evident needs are being denied, compelling arguments about rights are being rebuffed. This is a political predicament, not a semiotic one: there are no magic words that, if only we could find them, would do everything we want them to do.

Perhaps we are looking in the wrong place for the advantages of needs talk. Perhaps the advantage has to do not with clarity or effectiveness, but with morality. Talk of needs sounds somehow more compassionate, more open, more responsive, less aggressively individualistic, less *male*, than the table-thumping adversarial rhetoric of rights.

That may be so, but it is worth registering an initial caveat. In my experience (not wholly confined to California), the modern language of needs—"I really *need* this" and "You're not understanding my *needs*"—is every bit as querulous, individualistic, and self-absorbed as rights talk ever was. It certainly has dimensions of confessional and

---

23. Patricia Williams, *The Alchemy of Race and Rights: Diary of a Law Professor* (Cambridge: Harvard University Press, 1991), 151–52.

therapeutic narcissism that the comparatively formal and public language of rights lacks. Perhaps we should say that needs talk *presents* itself initially as being less adversarial and self-interested than other forms of political conversation. But it doesn't take long before that attribute too is being exploited by its users for the intensification of their demands.

There *is* a difference, though, and it is an important one. There seems to be something *passive* about needs talk; a person with needs addresses others as a potential recipient of their concern and assistance. This is not a universal truth, for one can also say, "I need space; leave me alone." But it is true, nevertheless, as to the general flavor of neediness. The language of rights has traditionally had connotations of independence and self-sufficiency. The right bearer is seen as someone vindicating their autonomy. If there is a positive value that others are supposed to respond to in that individual's rights, it is the establishment of that person's self as an agent with a life to lead on her or his own terms. The person who is needy, by contrast, is the one who is breaking down the fences of his or her independent agency and asking to be taken in by others. Needs talk is the language of supplicants. Those who are looking after their own necessities find other ways of expressing themselves.

We have to be careful, however, with these last formulations. Perhaps it is only needs *talk* that is passive and suppliant, not need itself. Humans, like other animals, are active and largely self-sustaining systems. If they need something, their natural tendency is to go out and try to get it, rather than to sit around waiting for it to come to them.[24] For this reason, surely the primary normative force of "need" (assuming it *has* normative force) is for the need bearer herself or himself: "P needs X" implies "P should try to get X." The concept is only secondarily normative for others: "Q should try to get X for P." Of course, if P is engaged in some communal mode of production, the cooperative actions calculated to satisfy P's needs are also at the same time calculated to satisfy the needs of others. Even so, cooperating is not the same as becoming the passive recipient of others' activity. Need remains active even when we act together.[25]

24. Cf. G. E. M. Anscombe, *Intention* (Ithaca: Cornell University Press, 1963), 23: "The primitive sign of wanting is trying to get."

25. I have stressed the active aspect of deprivation in "Homelessness and the Issue of Freedom," *UCLA Law Review* 39 (1991): 295–324, esp. 303–4 and 324.

It would be wrong to express a putative difference between needs and rights by saying that needs connect up more naturally with interpersonal *responsibilities* than rights do. Rights are necessarily correlative to duties: even the person who claims a right to be left alone is implying the existence of a corresponding responsibility on others.

Furthermore, rights talk is associated with moral theories and schemes of legal protection in which rights and duties are *reciprocal* as well as correlative. The person who says she or he has a right, and thus that others owe her or him a duty, usually does so in terms that are universalizable, that is, in terms indicating that the duty bearers also have a similar right that they are entitled to press against that person. Thus not only are P's rights correlative to Q's responsibilities, but those responsibilities are reciprocated by similar duties that P owes to Q. I remarked earlier that there is a much tighter conceptual connection between rights and duties than there is between needs and duties. That applies to the relation of correlativity; it also—inasmuch as *systems* of rights have been thought through more carefully than systems of needs[26]—applies to the relation of reciprocity. No one has ever done for needs talk what Kant did for rights in his *Metaphysical Elements of Justice* or in his image of the "kingdom of ends."[27]

If there is a difference, it has to do with the kinds of responsibilities that are recognized. Duties correlative to rights are often thought of as duties of noninterference, negative duties, duties of omission rather than positive action. If the background right in this tradition is liberty, the background responsibility is that of respecting interpersonal boundaries and refraining from crossing them.[28] Mary Ann Glendon

---

26. For "system of needs," we have to turn either to G. W. F. Hegel's comments about the market in *Elements of the Philosophy of Right*, trans. Allen Wood (Cambridge: Cambridge University Press, 1991), paras. 189–208, or to Karl Marx's desultory comments in the *Critique of the Gotha Program* (New York: International Publishers, 1966) and elsewhere.

27. Immanuel Kant, *Metaphysical Elements of Justice*, trans. J. Ladd (Indianapolis: Bobbs-Merrill, 1965). For the "kingdom of ends," see Kant, *Groundwork to the Metaphysics of Morals*, trans H. J. Paton, sub nom. *The Moral Law* (London: Hutchinson, 1948), chap. 2, 100–103. See also Martha Minow's excellent discussion in *Making All the Difference: Inclusion, Exclusion and American Law* (Ithaca: Cornell University Press, 1990), 277 ff.

28. It is easy to denigrate as a form of atomism this essentially liberal concern with establishing boundaries between persons. Patricia Williams reminds us that such denigration is unlikely to appeal to those whose historical experience has been "generations of existing in a world without any meaningful boundaries—and 'without boundary' for

cites Marx in this connection: the duties correlative to rights establish the right bearer "as an isolated monad . . . withdrawn into himself, . . . an individual withdrawn behind his private interests and whims and separated from the community."[29]

One way of putting this is to say that the responsibility correlative to the abstract idea of rights is the duty to *mind one's own business*. That is an important formulation because it indicates the possibility of *congruence* between the rights a person is supposed to have and the responsibilities the person has in relation to the similar rights of others. I have spoken so far of correlativity and reciprocity: my rights are correlative to your duties; and your duties are reciprocated by my similar duties to you. The relation of congruence is more subtle: the idea is that my rights and my duties are congruent when it is the case that fulfilling my duties promotes rather than detracts from the exercise of my rights.[30] By refraining from interfering with your projects, I can turn my full attention to my own, undistracted by moralistic worries about what you are up to: by not interfering with what is *your* business, I can better mind my own. In this sense, the requirement of noninterference seems an eminently reasonable one.[31]

By contrast, it is commonly thought that if the idea of needs generates responsibilities at all, it generates active responsibilities: duties to give, duties to assist, duties to rescue. Instead of a responsibility to mind my own business, the duties generated by needs require me to *go out of my way* to help you. A need becomes normatively relevant when a person lacks something that is necessary for life, health, flourishing, and so on. If P lacks something he or she needs and cannot get it himself or herself, then if the word *need* is to be endowed with any normative force, it must be that others should get it for P. Need-based responsibilities, then, connote our lack of self-sufficiency, the implication of our lives with others, our being at the mercy of each other's care and empathy.

---

blacks has meant not untrammeled vistas of possibility but the crushing weight of total—bodily and spiritual—*intrusion*" (Williams, *Alchemy of Race and Rights,* 164.)

29. Karl Marx, "On the Jewish Question," in *Nonsense Upon Stilts: Bentham, Burke and Marx on the Rights of Man,* ed. Jeremy Waldron (London: Methuen, 1987), 146–47, cited by Glendon, *Rights Talk,* 47.

30. The terminology is mine, but I owe the idea to Loren Lomasky.

31. This congruence will fail, however, if you and I are engaged in an essentially *competitive* struggle, for then not interfering with you may seem a way of undermining rather than promoting the successful exercise of my rights.

Moreover, need-based duties are duties to *attend to* or *be sensitive to* another's position. At a given time, a person will have some but not all of what he or she needs: one who responds properly to a duty to serve the needs of others must be able to find out what exactly is lacking and determine the best way to supply it. With traditional rights it is different. Everyone is simply to be left alone: we are to adopt the same hands-off policy, determined by the same evident boundaries of interpersonal integrity, with regard to each and every other. No special sensitivity is called for.

There is finally this difference between right-based and need-based responsibilities, as they are traditionally conceived: inasmuch as the former are duties of omission, they are likely to foster a sense of morality as a largely conflict-free system of absolutes. Since I can omit performing any number of actions at a given time, duties of omission are unlikely to generate moral conflicts: I am not going to have to choose between my duty not to torture and my duty not to kill. Duties of assistance, however, *may* generate conflict: if time and resources are scarce, the duty of assistance I owe to P may conflict with the duty of assistance I owe to Q. Since need-based responsibilities are characteristically of this kind, the morality comprising them will have a more compromised, less absolute or deontological aspect, than a traditional right-based morality has. Theorists divide on the question of whether this is an advantage or a disadvantage of the shift from rights to needs.[32]

Previously, I have talked of the way rights are *traditionally* perceived. They tend to be seen as moral relations vindicating freedom in a negative sense, and so they tend to be thought of as correlative to strict responsibilities of noninterference. It is, however, far from clear that this is an accurate perception of rights, or that it is a necessary feature of rights talk (as opposed to a contingent feature of various amendments to the 1787 Constitution of the United States.)

For one thing, we are perfectly comfortable with rights correlated to duties of positive action in private law. If I give you fifty dollars today to mend my roof tomorrow, then I have a right that you should help mend my roof and you have a positive duty to do so. The responsibility here is one of action and assistance, not omission. A critic may respond that such rights are all pursuant to special, contractual relations; and so

32. For a discussion, see Jeremy Waldron, "Rights in Conflict," *Ethics* 99 (1989): 503–19.

they are. The critic will point to the lack of any *general* duty to rescue and thus the lack of any general right to assistance from others in tort law and elsewhere.[33] For the moment, that is beside the point. The question is whether there is anything about the *form* of rights, the very language of rights talk, that disqualifies it from expressing ideas about the assistance we owe to one another. Is there anything about the logic or the connotations of "P has a right against Q to ____" that should dissuade us from filling in the blank with activist, interventionist, or welfarist responsibilities? I submit that there is not. The use of rights talk in contract to express duties of positive action as well as duties of noninterference shows that the language *as such* does not preclude the expression of claims about the things we owe one another in the way of cooperation and mutual aid.

For another thing, it is simply not true that traditional rights are correlated mainly to duties of noninterference. Marx insisted that many of the rights set out in contemporary proclamations were "political rights that are only exercised in community with other men. Their content is formed by participation in the common essence, the political essence, the essence of the state."[34] These were the rights of the citizen: the right to vote, to stand for public office, to hold public officials accountable, and to engage in the speech and conversations that are constitutive of public life. They cannot plausibly be regarded as the rights of "an isolated monad withdrawn into himself," nor can the corresponding responsibilities be regarded simply as duties of noninterference. In the case of voting rights, for example, the responsibility is to set up and maintain mechanisms of popular decision making in which each individual will have an equal voice. It is not enough to respect people's *liberty* to mark an "X" against the name of their favorite politician: respecting the right means going out of one's way to give that action meaning in the context of a flourishing democracy. As modern theorists explore the resonances of *citizenship* as a concept for understanding social and economic equality, it is clear that the idea of rights has always been associated with the sense of a shared political duty to provide a place for each individual in the fabric of common life.[35]

---

33. Glendon makes a big deal of this in chapter 4 of *Rights Talk*, "The Missing Language of Responsibility."

34. Marx, "On the Jewish Question," 144.

35. See T. H. Marshall, "Citizenship and Social Class," in his book *Class, Citizenship and Social Development* (New York: Doubleday, 1964); Ralf Dahrendorf, *The Modern Social*

Even in the seventeenth century, when the concept was by no means associated automatically with democratic citizenship, there was a sense that rights could express positive and substantive responsibilities. James Tyrrell and John Locke both based the acquisition of individual property—perhaps the paradigm of rights, according to the traditional view—on a background right to individual sustenance out of the natural resources created by God.[36] That Locke felt no difficulty or embarrassment in regarding this as the right-based ground for a duty of mutual aid is evident from the following passage:

> But we know that God hath not left one Man so to the Mercy of another, that he may starve him if he please: God the Lord and Father of all, has given no one of his Children such a Property, in his peculiar Portion of the things of this World, but that he has given his needy Brother *a Right* to the Surplusage of his Goods; so that *it cannot justly be denied him*, when his pressing wants call for it. . . . As Justice gives every Man a Title to the product of his honest Industry, and the fair Acquisitions of his Ancestors descended to him; so Charity gives every Man *a Title* to so much out of another's Plenty as will keep him from extream want, where he has no means to subsist otherwise; . . . [37]

To claim that Lockean rights were merely negative rights to noninterference is to show ignorance of the foundations (not just the detail) of early modern thought.[38]

Conflict: An Essay on the Politics of Liberty (London: Weidenfeld and Nicholson, 1988), chap. 2; Desmond King and Jeremy Waldron, "Citizenship, Social Citizenship and the Defense of Welfare Provision," *British Journal of Political Science* 18 (1988): 415–43.

36. See James Tyrrell, *Patriarcha non Monarcha* (1681), cited in Thomas A. Horne, *Property Rights and Poverty: Political Argument in Britain, 1605–1834* (Chapel Hill: University of North Carolina Press, 1990), 43. John Locke, *Two Treatises of Government*, vol. 1, sect. 86, pp. 204–5 and vol. 2, sect. 25, pp. 285–86.

37. Ibid., vol. 1, sect. 42, p. 170 (my emphasis).

38. Mary Ann Glendon asserts that Locke repudiated "the idea of the human person as 'naturally' situated within and constituted through relationships of care and dependency" (*Rights Talk*, 70). But a philosopher who begins his discussion of civil society with the following passage:

> God having made Man such a Creature, that, in his own Judgment, it was not good for him to be alone, put him under strong Obligations of Necessity, Convenience, and Inclination to drive him into Society, as well as fitted him with Understanding and Language to continue and enjoy it. The first Society was between

So rights *can* be used to express demands for assistance and positive action. It is true, however, that they do so in a certain style or spirit, which needs talk cannot capture. We should consider whether that spirit is really something we want to abandon.

Earlier, I quoted Patricia Williams saying that claims of need are seldom effective in combating racist injustice. Maybe things are different, Williams conceded, when someone white is describing need. "Shorn of the hypnotic rhythmicity that blacks are said to bring to their woe, white statements of black needs suddenly acquire the stark statistical authority that lawmakers can listen to and politicians hear."[39] But think what this entails. Right-laden whites become experts on blacks' needs so that those needs can be represented as a matter of calm, technocratic authority. In this way, we avoid the angry and unpredictable business of blacks using *their own voice* to confront the society in which they live. Talk of the *rights* of an oppressed people comes most naturally from their own lips, and it will sound disconcerting to those who think it wiser or more politic for the oppressed to keep quiet. Talk of needs has no such connotation: it sounds as natural in the mouth of a detached observer as in that of the needy person.

The link between needs and authority, objectivity, and expertise is well known to philosophers. The first thing students are taught in this area is the distinction between *needs* and *wants*. They learn that while no one can tell me what my wants are (for logically I am an authority on my subjective desires), the language of needs is an objective language.[40] A person has needs in the same sense an automobile

---

man and Wife, which gave beginning to that between Parents and Children; . . . (Locke, *Two Treatises of Government*, vol. 2, sect. 77, pp. 318–19)
can hardly be accused of atomism or of neglecting the natural interdependence of human beings. Locke had no difficulty in using the language of rights to describe family responsibilities. Children, he said, have "a Right to be nourish'd and maintained by their Parents" for "men being by a like Obligation bound to preserve what they have begotten as to preserve themselves, their issue come to have a Right in the Goods they are possessed of." (Ibid., vol. 1, sects 88–89, p. 207). [Incidentally, the passage cited by Glendon—*Two Treatises of Government*, vol. 1, I, sects. 57–58, p. 182—establishes only Locke's awareness of the fact that human practice does not necessarily coincide with natural law in this regard.]

39. Williams, *Alchemy of Race and Rights*, 152.

40. Thus David Miller, *Social Justice*, 129: "The point is that wanting is a psychological state, which is ascribed on the basis of a person's avowals and his behaviour (we use behaviour as a criterion when we cannot ask the person directly to tell us what he wants, or when we think he is being disingenuous). Needing, on the other hand, is *not*

does: if it is not serviced regularly, protected from the elements, and supplied with fuel, it will break down. A mechanic can be an authority on a car's needs (much more than the car or the owner can be) and similarly a nutritionist, a social scientist, or a therapist can be an authority on people's human needs. We saw earlier that the expert on needs will have to be sensitive to the detail of the person being studied; but again, that is true of the mechanic and the car. The point is that the human expert does not have to defer to the subject's conscious articulation of needs; the expert can do all she or he has to do with an understanding of how a person works (or how *this* person works) and what is the proper condition of human flourishing.[41]

Rights, by contrast, are claims made naturally in the voice of the person who is their bearer. Not exclusively: we talk of the rights of infants who cannot speak for themselves, and Amnesty International pursues rights on behalf of political prisoners everywhere.[42] We hope that for every Florestan there is a Leonora. But there is something especially appropriate about a person standing up for her or his own rights.[43] Rights are the claims one can put forward for one's own sake and on one's own behalf without the moral embarrassment usually associated with assertions of self-interest. Unlike needs, which may have no necessary presence in consciousness, rights are essentially articulate and self-conscious. Though it is not true that one has a right just because one thinks one does, still the truth about rights is supposed to reflect what everyone may properly think and assert about the exigencies of their own situation and the claims they have against others. To this extent, rights *do* embody a certain view of the human individual: the right bearer is one who is self-aware and vigorously

---

a psychological state, but rather a condition which is ascribed 'objectively' to the person who is its subject."

41. A suspicion of this sort of expertise explains much conservative opposition to needs talk: see, for example, Antony Flew, *The Politics of Procrustes: Contradictions of Enforced Equality* (London: Temple Smith, 1981), 117–37. But it should not be confined to the Right: the language of needs is, in Foucault's terms, the expert language of disciplinary power, the language of normalization and the science of the body. (See, e.g., Michel Foucault, "Two Lectures," in *Power/Knowledge: Selected Interviews and Other Writings, 1972–1977*, ed. Colin Gordon (New York: Pantheon Books, 1980), esp. 95–108.)

42. See the discussion in Waldron, *Nonsense Upon Stilts*, 195–200.

43. See Joel Feinberg, "The Nature and Value of Rights," in his *Rights, Justice and the Bounds of Liberty: Essays in Social Philosophy* (Princeton: Princeton University Press, 1980), and Thomas E. Hill, "Servility and Self-Respect," *Monist* 57 (1973).

conscious of what one is entitled to demand from others and who is not embarrassed about advancing those demands.

[The point can also be put like this. To the extent that there is anything *descriptive* in the assertion that people remain the bearers of rights even when they are being abused, it is that men and women have (or can develop) the capacity and virtue to stand bravely witness to, and indomitably defiant of, assaults on their dignity as persons.[44] To say that one has a *right* that is being abused or neglected is not just to heighten the pathos; it is to face one's oppressors, and bring to bear on the situation the dignity of that power of *being a person*. This descriptive aspect of the claim that people *are* the bearers of rights—that is, that *that* is the sort of beings they are—has perhaps been too much neglected in our haste to avoid the naturalistic fallacy by giving a purely normative sense to the idea that there are certain "common rights to which we are called *by nature*."[45]]

Thus rights talk and needs talk may both embody a form of respect; but only the language of rights conjoins in its very structure the idea of respect for persons and *self*-respect. Both rights and needs amount to a demand that certain interests be attended to; but only rights talk presents those interests in the voice of one who would be a full-fledged *member* of society, who is not going to go away, and who expects to be taken seriously as an enduring source of continuing demands. Patricia Williams again: "The concept of rights is the marker of our citizenship. . . . 'Rights' feels new in the mouths of most black people. It is still deliciously empowering to say."[46] She also says,

> For the historically disempowered, the conferring of rights is symbolic of all the denied aspects of their humanity: rights imply a respect that places one in the referential range of self and others, that elevates one's status from human body to social being. For blacks, then, the attainment of rights signifies the respectful behavior, the collective responsibility, properly owed by a society to one of its own.[47]

44. See Jeremy Waldron, "Florestan, Leonora, and the Virtue of Human Rights," manuscript on file with author.

45. Condorcet, "Sketch for the Progress of the Human Mind," in *Condorcet: Selected Writings*, ed. Keith Michael Baker (Indianapolis: Bobbs Merrill, 1976).

46. Williams, *Alchemy of Race and Rights*, 164.

47. Ibid., 153.

Of course it is true, she says, that constitutional rights in America have been "shaped by whites, ordained from on high in small favors, random insulting gratuities."[48] But that would be true of needs also. The difference is that the *idea* of rights, associated as it is with respect for persons, is essentially open-ended and continually demanding. Even as an ideal, it connotes not just that the subject in question is a focus of present or occasional concern; it says *here she or he is*, on her or his own behalf, with claims to press as a person. A concession of *any* claim put forward in the language of rights is implicitly a concession that nothing short of full rights will do, for rights are the rights of persons. The language of rights refers us to the full moral status of the claimant in a way that the language of needs, taken on its own, does not.

These considerations are, I think, sufficient to rebut Tushnet's suggestion that we abandon the language of rights. But they do not require us, on the other hand, to give up our talk of needs. That would be the myth of disjunction: the "either/or" that Tushnet and Williams seem both to subscribe to. Instead, what I have said here suggests that rights talk provides an indispensable *framework* in which talk of needs can be related to ideas about personhood, self-assertion, and dignity.

In addition, the framing of needs in terms of rights can help focus our attention on the network of duties and responsibilities that individual needs are supposed to give rise to. A claim of need, by itself, is merely a diagnosis—perhaps an expert diagnosis—of the predicament of some organism, animal or human: "That plant needs water," "The child needs protein," "You need therapy," and so on. By expressing some of these claims as rights—by taking needs, in other words, as a *basis* for rights, rather than as an alternative to rights—we can give them a certain integrity and dignity that claims of need do not always have on their own.

It is not that we simply *confer* that dignity by replacing "needs" in the above formulations by the magic phrase "has a right to." The idea is, rather, that we should do for needs what gets done for rights claims as a matter of course: we should seriously scrutinize their aspiration to fit into and play a part in an overall account of respect for persons.

---

48. Ibid., 164.

Martha Minow has pointed out that "when [a] system assigns rights to individuals, it actually sets in place patterns of relationships."[49] To claim a right is not just to trumpet one's own interests; it is (in a sense) to promise that a viable structure of relational responsibilities can be found to house the interests in question. Both formally and substantively—in their commitment to *equal* respect—theories of rights aspire to an integrity that is sometimes belied by their presentation as line-item claims on some enumerated charter or bill. A theory of rights is not simply a list of demands: since Kant, it has been taken to imply that the demands can be organized into a vision of society, a *Rechtstaat*, integrated around a concept of the person as the dominant single status of equality in moral and political life. If rights, as Minow suggests, are like a language,[50] then it is a language with a grammar, and one that makes serious demands upon its users: there is a responsibility that one assumes when one makes a claim about rights.

The test of any such claim is whether it can play a coherent part in defining systematically what a mass of people in society owe one another as equals. We have, in our three centuries or so of theorizing about rights, developed techniques for thinking about that systematicity. To say, therefore, that we should couch needs in the language of rights is to suggest—I think responsibly—that we submit them to this test, take advantage of that heritage, and integrate them into the ideal.

In talking about a test, I don't mean that rights are a sort of liberal club and that newcomers—claims of need—have to be examined by the existing members to see if they "fit in." The idea is not that the traditional rights to property and civil and political liberty are already there, and the question is only whether claims based on need—putative socioeconomic rights—should be admitted.

It is true, philosophers have sometimes written in those terms, complaining about a proliferation of rights, arguing that Articles 22 through 27 of the Universal Declaration debase the currency, and so on.[51] Robert Nozick is typical in his complaint that

---

49. Minow, *Making All the Difference,* 277.
50. Ibid., 307–8.
51. See Maurice Cranston, "Human Rights—Real and Supposed," in *Political Theory and the Rights of Man,* ed. D. D. Raphael (1967).

> The major objection to speaking of everyone's having a right *to* various things such as equality of opportunity, life, and so on, . . . is that these "rights" require a substructure of things and materials and actions; and *other* people may have rights and entitlements over these. . . . There are particular rights over particular things held by particular persons, and particular rights to reach agreements with others. . . . No rights exist in conflict with this substructure of particular rights. Since no neatly contoured right to reach a goal [or serve a need] will avoid incompatibility with this substructure, no such rights exist. The particular rights over things fill the space of rights, leaving no room for general rights to be in a certain material condition.[52]

His objection assumes that claims based on need occupy a relatively superficial role in a general theory of entitlement. It is as though we *first* determine who owns what, and *then* determine whose needs are left unsatisfied and what is to be done about them. The alternative, he says, would be to stipulate the need-based rights first, then try to fit particular property entitlements around them: "To my knowledge, no serious attempt has been made to state this 'reverse' theory."[53]

I doubt that he is correct in that last point,[54] but, at any rate, he is right to notice the challenge. A claim based on need may disturb our existing understanding of ownership and justice. Traditional views about individuality, property, economy, and markets are theoretically well structured and coherently thought through. Those who defend them have a right to ask whether anything similar can be developed to accommodate the new claims based on need. However, in responding to this inquiry, there is no reason why the proponents of need should not throw the whole structure into question. Once they have raised their challenge, all bets are off. Now no rights have any priority. The

52. Robert Nozick, *Anarchy, State and Utopia* (Oxford: Basil Blackwell, 1974), 238.

53. Ibid.

54. See the discussion in Jeremy Waldron, *The Right to Private Property* (Oxford: Clarendon Press, 1988), 283, referring, for example, to John Locke's emphasis on the priority of need over individual property rights in *Two Treatises of Government*, vol. 1, sect. 42 and vol. 2, sect. 25, and to Rawls's insistence in *A Theory of Justice*, 64, 88, and 270 ff., that the determination of a basic structure by principles that respect everyone's interest in fair access to primary goods has priority over particular allocations and even over the decision as to whether there is to be private property in a whole range of resources.

newcomers' task is to devise a *Rechtstaat* that can accommodate all the claims of right that *they* propose to recognize; it is not their job to accommodate their demands to the claims or the systems that others have put forward. So when I said that a person asserting a new right has a responsibility to define a relational structure in which it can take its place, I did not mean that structure should be a comfortable or a familiar one. Accordingly, the demandingness of rights discourse that I have emphasized need not be thought of as an obstacle to radical reform or comprehensive social criticism.

Historically, the radical power of the rights ideal has always consisted in its commitment to *theory*. Those who demanded religious toleration, civil liberty, and the democratic franchise did not confine themselves to particular demands. They made claims about the rights of the person; and they presented those claims not on behalf of just one or a few individuals, but as a coherent new vision of a kingdom of ends. They were confronted not just with instances of oppression, but with well-defined structures of thought about monarchy, religious establishment, and patriarchal domination. It was the republication of Robert Filmer's writings, not just the antics of Charles Stuart and his brother, that was the occasion for John Locke's pioneering work on natural rights. The challenge was not just to batter at these edifices with individual demands, but to come up with theories that were at least as articulate and as structured as the institutions they opposed.

Nothing less is promised by the integration of social and economic needs into a theory of rights. By themselves, claims of need are nothing more than particular suppliant pleas. But taking their place in a theory of rights, they challenge us to develop new structures of thought about personhood, citizenship, universality, community, and equality. The language of rights offers a framework and a sense of responsibility for articulating that challenge.

It is true that rights have been associated in the past with the organized power of capital, and that there are relics of that association in the archaeology of our constitutional jurisprudence. Some critics—Tushnet is one of them[55]—talk as though the language of rights has been hopelessly tainted by that association, as though it will lay a curse now on any activist who comes near it. If so, then the language

---

55. Tushnet, "An Essay on Rights," 1386–94.

of social democracy has been cursed by Stalin, the language of community has been compromised by ethnic cleansing, and the language of equality blighted by Pol Pot.

The wiser course is surely to profit rather than suffer from the fact that we share a vocabulary with our ideological opponents. It means we can talk to them, and also that in framing their ideas they may contribute, even if inadvertently, to the shared enterprise of developing the concepts and apparatus of political argument.

We may take a narrow view and say it is only the expression of our concerns about need that matters: who cares what concepts the bourgeois use? Still, as I have tried to show in this chapter, there is a contribution that the bourgeois language of rights can make to the articulation of our concerns. No doubt the contribution is formal. But by connecting *needs* with *the person*, by stressing the importance of a person speaking for himself or herself, *in his or her own voice*, and by relating all that to the *theory* of a society of such individuals addressing one another as equals, the formalism of rights can give our claims a coherence and a dignity that they otherwise lack. It would be a pity if—for the sake of purity or on the basis of contingent historical associations—we were to revert instead to less articulate forms of political demand.

Part 2
The Foundations of Rights
or Rights without
Foundations

Justifying the Rights of Academic Freedom in the Era of "Power/Knowledge"

Thomas L. Haskell

A hundred years ago, when the old-time colleges seemed to have lost their way and the modern university system was still struggling to be born, American academics worried about an entire range of questions that hardly anyone asks today. Broadly speaking, the questions lay at the intersection of epistemology and intellectual authority. How is knowledge best cultivated? What institutional setting is most conducive to intellectual authority? How is the professoriate to justify its existence to those who pay the bills? What is the university *for?*

Questions of this kind, which carry no special charge today, seemed urgent indeed at the turn of the century, when less than 4 percent of the college-age population was attending college and the university had not yet become securely ensconced as gatekeeper to the professions. The Victorian reformers whom we now remember as the architects of the modern American university—Charles William Eliot of Harvard, Andrew Dickson White of Cornell, Daniel Coit Gilman of Johns Hopkins, and many others whose names are less well known—confronted questions of intellectual authority every day, and

I am indebted to more people for advice about this chapter than I can mention here. Special pains were taken by Steven Crowell, Sanford Levinson, Randall McGowen, Louis Menand, Walter Metzger, Robert Post, and Carol Quillen. Advice sometimes took the form of vigorous dissent, so no one is to be blamed for the final product but me. Various versions of the chapter were presented as papers at conferences at Amherst College in November 1992 and at the Swedish Collegium for Advance Study in the Social Sciences in September 1994; and at the history departments of the University of Oregon in October 1993 and Rice University in September 1994.

they did not have the luxury of suspending judgment. They had to get on with the practical business of building universities, for expanding enrollments and lavish infusions of capital from a burgeoning industrial economy were opening up a world of new possibilities in higher education.[1]

The same developments also brought crude demands for orthodoxy. State legislators and wealthy private donors alike took it for granted that "he who pays the piper, calls the tune," an assumption strongly seconded by the prevailing legal doctrines of the era. Faced with contradictory possibilities and pressures, Victorian reformers thought long and hard about authority and professional autonomy. They drew inspiration from ancient precedents of faculty self-governance in England and from the full-bodied traditions of academic freedom that many of them had seen firsthand during their own student days in Germany. Their thinking and worrying bore practical fruit during the decades following the Civil War, and we who teach and work in the American university system today are the beneficiaries of what they wrought. Nowhere is the success of their handiwork more evident than in the easy complacency with which we take for granted the intellectual authority of the university and those who work within it.

My aim is to dispel that complacency, at least momentarily, by doing what historians so often do: tell stories about how things came to be the way they are. The story I will tell draws heavily on the work of Walter Metzger, Mary Furner, William Van Alstyne, and other scholars. I will have little to say about either the captains of industry who financed the modern university or the educational entrepreneurs,

---

1. College attendance ratios appear in Fritz Machlup, *The Production and Distribution of Knowledge in the United States* (Princeton: Princeton University Press, 1962), 78. On the development of the modern American university, see Richard Hofstadter and Walter Metzger, *The Development of Academic Freedom in the United States* (New York: Columbia University Press, 1955); Laurence R. Veysey, *The Emergence of the American University* (Chicago: University of Chicago Press, 1965); Hugh Hawkins, *Pioneer: A History of the Johns Hopkins University 1874–1889* (Ithaca: Cornell University Press, 1960); Thomas Bender, *Intellect and Public Life: Essays on the Social History of Academic Intellectuals in the United States* (Baltimore and London: Johns Hopkins University Press, 1993); Dorothy Ross, *Origins of American Social Science* (Cambridge: Cambridge University Press, 1991); Burton J. Bledstein, *The Culture of Professionalism: The Middle Class and the Development of Higher Education in America* (New York: Norton, 1976); and Thomas L. Haskell, *The Emergence of Professional Social Science: The American Social Science Association and the Nineteenth Century Crisis of Authority* (Urbana: University of Illinois Press, 1977).

such as Eliot, White, and Gilman, who superintended its construction. Nor will I say much about martyrs to academic freedom, with the single exception of Edward A. Ross. His case deserves special attention because it illustrates the late emergence and fragility of the rights we take for granted and helps us recall the circumstances under which the American Association of University Professors (AAUP) was founded. The focal point of my story is the emergence of the disciplines, such as history, chemistry, sociology, mechanical engineering, and so forth, in which we academics do our work today. These "communities of the competent" were, I believe, the seed crystals around which the modern university formed. Defending their authority is, in my view, what academic freedom is principally about. What concerns me are two things that imperil that authority: (1) the decay of the epistemological assumptions that originally underwrote the founding of disciplinary communities, and (2) a growing assimilation of academic freedom to First Amendment law, a development that has brought immense benefits, but at the expense of obscuring both the function of the disciplinary community and its intimate relation to academic freedom. My aim is not to put forth a new justification for academic freedom, but to call attention to the limitations of the old one and hold up for critical examination some of the obstacles that stand in our way as we seek a formulation more adequate to our needs.

Appearances to the contrary notwithstanding, the comfortable state of affairs in which we find ourselves today was not foreordained. What brought it about was a process of institutional development that proceeded in two overlapping phases, each vital to the success of the other. The first created communities of competent inquirers, the second used them to establish authority in specialized domains of knowledge. The history of the community of the competent is long and honorable but only sketchily documented. It has roots that go far back into the history of ecclesiastical establishments, on the one hand, and science, on the other, and which intertwine at every stage with controversies over heresy and communal autonomy. The rudiments of an always edgy and competitive communal solidarity among competent inquirers date back to the founding of the first European universities. By the eighteenth century the changing technology and economics of print culture had decisively surpassed personal acquaintance and pri-

vate correspondence as a means of knitting inquirers together, giving
rise to a nascent division of intellectual labor and prompting much
speculation about the growing influence of the "republic of letters."[2]

The nineteenth century brought changes of scale so great as to
constitute a qualitative transformation of the conditions of intellectual endeavor.[3] Population growth, rising literacy rates, growing per
capita income, and the rapid spread of a predominantly urban form
of life joined with immense improvements in the ease and speed of
communication to make the fruits of specialized intellectual competence relevant and accessible to a larger public than ever before.
Architects of the modern American university such as Daniel Coit
Gilman at Hopkins capitalized on these changes, not only by constructing ivy-covered classrooms and dormitories to house an expanding clientele of students, but also by founding academic jour-
nals, reshaping undergraduate libraries to the needs of research,
funding graduate fellowships, and encouraging their faculties to
seek reputations of national and international scope. The most visible manifestation of the maturing communities around which the
university formed were the specialized disciplinary associations that
began organizing on a national basis in the 1880s: the Modern Language Association (1883), the American Historical Association (1884),
the American Economic Association (1885), and many others in suc-
ceeding years.[4] By the time of World War I, a new intellectual division of labor had taken shape as college and university campuses all
over the country reorganized themselves around "departments," local outposts of the fields of learning staked out by the national specialist associations. Neither the departments nor the national professional associations they represented were of any great consequence
in themselves, but the maturing communities of the competent for
which they stood had profound effects on the lives of their members

2. Lorraine Daston, "The Ideal and the Reality of the Republic of Letters in the
Enlightenment," *Science in Context* 4 (autumn 1991): 367–86.

3. The reforms of the nineteenth century were made possible by a long and rich
tradition of academic freedom, which is carefully developed in the classic work by
Hofstadter and Metzger, *Development of Academic Freedom*.

4. The term *community of the competent* comes from Francis E. Abbot, who was a
member of the "Metaphysical Club" where Charles Peirce and William James worked
out the basic ideas of pragmatism in the 1870s. Stow Persons, *Free Religion: An American
Faith* (New Haven: Yale University Press, 1947), 31, 125–29; Philip P. Wiener, *Evolution
and the Founders of Pragmatism* (New York: Harper & Row, 1965), 41–48.

and utterly transformed the character of higher education in this country.

The importance of these newly defined communities lay in the opportunity they provided for professors to divide their loyalties, thereby complicating their identity and enhancing their authority. Professors would, of course, continue to be teachers, dependent as always on a particular college or university for a salary and for provision of the mainly undergraduate classrooms in which they earned their keep. But they would also become something new: research scholars. As such, their employment credentials, even in their traditional role as teachers of undergraduates, would become contingent upon membership and reputation within translocal communities made up of fellow research specialists. By keeping up a constant exchange of communications in the form of journal articles and books, as well as private correspondence and face-to-face conversations at periodic conventions, the members of these far-flung communities, or *Kommunikationgemeinschaft*, as Karl-Otto Apel calls them, would police each other's opinions and thus provide, in theory at least, a collective warrant for one another's authority.[5] Knit together not by affection, but by the respectful attention that experts owe their peers, these densely interactive communities effectively constitute the specialized universes within which scholarly discourse proceeds today.[6] Although they have undeniably generated their share of ponderous mystifications over the years, when all is said and done they created a space for originality and critical thinking without which modern culture would almost certainly be the poorer.

The second phase of reform harvested what the first planted. Insofar as a distinct community of competent investigators could be said to exist in a given field, the keystone of professional autonomy

5. Karl-Otto Apel, *Charles S. Peirce: From Pragmatism to Pragmaticism*, trans. J. M. Krois (Amherst: University of Massachusetts Press, 1981), xvi; and Apel, *Toward a Transformation of Philosophy*, trans. G. Adey and D. Frisby (London, Boston, and Henley: Routledge and Kegan Paul, 1980).

6. An early pioneer was Friedrich August Wolf, founder of a famous seminar in classical studies at Halle in the 1780s, who borrowed the ideology of cultivation *(Bildung)* from Humboldt and used it, paradoxically, to elevate research above teaching so as to achieve a level of authority that pedagogy alone could not supply. See Anthony J. La Vopa, "Specialists Against Specialization: Hellenism as Professional Ideology in German Classical Studies," in *German Professions, 1800–1950*, ed. Geoffrey Cocks and Konrad H. Jarausch (New York and Oxford: Oxford University Press, 1990), 27–45.

was already in place, for the individual members of such a community were empowered by its very existence to speak in a quasi-corporate voice. Having acknowledged one another as peers, and thus relieved one another of the heavy burdens of anonymity and idiosyncrasy, they were well situated to deflect criticism originating outside the community's borders and deflate truth claims unable to win communal support. The result of the sharpened identity and growing solidarity of specialists was an effective monopoly on "sound opinion" within their domain. The cardinal principle of professional autonomy is collegial self-governance; its inescapable corollary is that only one's peers are competent to judge one's performance. *Monopoly* is not an inappropriate term to describe the resulting advantage enjoyed by communally sponsored opinion, yet it carries implications that tend to obscure the defining feature of the community. It is vital to remember that this sort of monopoly comes about by *intensifying* competition between producers (in this case, of ideas), not by sheltering them from it, as in the classic case of economic monopoly. *The price of participation in the community of the competent is perpetual exposure to criticism.* If there is anything at all that justifies the special authority and trustworthiness of community-sponsored opinions, as I believe there is, it lies in the fact that these truth claims have weathered competition more severe than would be thought acceptable in ordinary human communities.[7]

All that remained was to reach an understanding about the practical limits of solidarity. What degrees and kinds of politically sensitive expression would the professoriate be willing actually to defend through collective action? Where was the pale beyond which the outspoken individual would be left to twist in the wind? That understanding gradually took shape in the political turbulence of the Populist and Progressive eras, as young social scientists, in particular, espoused unpopular views that triggered explosive controversies on campus after campus. Out of this crucible of controversy a tacit set of stan-

7. The inadequacies of the economic monopoly model are developed more fully in my essay "Professionalism versus Capitalism: R. H. Tawney, Emile Durkheim, and C. S. Peirce on the Disinterestedness of Professional Communities," in *The Authority of Experts: Studies in History and Theory*, ed. Thomas L. Haskell (Bloomington: Indiana University Press, 1984), 180–225. On the "culture of critical discourse" fostered by these communities, see Alvin Gouldner, *The Future of the Intellectuals and the Rise of the New Class* (New York: Continuum, 1979).

dards and expectations finally crystallized in 1915, with the founding of the American Association of University Professors (AAUP) and the publication of its first report on Academic Freedom and Tenure.

Although the AAUP code would be severely tested in the patriotic fervor of World War I and placed under heavy strain again in the loyalty controversies of the McCarthy period, it served as a kind of capstone, bringing to completion the institutional edifice the Victorians planned and built out of their concern to provide safe havens for sound opinion. Today, although the professoriate is less influential (and less affluent) than it would like to be, it speaks with unchallenged authority in many spheres of life and is substantially free to play whatever tunes it likes, without begging permission from those who pay the piper. Some recent Supreme Court decisions might even be taken to indicate that professional autonomy, suitably garbed in the lofty language of rights and academic freedom, is today not only secure, but as close to sacred as a secular society can make it. Our Victorian predecessors never dared hope that academic freedom had been high on the agenda of the nation's Founding Fathers. Yet in 1967, speaking for the majority of the Supreme Court in *Keyishian v. Board of Regents*, Justice Brennan did not hesitate to say that "academic freedom . . . is of transcendent value to all of us and not merely to the teachers concerned. That freedom is therefore a special concern of the First Amendment, which does not tolerate laws that cast a pall of orthodoxy over the classroom."[8]

Ironically, even as Justice Brennan crowned the Victorian project with a victory more complete than its architects had envisioned, the tide was running out on the intellectual premises that had sustained it in the first place. None of us today are likely to feel entirely comfortable with the assumptions on which our ancestors built the modern academic order. The problem is most severe for those among us who unreservedly identify themselves as "postmodern," from whose vantage point the assumptions that propelled the Victorians are likely to seem at least naive, and possibly sinister. Consider, for

---

8. Brennan quoted in William W. Van Alstyne, "Academic Freedom and the First Amendment in the Supreme Court of the United States: An Unhurried Historical Review," *Freedom and Tenure in the Academy: The Fiftieth Anniversary of the 1940 Statement of Principles,* William Van Alstyne, special editor, *Law and Contemporary Problems* 53 (summer 1990): 114.

example, the familiar Foucauldian notion that power and knowledge, far from constituting a natural opposition, are locked in a mutually supportive embrace so tight that they should be written "power/knowledge," as if two sides of a single coin.[9] Nothing could be more alien to the thinking of our Victorian predecessors, for whom the whole point of academic freedom was to expand the sphere of disinterested knowledge and fence it off from power.[10] Obvious questions present themselves. If a day should come when the premises of academic freedom no longer seem plausible even within the academy, how long can they be expected to prevail in the world at large? And if, as I have contended, academic freedom is but the exposed cutting edge of the drive toward autonomy that every community of the competent must undertake if it is to do its work of authorizing sound opinion, what does the decay of those premises portend for the university?

---

9. Michel Foucault, *Power/Knowledge: Selected Interviews and Other Writings 1972–1977*, ed. Colin Gordon (New York: Pantheon, 1980). In *Discipline and Punish*, Foucault's formulation took this practical form: "Instead of treating the history of penal law and the history of the human sciences as two separate series [that merely have effects on one another, my aim is to] see whether there is some common matrix or . . . single process of 'epistemological-juridical' formation; in short, [to] make the technology of power the very principle both of the humanization of the penal system and of the knowledge of man." The problem is that in making the "technology of power" the *"very principle"* of humanitarian reform and knowledge of man, one reduces knowledge and justice to power. Or, to take him at his word, Foucault does not *reduce* one to the other, but argues for their simultaneous production in a "single process," which blurs the opposition between them just as surely as reduction would. Blurring that opposition means obscuring the difference between education and indoctrination, scholarship and propaganda, history and fiction, right and might, consent and coercion, and so on, tending to make these and other classic oppositions, as I put it earlier, "two sides of a single coin." Michel Foucault, *Discipline and Punish: The Birth of the Prison*, trans. A. Sheridan (New York: Pantheon, 1977), 23.

10. Committed Foucauldians will remind us that distinguishing between power and disinterested knowledge can itself be construed as an exercise in power. Indeed it can. The problem is that once one accepts the proposition that power is the only game in town, power relations can and will be teased out of anything at all. The same could be said for sex, religion, or any number of other grand obsessions. Any master key, once subscribed to, will seem to open all locks. The dangers of reducing everything to power relations are twofold. First, making power the master category obscures a vital distinction between force and persuasion that is constitutive for liberal politics. Second, unlike sex, religion, and other interpretive obsessions, the presumption that power is the master motive is a classic example of the self-fulfilling prophecy. One who insists upon construing dancing as sex by other means is merely a bore; but one who construes scholarship as politics by other means is very likely to act in such a way as to breed in others the very motives imputed to them.

Turning up the level of magnification a bit will help us gauge the chasm that is opening between the Victorians and ourselves. In 1896, at the height of Populist agitation against the gold standard, Edward A. Ross, a young economist who had just arrived at Stanford, made several speeches in support of William Jennings Bryan and published a campaign pamphlet titled "Honest Dollars." At a time when respectability and Republican party loyalty were expected to go hand in hand, Ross became the first academic economist to openly endorse the idea of free silver. He was no lightweight. Trained at the University of Berlin and Johns Hopkins University, Ross was married to the niece of social theorist Lester Frank Ward and had recently become secretary of the American Economic Association. Although only thirty years old, he had already achieved high visibility in his field, both as a scholar and as an outspoken reformer at Indiana University and Cornell. When David Starr Jordan left the presidency of Indiana to take over the new university that Leland Stanford was building in California, he invited Ross to come along. With Indiana, Stanford, Northwestern, and Cornell all courting him, Ross put Jordan off twice before accepting his third offer.

Jordan's admiration for Ross was soon put to the test by Mrs. Jane Lothrop Stanford, who had been left in sole command of the university by her husband's death. Offended by Ross's activism, she demanded that Jordan dismiss him. Stalling for time, Jordan persuaded Mrs. Stanford to give Ross a sabbatical leave in 1898–99 with the understanding that he would look for another position and resign a year later if still considered unsuitable. Simultaneously Jordan transferred Ross out of economics and made him professor of sociology.

Although he was professionally well connected and had a friend in power, Ross had good reason to wonder how much support he could count on. San Francisco newspapers reported that six out of every seven Stanford faculty members supported McKinley and the gold standard. Leading economists viewed Ross's activism with mixed feelings at best. Frank Taussig of Harvard cautioned Ross that flamboyant popular pronouncements on economic issues were "undignified and objectionable." Taussig was a man of conservative temperament, but even fellow radical Simon Nelson Patten asked: "Have you not been giving a little too much time to politics lately? . . . That miserable money problem gets much more attention than it deserves and I never see an article of yours on it but what I feel that intellectual force has been wasted which might have produced far greater results in other directions."[11]

There was no such thing as tenure at Stanford University in 1896, and no one could say just how far an outspoken scholar could go. A colleague of Ross's, H. H. Powers, clearly went too far when he had the misfortune not to notice Mrs. Stanford, an orthodox Catholic, sitting in a predominantly student audience as he spoke on religion. The "pessimism and heterodoxy" of his remarks offended her.[12] When Powers added insult to injury by challenging the gold standard as well, she demanded his resignation. Comparatively unpublished and not nearly as well connected as Ross, Powers understandably regarded publicity as a profound threat to his career. He had little choice but to accept his fate in silence. Ross showed him no great sympathy and in fact helped the administration smooth his departure by taking over some of his assignments. By the end of 1897 Ross felt confident that his own safety was assured, as long as he confined himself to questions "about which it was my business to know."[13] Sure enough, at the end of his cooling-off sabbatical Jordan notified him that in spite of Mrs. Stanford's threats, his annual appointment would be resumed in 1899–1900.

By this time Mrs. Stanford had issued a total ban on faculty political activity. Her aim, she said, was to preserve the neutrality of the institution. Ross flouted the ban so brazenly on his return that one cannot rule out the possibility that he had, perhaps, already made up his mind to leave. Speaking before a group of San Francisco labor leaders in 1900, he condemned coolie immigration and issued a plea for Anglo-Saxon racial purity, going so far as to assert, according to some reports, that vessels bringing Asian laborers to these shores should be fired on to prevent their landing. Ross's ugly racial chauvinism was unexceptional in the context of the times. What made his comments inflammatory was the fact that the Stanford fortune had been built on coolie labor. In another address at about the same time, Ross predicted that in the twentieth century all natural monopolies, including railroads, would pass into public ownership. Outraged once again; concerned about the "socialistic" elements that Ross

11. Mary O. Furner, *Advocacy and Objectivity: A Crisis in the Professionalization of American Social Science, 1865–1905* (Lexington: University Press of Kentucky, 1975), 234.
12. Ibid.
13. Ibid., 235.

seemed to be courting; and feeling pressure from her late husband's business associates, Mrs. Stanford ordered Jordan to fire Ross, giving him six months to wrap up his affairs.[14]

Not one to play the passive victim, except when doing so in public might work to his advantage, Ross carefully timed the announcement of his firing to coincide with publication of his major book, *Social Control*. At a well-managed press conference in November 1900, Ross turned on his friend in power, depicting himself as the victim not only of Mrs. Stanford and big money, but also of a university president who lacked the courage to defend free speech.[15] His self-conceived role was that of the scientific expert, duty bound to announce truths arduously wrested from nature and corporately sanctioned by a community of peers. "I cannot with self-respect decline to speak on topics to which I have given years of investigation," he said. "It is my duty as an economist to impart, on occasion, to sober people, and in a scientific spirit, my conclusions on subjects with which I am expert. . . . The scientist's business is to know some things clear to the bottom, and if he hides what he knows he loses his virtue."[16]

George Howard, head of the Stanford history department, went before his French Revolution class two days later and likened the university's termination of Ross to the tyrannies of the ancien régime. When subsequently Howard refused to apologize for this outburst, he too was ousted. In the ensuing turmoil, thirty-seven of forty-eight senior faculty members pledged their loyalty to Jordan, but all those in the social sciences who could afford the gesture resigned, virtually wiping out the fields of economics, history, and sociology. Frank Fetter, a prominent economist who had just come from Cornell to take over economics, asked for assurances of free inquiry and expression for all faculty in the future; when it was not forthcoming, he resigned. So did Arthur Lovejoy, Stanford's first and, at the time, only philosopher. Ross may well have shaped the encounter in self-serving ways, but there is no denying that his flair for the dramatic gesture achieved what no other academic freedom case of the era did: it overrode

---

14. Ibid., 235–36.

15. James C. Mohr, "Academic Turmoil and Public Opinion: The Ross Case at Stanford," *Pacific Historical Review* 39 (February 1970): 39–61; Furner, *Advocacy and Objectivity*, 238.

16. Ross quoted in Furner, *Advocacy and Objectivity*, 238.

political differences, galvanized opinion, and produced united action by the professoriate to defend one of its own.[17]

At the annual convention of the American Economic Association (AEA) in December 1900, Edwin R. A. Seligman, one of the most widely respected American economists of his generation, stage-managed a quasi-formal vindication of Ross. The president of the AEA at the time was Richard T. Ely, whose own radicalism had triggered an academic freedom case at Wisconsin in 1894, in which he received only lukewarm support from the profession. Still thought by some to be too much the Chautauqua speaker and Christian socialist and too little the scholar, Ely's name would have had to head the list of signatures if the association had officially declared its support for Ross. Apparently in hopes of avoiding that outcome and bringing together both ends of the political spectrum in defense of Ross, Seligman preferred to act informally, even though that meant not having the official imprimatur of the AEA. Accordingly, Ross made a dramatic appearance before a meeting of about forty economists and then sat silently as Seligman read excerpts from Jordan's letters to show that he was being unjustly persecuted. The AEA members present then created a committee to investigate the case. "With this declaration," says Walter Metzger, "the first professorial inquiry into an academic freedom case was conceived and brought into being—the predecessor if not directly the parent of Committee A of the AAUP."[18]

Given the cold shoulder by President Jordan and many members of the Stanford University faculty, the inquiry rapidly bogged down in futile efforts to unravel Mrs. Stanford's motives. Lacking the imprimatur of the AEA, its report was fair game for critics. Magazines and newspapers that were unfavorably disposed dismissed it as a partisan document. Thus, in spite of receiving strong support even from conservative economists, the inquiry fell flat. Seligman and others tried to organize a boycott of the university. They succeeded in persuading several job candidates to withdraw from consideration, but when it came to a choice between professional solidarity and placing one's graduate students advantageously, solidarity evaporated. Much to the chagrin of Harvard social scientists, new Ph.D. recipients from Harvard promptly filled the empty slots in Stanford's history department. Although efforts were made to find a desirable post for Ross, he left

17. Ibid., 239–41.
18. Ibid., 245; Hofstadter and Metzger, *Development of Academic Freedom*, 442–43.

Palo Alto for the academic wilderness of Nebraska, where another martyr to academic freedom, E. Benjamin Andrews, was president. Five years later, as memories faded, Ross moved to Wisconsin, where his career flourished for the next thirty years. The warm-hearted historian of the ancien régime, George Howard, went to Nebraska for good.[19]

The Ross case was a happy fluke that enabled Ross and his supporters to publicize the issues of academic freedom in uncharacteristically stark, black-and-white terms. The imperious "Dowager of Palo Alto," as sociologist Albion Small called her, could not have played her role better if Ross had been writing the script.[20] Yet even in convenient caricature, the issues of academic freedom are sufficiently murky that the case also illustrates the fragility of intellectual authority and the difficulty of mobilizing effective support on behalf of a scholar confronted with demands for political conformity. Rescuing Ross was no piece of cake. Had events fallen out a little differently, things could have turned out a lot worse than they did. Needless to say, in the absence of a well-organized and highly self-conscious community of the competent, forearmed with values appropriate to the task, there would have been no one to come to Ross's rescue, and she who paid the piper would have called the tune—or hired another piper.

Some may imagine that with the resources of the First Amendment at his disposal, Ross and the cause of academic freedom were bound ultimately to prevail. Those resources were not yet available, however. Justice Oliver Wendell Holmes did as much as anyone to make them available, but not until after World War I. Holmes's famous dissent in *Abrams v. United States* came in 1919: "The best test of truth is the power of thought to get itself accepted in the competition of the market. . . . [W]e should be eternally vigilant against attempts to check the expression of opinions that we loathe and believe to be fraught with death, unless they so imminently threaten immediate interference with the lawful and pressing purposes of the law that an immediate check is required to save the country." In contrast, back in 1892, while still a justice of the Massachusetts Supreme Court, Holmes had no compunctions about making freedom of expression contingent upon contractual obligations. In keeping with legal doctrines that prevailed

19. Furner, *Advocacy and Objectivity*, 246, 251, 252–53.
20. Small quoted in Hofstadter and Metzger, *Development of Academic Freedom*, 443.

at the time, he then construed the First Amendment only as a prohibition on prior restraint, not a guarantee of immunity against the consequences of expression. In the case of a police officer who had been fired after criticizing his department, Holmes held that

> The petitioner may have a constitutional right to talk politics, but he has no constitutional right to be a policeman. There are few employments for hire in which the servant does not agree to suspend his constitutional right of free speech, as well as of idleness, by the implied terms of his contract. The servant cannot complain, as he takes the employment on the terms which are offered him.[21]

The Ross case not only was a trial run for the investigative modus operandi that the AAUP would later make its stock in trade, it also brought together the two men who, more than anyone else, brought the AAUP into existence. Arthur Lovejoy, the Stanford philosopher who resigned in protest over Ross's ouster, would become secretary of the organization at its founding in 1915. E. R. A. Seligman, the Columbia economist who arranged for Ross's quasi-official vindication, wrote the first draft of the 1915 Report on Academic Freedom and Tenure. Lovejoy then rewrote the text so extensively that Walter Metzger, our premier historian of academic freedom, credits him with being virtually coauthor. Both later served as president of the organization. It was Lovejoy and a group of seventeen colleagues at Johns Hopkins University who hosted the first intercollegiate meeting aimed at the construction of a national association of university professors. Since Hopkins faculty had also founded the MLA, the AHA, the AEA, and most of the other specialist organizations that defined the new intellectual division of labor, it was only fitting that they would take the lead in adding this capstone to their professionalizing labors.

The word *capstone* needs stressing. This is how I, as a historian, would *define* academic freedom: as the capstone of the institutional edifice that Victorian reformers constructed in hopes of establishing authority and cultivating reliable knowledge. The metaphor implies a

21. Holmes quoted in Van Alstyne, "Academic Freedom and the First Amendment," 98, 84. Even today, of course, the legal protections of the First Amendment extend only to public institutions, but I assume that that has been far enough to decisively influence the culture of the private sphere as well.

stronger linkage between academic freedom and professionalization than is commonly recognized today. The connection often goes unacknowledged, partly because in our generation professors have been extremely loath to admit their kinship to lawyers, physicians, and other fee-for-service professionals. Here etymological common sense should be our guide: *Professor* could hardly help but be a variety of *professional.*[22] The founders of the AAUP were not so skittish about their professional aspirations. They explicitly identified their organization as a complement to the specialist societies and deliberately modeled it on the American Bar Association and the American Medical Association:

> The scientific and specialized interests of members of American university faculties are well cared for by various learned societies. No organization exists, however, which at once represents the common interests of the teaching staffs and deals with the general problems of university policy. Believing that a society comparable to the American Bar Association and the American Medical Association in kindred professions, could be of substantial service to the ends for which universities exist, members of the faculties of a number of institutions have undertaken to bring about the formation of a national Association of University Professors.[23]

22. The kinship of professors and professionals was especially close in the case of the social science disciplines, which received unprecedented prominence in the modern American university and provided the most frequent setting for academic freedom controversies. The pioneering members of the American Social Science Association, which began meeting in 1865 and spawned the AHA in 1884 and the AEA in 1885, were for the most part forward-looking professional men in whose eyes the social sciences were elaborations of a professional division of labor that extended far beyond the university and defined the wisdom and knowledge necessary for exercising leadership in a merit-based liberal democracy. See Haskell, *Emergence of Professional Social Science*, 100–110. Stephen Bann brings out the intimate dependence of the historians' mode of discourse on that deployed by physicians, lawyers, and ministers. See Bann, "History and Her Siblings: Law, Medicine and Theology," in *The Inventions of History: Essays on the Representation of the Past* (Manchester and New York: Manchester University Press, 1990), 12–32.

23. These words appear in the three-page brochure sent out by the "committee on organization" in November 1914, announcing the founding session to be held in January. The passage continues as follows: "The general purposes of such an Association would be to facilitate a more effective cooperation among the members of the profession in the discharge of their special responsibilities as custodians of the interests of higher education and research in America; to promote a more general and methodical discussion of problems related to education in higher institutions of learning; to create means for the authoritative expression of the public opinion of college and university

Still more important, the linkage between professionalization and academic freedom has been obscured by the stupendous growth of First Amendment law over the past half century. The rising tide of First Amendment protections has undeniably lifted academic freedom to new heights, and today it does indeed make good sense, legally speaking, to think of academic freedom as a subset of First Amendment liberties. But academic freedom and free speech overlap and reinforce one another only at certain points. Any effort to completely assimilate the former to the latter would be disastrous. Historically speaking, the heart and soul of academic freedom lies not in free speech but in professional autonomy and collegial self-governance. Academic freedom came into being as a defense of the disciplinary community (or, more exactly, the university conceived as an ensemble of such communities), and if it is to do the work we expect of it, it must continue to be at bottom a denial that anyone outside the community is fully competent to pass judgment on matters falling within the community's domain. From my standpoint, no justification for academic freedom can succeed unless it provides ample resources for justifying the autonomy and self-governance of the community. For this task, the First Amendment is ill suited.[24]

One way to highlight the difference is simply to observe that the founders of the modern university were not so much libertarians as communitarians. They wanted to liberate individual practitioners such as Ross from the dictates of their employers, not as an end in itself, but as a way of enhancing the authority of the entire community of practitioners.[25] It was a generation whose members, like Matthew

---

teachers; and to maintain and advance the standards and ideals of the profession." AAUP Archives, file marked "A. O. Lovejoy 1914," also published in *Bulletin of the AAUP* 2 (March 1916): 11–13.

24. I follow the lead of Walter Metzger in stressing the tension between two definitions of academic freedom, the "professional" and the "constitutional" (the latter deriving from the First Amendment): see Metzger, "Profession and Constitution: Two Definitions of Academic Freedom in America," *Texas Law Review* 66 (June 1988): 1265–1322. For a somewhat divergent view, see David M. Rabban, "A Functional Analysis of 'Individual' and 'Institutional' Academic Freedom under the First Amendment," *Freedom and Tenure in the Academy: The Fiftieth Anniversary of the 1940 Statement of Principles,* William Van Alstyne, special editor, *Law and Contemporary Problems* 53 (summer 1990): 227–301.

25. On this point the charter document of the AAUP, the 1915 Report on Academic Freedom and Tenure, is explicit: "It is, in short, not the absolute freedom of utterance of the individual scholar, but the absolute freedom of thought, of inquiry, of discussion and of teaching, of the academic profession, that is asserted by this declaration of principles."

Arnold, were not much impressed by the freedom merely to do (or say) whatever one pleases. They looked askance at individualistic values and felt no embarrassment about imposing a wholesome discipline on the crude, market-driven society that was growing by leaps and bounds around them. They set out to professionalize higher education because they wanted to establish the good, the true, and the beautiful on a firmer base. Of all the institutions they founded, none are more characteristic or more aptly named than the "disciplines," which even today define the division of intellectual labor within the university.

To sharpen the contrast still more, consider the continuing controversy over the teaching of Darwin's evolutionary theory. If our point of departure were free speech alone, it would not be at all easy to justify the exclusion of "creation science" from the curriculum. After all, when biblical literalists say that evolution is "only a theory," they are not wrong. Like all scientific theories, Darwin's is contestable and will one day be superseded. Why give it a privileged place in the curriculum? The only persuasive answer lies in the authority that inheres in a well-established disciplinary community. Darwin's theory deserves a privileged place because it, unlike "creation science," enjoys the support of a strong consensus of competent biological investigators, who have organized themselves in such a way as to foster mutual criticism and drive out of circulation truth claims that cannot take the heat.

We academics are prone to hide from ourselves the degree to which we ourselves rely on authority and count on others to do the same. I once heard a prominent sociologist blithely announce that "authority has no place in the classroom." He meant that teachers should encourage discussion, tolerate dissent, and bend over backwards to avoid silencing or penalizing students whose politics offend them. These are admirable values, too often honored in the breach, but it would be the height of naïveté to think that authority plays no role in the classroom, or that professors and students meet on a level playing field. We professors walk into a classroom and the students

---

AAUP, "General Report of the Committee on Academic Freedom and Academic Tenure (1915)," included as Appendix A of *Freedom and Tenure in the Academy: The Fiftieth Anniversary of the 1940 Statement of Principles,* William Van Alstyne, special editor, *Law and Contemporary Problems* 53 (summer 1990): 404–5 [hereafter referred to as AAUP, "The 1915 Report on Academic Freedom and Tenure"].

cease their chatter, get out pen and paper, and wait dutifully for us to begin. Surely no one dreams that this effect is produced merely by personal charisma or sheer mental power. Teachers occupy one role and students another in an institution cunningly designed to make it in the student's interest to pay attention, to listen up, to defer to our authority. We appear before them not as mere citizens, but as delegates of a community of inquiry, made up of members who earn their keep by engaging in mutual criticism. When we defend academic freedom, we are defending that authority.

The very mention of authority makes late-twentieth-century academics nervous, yet we all routinely defer to the authority of experts. Deference undergirds even our most fundamental assumptions about ourselves and the world we inhabit. For example, I believe in evolution with nearly the same degree of confidence I feel about the existence of the table I am writing on or the accuracy of an account I might give of some episode in my own life, based on personal experience and recollection. Yet my belief in evolution rests on no firmer basis than deference to expert authority. I have not inspected the fossil record for myself or worked my way through the intricate details of Darwin's argument in *The Origin of Species*. Much less have I followed the tangle of debates that lead up to the present version of the theory. Many imagine that the story of divine creation is *intrinsically* less plausible than evolution. They claim to find in the idea of one-celled primeval slime gradually evolving into complex forms of life under the directionless pressure of natural selection a virtually self-evident truth. I am not persuaded. The compelling quality they attribute to the idea of natural selection itself I would attribute instead to the institutional arrangements that have succeeded in making belief in evolution a recognized badge of intelligence and educational attainment in our culture. We nonfundamentalists who are not trained in biology believe in evolution, not because we are more rational than biblical literalists, not because we can recite the "good reasons" that a fully rational judgment would require, and not because we have in mind the evidence and experience it would take to envision the process and grasp it in the way biologists do. We believe because we trust biologists.[26]

---

26. This and the next paragraph borrow from my introduction in *The Authority of Experts: Studies in History and Theory,* ed. Thomas L. Haskell (Bloomington: Indiana University Press, 1984), x–xi.

Our trust is not blind, of course. We willingly defer to the judgment of biologists in large part because we feel sure they have good reasons for their beliefs and could display those reasons to us if we were willing to take the time. But my confidence that good reasons exist does not alter the plain fact that my present acceptance of the theory of evolution is based not on those uninspected reasons but on deference to authority. What shapes my belief is as much psychological and sociological as logical. And although I think the thought process that leads me to my belief is far sounder than the one that leads the creationist to hers or his, the difference is not a matter of the creationist's clinging to authority while I rely on reason: we both submit to authority, but to different authorities. For this no apologies are needed. Up to a point, we are better off for our willingness to defer to experts. Even though deference to authority short-circuits the quintessentially rational processes of personally weighing the evidence and following out a chain of logic to one's own inner satisfaction, deferring to experts brings real advantages insofar as it enables us to gain vicariously from others' experience and compensate for the limited range of our own. Sometimes deferring to expert authority is the rational thing to do.

If, as I have been arguing, academic freedom was the capstone of an effort to establish authority by fostering the development of communities of the competent, we should expect to find evidence supporting that claim in the AAUP's charter document, the 1915 Report on Academic Freedom and Tenure. The expectation is amply borne out. As we shall see, Seligman and Lovejoy in writing that document addressed themselves most explicitly to the rights of scholars, the duties of trustees, and the needs of the lay public—the nuts and bolts, as it were, of academic freedom—but at every stage they self-consciously advocated deference to expert authority and took for granted the epistemological efficacy of disciplinary communities. Notice that in doing so they were already moving far beyond any simple correspondence theory of truth. However much they may differ from us, the late Victorians were not epistemologically naive. After all, the first "crisis of historicism" occurred during their watch, and no one since has plumbed the depths of the crisis any more deeply than that renegade Victorian, Friedrich Nietzsche. The generation of the 1890s, of which the founders of the modern university were a part, was already energetically embarked on what H. Stuart Hughes has called a "revolt against positivism." The lessons of fallibilism and the un-avoidable subjectivity of perception were widely appreciated at the turn of the century. The insight that truth was a collective, communal enterprise, rather than a solitary, culturally unmediated one—the en-abling idea behind the community of the competent—was itself one of the products of the Victorians' struggle to come to terms with the uncertainties that historicism notoriously breeds.[27] The words of the AAUP's 1915 report testify to greater confidence in the power of rea-son than is commonly acknowledged today and may seem to some readers quaint. But it remains to be seen whether the radical forms of historicism in circulation today will prove as durable as the more moderate varieties that were already firmly in place at the beginning of the century.

In drafting the 1915 report, Lovejoy and Seligman most certainly did not proceed on the Foucauldian premise that power and knowl-edge were two sides of a single coin. They took the possibilities of disinterestedness and objectivity with utmost seriousness, not as re-sults easily attained, but as ideals well worth pursuing. The univer-sity, they said, should be an "intellectual experiment station" and an "inviolable refuge" against the equally dangerous tyrannies of public opinion and political autocracy. If scholars were to solve the problems of society, "the disinterestedness and impartiality of their inquiries and their conclusions [would have to be], so far as it is humanly possible, beyond the reach of suspicion."[28] Warding off suspicion meant that the line between authentic scholarship and political propa-ganda would have to be sharp and clear (the implication again being "so far as it is humanly possible"). They warned against teachers who would take "unfair advantage of the student's immaturity by indoctri-nating him with the teacher's own opinions." They associated the right of academic freedom with a duty on the part of the academic profession to police its ranks and rigorously uphold standards. "If this profession," they wrote, "should prove itself unwilling to purge its ranks of the incompetent and unworthy, or to prevent the freedom it claims in the name of science from being used as a shelter for ineffi-

27. H. Stuart Hughes, *Consciousness and Society: The Reorientation of European Social Thought, 1890–1930* (New York: Knopf, 1958), chap. 2; James Kloppenberg, *Uncertain Victory: Social Democracy and Progressivism in European and American Thought, 1870–1920* (New York and Oxford: Oxford University Press, 1986).

28. AAUP, "The 1915 Report on Academic Freedom and Tenure," 399.

ciency, for superficiality, for uncritical and intemperate partisanship, it is certain that the task will be performed by others." Although they specifically moved beyond the German model of academic freedom by claiming protection for extramural as well as intramural utterances, they never doubted the desirability of teachers having "minds untrammeled by party loyalties, unexcited by party enthusiasms, and unbiased by personal political ambitions."[29]

The first section of the 1915 report bears a revealing title: "The Basis of Academic Authority." The section is in its entirety organized around a distinction between real universities, engaged in the pursuit of truth, and "proprietary school[s] . . . designed for the propagation of specific doctrines." The latter are bound by their founders "to a propagandist duty." Seligman and Lovejoy grudgingly acknowledged the legitimacy of proprietary schools (usually religious), but only for the sake of relegating them and their propagandistic function to the lowest ranks of postsecondary education. "Any university which lays restrictions upon the intellectual freedom of its professors," they asserted, "proclaims itself a proprietary institution, and should be so described when it makes a general appeal for funds." By their standard, any institution that withheld from its faculty the rights of academic freedom in the interest of serving a propagandistic function could not claim the authority of a true university and would deserve the support only of fellow sectarians, not that of the general public.[30]

The central thrust of the 1915 report was to displace trustees as sole interpreters of the public interest and put forth a strong claim for the corporate authority of professional communities. As Seligman and Lovejoy put it, "the responsibility of the university teacher is primarily to the public itself, and to the judgment of his own profession."[31] In a nutshell, they were defining the university as a loose-knit

29. Ibid., 400, 402, 404.
30. Ibid., 394–95.
31. Ibid., 397. The 1915 report also presented "practical proposals" calling for faculty representation on committees considering reappointment; judicial hearings and formulation of explicit grounds in cases of dismissal; and permanent tenure for all positions above the grade of instructor after ten (not seven) years of service. The practical nuts and bolts underpinning academic freedom were further developed in a second landmark AAUP document, which continues to enjoy something approaching constitutional status today, the "1940 Statement of Principles on Academic Freedom and Tenure." By that date, although as many as half of all colleges and universities may

family of specialized disciplinary communities and making the family's integrity conditional on the degree of self-governance attained both by the whole and by its constituent parts. The role of the community looms largest in the second section of the report, titled "The Nature of the Academic Profession," where they spelled out the "distinctive and important function" of the professional scholar:

> That function is to deal at first hand, after prolonged and specialized technical training, with the sources of knowledge; and to impart the results of their own and of their fellow-specialists' investigations and reflection, both to students and the general public, without fear or favor. The proper discharge of this function requires (among other things) that the university teacher shall be exempt from pecuniary motive or inducement to hold, or to express, any conclusion which is not the genuine and uncolored product of his own study or that of fellow-specialists. Indeed, the proper fulfillment of the work of the professorate [sic] requires that our universities shall be so free that no fair-minded person shall find any excuse for even a suspicion that the utterances of university teachers are shaped or restricted by the judgment, not of professional scholars, but of inexpert and possibly not wholly disinterested persons outside their ranks.[32]

Notice that the authors of the 1915 report did not imagine that the problem of intellectual authority was to be solved merely by appeals to disinterestedness. In common with other members of their genera-

---

have still been appointing faculty on an annual basis, hiring practices had become sufficiently uniform at the leading institutions that the AAUP made a bid to install tenure as the keystone of academic freedom. It called for permanent tenure for all academics after a probationary period, normally not exceeding seven years, and allowed for termination only at retirement, upon demonstration of adequate cause, or because of extraordinary financial exigencies. The 1940 statement, which of course does not have the force of law, was a compromise jointly authored by teachers in the AAUP and administrators in the American Association of Colleges. The premier association of administrators, the American Association of Universities, has never endorsed the 1940 principles, although its member institutions probably uphold them at least as scrupulously as other schools do. See Walter P. Metzger, "The 1940 Statement of Principles on Academic Freedom and Tenure," *Freedom and Tenure in the Academy: The Fiftieth Anniversary of the 1940 Statement of Principles*, William Van Alstyne, special editor, *Law and Contemporary Problems* 53 (summer 1990): 1–77.

32. AAUP, "1915 Report on Academic Freedom and Tenure," 396–97.

tion, they did of course take it for granted that scholars would display a large measure of that self-denying quality of asceticism that Nietzsche so merrily skewered in the third essay of *The Genealogy of Morals*. But if scholars were to speak without "fear or favor"—and, equally important, be *seen* as speaking thus, so as to earn the deference of the general public—they would not only have to purge themselves of interest, insofar as possible, but generally distance themselves from all influences extrinsic to their work. The latter task was understood by Seligman and Lovejoy as inherently collective: accomplishing it required the existence of a community so intense that its internal relations would overshadow external influences, as members strove above all to earn and retain one another's respect according to standards specifically tailored to the work at hand. Their conception of the ideal community differs little from that of Jürgen Habermas, who defines the "ideal speech situation" as one in which "no force except that of the better argument is exercised; and, . . . as a result, all motives except that of the cooperative search for truth are excluded."[33]

Thus Seligman and Lovejoy's discussion of "The Nature of the Academic Profession" continues:

> The lay public is under no compulsion to accept or act upon the opinions of the scientific experts whom, through the universities, it employs. But it is highly needful, in the interest of society at large, that what purport to be the conclusions of men trained for, and dedicated to, the quest for truth, shall in fact be the conclusions of such men, and not echoes of the opinions of the lay public, or of the individuals who endow or manage universities. To the degree that professional scholars, in the formation and promulgation of their opinions, are, or by the character of their tenure, appear to be, subject to any motive other than their own scientific conscience and a desire for the respect of their fellow-experts, to that degree the university teaching profession is corrupted; its proper influence upon public opinion is diminished and vitiated; and society at large fails to get from its scholars, in an unadulterated form, the peculiar and necessary service which it is the office of the professional scholar to furnish.[34]

33. Habermas, *Legitimation Crisis* (Boston: Beacon Press, 1975), 107–8.
34. AAUP, "1915 Report on Academic Freedom and Tenure," 396–97.

In the vision set forth by Seligman and Lovejoy, the psychological, institutional, and legal dimensions of the problem of intellectual authority fit together and reinforce one another like the nested boxes of a Chinese puzzle. To speak with authority one must visibly enjoy the respect of one's peers, organized as a self-governing community. In order for the community to exist and be self-governing, its members must, in the work at hand, defer only to one another and be ready to resist the influence of nonpractitioners in matters intrinsic to the community's domain. The legal rights of academic freedom stake out the vital boundary between matters intrinsic and extrinsic, distinguishing those who are competent to judge a practitioner's work from those who are not. In the words of Seligman and Lovejoy, it would be "inadmissible that the power of determining when departures from the requirements of the scientific spirit and method have occurred, should be vested in bodies not composed of the members of the academic profession. Such bodies necessarily lack full competency to judge of those requirements."[35] The proper relationship, then, between professors and trustees is not that of employees to employers. The relation should instead be analogous to that of federal judges and the chief executive who appoints them but then has no authority over their decisions. Leaving unchallenged the power of trustees and administrators to appoint faculty, Seligman and Lovejoy denied that those exercising that power could properly retain any control over the intellectual productions of those whom they appointed, and they insisted that appointment itself be based on criteria established within the community by the candidate's peers.[36]

There is no single author who can be said to have exhaustively conceptualized the widespread assumptions about truth and inquiry that Seligman and Lovejoy were trying to distill in their 1915 report. But Charles Sanders Peirce, arguably the most original of the Pragmatists and the author of the strongest claims for a communal theory of truth ever written, did more than anyone else of his generation to articulate the presuppositions that I believe underlay Victorian reform. My claim is not that his philosophical writings influenced any large number of people or served as a blueprint for action. Peirce's writings on commu-

35. Ibid., 402.
36. Ibid., 402, 397.

nity and the social basis of scientific endeavor were, as a matter of fact, influential among Harvard philosophers while Lovejoy was a graduate student there, but professionalization was a social process with great momentum in late-nineteenth-century life: it did not wait upon theoretical articulation. It is, I believe, no coincidence that Charles Peirce was the son of one of the foremost professionalizers of science in the antebellum period, the eminent Harvard astronomer and mathematician Benjamin Peirce. Member of a self-selected elite of scientists known as the Lazzaroni, the elder Peirce helped organize the Lawrence Scientific School at Harvard, helped write the constitution of the American Association for the Advancement of Science, and helped push through Congress the bill creating the National Academy of Sciences.[37] Charles Peirce's communitarian theory of truth can stand on its own philosophical legs, but for my purposes it would suffice to regard it as an idealized extrapolation from the practical processes of professionalization that were transforming society during his lifetime. Peirce's theory suits my purposes especially well because it invites comparison with the communitarian theorizing of recent writers such as Thomas Kuhn, Richard Rorty, and Stanley Fish.[38] These three authors share Peirce's basic conviction that communal solidarity among inquirers can function epistemologically, and thus their differences with him— substantial, as we shall see—give us a way of gauging the gap between the Victorians and ourselves.[39]

Charles Peirce believed that the very possibility of attaining truth

37. For a fuller discussion of the two Peirces and the theme of professionalization, see my *Emergence of Professional Social Science* and "Professionalization versus Capitalism," 208. On Peirce's influence at Harvard, see Bruce Kuklick, *The Rise of American Philosophy: Cambridge, Massachusetts, 1860–1930* (New Haven and London: Yale University Press, 1977).

38. Thomas Kuhn, *The Structure of Scientific Revolutions*, 2d ed. (Chicago: University of Chicago Press, 1970); Richard Rorty, *Philosophy and the Mirror of Nature* (Princeton: Princeton University Press, 1979); Stanley Fish, *Is There a Text in This Class? The Authority of Interpretive Communities* (Cambridge: Harvard University Press, 1980), and "Anti-Professionalism," in Fish, *Doing What Comes Naturally: Change, Rhetoric, and the Place of Theory in Literary and Legal Studies* (Durham and London: Duke University Press, 1989), chap. 11.

39. Stephen Toulmin never mentions Peirce but presents an account of knowledge that is comparably community oriented in *Human Understanding: The Collective Use and Evolution of Concepts* (Princeton: Princeton University Press, 1972). An explosion of interest in Peirce is under way today; among many recent publications, most relevant is C. J. Misak, *Truth and the End of Inquiry* (Oxford: Oxford University Press, 1991).

depended on transcending one's self and entering into intensely communal relations with other competent investigators. As if to repudiate Ralph Waldo Emerson's advice to "trust thyself," Peirce contended that no individual, least of all one's self, could ever be worthy of trust. "The individual man, since his separate existence is manifested only by ignorance and error . . . is only a negation."[40] Peirce's advice was to trust instead the community of inquirers. "What anything really is," argued Peirce, "is what it may finally come to be known to be in the ideal state of complete information. . . . " Since information cannot be complete in my lifetime or yours, our best conceptions are riddled with error, and the truth can only be known by the last survivors of a community of inquirers that includes the yet-to-be-born as well as the living and extends indefinitely far into the future. "The real, then," said Peirce in a famous passage, "is that which, sooner or later, information and reasoning would finally result in, and which is independent of the vagaries of me and you. Thus, the very origin of the conception of reality shows that this conception essentially involves the notion of a COMMUNITY, without definite limits, and capable of a definite increase in knowledge."[41]

It may have been his prickly personality and status as an outsider who never found permanent employment in the academic world that sensitized Peirce to the social, consensual quality of all that passes for truth among human beings. Yet in his conception there is no trace of cynicism. The ultimate consensus to be reached by his community of inquiry is of a very special kind, and his theory of reality, though indubitably social, is not at all relativistic, as twentieth-century analogues have tended to be. Like Kuhn, Rorty, and Fish, modern thinkers who have advanced arguments that sound quite Peircean, Peirce himself clearly regarded science and scholarship as the practical accomplishment, not of individuals, but of a community of researchers. Unlike Kuhn, Rorty, and Fish, however, Peirce was a philosophical realist: he supposed that the universe was so made that an ultimate convergence of opinion was virtually predestined and that the reality

---

40. Charles S. Peirce, *Collected Papers*, ed. Charles Hartshorne and Paul Weiss (Cambridge: Harvard University Press, 1931–60), 5:317 [reference is to volume and paragraph]. This and the next five paragraphs are based on my essay "Professionalism versus Capitalism," which is an extension and revision of my comments on Peirce in *Emergence of Professional Social Science*.

41. Peirce, *Collected Papers*, 5:316, 311 (emphasis in the original).

toward which opinion converged was utterly independent, not of thought in general, but of what any finite number of human beings thought about it. For him reality was socially discovered but not socially constructed. When pressed by a critic, he allowed that the ultimate convergence of opinion might be incomplete in some matters and that convergence was a "hope" rather than an inevitability. But he insisted that the hope was of the same indispensable character as the expectation of survival that a person struggling for his life must feel. To live is to hope: similarly, to inquire is to suppose that opinions ultimately converge toward the real. The following passage catches the spirit of Peirce's discussion of the community better than any other I know.

> This activity of thought by which we are carried, not where we wish, but to a fore-ordained goal, is like the operation of destiny. No modification of the point of view taken, no selection of other facts for study, no natural bent of mind even, can enable a man to escape the predestinate opinion. This great hope [originally he wrote *law*] is embodied in the conception of truth and reality. The opinion which is fated to be agreed to by all who investigate, is what we mean by the truth, and the object represented in this opinion is the real. That is the way I would explain reality.[42]

Peirce was no ideologue. He had no intention whatsoever of supplying existing communities of inquiry in physics, chemistry, or biology with a philosophical warrant for their authority. Much less did he intend to buttress the claims of quasi sciences such as law, medicine, or historical studies. He expressly rejected the "method of authority" as a means of fixing belief, and he equated that method with the claims of priesthoods, aristocracies, guilds, and other "association[s] . . . of men whose interests depend . . . on certain propositions."[43] As long as we interpret Peirce's words strictly, as he no doubt wished us to do, his theory bundles truth off into an infinite progression where it is too remote to serve *any* interest or strengthen any particular claim to knowledge. But if his theory undermines all existing authorities and courts radical skepticism when strictly interpreted—offering no guidance at

---

42. Ibid., 5:407, 408; 6:610.
43. Ibid., 5:379.

all when we ask, "Which present claim is true?" or "What belief shall I now act on?"—it performs the opposite function of building bulwarks against skepticism when loosely interpreted. And how can we resist interpreting it loosely? As the philosopher John E. Smith has said, "reality in the end for Peirce is future experience, and this is not enough."[44] Peirce conceived of the truth in such a way as to make it literally useless, for no one can claim to know the truth, once it has been defined as the final opinion of a community that extends indefinitely into the future. However, once we accept Peirce's identification of truth as the outcome of a community's striving, then, if a community of inquiry exists in a field that interests us, it is difficult to resist the implication that its *current best opinion* is, in practice, the closest approach to the truth we can possibly hope for. Given a choice between these two interpretations, it may well be that the strict one is closest to Peirce's own intentions. But even if this is so, the most important thing to observe about Peirce's communal theory of reality may be that the more persuasive we find it, the more likely we are to live by the loose interpretation of it. Identifying truth with the community but lacking the community's final opinion, we are bound to prefer its current best opinion to a chaos of indistinguishable truth claims, which is the only alternative Peirce's line of reasoning leaves us.

No writer today would dare attribute to the community of inquiry quite the same truth-finding power that Peirce assigned it. Of the writers I have mentioned, Kuhn comes closest to Peirce. Certainly in Kuhn's world there is no standard higher than the current best opinion of the relevant scientific community. If one asks, "Why should taxpayers foot the bill for professors who devote more time to research than to teaching?" or "Why should trustees tolerate the expression of views they loathe?" Kuhn supplies us with a compelling answer: The community is epistemologically efficacious. Without it, our grasp of reality would be immeasurably weaker. Yet Kuhn's community is not nearly as efficacious as Peirce's, for Kuhn is not nearly the realist Peirce was. The relationship between the community's current best opinion and anything that deserves the name "truth" becomes problematic in Kuhn's treatment. He retains a trace of realism by holding that the sequence of conceptions espoused by a scientific

---

44. John E. Smith, "Community and Reality, " in *Perspectives on Peirce*, ed. Richard J. Bernstein (New Haven: Yale University Press, 1965), 118.

community takes the shape of an irreversible branching tree. A kind of development not altogether different from progress is, therefore, involved—but this is "progress" away from confusion, rather than toward any antecedent reality existing "out there," independent of human consciousness, awaiting our apprehension of it. How much epistemological comfort we are entitled to draw from this sort of development, especially in fields other than natural science, is an open question.[45]

If the Peircean rationale for disciplinary autonomy is left looking a bit frayed around the edges by Kuhn, it is left in tatters by others who have been inspired by Kuhn's writings. Rorty and Fish both pay homage to Kuhn, but their own posture is that of uncompromising antirealism. Unlike Kuhn, who is ambivalent and who frankly confesses that although he is disenchanted with the realist view, no existing alternative seems an adequate replacement for it, Rorty and Fish flatly deny that there is any important sense in which ideas can be said to converge on, approximate, correspond with, or be adequate to the real. For them, the real is socially and linguistically constructed, through and through. Rorty declares the entire enterprise of epistemology wrongheaded. He joins Jacques Derrida in recommending that we overcome our nostalgic longing for "foundations" and throw overboard the entire "metaphysics of presence." Even Derrida's most notorious antirealist sally, "There is nothing outside the text," wins from Rorty a blithe nod of approval. Rorty asks us to believe that the tradition inaugurated by Plato and called "philosophy" has quite simply lost its usefulness and ought to be discontinued in favor of conversations that aim at nothing more than "edification." "The notion of 'accurate representation,'" he says, "is simply an automatic and empty compliment which we pay to those beliefs which are successful in helping us do what we want to do."[46]

---

45. Kuhn, *Structure of Scientific Revolutions*, 205–6, 170–72.
46. For Kuhn's ambivalence, see ibid., 121, 126, 170–73; for Rorty, *Philosophy and the Mirror of Nature*, 10; *Consequences of Pragmatism: (Essays: 1972–1980)* (Minneapolis: University of Minnesota Press, 1982), xiv, 96–98. In an unpublished 1984 paper titled "Rhetoric and Liberation," Kuhn, commenting on a paper by Rorty titled "Solidarity or Objectivity?" expressed his dissent from Rorty's sweeping rejection of objectivity and warm embrace of solidarity as an adequate standard of correct belief. Kuhn warned of a "profound misconception of the human condition, a misconception here manifest in an insufficient respect for the intrinsic authority of language. . . . I said I would speak as Cassandra, and I have been doing so. What I fear are attempts to separate language or

The immediate target of Rorty's campaign on behalf of edifying conversation is none other than Arthur Lovejoy, one of the heroes of the Ross case and a founder of the AAUP. It was Lovejoy who, in his presidential address to the American Philosophical Association (APA) in 1916, called upon philosophers to choose between edification and verification, hoping they would choose the latter. In picking up the banner of edification, Rorty seeks to turn Lovejoy's Victorian project upside down. Lovejoy epitomizes for Rorty the antipragmatic disciplinarian, who spurns the gentle delights of edification and makes a fetish of rigor and circumspection. "Echoing what was being said simultaneously by Russell in England and Husserl in Germany, Lovejoy urged the sixteenth annual meeting of the APA to aim at making philosophy into a science," reports Rorty. "Lovejoy insisted that philosophy could either be edifying and visionary *or* could produce 'objective, verifiable, and clearly communicable truths,' but not both." William James agreed that the two aims were incompatible, Rorty observes, but wisely preferred edification to science. To Rorty's dismay, "Lovejoy . . . won this battle." The mainstream of the philosophical profession chose the analytical path over edification.[47]

There is no denying that Lovejoy was a devotee of rigor. His belief that philosophy's family quarrels were a "standing scandal" that threatened to bring "discredit upon the entire business" seems to me misguided, and his plan for the production of a catalogue raisonné of "considerations" pertaining to all important issues in philosophy— a modern "*Summa Metaphysica*," as he himself called it—seems both misguided and grandiose.[48] I readily confess that if I were choosing books for a year's sojourn on a desert island, Rorty's *Mirror of Nature* would be a more likely choice than Lovejoy's *Great Chain of Being*, important though the latter is.

These things said, there remains room to argue that Lovejoy was not the Dr. Strangelove that Rorty makes him out to be. In calling for

discourse from the real and to do so in the name of freedom." Rorty's paper was published in *Post-Analytic Philosophy*, ed. John Rajchman and Cornel West (New York: Columbia University Press, 1985).

47. Rorty, *Consequences of Pragmatism*, 169–70 (emphasis in original). On the issue of edification vs. verification, see Arthur Lovejoy, "On Some Conditions of Progress in Philosophical Inquiry," *Philosophical Review* 26 (March 1917): 131–38, and Daniel J. Wilson, *Arthur O. Lovejoy and the Quest for Intelligibility* (Chapel Hill: University of North Carolina Press, 1980), 92.

48. Lovejoy, "On Some Conditions of Progress," 130, 159–60.

philosophy to become a science, Lovejoy meant only that it should be
a Wissenschaft, an "organized body of knowledge," not that it should
mindlessly imitate physics or chemistry.[49] Lovejoy's essays on pragmatism are, in my view, the sort of close, respectful criticism that any
school of thought should count itself lucky to receive. One of them,
titled "William James as a Philosopher," is as warm, generous, and
open-minded a tribute as any scholar ever rendered to a rival.[50] Lovejoy's point about edification was not that it was an unworthy goal, but
that philosophy may not be the best way to achieve it. He acknowledged that "the philosopher's reasonings" may only be his or her
"peculiar way of uttering the burden of his soul and of edifying the
like-minded," but, he continued, if edification is the goal, "poetry is
surely a happier medium."[51]

Convinced, just as Peirce was, that "philosophizing is a collective
process," Lovejoy thought philosophers should never concede the incommensurability of rival positions at the start of an argument, but
should instead obstinately hold out the "possibility of unanimity" as a
regulative ideal. After all, he observed, the prospect of really achieving
unanimity was "scarcely so imminent as to justify alarm." As these
words suggest, Lovejoy was not naive about the likelihood of convergence. His aim was to strengthen the community of inquiry by making
communication between its members more complete and harder to
evade, thus intensifying the half-competitive, half-cooperative exchange of opinions that constitutes the life process of such communities. He shared Walter Bagehot's admiration for a "polity of discussion," in which the obligation to talk things over and seek agreement
would always act as a check on precipitate action. Like most Victorians,
including Peirce (whose essay "Evolutionary Love" is a sermon on the
subject), Lovejoy blamed human ignorance largely on "subjective
sources of error" and looked to socialization for the cure. We guard
against the snares of subjectivity, he wrote, by

> seeking the complementary and correcting action of other minds
> upon our own; and not of dead men's minds, alone, but of con-
> temporaries with whose thoughts ours may establish genuine

49. Ibid., 160.
50. Arthur Lovejoy, *The Thirteen Pragmatisms and Other Essays* (Baltimore: Johns
Hopkins University Press, 1963).
51. Lovejoy, "On Some Conditions of Progress," 131.

and vital contact, to whom we may explain and re-explain our own thoughts, who will patiently "follow the argument" with us, who will drive their meanings into our consciousness with friendly violence if necessary, and will gladly submit to like violence in return.[52]

Rorty has little use for either Peirce's communal theory of truth or Lovejoy's "friendly violence." The problem with both, apparently, is that by holding out the possibility of rational convergence, they breed confrontation. Unlike the Victorians, who prized criticism and accepted the need for confrontation, Rorty looks forward to a culture devoted to edifying conversation, which he specifically likens to Kuhn's "abnormal" or "revolutionary" science and associates with the perpetual incommensurability of rival vantage points. Since the contributors to Rorty's conversation would by definition share few common presuppositions, their contributions would be largely incommensurable, leading no doubt to an abundance of divergent opinions but seldom to confrontation in the classic sense of a rigorous encounter from which only the truth can emerge unscathed. Everyone's views would be different; no one's would be right or wrong. Most important, no view would qualify even potentially as "normal." Lacking foundations, absent any hope of rational convergence or correspondence with the real, confrontation loses its point and becomes difficult to distinguish from aimless aggression.

Rorty's aversion to convergence-oriented confrontation (perfectly compatible with polemical brilliance, as we shall see) most often manifests itself in his frustrating habit of sidestepping bothersome questions. As Stefan Collini has remarked, Rorty frequently announces "with a studied off-handedness that some find exhilarating and others infuriating, that a large number of time-honoured questions just are not interesting questions any more." Granting the exceptional range and brilliance of Rorty's contribution, Collini nonetheless complains that "the range of questions which 'we pragmatists' would say there is no point in asking threatens to shrink the horizons of intellectual inquiry," possibly encouraging a kind of "anti-intellectualism."[53]

---

52. Ibid., 150, 133, 132, 151–52.
53. Stefan Collini, ed., *Interpretation and Overinterpretation: Umberto Eco with Richard Rorty, Jonathan Culler, Christine Brooke-Rose* (Cambridge: Cambridge University Press, 1992), 12, 19.

Rorty assigns top priority not to the characteristically Victorian task of pruning back error in hopes of expanding the domain of reliable knowledge, but instead to the distinctively post-Holocaust task of encouraging respect for otherness and cultivating sensitivity to the lush multiplicity of human perspectives. Rorty's priorities are eminently decent and readily understandable in view of the ethnic clashes and seemingly endless dilemmas of difference that beset the world today. I have no quarrel with those priorities, except insofar as they block historical understanding and tempt us to think we can get away without having any adequate justification for academic freedom. Rorty evidently believes that we academicians have it in our power to help reduce bloodshed and brutality in the world at large simply by adopting a kinder and gentler mode of intellectual exchange within the academy. I demur because I doubt that the academy's influence takes quite that form and because I feel that the intellectual price Rorty is prepared to pay is too high. If I read Lovejoy correctly, he understood full well that many of the great debates in philosophy originate in incommensurable premises and are unlikely ever to yield consensus. What he opposed was a premature abandonment of consensus as an *ideal*, a target one aims at without expecting to reach. That ideal is as indispensable as ever, for the community of the competent cannot do its work of cultivating and authorizing sound opinion unless its members confront one another and engage in mutual criticism. Unless I miss my guess, Lovejoy could have said about philosophy what Clifford Geertz said of anthropology: that it is "a science whose progress is marked less by a perfection of consensus than by a refinement of debate. What gets better is the precision with which we vex each other."[54] Still, Lovejoy would have added, Peirce was right: to inquire at all is to hold out the possibility of convergence.

Although Rorty (unlike Fish, as we shall see) is not the sort of person to treat ideals dismissively, this particular ideal gets short shrift in his "conversation of the West." Conversation and consensus figure prominently in his thinking, but their role is therapeutic rather than rigorous, remissive rather than exacting. Conversation he recommends not as a means of exposing error but, rather, as an opportunity to savor the kaleidoscopic variety of the human experience. He values consensus less as a regulative ideal, the pursuit of which may provoke

54. Clifford Geertz, *The Interpretation of Cultures* (New York: Basic Books, 1973), 29.

confrontation and inflame passion, than as our last hope of solace in a world that lacks foundations. Threatened as we all are by the eruption of violence, he judges the sacrifice of rigor a small price to pay for greater solidarity.

Given Rorty's aversion to confrontation, we should not be surprised that his revival of pragmatism, unlike those of Richard Bernstein, Hilary Putnam, or Jürgen Habermas, pointedly excludes Peirce from the front ranks of the tradition.[55] A "tendency to overpraise Peirce," he says, is the first symptom of a mistaken conception of what pragmatism is all about.[56] One might think that Peirce's perpetually postponed truth, never accessible in any human "present," would be sufficiently remote and impractical to at least seem harmless, but Rorty detects within it the bitter seeds of tyranny. "The pragmatist must avoid saying, with Peirce, that truth is *fated* to win. He must even avoid saying that the truth *will* win." So deep is Rorty's distaste for this aspect of Peirce's thinking that he appears to sympathize even with an imaginary antipragmatic interlocutor of his own devising, the "traditional philosopher," who asks rhetorically, "When tyrants employ Lenin's blood-curdling sense of 'objective' to describe their lies as 'objectively true,' what is to prevent them from citing Peirce in Lenin's defense?"[57]

At first glance arguments like these seem to sound a death knell for the dream of epistemological efficacy that Charles Peirce articulated at the dawn of the modern American university system. If convergence is unacceptable, even as an ideal, the disciplinary community cannot serve as a crucible of criticism and so cannot claim any special authority for the ideas it sponsors. Indeed, if Rorty really believes that the very idea of "truth" is dangerous, because of the encouragement it gives tyrants, then it is not just Peirce we need to renounce, but the university itself, for the university has always been and is likely to remain a hotbed of aspirations for truth, sound opin-

---

55. See, for examples, Richard J. Bernstein, *Beyond Objectivism and Relativism: Science, Hermeneutics, and Praxis* (Philadelphia: University of Pennsylvania Press, 1988), 36, 69, 71; Hilary Putnam, *Realism With a Human Face*, ed. James Conant (Cambridge and London: Harvard University Press, 1990), 21–22; and Jürgen Habermas, *Postmetaphysical Thinking: Philosophical Essays*, trans. William Mark Hehengarten (Cambridge and London: MIT Press, 1992), chap. 5, "Peirce and Communication."

56. Rorty, *Consequences of Pragmatism*, 160.

57. Ibid., 173 (emphasis in the original). The order of the quoted passages has been altered. See other comments about Peirce, ibid., 160–61, xlv.

ion, and other invidious distinctions between better and worse ways of thinking. In the words of John Dewey, whom of course Rorty holds in very high regard, and whose conception of truth was not naive, "the university function is the truth function."[58] Dewey published these words in 1902, two years after Ross's dismissal from Stanford and thirteen before taking office as the founding president of the AAUP. In his AAUP inaugural address in 1915, Dewey spoke in the same vein, calling for the "judgment, the courage, and the self sacrifice commensurate with reverence for our calling, which is none other than the discovery and diffusion of truth."[59]

Rorty's conflation of Peircean fallibilism with Leninist objectivism need not be taken as his last word on the subject. Clearly Peirce's theory of truth is not acceptable to him and the community of the competent does not, as such, play a prominent role in his thinking. Still, there are important similarities. The philosopher whom William James credited with founding pragmatism and who wanted to write on every wall of the city of philosophy, "Do not block the way of inquiry," cannot truly be a dangerous man in Rorty's eyes.[60]

One might argue that the two pragmatists differ more sharply at the level of tactics than ultimate goals. Both want to substitute persuasion for force. Whether to aim at that goal directly and try to extend its benefits to an entire society at once or to approach it obliquely, relying for the foreseeable future on an elite vanguard of inquirers, is where

---

58. The passage is worth quoting at greater length. Notice that neither literally nor in spirit did Dewey put the word *truth* in quotation marks. Rorty's proto-Nietzschean Dewey is not easily detected in passages such as this: "It is clear that . . . any attack, or even any restriction, upon academic freedom is directed against the university itself. To investigate truth; critically to verify fact; to reach conclusions by means of the best methods at command, untrammeled by external fear or favor, to communicate this truth to the student; to interpret to him its bearing on the questions he will have to face in life—this is precisely the aim and object of the university. To aim a blow at any one of these operations is to deal a vital wound to the university itself. The university function is the truth function. At one time it may be more concerned with the tradition or transmission of truth, and at another time with its discovery. . . . The one thing that is inherent and essential is the idea of truth." Dewey, "Academic Freedom," *Educational Review* 23 (1902): 3 [reprinted in *The American Concept of Academic Freedom in Formation: A Collection of Essays and Reports*, ed. Walter P . Metzger (New York: Arno Press, 1977)].

59. Dewey's speech appears in *Science*, n.s. 41 (29 January 1915): 150.

60. This famous line of Peirce's is given a place of honor in a recent ringing defense of free speech by Jonathan Rauch, *Kindly Inquisitors: The New Attacks on Free Thought* (Chicago and London: University of Chicago Press, 1993), vii.

they seem to differ most concretely. Rorty's "conversation of the West" is conceived in an inclusive spirit of romantic egalitarianism that embraces an entire ethnos and all who partake of it, leaving no specified role for intellectual elites or disciplinary institutions. In effect, Rorty's vision of the ideal liberal society tacitly anticipates the extension to everyone of the life of inquiry and persuasion that Peirce assigned to a scholarly elite. Rorty's utopia, in short, looks rather like Peirce's community of inquiry writ large—larger than Peirce would have thought appropriate or feasible.[61] Having given up all foundationalist hopes, and having expanded the circle of the "we" to embrace all willing recruits, Rorty's version of the good society presumably would downplay degrees of competence, extending to all citizens the opportunity of engaging as equals in the "conversation" through which reality is socially constructed. Rorty's utopia could even acknowledge a pale surrogate for Peirce's objectivity, defining it as that which wins "unforced agreement."[62] And although Rorty's liberal utopia would most assuredly not be devoted to the pursuit of Truth, he assures us that it would honor "truth," decapitalized and safely quarantined within quotation marks:

> It is central to the idea of liberal society that, in respect to words as opposed to deeds, persuasion as opposed to force, anything goes. This openmindedness should not be fostered because, as Scripture teaches, Truth is great and will prevail, nor because, as Milton suggests, Truth will always win in a free and open encounter. It should be fostered for its own sake. A liberal society is one which is content to call "true" whatever the upshot of such encounters turns out to be.[63]

Here it is tempting to think that Rorty and Peirce come within hailing distance, for Peirce, too, was content (at least on the "loose"

61. Rorty sometimes uses the term *community of inquiry* as a near synonym for culture or society: "We can always enlarge the scope of 'us' by regarding other people, or cultures, as members of the same community of inquiry as ourselves—by treating them as part of the group among whom unforced agreement is to be sought." Richard Rorty, *Objectivity, Relativism, and Truth: Philosophical Papers*, vol. 1 (Cambridge: Cambridge University Press, 1991), 38.

62. Ibid., 38, 41, 88.

63. Richard Rorty, *Contingency, Irony, and Solidarity* (Cambridge: Cambridge University Press, 1989), 51–52.

interpretation of his doctrine) to call "true" the upshot of the community's debates—true for now, anyway. Yet the differences remain fundamental. The reality-discovering task that Peirce assigned to the community of the competent, Rorty assigns to liberal society as a whole, and he adds the antirealist proviso—fatal, from Peirce's standpoint—that reality is something we construct, not discover. For much the same reason, relaxed "conversation" replaces confrontational debate. The disciplinary function disappears; the free expression of ideas no longer serves as a means of winnowing truth, having been defined by Rorty as an end in itself. Intellect is dethroned and takes its cue from sociability. In the last analysis, our choice between the two visions is likely to hinge on our estimate of the feasibility and desirability of Rorty's effort to extend to everyone the essential features of a form of life thus far inhabited only by scholars.[64] Not only is it uncertain that all aspire to such a life, many are not well suited for it, making their opportunity to contribute to the conversation merely formal. The history of professionalization over the past century and a half suggests that dense, fast-paced scholarly "conversations" of the sort Rorty admires have greater momentum and will be more difficult for novices to break into than he acknowledges. Indeed, they have proved to be formidable sources of privilege and authority for those who possess the skills to excel in them: democratizing them would be no easy matter.

The most intractable difference between Peirce and Rorty appears to lie in the question of realism. There are of course many versions of realism, and it is not inconceivable that a version making the right sort of concessions to history, perspective, and social convention might earn Rorty's grudging acceptance. But as long as there is no respectable sense (not even a largely social and conventional one) in which we are entitled to say that there is a "nature of things" for inquirers to "get right," then one cannot help wondering what the community of inquiry is for.[65] If nothing at all constrains inquiry, apart from the will

<hr>

64. Rorty is not the first to see in the values of the academic community a way of life suitable for the larger society. For similar gestures at the turn of the century by R. H. Tawney and Emile Durkheim, see my essay "Professionalism versus Capitalism."

65. What I have in mind is something corresponding roughly to the "moderate realism" Mary Hesse proposes for science, which steers a middle course between instrumentalism and the "strong realism" of, say, Plato. "Such a moderate realism of scientific knowledge turns out to be particular rather than general, local rather than universal, approximate rather than exact, immediately describable and verifiable rather

of the inquirers and whatever value they may assign to the traditions of their ethnos, why should anyone defer to the community's judgment, pay its expenses, or bend over backwards to tolerate its "findings" when they are unsettling? Peirce's realism had ready answers to such questions because it acknowledged other constraints, clinging fiercely to the possibility of truth even as it admitted truth's elusiveness and hammered home the lesson of fallibility. Antirealism, even Rorty's comparatively domesticated version of it, necessarily annihilates error along with its opposite, truth, making fallibilism an untenable posture: Where no opinions can be right, neither can any be wrong. Even disregarding the deeper ontological question and focusing on the rhetorical consequences alone, the death of fallibilism has ominous implications, for it narrows the number of argumentative positions available to us, threatening to reduce all intellectual exchanges to a naked clash of wills. If there is no such thing as truth, but only a variety of incommensurable perspectives in criterionless competition with one another, then giving up one's own initial perspective and adopting that of an interlocutor can never signify anything more than submission to superior force, be it physical or rhetorical. The honorable option of bowing to reason and willingly renouncing error for the sake of impersonal truth drops out, leaving only "me versus you" or "us versus them." Down this path lies Nietzsche's world, where not only power and knowledge blur together, but might and right as well.

The consequences of doing away with truth (or shrinking it to a vestigial synonym for whatever we want to believe, which comes to the same thing) do not all point in the same direction. The problem is not simply that Rorty has retreated too far from Peircean claims of epistemological efficacy and thus called into question the raison d'être

---

than theoretically deep and reductive. It is not the theoretical frameworks as such that validate the claim of science to be a distinctive and reliable body of knowledge, but rather the way they are used to further the feedback method of successful prediction and control." Mary B. Hesse, "Models, Metaphors and Truth," in *Knowledge and Languange*, vol. 3 of *Metaphor and Knowledge*, ed. F. R. Ankersmit and J. J. A. Mooij (Dordrecht: Kluwer, 1993), 49–66. Along similar lines, one thinks of Stephen Toulmin's comment that "Questions of 'rationality' are concerned, precisely, not with the particular intellectual doctrines that a man—or a professional group—adopts at any given time, but rather with the conditions on which, and the manner in which, he is prepared to criticize and change those doctrines as time goes on." Stephen Toulmin, *Human Understanding: The Collective Use and Evolution of Concepts* (Princeton: Princeton University Press, 1972), 84.

of the community of the competent. As Stanley Fish has seen as clearly as anyone, there is a curious sense in which the historicist standpoint, if carried far enough, also makes it possible to impute to such communities an authority more august than Peirce would have dared claim even in his most extravagant moments. For in keeping with the "linguistic turn," one can argue that if there is no reality with a capital *R*, then the conversation of inquirers can be regarded not merely as approximating knowledge of the real, but as actually *constituting* the only socially constructed, small-*r* reality that human beings can ever hope to know. Antirealism points paradoxically in two opposed directions, neither reassuring. It is not easy to say which we should think more worrisome: the retreat from Peircean claims of epistemological efficacy, on the one hand, or the imperious claim that academic conversations actually constitute reality on the other.[66] Either way, we lack any adequate rationale for the autonomy academic freedom is meant to defend. If we take the modest tack, admitting that our communities aim at nothing more than edification, it becomes unclear why anyone should defer to our judgment. Alternatively, if reality comes to be seen as entirely a social construction, incapable of representing or corresponding to anything outside language, the lay public would have to be incredibly trusting, even gullible, to let us academics retain the disproportionate voice we now have in the language games that are said to make the world what it is.

Whether the greater danger is timidity or hubris, the question we must face about academic freedom today is why, on antirealist premises, trustees and legislators should ever consent to the propagation of a reality not to their taste. Indeed, in the hands of antirealists more radical than Rorty, the pertinent question becomes: *How, in good political conscience, could anyone who has the resources to shape the very construction of reality—say, by changing the curriculum or influencing the selection of teachers or regulating the discourse of students about gender, ethnicity, or other sensitive issues—pass up such an opportunity? Is not abstention from the use of power on behalf of the good an abdication of responsibility?* The fate of academic freedom cannot be disentangled from prevailing conceptions of the good and the real. Insofar as reality is understood to be a malleable collective construction, political at its core, no person or

---

66. For an amusing and trenchant response to this imperial prospect, see David A. Hollinger, "Giving at the Office in the Age of Power/Knowledge," *Michigan Quarterly Review* 29 (winter 1990): 123–32.

group in a democratic society could be entitled to any sort of privileged voice—that is, an autonomous and authoritative voice—in its definition. We have seen that the founders of the modern university were not wedded to a naive correspondence theory of truth and made important concessions to truth's historicity, to its conventionality, and occasionally even to its cultural variability. Fallibility they accepted, but they did not doubt that some interpretations were better than others, better in a strong sense that did not necessarily depend on correspondence and yet was not reducible to perspective. If they were wrong about this—if "truth" is so much a matter of perspective that it belongs always inside quotation marks, as befits a claim made only half-seriously—must not the "rights of academic freedom" be enclosed within quotation marks, too?[67]

Here we must step back from Rorty's rhetorical posture and begin taking into account his practice, for although he has delivered powerful blows against the assumptions that have traditionally been used to justify the rights of academic freedom, anyone familiar with the whole tenor and spirit of his writings will know perfectly well that he means no harm to the university or to the disciplinary communities it harbors. If push came to shove, he is among the first I would expect to find in the foxholes, risking his own safety in defense of academic freedom. The point of my discussion has not been to indict Rorty as a reckless nihilist, which he most certainly is not, but to highlight the tendency of his antirealist rhetoric to generate implications that spill beyond the limits he evidently intends. Between his words and his intentions a touch of hyperbole often intrudes. There is, for example, room to suspect that, as a recent president of the APA, he may not be altogether serious about doing away with philosophy. His writings, after all, are from a lay point of view not something other than philosophy, but a delightfully lucid example of it, and one that could never have been produced were he not the member of a thriving and well-disciplined community of the competent. His pages bristle with all the telltale name-dropping, alliance building, and allusive arm wrestling of a scholar whose every thought is conditioned by the network of rivalrous relationships in which the professional community inserts him. Against confrontation? Why, Rorty thrives on it, even as he impugns the epistemological assumptions that would dis-

---

67. I am obliged to David Rabban for this succinct formulation of the problem.

tinguish it from aimless aggression. Like the biblical David with his sling, he has taken on the entire analytical mainstream of his profession at once, as if to prove how fruitful confrontation can be. His own words to the contrary notwithstanding, Rorty is too much the virtuoso of the community of the competent to knowingly contemplate any reduction in its authority.

What, then, are we to make of his antiprofessional posture? A useful corrective to Rorty's underestimation of the role that disciplinary influences play in shaping the way we think can be found in Stanley Fish's witty and perverse defense of professionalism. As will become clear, I have grave reservations about Fish's conception of the professional community, but no one has displayed a keener awareness of the ways in which the community defines the lifeworld of its members. Drawing on Kuhn's portrait of revolutionary science as a clash between rival groups whose professional worldviews are defined by the paradigmatic, world-making assumptions of their members, Fish argues that in an era of illimitable interpretation such as ours it is the professional community that prevents opinion from becoming merely arbitrary. To be sure, not even the professional community can provide a firm foundation for interpretation. Fish would be the last to suggest that membership in the community enables anyone to transcend time and place or attain Truth. Still, the current state of opinion within the professional community, even though ultimately a matter of fashion, is all he thinks we need for intelligibility. Just how impressed the public should be with the level of intelligibility currently being sustained in the academy is debatable, but in any event Fish accords to the disciplinary community an important and at least quasi-epistemological function in fixing collective opinion.[68]

Fish sees in antiprofessionalism a posture that serves distinctly professional ends. The relationship he has in mind between individuals and institutions appears to be broadly Freudian. Just as civilization breeds discontent by thwarting instinctual gratification, so on Fish's conception the disciplinary community unavoidably breeds resentment among its members in the course of defining their lifeworld. The result is a state of consciousness that is not only "false," but inverted, as the community's members conceal from themselves their utter dependence on it by indulging in fantasies of solitude and self-sufficiency, all

68. Fish, *Is There a Text in this Class?*

the while complaining about the shallowness and parochialism of communal life. Far from suggesting the imminent breakdown of the community, these complaints and escapist fantasies may signify that a
healthy balance has been achieved between individual initiative and
communal constraint. Fish construes his own profession of literary
criticism as one that depends vitally on imagining itself to be something
other than it is. "Anti-professionalism," he says, "is a form of professional behavior engaged in for the purpose of furthering some professional project." That is how Fish would explain what he calls the
"virulence" of antiprofessionalism among literary critics: "While most
professions are criticized for betraying their ideals," Fish observes,
"this profession betrays its ideals by being practiced at all, by being, as
a professor of medicine once put it to me, 'a parasite on the carcass of
literature.' "[69] Thus it becomes obligatory within some academic circles
to present oneself to the world as a free spirit, spontaneous to the point
of idiosyncrasy, who disdains everything that smacks of calculation
and self-advancement and lives only for the love of art and justice.
Successfully managing such a self-presentation can be the key to professional advancement, precisely because it prominently displays a disposition to subordinate self-advancement to other, higher values.

Fish's point, however, is not simply that conspicuous renunciation
of careerist aims can be an effective strategy for their attainment. The
larger and less cynical point is that in order for such a community to
function effectively, it may be necessary for its members to imagine that
they are boldly improvising, even when they are playing roles the
community defines for them. Antiprofessionalism in this largest sense,
says Fish, is the "founding gesture of the profession," in that it supplies
members with a "vocabulary of transcendence" and enables them to
ward off fears of heteronomy. "A professional must find a way to
operate in the context of purposes, motivations, and possibilities that
precede and even define him and yet maintain the conviction that he is
'essentially the proprietor of his own person and capacities'. *The way he
finds is anti-professionalism.*" "To be a professional," says, Fish "is to
think of oneself as motivated by something larger than market conditions." From this standpoint the community not only can tolerate a
high level of antiprofessionalism, but also needs it to offset the pressures for consensus and rigor (and perhaps also scholasticism and

69. Fish, *Doing What Comes Naturally*, 207, 201.

conformity) that are bred by communal life. Antiprofessionalism of the sort that Rorty displays thus becomes an ironic but integral part of the ideology of professionalism. At the end of his essay titled "Anti-Professionalism," Fish admits that "in my efforts to rehabilitate professionalism, I have come full circle and have ended up by rehabilitating anti-professionalism too."[70]

Alas, Fish's admirable insight that the community must, *for its own good*, leave a niche for personal autonomy is squandered by his insistence that this niche can never be anything more than a mirage. Freedom for Fish is a myth to which we cling out of hunger for self-esteem. If Rorty's view of the professional scholar is "undersocialized" in its failure to acknowledge the immensity of the intellectual debt each of us owes to the disciplinary matrix within which we work, Fish's view is, in the last analysis, "oversocialized," for in the end his professionals turn out to be nothing more than passive reflexes of their professional surroundings, incapable of voicing any opinion not prefabricated by the community. Taking thought; putting one's affairs in a larger perspective; heightening one's awareness of one's place in the world; attaining higher stages of self-consciousness—all these inward operations performed by the thinking self he dismisses as illusory. "The demand for self-consciousness," he says, "is a demand for a state of consciousness in which nothing has yet been settled and choices can therefore be truly rational." No such state of mind exists. "If you are a finite being, and therefore situated, you are wholly situated, and no part of you or your experience is asituational; your every capability is positive, a reflection and extension of the system of belief that bespeaks you and your possibilities, and there is nothing negative (detached, independent, free) to nurture." Careening over the edge, Fish concludes that "freedom, in whatever shape it appears, is another name for constraint."[71]

Surely this goes too far. It does not follow that since we are situated (constrained by circumstance), we must be "wholly situated"

---

70. Fish, *Doing What Comes Naturally,* 179, 201–2, 244, 177, 246 (emphasis in the original). Fish quotes Magali Sarfatti Larson, *The Rise of Professionalism: A Sociological Analysis* (Berkeley: University of California Press, 1977), 221–22.

71. Fish, *Doing What Comes Naturally,* 394, 430, 459. These three quotations, all concerned with the critical legal studies movement, come from three different articles. The immediate context of the first is a discussion of the work of Mark Kelman; of the last two a discussion of the work of Roberto Unger. Since Kelman and Unger are members of the same movement, bringing the passages together does not, I think, deprive them of an appropriate context.

(fated, incapable of authentic choice). The idea of freedom is riddled with paradox, and there is plenty of room to criticize commonsense understandings of it, but our vivid everyday experience of choice and decision has to be taken more seriously than this. Nor is it enough to add, as Fish so characteristically does, that perceptions of freedom, although illusory, are built into the human condition and so cannot finally be doubted or set aside, any more than can mortality itself.[72] Fish's own doubts about the authenticity of freedom are on record, and he carries them out in practice. Caught up in the exuberance of his own rhetoric, he is not content to describe scholars as independent agents or even as participating members of a community whose every thought bears traces of its corporate origins. Instead, they are mere "extensions" and "reflections" coughed up by a soulless sociocognitive machine that "bespeaks" them and their possibilities—not a promising place to begin if one is trying to justify academic or any other variety of freedom.

What if the customary rights and privileges of academic freedom were to come under attack: Would Fish defend them? I have no doubt that he would, but only because he is utterly fearless when it comes to incurring charges of inconsistency and expediency. As a self-identified member of the species *"homo rhetoricus,"* who is used to being accused of a morally paralyzing relativism, Fish is quick to insist that we are *always* entitled to assert our interests and resist actions that have deplorable consequences.[73] The adequacy of our justification would not concern him: we defend academic freedom because it is in our interest to do so, and the justificatory rhetoric we employ is adequate insofar as it carries the day—no internal or logical criterion of adequacy applies. Some readers may wonder how anyone who sees so little difference between freedom and unfreedom, and who has so much disdain for the "vocabulary of transcendence," could defend academic freedom with a good intellectual conscience, but from Fish's perspective this is not only a tenderminded response, but also an obfuscating one, because of its easy distinction between those who act on conscience and those who do not. This being a Darwinian world, motives unmindful of the self promise extinction. Us versus them, me versus you: that's life. Nietz-

---

72. Ibid., 246.
73. Ibid., 482–83.

sche's slippery slope holds no terror for Fish. We have been there all along; there is no other place to be.

In a recent essay impishly titled, "There's No Such Thing as Free Speech and It's a Good Thing Too," Fish shrugs aside the conventional wisdom that free speech is a right of "independent value"—that is, a value we should uphold for its long-term benefits regardless of whose speech is in question and how well our own immediate interests and preferences are served by it. The alternative, one gathers, is to regard free speech as a *dependent* value, and what it most depends on is whether or not it serves one's own personal or political interests. Fish observes, accurately enough, that no society ever has protected or ever could protect all speech whatsoever, that a limit must always be set somewhere. From this familiar and uncontroversial fact he brings forth the astonishing non sequitur that, all pretenses aside, free speech has never been anything more than a dependent value and therefore we would be fools to honor the right of free speech when it does not serve our interests. If, in a particular instance, acknowledging a right of free speech would be inconvenient, or suit the other person's interests better than your own, well then, says Fish, just don't acknowledge it. In the essay's introductory paragraph he lays out its lesson without a trace of embarrassment:

> Free speech is not an independent value but a political prize, and if that prize has been captured by a politics opposed to yours, it can no longer be invoked in ways that further your purposes for it is now an obstacle to those purposes. This is something that the liberal left has yet to understand and what follows is an attempt to pry its members loose from a vocabulary that may now be a disservice to them.[74]

Fish spells out the lesson again near the essay's end: "My counsel is therefore pragmatic rather than draconian: so long as so-called 'free

---

74. Stanley Fish, "There's No Such Thing as Free Speech and It's a Good Thing Too," *Boston Review* 17 (February 1992): 3, also published in *Debating PC: The Controversy over Political Correctness on College Campuses*, ed. Paul Berman (New York: Dell, 1992) and in Stanley Fish, *There's No Such Thing as Free Speech and It's a Good Thing Too* (New York and Oxford: Oxford University Press, 1994), 102–15. See also his "postscript," pp. 115–19, where he gives us fair warning that he is working on "an argument for the emptiness of any gesture that invokes a regulative ideal." (116).

speech principles' have been fashioned by your enemies, contest their relevance to the issue at hand; but if you manage to refashion them in line with your purposes, urge them with a vengeance."[75] In short, free speech, being a privilege, is best reserved for oneself and one's allies. When in the presence of those who mistake free speech for an "independent value," demand it as a right; but do not be so naive as to extend reciprocal rights to them, or anyone else, as long as you can get away without doing so. Fish's Machiavellian advice transforms free speech from a matter of obligation that may constrain us to act against our own wishes into a rhetorical ruse that liberates us to take advantage of suckers, including all who believe in such ephemeral things as "independent value." Here the message is delivered in a soothing context of concern about the harmful effects of hate speech, but Fish has delivered similar messages on other occasions and, whatever the occasion, his basic assumptions remain the same. These assumptions, widely shared in the era of power/knowledge, are not hard to enumerate: It's a jungle out there. Politics is the only game in town, all appearances to the contrary notwithstanding. Playing politics means being rhetorical, at least until the violence begins. Only the tender-minded take ideals, principles, and procedural scruples to be actual rules of conduct; everyone else knows them to be nothing more than masks, means of persuasion, moves in a struggle that aims always at dominance. The only operative rules are catch as catch can, winner take all, dupe or be duped.

Given these assumptions, all the agonizing complexities posed by hate speech evaporate into thin air:

> When someone observes, as someone surely will, that anti-harassment codes chill speech, one could reply that since speech only becomes intelligible against the background of what isn't being said, the background of what has already been silenced, *the only question is the political one of which speech is going to be chilled,* and all things considered, it seems like a good thing to chill speech like "nigger," "cunt," "kike," and "faggot." And if someone then says, "But what happened to free speech principles?" one could say what I have now said a dozen times, free speech principles don't exist except as a component in a bad argument in

75. Ibid., 26.

which such principles are invoked to mask motives that would not stand close scrutiny.[76]

Although the raw examples Fish lists would seem potentially to qualify as "fighting words," and thus to be actionable under the principle adopted by the Supreme Court in *Chaplinsky v. New Hampshire* (1942), not even that principle carries any weight with him, for "every idea is an incitement to somebody."[77] Against the dangers of the jungle, principle is powerless, the resort to force inescapable.

It is not hard to imagine what would become of academic freedom if trustees took to heart Fish's lesson that free speech is inescapably a "dependent value," to be honored or ignored depending on how well it serves one's own interests. I argued previously that academic freedom could not be fully assimilated to free speech protections without grave loss, but the two obviously overlap extensively, and the fate of academic freedom can no more be disentangled from free speech protections than it can from epistemological assumptions. If free speech is not an "independent value," then neither is academic freedom. Fish claims merely to be refining our understanding of free speech conventions, which he admits usefully "channel" political debate and "protect society against over-hasty outcomes," but in truth widespread adoption of his "refinements" would reduce those conventions to rubble.[78] Insofar as free speech and academic freedom are selectively applied and made "dependent" on political consequences, they lose their independent status as "values" and become incapable of channeling debate. Deprived of independence, they exert no force of their own and merely augment whatever political interest has overpowered them.

Defining academic freedom as a "dependent value" would carry us back to the state of affairs that existed in the 1890s, at the time of Edward A. Ross's dismissal. By Fish's Orwellian standard, Jane Lothrop Stanford committed no sin against academic freedom, she just construed it realistically, as a dependent value. Her decision to

---

76. Ibid., 25 (emphasis added).
77. Ibid., 23. Fish presents his own position as an alternative to "First Amendment absolutism," but his dismissive attitude toward the "fighting words" test puts him in opposition to many nonabsolutists, such as myself, who are worried about the growing spirit of censoriousness of the academic left but who also believe that the most abusive and persistent hate speech should be punished.
78. Ibid., 26.

fire Ross depended on his politics, which Fish recognizes as a good and sufficient reason for withholding free speech protections. Of course Fish might disapprove of her politics and therefore accuse her of violating Ross's rights, but only as a theatrical ploy on behalf of his own politics. The goal of the Victorian project that was brought to completion by the founding of the AAUP in 1915 was to insure that politics and other influences deemed extrinsic to intellectual work would not be the sole, the primary, or even the major determinants of scholarly expression. For Fish such a project can be one of two things: an exercise in futility (if the projectors are sincere about their intentions) or deception (if not). Not that deception would be out of bounds. "The only question," as he says, "is the political one of which speech is going to be chilled."

> People cling to First Amendment pieties because they do not wish to face what they correctly take to be the alternative. That alternative is *politics*, the realization . . . that decisions about what is and is not protected in the realm of expression will rest not on principle or firm doctrine, but on the ability of some persons to interpret—recharacterize or rewrite—principle and doctrine in ways that lead to the protection of speech they want heard and the regulation of speech they want silenced. (That is how George Bush can argue *for* flag-burning statutes and *against* campus hate-speech codes.) When the First Amendment is successfully invoked the result is not a victory for free speech in the face of a challenge from politics, but a *political victory* won by the party that has managed to wrap its agenda in the mantle of free speech. . . . In short, the name of the game has always been politics, even when (indeed, especially when) it is played by stigmatizing politics as the area to be avoided.[79]

The primacy of the political: Here is an article of faith so rich in implications as to be virtually constitutive of the era of power/knowledge. It is deeply inimical to academic freedom, presumably another of the "pieties" like free speech to which Fish says the timid "cling." For those who subscribe to this web of assumptions, politics extends seamlessly into every nook and cranny of life, making un-

---

79. Ibid., 25 (emphasis in the original).

thinkable the very ideas of the unpolitical and the nonpartisan (not to mention the disinterested). Even the thought that politics is a matter of degree, that some decisions or motives are *less* political than others, is taken by the faithful to be an evasion of this all-revealing truth about the universal sway of political motivation. The pervasiveness of the political is commonly presented as a plain and palpable fact of the sort that only fools or knaves could deny, but in fact it is the predictable outcome of a hermeneutics of suspicion to which all of us resort in our most cynical moments, when we are eager to project our own aggression outward into the world. The presumption that everything is political reproduces at the level of policy the character ideal specific to a "therapeutic" culture, in which the goal of personal autonomy has resolved itself into the crass problem of knowing how to use others without being used by them. Just as the inhabitants of a therapeutic culture, in Philip Rieff's words, "cannot conceive of an action that is not self-serving, however it may be disguised or transformed," neither can they imagine anything standing outside the struggle for political advantage. "This is a culture in which each views the other, in the fullness of self-knowledge, as 'trash.'"[80] One's guard instinctively goes up in the presence of those who mutter, "It's a jungle out there!" for we never know whether these words are really the incantation of innocents, who fear becoming prey, or of predators, who are eager to dilute their guilt by universalizing it.

The "politics" that is said to be so ubiquitous is a thin, one-dimensional affair, bearing little resemblance either to the bookish subject taught by political science or to the turbulent panorama of horse trading, arm-twisting, rule making, and rule bending—by turns ennobling and degrading—that is on display daily in legislatures, court houses, and town councils across the land. "Politics" stands simply for the lawlessness of the jungle. It is a nightmare vision, devoid of empirical substance and animated by bruised innocence. There is little room in it for the rich assortment of institutions, devices, and strategies by which wise diplomats have tried to deflect power, diffuse antagonisms, outwait confrontations, and set baffles in the way of force, for from the vantage point Fish occupies, all these measures (like academic freedom) smack of otherworldliness, of the

80. Philip Rieff, *The Triumph of the Therapeutic: The Uses of Faith After Freud* (Chicago and London: University of Chicago Press, 1987), 61.

flight from the political, of vain attempts to make of ourselves something more than creatures of the jungle.

Thus, in the long passage I have quoted, Fish characteristically
identifies politics with the stark "realization" (no mere "supposition"
or "hypothesis," contingent on the facts of the case) that our *principles* and *doctrines* count for nothing; that the only important question
is who gets to *interpret* them. He thereby obscures the elementary
political lesson that principles and doctrines can usefully narrow an
officeholder's range of personal discretion; that personality, principle, and doctrine *all* have a hand in shaping political outcomes; that
neither the interpreter nor what is interpreted determines everything. In the same vein, he dismisses the argument that the short-
run benefits of silencing haters might be offset by the detrimental
long-term consequences of chilling free expression. He does so
archly, on the grounds that such an argument "could be seen" as the
mask that hate wears. Even when not a mask, he contends, the
argument is just the secular residue of the "Puritan celebration of
millenarian hopes," plausible only to those who put their faith in the
"Holy Spirit" and the indefinite future, instead of this world and the
present.[81] When it comes to regulative ideals, Fish simply has a tin
ear. He would no more pursue a goal that he knew in advance could
be only imperfectly attained than go shopping in a museum. Shopping is for malls, where dollars count and consumers get what they
ask for. Why want something that eludes your grasp, that you cannot wrap up and take home with you?

Some of the premises underlying academic freedom are open to
serious objections, but the Victorians were not wrong to distinguish
between motives more and less political. Those who see ominous
political implications lurking beneath every bed and hiding behind
every door do so not because "that is the way the world is"—an
impermissible formulation on their own premises, after all—but because of assumptions they deploy as a matter of choice. The skillful
deployment of these assumptions is a kind of game. Foucault was
past master and Fish a world-class practitioner, but anyone can play.
Here's how: First, acknowledge no limits to interpretation. Second,
acknowledge no difference between intended and unintended consequences. Third, disregard all distinctions between acts of commission

---

81. Fish, "There's No Such Thing," 25.

and acts of omission. Fourth, firmly embrace (as if true) the logical fallacy of supposing that whoever is not for your cause is against it.

These axioms constitute a blank check for tendentiousness. Adopt them and you, too, will find that politics has expanded to fill your entire universe. Threatening agendas and scandalous breaches of responsibility will rear up on all sides; masks will fall away and sordid motives leap into view. Advocates of speech codes will be revealed (in the eyes of their opponents) as stealthy Stalinists; advocates of free speech will be revealed (in the eyes of *their* opponents) as covert bigots. Actions and inactions, words and silences, choices and accidents, things done and things left undone—all acts and omissions to act will testify to the universality of selfish motives and the pervasiveness of political machination. Anyone who rebuffs your idea of a proper solution will be "part of the problem"; anyone who argues for an understanding of events more complicated than your own will be guilty of "blaming the victim." Once these strategic premises are in place, responsibility will have been transformed from a concrete relation into a diffuse quality that floats freely through all relations, ready to be imputed to anyone, anytime. If it suits your needs, you can find fault with the person who sends an annual charitable donation to Amnesty International for not caring enough about world hunger, while simultaneously accusing the person who sends a contribution to Oxfam of being indifferent to torture—for from this standpoint nothing evil "just happens." Remember, good acts omitted are no less incriminating than evils committed; the indirect consequences of a person's acts may signify unconscious wishes, even if not conscious intention; moral liability extends as far as interpretation can carry it. And interpretation knows no bounds.[82]

---

82. This is not the place to spell out the way these assumptions operate in the work of Foucault and other recent writers, but many readers will recognize them as the foundational assumptions, as it were, of antifoundationalism. Even so sympathetic a reader as Charles Taylor rejects what he calls Foucault's "case for the invasion of everyday understanding by relations of power," formidable though he admits it is. "Only if we could show that relations of domination, and the strategies which create and sustain them, have totally invaded the world of everyday self-understanding could we adopt the narrow, neo-Clausewitzian interpretation [according to which intellectual debate is war by other means] and make all dominant ideas the outcome of conflicts which centre on war and the struggle for power." Taylor, "The Hermeneutics of Conflict," in *Meaning and Context: Quentin Skinner and his Critics*, ed. James Tully (Princeton: Princeton University Press, 1988), 226. For telling second thoughts about the supposed boundlessness of interpretation (by an influential early advocate of the reader's power

Once this perspective is adopted, Fish's description is undeniable: politics floods the world, leaving, as he says, "no safe place."[83] It is a perspective from which academic freedom can be seen as an enviable political prize, well worth hanging onto; but also one from which all efforts at justification have to be interpreted as self-serving rhetoric. Illogical though the assumptions underlying this perspective plainly are, their appeal today is great. Rieff may be right; we may already live in a culture that cannot conceive of acts that are not self-serving and can only define autonomy as the opportunity to use without being used. If so, the "safe place" the Victorian founders of the university tried to create under the banner of academic freedom is beyond any possibility of justification. One can only hope and trust that this is not the case.

I have examined the views of Rorty and Fish at some length because, in their very different ways, they (along with Kuhn) are heirs of the tradition in which Peirce, Lovejoy, and Seligman stood. The fragility and inconclusiveness of the support they render to the community of the competent is therefore all the more revealing of the chasm that has already opened between the Victorians and ourselves. If those who share in the traditions of the community can speak of it only in the equivocal manner of Rorty and Fish, what of critics who subscribe to rival traditions? In particular we should ask how the autonomy of the disciplinary community can continue to be defended in the face of sweeping doubts about "disciplinization," such as those advanced by Hayden White, to whose arguments I now turn in conclusion.

Up to this point my purpose in this chapter has not been to weigh the substantive merits and demerits of the disciplinary community but, rather, to trace the shifting fortunes of its rationale at the level of "rights talk," which of course marches under the banner of academic freedom. That the community is but a flawed and imperfect means of attaining reliable knowledge was conceded even by its greatest champion, the fallibilist, Charles Peirce. In this closing section of the chapter I will briefly rehearse some of its limitations and liabilities, partly for the sake of presenting a balanced picture, but also to sharpen the contrast between moderate and radical forms of criticism. I have no

---

to "produce" the meaning of a text), see Umberto Eco's contribution to Collini, ed., *Interpretation and Overinterpretation*.

83. Fish, "There's No Such Thing," 26.

quarrel with those critics who remind us of the community's limitations or its susceptibility to misuse in unskilled hands. What concerns me are criticisms such as those voiced by White that, if widely accepted, would leave disciplinary communities without a justificatory leg to stand on, either epistemologically or ethically. White's doubts about "disciplinization" are more far-reaching than any we have yet considered; to assess them we need first to mention the warts and blemishes that even the strongest friends of the community should be prepared to admit.

The most common complaint today about disciplinary communities concerns the underrepresentation of women and members of minority groups. These complaints sometimes oversimplify the question of responsibility and exaggerate the ease of reform—ignoring, for example, the wide acceptance by women themselves of the now hated gender conventions of the not-so-distant past or failing to acknowledge the continuing shallowness of the pool of qualified applicants from some minority groups, even after two decades of energetic efforts to deepen it. But there is no denying that white males are disproportionately represented. Reform is well under way. It will not be complete in our lifetimes; there will be tarnished standards, travesties of justice, and much hypocrisy along the way. But fulfilling the community's own ideal of admitting to membership all who demonstrate competence reaffirms its deepest commitments and can only strengthen it in the long run.

A more troubling criticism has been set forth by critics who lament the demise of the "public intellectual" and blame that complex development largely on the rise of academic professionalism. Louis Menand, for example, justly complains that the very existence of a professionally organized community imposes hardships and disabling restrictions on amateurs, outsiders who in some cases are more talented than those who flourish professional credentials.[84] The community obviously desecrates its own deepest commitments when it rewards mediocre "insiders" over talented "outsiders," but the problem is hard to address because the vice of premature closure is not easily disentangled from the virtue of professional autonomy. Even insiders become victims of professional closure when the quest for

---

84. Louis Menand, "The Future of Academic Freedom," *Academe* 79 (May/June 1993): 13.

autonomy becomes so inward turning and self-enclosing that it shrinks the ethical or intellectual horizons of its members. Thomas Bender has issued eloquent warnings against the "mystified but determined careerism" that "animates and supplies a pattern to contemporary academic intellect." He calls for a shift of priorities, away from autonomy, to "the opening up of the disciplines, the ventilating of professional communities that have come to share too much and that have become self-referential."[85]

These liabilities are authentic and largely irremediable. In the absence of countervailing forces, it is probably true that all human organizations tend to devolve into country clubs and fraternal lodges. Unchecked, the republic of letters becomes a republic of pals. The only remedy for this degenerative tendency is for individuals deliberately to embrace values that offset and counterbalance it. The importance and fruitfulness of countervailing values is what Richard Rorty had in mind when he singled out the ethnos of the West as one that "prides itself on suspicion of ethnocentrism" and therefore stands out as a model worthy of respect and even emulation around the globe.[86] Rorty was not saying that the West has overcome the dangers of ethnocentrism; his point was that the culture of the West has made suspicion of ethnocentrism a "norm," or "value," or "ideal," powerful enough to significantly influence conduct, thus giving it a limited but hopeful capacity for self-correction. It is in the same spirit that I endorse the community of the competent: not because it is all we might desire, but because insofar as its members genuinely engage in mutual criticism and pride themselves on suspicion of professional closure, they make it, too, a partially self-correcting enterprise.

To make the need for countervailing values clearer, we might do well to think of disciplinary communities as dangerous tools designed to fight fire with fire. In their effort to establish authority, Victorian reformers embraced a broadly Tocquevillian analysis of democracy, taking it for granted that democracy's great liability was the tyranny of the majority and its great strength the art of "voluntary associa-

85. Thomas Bender, *Intellect and Public Life: Essays on the Social History of Academic Intellectuals in the United States* (Baltimore and London: Johns Hopkins University Press, 1993), 142–43.

86. Rorty, *Objectivity, Relativism, and Truth*, 2. For a brilliant commentary on Rorty's use of the concept of ethnocentrism and related issues, see David Hollinger, "How Wide the Circle of the 'We'? American Intellectuals and the Problem of the Ethnos Since World War II," *American Historical Review* 98 (April 1993): 317–53.

tion." The community of the competent is, after all, a special kind of voluntary association, one that offers its members (and through them, indirectly, the entire culture) a degree of protection against the tyrannous tendencies of unchecked public opinion. What usually escapes notice is that it achieves this laudable end only by exposing them to a rival source of majoritarian pressures, internal to the community. When individuals become members of such a community, they are elevated above laypersons and made somewhat independent of public opinion, but at the same time they are made more dependent on their professional peers and less able to resist the consensus of the competent.[87] Their heightened susceptibility to peer-group majorities is what gives them both the incentive and the ability to resist the majoritarian excesses to which the larger society is prone.

Thinking of the disciplinary community in this way might help us remember that it is a potential engine of orthodoxy, which uses the tyrannical proclivities of an *internal* majority to offset and counterbalance the even more dangerous proclivities of an *external* majority. This is, to paraphrase what James Madison said about the Constitution, a majoritarian remedy for the defects of majoritarianism. The use of such a toxic remedy can be justified only by the greater dangers of stultification and conformity that might result from the unchecked majoritarian tendencies of the larger democratic culture, which are no more benign today than they were in Tocqueville's time. Although suspending individuals between two rival centers of conformity opens up opportunities for independence, that outcome is by no means guaranteed. This intricate system of checks and balances is not complete unless it extends to the conscious preferences and values of the individuals who constitute the community, for in the last analysis what keeps the community from becoming a tyrannical fount of orthodoxy in its own right are the countervailing values of the individuals who work within it. When individual scholars lose their suspicion of professional closure, become impatient with dissent against their own views, or cease going out of their way to encourage originality and diversity of opinion within the community, especially in matters political, then they themselves generate the orthodoxy that academic freedom was created to resist.

---

87. Alexis de Tocqueville, *Democracy in America*, 2 vols., trans. H. Reeve (New York: Schocken Books, 1961), 1:309–12. Some of the language of this paragraph is drawn from my *Emergence of Professional Social Science*, 75.

Some of the thorniest academic freedom issues of recent years have been produced by demands for political orthodoxy coming not from powerful outsiders, as in the classic case of Edward A. Ross, but from a politically mobilized faction of peers *within* the scholarly community, relentlessly pursuing its own vision of righteousness.[88] President Kingman Brewster of Yale once suggested that the principal threats to academic freedom at major universities come from within faculty ranks. Some of the glaring failures of the academy to defend endangered members during World War I and the McCarthy era might be similarly explained in terms of the community's susceptibility to waves of majoritarian excess—not just *external* waves that overwhelm the community's defenses, but also internal, self-generated ones that permit an incensed political faction to assume for a time the mantle of truth intended for those who articulate the community's "current best opinion."[89]

The sobering truth is that, acting collectively and employing the routine mechanisms of peer review established by their professional disciplines, academicians have it in their power (through hiring decisions, selective admission of graduate students, refereeing of one another's work, allocating of grants, control of professional associations, and so on) to impose on one another an orthodoxy more complete than Jane Lothrop Stanford could have imagined. This perversion of the community's purpose will be perpetrated with a clear political conscience as long as scholars continue to embrace the self-indulgent illusion that their own efforts to enforce political orthodoxy—originating inside the community and unaccompanied by the administrator's di-

---

88. A case in point is the conduct of feminist historians, outraged that one of their number had chosen to testify as an expert witness for Sears & Roebuck and against the EEOC in a case involving charges of sexual discrimination. For an account of the case and citations to the substantial literature it spawned, see Thomas L. Haskell and Sanford Levinson, "Academic Freedom and Expert Witnessing: Historians and the *Sears* Case," *Symposium on Academic Freedom: Texas Law Review* 66 (June 1988): 1629–59; Alice Kessler-Harris, "Academic Freedom and Expert Witnessing: A Response to Haskell and Levinson," *Texas Law Review* 67 (December 1988): 429–40; Haskell and Levinson, "On Academic Freedom and Hypothetical Pools: A Reply to Alice Kessler-Harris," *Texas Law Review* 67 (June 1989): 1591–1604. For more on internally originated pressure for orthodoxy, see David M. Rabban, "Does Academic Freedom Limit Faculty Autonomy?" *Symposium on Academic Freedom: Texas Law Review* 66 (June 1988): 1405–30.

89. Kingman Brewster, "On Tenure," *AAUP Bulletin* 58 (1972): 381, 382. See also Fritz Machlup, "On Some Misconceptions Concerning Academic Freedom," in *Academic Freedom and Tenure*, ed. L. Joughin (Madison: University of Wisconsin Press, 1967). Both are cited in Rabban, "Does Academic Freedom Limit Faculty Autonomy?"

rect threat of job termination—simply do not count as offenses against academic freedom. On the contrary: The enemies of academic freedom are those who try to enforce orthodoxy, whether inside or outside the community. The danger will be averted only insofar as the members of the community conduct themselves with the caution and restraint appropriate to people who understand that they share in the operation of a risky instrument, one that when misused can be every bit as hazardous to independent thinking as the majoritarian tyranny it is meant to hold in check.

The truths of the disciplinary community are perishable, its side effects are regrettable, and when misused it compounds the very problems it is meant to rectify. These blemishes remind us that a significant gap exists between the community's ideals and the reality of its operation, but few readers will think imperfections of this sort weighty enough to discredit the disciplinary enterprise itself. The same cannot be said of Hayden White's very different criticism, in which the assumptions of power/knowledge might be said to reach their logical conclusion. In a brilliant and controversial 1982 essay, "The Politics of Interpretation," White confined his attention to a single discipline, history, but set forth an argument that takes as its target "disciplinization."[90] His argument seems to me to confirm the improbability that any justification of academic freedom could ever be reconciled with the highly skeptical epistemological views that have gained currency in recent years. White never speaks of the community of the competent as such and displays little interest in the social or institutional mechanisms by which "disciplinization" was accomplished, but the process he has in mind is obviously produced by the community of the competent.

White's thesis claims to unmask the deep political significance of disciplinization and therefore of the disciplinary community itself. Its central claim is easily stated: The nineteenth-century transformation of historical studies into an empirical discipline, distinct from both belles lettres and speculative philosophy, came about because of the "ideological benefits to new social classes and political constituencies that professional, academic historiography served and, *mutatis mutandis*, continues to serve down to our own time." The ideological function of

---

90. Hayden White, "The Politics of Historical Interpretation: Discipline and De-Sublimation," in his *The Content of the Form: Narrative Discourse and Historical Representation* (Baltimore and London: Johns Hopkins University Press, 1987), 58–82.

disciplinization boils down, in White's view, to the development of a "standard of realism in political thought and action," a standard that dignifies history as a superior alternative to fiction and distinguishes sharply between verifiable "facts," on the one hand, and speculative philosophies or theories of historical development, on the other. The very existence of such a standard, White believes, favors the political center by enshrining common sense and marking out for repression "utopian thinking in all its forms (religious, social, and above all political)." Utopian thinking he further defines as "the kind of thinking without which revolutionary politics, whether of the Left or the Right, becomes unthinkable."[91]

Disciplinization thus brings about a "domestication of historical consciousness" that narrows the political spectrum and, in White's view, tragically deprives oppressed peoples of the opportunity for "visionary politics."[92] He never specifies exactly who has been deprived or what a "visionary politics" might consist of, but presumably he has in mind "the wretched of the earth" and a politics that would enable them to cope with the mounting demographic and economic crises of the Third World. This supposed tendency of professional historiography to repress visionary politics is not a function of the individual historian's preferences or ideological convictions. Marxist historiography is as guilty as liberal is. Not only have both schools of thought aspired to a "science" of history, even more fundamentally, both have shared the conviction—unwarranted and presumptuous in White's eyes—that "history is not a *sublime spectacle* but a *comprehensible process* the various parts, stages, epochs, and even individual events of which are transparent to a consciousness endowed with the means to make sense of it in one way or another."[93]

---

91. Ibid., 61–63.
92. Ibid., 75, 73.
93. Ibid., 73 (emphasis added). It is easy to underestimate White's radicalism here. His doubts are not confined to overconfident varieties of historiography that claim to settle "scientifically" matters generally recognized as debatable. His doubts extend to any account cast in narrative form that claims to represent the real. Narrative form, in his view, distorts the mere meaningless sequence of reality, imparting to it the "odor of the ideal." It does so, moreover, in the service of a "moralizing impulse" that inevitably seeks to authorize a particular social order. See "The Value of Narrativity in the Representation of Reality," in *Content of Form*, 21, 24, 13. White quotes Roland Barthes's unequivocal claim that "historical discourse is in its essence a form of ideological elaboration," without either embracing or rejecting it: "The Question of Narrative in Contemporary Historical Theory," in *Content of Form*, 36.

It is precisely the success of disciplinization in rendering the past comprehensible that White deplores. After all, he argues, "the conviction that one can make sense of history stands on the same level of epistemic plausibility as the conviction that it makes no sense whatsoever." Following Schiller and other early romantic theorists of the "sublime," he suggests that many of the world's peoples would be better off to regard their own past as a terrifying and incomprehensible spectacle of confusion, uncertainty, and moral anarchy, for only this perspective would provoke them to take command of their lives and forge from their miseries a more satisfying future. "In my view," he argues,

> the theorists of the sublime . . . correctly divined that whatever freedom and dignity human beings could lay claim to could come only by way of what Freud called a "reaction-formation" to an apperception of history's meaninglessness. . . . Modern ideologies [such as liberalism or Marxism] impute a meaning to history that renders its manifest confusion comprehensible to either reason, understanding, or aesthetic sensibility. To the extent that they succeed in doing so, these ideologies deprive history of the kind of meaninglessness that alone can goad living human beings to make their lives different for themselves and their children.[94]

One might expect that anyone expressing concern about the anti-utopian, antirevolutionary bias of disciplinization would do so in hopes of reopening revolutionary options, but White denies having any such motive. "I am against revolutions," he disarmingly announces. Even more surprisingly, he expresses the "wish" that politicians and political thinkers might continue to be guided by "the kind of realism to which a disciplined historical consciousness conduces." The only motive he imputes to himself is intellectual curiosity: a concern to resolve differences of opinion at the level of "interpretative theory." He thus credits himself with a level of scholarly detachment and independence from political considerations that is strikingly at odds with the central thrust of his argument, which is to construe disciplinization as an epiphenomenon of political domination and scholarship itself as the willing servant of power.

---

94. Ibid., 72.

There is no satisfying a critic who prefers his history incomprehensible. Tempting though it is for historians to dismiss White's concerns out of hand, the brilliance of his provocation is undeniable, and there are lessons to learn from it. The controversy that has swirled about his essay since its publication, much of which is not germane to my immediate purposes, centers on the Holocaust and the extreme limits of representation. Passion has run high because White chose—out of intellectual honesty, I believe, not malice—to tackle head-on the question always thrown up at relativists: "What about the Nazis?" He also candidly admitted that his own fascination with the "historical sublime" bears more than a passing resemblance to that of fascist theorists such as Giovanni Gentile. So far as I can tell, White is as horrified by the Holocaust as anyone, but he is also unwilling to duck the implications of his own epistemological commitments. Those commitments he has spelled out in *Metahistory* and other writings, and they define him as a thoroughgoing ironist and antirealist for whom the writing of history and the construction of political ideologies necessarily blur into a single enterprise. There is, in his view, nothing stable and independent about the past for the historian to "get right"; nothing for historical interpretation to "correspond with" or to which it might "be adequate." All attempts to distinguish between scholarship and propaganda, or to array knowledge against power, are doomed merely to manifest the political passion they pretend to circumscribe. When historians set out to discover the meaning of the past, all they can possibly find, in White's view, are the tropological artifacts of their own will and imagination, more or less consciously projected onto a medium that is, in itself, shapeless and unresisting. A certain notoriety has been achieved by White's far-reaching and highly characteristic claim that "the best grounds for choosing one perspective on history rather than another are ultimately aesthetic or moral rather than epistemological."[95]

Confronting critics who have accused him of promoting a "debilitating relativism" that permits, as he says, "even a Nazi version of Nazism's history to claim a certain minimal credibility," White unflinchingly turns in "The Politics of Interpretation" to what he calls the

95. Ibid., 74; Hayden White, *Metahistory: The Historical Imagination in Nineteenth-Century Europe* (Baltimore and London: Johns Hopkins University Press, 1973), xii. For a powerful reconsideration by a scholar who has long admired White and still credits him with setting the terms of debate, see Lionel Gossman, *Towards a Rational Historiography: Transactions of the American Philosophical Society* 79, part 3 (1989).

"bottom line," the claim of revisionists that the Holocaust never occurred. "Do you mean to say," he asks himself rhetorically, "that the
occurrence and nature of the Holocaust is only a matter of opinion
and that one can write its history in whatever way one pleases?"[96]

Common sense and old-fashioned "positivist" historiography answer with a forthright no. In contrast, White's response is extremely
roundabout. He finally gives his grudging assent to the judgment of a
professional historian, Pierre Vidal-Naquet, who says that Holocaust
revisionists are quite simply putting forth a "total lie."[97] But White
observes that Vidal-Naquet was not content to distinguish lies from
truth. Having done that, Vidal-Naquet then invoked the authority of
the professional historical community to carve out a third category,
situated somewhere between "historical truth" and outright "lies," a
category made up of "ideological distortions" and "untruths" that do
not go so far as to deny the very occurrence of the Holocaust, but
twist its meaning farther than the facts will allow. These interpretations, spurned by professional historians, are produced by passionately interested parties; Vidal-Naquet's own example was Zionists
who contend that "Auschwitz was the ineluctable, logical outcome of
life lived in the Diaspora, and all the victims of the death camps were
destined to become Israeli citizens."[98]

The claim that ideologically driven history is "distorted" and can
be relegated to the inferior category of "untruth," even though not an
outright "lie," provokes from White a crucial objection that goes to
the very heart of his quarrel with disciplinization:

> Vidal-Naquet is inclined—too hastily, I think—to consign the
> Zionist interpretation of the Holocaust . . . to the category of un-
> truth. In fact, its truth, as a historical interpretation, consists pre-
> cisely of its *effectiveness* in justifying a wide range of current Israeli
> policies that, from the standpoint of those who articulate them, are
> crucial to the security of and indeed the very existence of the
> Jewish people. . . . Who is to say that this ideology is a product of a

96. White, "Politics of Historical Interpretation," 76.

97. This is not an insignificant concession, for if we can know that some interpretations are completely beyond the pale, that would seem to imply the existence of a
nonrelative standard enabling us to assess degrees of plausibility rationally. White does
not pause to consider this line of thought.

98. White, "Politics of Historical Interpretation," 77.

distorted conception of history? . . . The effort of the Palestinian people to mount a politically *effective* response to Israeli policies [some aspects of which White believes are themselves "totalitarian, not to say fascist"] entails the production of a similarly *effective* ideology, complete with an interpretation of their history capable of endowing it with a meaning that it has hitherto lacked . . . [99]

Highlighting White's repeated use of the word *effective*, just as I have done above, the historian Carlo Ginzburg has exposed to view the deeply disturbing implications of White's position. Having concluded that "there are no grounds to be found in the historical record itself for preferring one way of construing its meaning over another," White, like Nietzsche before him, seems tacitly to have accepted in the notion of *"effectiveness"* a criterion with appalling implications. By assuming that the only truth a historical interpretation can ever have is relative to the ideology it serves (one more instantiation of the assumption that power and knowledge are two sides of a coin), he gives up any defensible basis for passing moral judgment on historical developments and makes "right" the passive reflex of "might." For, as Ginzburg says, if the historical interpretation advanced by Holocaust revisionists were ever to prove *effective*, in the sense, say, of winning a strong popular following or being incorporated into the official policy of a state, then White would presumably regard it as being no less "true" than the Palestinian and Zionist interpretations that he endorses in the foregoing passage. Even the revisionists' "total lie" could become historically "effective" in White's sense, and once it did, it would presumably "justify" current policies deemed "crucial" by those who articulate them and endow history with "a meaning that it has hitherto lacked."[100]

White's understanding of the politics of interpretation is, I think, deeply flawed, but I give him full credit for following his skeptical assumptions to honest conclusions. It appears to me, as it does to him, that skepticism this radical deprives the disciplinary community of any basis whatsoever for claims of epistemological efficacy.[101] It

---

99. Ibid., 80 (emphasis added).
100. Ibid., 75. Carlo Ginzburg, "Just One Witness," in *Probing the Limits of Representation: Nazism and the "Final Solution,"* ed. Saul Friedlander (Cambridge and London: Harvard University Press, 1992), 93.
101. This would appear also to be the judgment of Martin Jay, who, in the concluding section of his own very sympathetic commentary on White's paper, acknowledges

thereby also appears to me to cut the ground out from under all existing justifications for the right of academic freedom. If I am right in this, it will not do just to paper the matter over, expecting the general public to continue accepting the traditional rationale for academic freedom, even though we undeceived sophisticates have come to regard it as poppycock. If the old rationale has lost its power to convince, then we need a new one in which both we and the educated public can believe. If no such rationale can be formulated, then the right should be allowed to perish, along with other unjustifiable practices. It is of course possible that the practice will continue to generate deeper convictions and stronger loyalties (both among academics and the public) than any of the theoretical considerations that tell against it. Should that be the case, presumably our theoreticians will take a cue from common sense, as theory has so often done in the past, and return to their epistemological drawing boards.

But of course my inability to formulate an adequate justification on the basis of au courant epistemologies may signify nothing more than my own personal limitations, of which the writing of this chapter has made me more than usually aware. Insofar as this is the case, one can only hope and trust that my errors, now in the public domain, will provoke a corrective response from others. Fortunately for my generation, even if the autonomy of disciplinary communities currently lacks any adequate justification, such communities do still exist, and their very existence gives some assurance that no one's incompetence is likely to hold the floor for long. In spite of all the sound and fury of the current Kulturkampf, the minimalist case for the authority of the disciplinary community remains hard to gainsay. Timothy

that the entire raison d'être of scholarly discourse is placed in jeopardy by White's analysis: "Although it would be foolish to assume that the uncoerced consensus of opinion, which is the *telos* of the discursive process, can be more than a regulative ideal never to be fully realized, it is still the case that scholars striving to convince each other live by it. However complicated the process may be made by the interference of nondiscursive elements, however inconclusive the outcome always is, the professional institutionalization of communicative rationality means that "effectiveness" [an allusion both to White's essay and to Ginzburg's criticism of it] can be more than merely a neutral description of what the majority believes is true or right. It may, to be sure, sometimes be little more than that, but there is no reason to despair of a more compelling alternative. Indeed, otherwise the entire raison d'être of scholarly discourse is undone." Martin Jay, "Of Plots, Witnesses, and Judgments," in *Probing the Limits of Representation: Nazism and the "Final Solution,"* ed. Saul Friedlander (Cambridge and London: Harvard University Press, 1992), 106.

Garton Ash set it forth unguardedly in a review of the controversial films *Heimat* and *Shoah*. Like White, Ash sees in the Holocaust an acid test of disciplinization, but he draws the opposite conclusion.

> The one conclusion to which [both films] lead me is: Thank God for historians! Only the professional historians, with their tested methods of research, their explicit principles of selection and use of evidence, only they can give us the weapons with which we may begin to look the thing in the face. Only the historians give us the standards by which we can judge and "place" Heimat and Shoah. Not that any one historian is necessarily more impartial than any one film director. But (at least in a free society) the terms of the historian's trade make them responsible and open to mutual attack, like politicians in a democracy.[102]

The "terms of the historian's trade" are those of all disciplinary communities, whatever their subject. A full description of those terms would fill volumes and require the skills of an ethnographer, but at their heart are some elementary provisions: that practitioners should constitute a professional community; that they should be in competitive communication with one another ("open to mutual attack"); that their decision-making process should be as public as possible (a matter of "tested" methods and "explicit" principles). The truths that such communities generate fall short of being universal or "foundational." Anyone who relies on such truths takes a calculated risk, not only that the community's current opinion may not be right, but that the community's own internal dynamics may render it obsolete tomorrow. In many parts of the world these truths will seem too frail to be valued, and even where valued they may prove too lacking in charismatic authority to compete against other, more visceral sources of conviction. Whether the truth claims of disciplinary communities are sustainable today, in a world very different from that faced by the Victorians, is the great question before us. I for one believe they are, but not until we reestablish through candid debate a plausible relationship between, on the one hand, our epistemological convictions, and on the other, our claims to authority and the rights of academic freedom.

---

102. Ash quoted in Gossman, *Towards a Rational Historiography*, 68.

The New Jural Mind:
Rights without Grounds,
without Truths, and without
Things That Are Truly Rightful

Hadley Arkes

It is never inapt to recall the exchange that took place in *Huckleberry Finn*, when Huck contrived a story and told Aunt Sally that his boat was delayed because "we blowed out a cylinder-head." Aunt Sally reacted: "Good gracious! anybody hurt?" "No'm. Killed a nigger." "Well, it's lucky; because sometimes people do get hurt."

I need not linger here to draw out, for this audience, the lessons in the story. We are reminded of the filter that may be placed on our lens, as we block from our view a whole class of beings that we do not exactly recognize as beings with any special claim to our concern, or as beings who are bearers of rights. The story is never inapt, because the obtuseness it reveals is always with us. It may be displayed by the most educated among us, for there is no immunity to be gained here by people covered over with degrees. In fact, there may be something about a deep seasoning in the law that renders lawyers especially vulnerable to this state of mind. I offer, as a notable case in point, Archibald Cox, who has certainly been quite seasoned in the law as a professor and a public man—as the solicitor general of the United States and as special prosecutor in the days of Watergate.

When he was solicitor general, Cox argued successfully for the government in upholding provisions of the Voting Rights Act in the redoubtable case of *Katzenbach v. Morgan* (1966).[1] At issue in that

1. Katzenbach v. Morgan, 384 U.S. 641 (1966).

case was the provision of the Voting Rights Act that swept away the tests of literacy, in voting, for people who had been enrolled in so-called American flag schools up through the sixth grade. This provision had been attached by Robert Kennedy as a rider to the Voting Rights Act; its purpose was to enfranchise, in a stroke, all of those Puerto Ricans in New York who were being inhibited from voting by the requirement of literacy, which was still part of the laws of New York State. No one alleged that Puerto Ricans were being subject to discrimination in the liberal politics of New York. There was no reason to think that the law was being used in a discriminatory way, or that there were not ample levers available, in New York, to correct this legislation if it were being misused. Nor would there have been any want of political figures anxious to add to their credits by taking on this issue. But Robert Kennedy saw a means of using the levers of the national government for the sake of "fixing" this particular problem quickly, without the need to work through the politics of legislation in New York State. And he could fix it without the need to consider again those ancient arguments as to why literacy was a fitting requirement for the act of citizenship involved in voting. Only seven years earlier, it appeared to the Supreme Court that this traditional understanding had retained its plausibility, for the Court had sustained these tests of literacy as quite compatible with the Constitution, and not at odds with the Fourteenth Amendment.[2]

But with Archibald Cox on the briefs, the Court sustained this part of the Voting Rights Act against a rather stern warning by Justice Harlan in dissent. Harlan found something ominous in this move, on the part of Congress, to dabble in the laws of a state simply as a matter of policy or, even worse, as a matter of constitutional interpretation. The Court had already held that tests of literacy, applied without bias, were constitutional. If the Congress now came to the judgment that these tests were incompatible with the "equal protection of the laws," the Congress would seem to be claiming a certain power to revise, through ordinary legislation, the judgments established by the Court on the requirements of the Constitution.

I should say that I have never been persuaded by Harlan's argument there, and in resisting that argument the majority seemed to

2. See Lassiter v. Northampton, 360 U.S. 45 (1959).

confirm, for the Congress and the president, a competence that had
long been recognized: namely, that the president and the Congress do
indeed have the obligation to reflect on whether the measures that
come under their hands are compatible with the principles of the
Constitution.[3] In this particular case, of *Katzenbach v. Morgan*, the
Court held then that there could in fact be a difference of judgment
between the Congress and the Court on a matter of constitutional
interpretation—and that the Congress did not have to give way before the Court.

Harlan had twitted his colleagues in opposition: In this case, they
would seem to be expanding the claims of rights, but if Congress may
remove some constitutional inhibitions for the sake of expanding certain rights, why may it not also add to those inhibitions or act for the
sake of contracting, or diminishing, the range of constitutional rights?
To this argument Justice Brennan replied, in a famous footnote, that
there is no going back. This authority, conceded to the Congress, may
be used only for *expanding* constitutional rights, not for contracting
them: The power of Congress under Section 5 of the Fourteenth
Amendment is "limited to adopting measures to enforce the guarantees of the Amendment; [Section 5] grants Congress no power to
restrict, abrogate, or dilute these guarantees."[4]

But, of course, the rejoinder should come readily to the lips of
any schoolchild: Does that not rather depend on just whose rights are
being expanded or contracted—or again, on just whom we happen to
notice as the bearers of rights? If we expanded the rights of workers,
say, at an expense borne by their private employers, we are diminishing the rights of employers. If Congress restricts the right to abortion,
or to put it another way, if it moves to the protection of unborn
children, it would be recognizing, and enlarging, the "rights" of unborn children to receive the protections of the law. There would be no
"abrogating" or "diluting" of rights under the Fourteenth Amendment. A policy that permits 1.5 million abortions each year without
the need to render a justification is a policy that would appear to

---

3. See, in this vein, some of my own pieces: "On the Moral Standing of the
President as an Interpreter of the Constitution: Some Reflections on Our Current
'Crises,'" *Political Science* (summer 1987): 637–42; *First Things* (Princeton: Princeton
University Press, 1986), 416–22; "On the Public Funding of Abortions," in *Abortion
Parley*, ed. James Burtchaell (New York: Andrews & McMeel, 1980), 237–64.

4. *Katzenbach v. Morgan*, 651 n.10.

generate victims on a grand scale—unless there are no "victims" because there is no one there to be killed. We can screen from ourselves any recognition of victims, or of rights being denied to a whole class of beings, if it is simply the case that the child in the womb does not count, that it has no weight in the law, as a being with interests and rights that deserve to be reckoned.

But again, all of this would seem to be so evident that it should hardly need stating. And yet, Archibald Cox affected not to notice it. He affected, that is, the most serene indifference to this point when the issue arose again in 1981, and the doctrine in *Katzenbach v. Morgan* was invoked by people who were not apparently supposed to use it. I speak here of the movement in 1981 on behalf of the human life bill, when the Reagan administration and the Republicans in the Congress sought to use that authority conceded by the Court in *Katzenbach v. Morgan*. The Court had proclaimed in *Roe v. Wade* that it could not pronounce on the question of when human life began and when that nascent life would be subject to the protections of the law. The Congress now offered to intercede, with vastly larger resources for taking testimony and consulting evidence in extended hearings. The Congress would supply to the Court an understanding of the beginning of human life, or the status of the being inside the womb. And in a rather venerable tradition, the Congress would encourage the Court to take a sober second look at one of its holdings (in this instance, the judgment in *Roe v. Wade*) and consider whether it might have been mistaken.

In pursuing this project, the congressional leaders were willing, as I say, to invoke the precedent of *Katzenbach v. Morgan*: that the Congress and the Court may come to a difference of judgment on the command of the Constitution, or on the beings who are being protected by the Constitution, *and the Congress need not recede*. The Congress had exercised that same authority in 1862 when it checked and countered the decision by the Court, in the Dred Scott case, that black people had no rights that white people were obliged to respect. The Congress on that occasion had moved, against the judgment of the Court, to bar a right of property in slaves in the territories of the United States. And with the same understanding of its powers, the Congress was seeking now to restore protection to a whole class of beings that the Court had removed from the protections of the law.

But when this issue became the subject of hearings in Congress, the attorney on the brief for the government in *Katzenbach v. Morgan* now testified that the precedent could not be used in that way here, for the sake of protecting fetuses or unborn children. As the anchor of his opposition, Cox relied on that footnote in *Katzenbach v. Morgan*, where Justice Brennan had declared that the decision of the Court conceded no power to Congress "to restrict, abrogate, or dilute" the guarantees of the Constitution. And in this case, as Cox argued, the human life bill "would cut back upon the established constitutional right of a woman to decide during the first two trimesters of pregnancy whether she wishes to bear a child."[5] I put aside this misstatement of *Roe v. Wade* and *Doe v. Bolton* to return to my original point about masking, or altering, the lens on the jural landscape. If we did use the lens that evidently affected Cox, if we viewed the matter in the way that the movers of the bill viewed it, there were over one million unborn children being destroyed every year in abortions. If one took seriously the notion that these were human lives, and human beings, then a bill to protect those lives was going to the rescue of over one million persons. Those persons, numbering in the millions, were not having their rights restricted here. *Their* rights were now being recognized, and therefore expanded, notably, from the condition of those rights under *Roe v. Wade*, which was virtually nonexistent. There is no need for me to argue at this moment the correctness of my own view, and I make no claim to persuade anyone today to my judgment on abortion. I point out simply that the constitutional question surely had to be affected by the question of whether human lives were being destroyed in abortions. If it is arguable that they were, it should have been evident, even to Archibald Cox, that this bill would not contract or reduce rights, and therefore the bill would not fail that formulaic test from *Katzenbach v. Morgan*. Cox's discourse on the commands of the Constitution, or the distribution of authority, could go forward only if he managed to screen, from the outset, any recognition of children in the womb as real human beings, as real objects of concern, and as beings who might well be the bearers of rights.

Nothing in the text of the Constitution provided that screening. And that indeed was at the heart of this dispute now between Congress and the Court. When Congress had resisted the Court on the

5. Senate Committee on the Judiciary, *Hearings on S. 158* [the human life bill], 97th Cong., 1st sess., 1981, 338.

Dred Scott case, the argument had to run to the question of just who properly came within the class of beings that the Constitution may protect. Cox had conceded, in *Katzenbach v. Morgan*, that the Congress and the Court may differ on a matter of interpreting the Constitution, but now he seemed to rule out the possibility that the difference may tenably involve a serious dispute about the nature of the beings who are protected. Congress may apparently deliberate and argue, but not about the question of substance that stands at the heart of the case and the assignment of "rights"—namely, whether we are dealing with beings who can be the bearers of rights.

As Cox sought to defend his position, he would mark off an understanding of the properties that attach to "rights." But as he elaborated his case, I would argue that he undercut the coherence of his original position in *Katzenbach v. Morgan*. In fact, the argument he put forward would have undercut the work of the Civil War Congresses in establishing protections for black people. In the first place, said Cox, the Congress was not working here, in the human life bill, to expand constitutional rights that were already established. It was seeking, rather, to alter our understanding of what constituted a "person," and therefore it was seeking to "create new constitutional rights."[6] But "only persons within the meaning of the Constitution have Fourteenth Amendment rights," he said.[7] And it was settled under "established constitutional law that the unborn are not 'persons' within the meaning of the Fourteenth Amendment."[8]

Established by what or by whom? As Cox himself had pointed out, along with liberals such as Robert Hart Ely, that definition of persons, or of a right to an abortion, was not contained in the text of the Constitution. That reading had been established only recently, by the Court, and that was precisely what was at issue. One might as well have told Lincoln and his Congress that it was established, after all, that black persons were not persons with rights that can be protected under the Constitution; that the Congress was simply obliged to work with the notion of "rights," or the definition of "persons," which had been supplied by the Court in the Dred Scott case.

In Cox's construction, the Congress and the Court may differ over a matter of constitutional interpretation and a constitutional

6. Ibid., 336.
7. Ibid., 337.
8. Ibid., 338.

right, say, to be free from tests of literacy in voting. And yet, curiously, the Congress may not argue over the substance of the right or
the identity of the agents who bear those rights. In this respect, Cox
seemed to fashion a strange distinction between a "right" as a moral
postulate, and certain questions of "fact," as though the claim of
rights was detached from questions of evidence, or from the prospect
of testing reasons. As Cox put it, "*Katzenbach v. Morgan* involved only
*deference to congressional determinations upon what are truly questions of
fact.*"[9] But here, Cox drifts into a bit of haze, since the "facts" he
thought were at issue in the Morgan case were not facts at all, but
speculations. In Cox's understanding, the literacy requirement in
New York rested on certain presumptions of fact:

> [I]t turned upon such considerations as the extent to which the
> requirement served as an incentive to learn English and ease the
> process of assimilation, the availability of Spanish-language news-
> papers and their sufficiency to enable non-English-speaking vot-
> ers to exercise the franchise intelligently, the importance of the
> franchise, and the relative effectiveness of other inducements to
> learn English.[10]

These were hardly facts, but predictions. And the Congress did
not overcome these presumptions of fact by disproving them with the
assembling of real facts. The Congress merely displaced one set of
predictions with another, namely, that the literacy requirement would
have the effect of diminishing the numbers of Puerto Ricans who were
voting, and in that way it would diminish the levers available to Puerto
Ricans in warding off discrimination. What Cox treated as a factual
dispute was merely a difference in speculations about the way in which
the literacy requirement would work in practice. And yet, it should
have been evident that the Congress was seeking to do far more than
offer an essay in social science: It seemed to be apparent to everyone
else that Congress was affirming something about the *rightness* or the
desirability of voting. In fact, it would be far more intelligible to understand the congressional act as quite the reverse of the construction
offered by Cox: Congress seemed to come closer to saying that there

---

9. Ibid., 339 (emphasis in the original).
10. Ibid., 340.

was something in principle good about voting; that voting was too important, as an attribute of citizenship, to be restricted on the basis of mere speculations about the effect that a literacy requirement might have in encouraging people to learn English and read newspapers.

But even if we worked for a moment in the cast defined by Cox— even if we confined the Congress to determinations of fact—the Congress seemed to meet Cox's standards even more handsomely in the work on the human life bill. For the Congress did not merely assemble speculations about the beginning of human life. It assembled the teachings from all the leading textbooks on embryology and obstetrics. It called in experts in embryology and fetology to consider what we *knew* in fact about the nature of the organism in the womb. And on the basis of that testimony, it sought to establish, as a new, corrected premise in the law, the understanding of human life contained in the textbooks. After all, Justice Blackmun had declared, in *Roe v. Wade*, that there were no truths that science and philosophy could declare on the beginning of human life. On that premise, the Court held back from regarding the child in the womb as a "human life" that the law was obliged to respect. But if the right to abortion was actually predicated on that account of science and philosophy, the moral claim of a "right" to an abortion surely had to be affected by any truth that science could pronounce on the nature of that being in the womb.

But no, Cox insisted: these were not matters of fact, after all. This bill to protect children in the womb "rests entirely," said Cox, "upon giving a particular meaning to the word 'life.' [But] What is 'life' is not simply a question of fact."[11] Perhaps Cox was still mired in the logical positivism that flourished in his youth; but only the most unreconstructed positivist could have insisted on such a radical disconnection between moral judgments and "facts." The Constitution speaks in two places about protecting "life" from being taken without due process of law. The Constitution tries to suggest principles, but it does not supply a lexicon. Still, it seemed to be assumed in the text that we could recognize the lives that were subject to protection under the Constitution. Or it was assumed, I think, that the matter was *open to deliberation* if we were in doubt. The Congress moved, in the 1860s, to bring black people under these protections of life and liberty; it sought to bar any arbitrary taking of life, or any restriction of liberty, on the basis of race.

---

11. Ibid., 340–41.

Now, let us suppose for a moment that we passed the Civil War Amendments and the Civil Rights Acts, but that legislatures in the South came forward with a version of Cox's argument. They might have said, "Of course we understand that the Constitution means to enforce freedom for human beings, and protect their lives, but you must know that there has been a serious disagreement over the years as to whether these black people are human beings. We happen to think that there is a gradation of colors, or shades, that finally helps us to discriminate between beings that are human because they are more like us. And we can actually supply the color wheel, or the book of shadings that we use in reaching our judgments."

If Cox's argument is regarded as plausible, that we cannot in fact legislate our understanding of human life, then I submit that his argument would disarm us in the face of assertions of this kind made by the Southern states. But that is to say, his argument would undercut, or render vacuous, the protections for "life" in the Fifth and Fourteenth Amendments. Those protections would be empty if any attempt to enforce them could be defeated by the claim that we do not know, after all, what life is—that the presence of a human life is not, strictly speaking, a factual question, but a metaphysical or a moral question, and that a moral question is cut off from the prospect of considering evidence and weighing reasons.

And yet, I think we could anticipate the way in which courts would respond if a legislature came forth with the color scheme I have just mentioned. The judges would probably insist that the legislature justify its judgment by proving the validity of the measures—by showing what was so dramatically different in the personal attributes of people located at different points along the gradation of shadings. And even if people were darker, swifter, more or less intelligent, why would any of these attributes mark off the difference between beings who were human or less than human? But if these shadings of color were given the status of standards in the law, they provide the most arbitrary ground of judgment for removing some human beings from a class in which they are the bearers of rights and objects of protection under the law. An immense moral shift would have taken place on the basis of attributes that finally command no moral significance and supply no justification for the removal of rights.

My argument, as you have no doubt gathered by now, is that the same kind of shift had been carried out in *Roe v. Wade*. The purpose of the human life bill was precisely to call that change into question, to challenge its premises, and to settle more justly the assignment of rights. Cox had recognized earlier the authority of the Congress to engage in that kind of project, in interpreting the Constitution. His refusal to support the human life bill could be attributed, of course, to his own political leanings or to his judgments, finally, on the rights and wrongs of abortion. But if we take him at his word, he recoiled from this bill because he earnestly could not see any "rights" engaged in this matter apart from the right of a woman to choose an abortion. And he could view the matter in this way, with this rather constricted vision, only if he did not manage to see that the understanding of rights may depend, not on assertion or promulgation, but on a certain deliberation, guided by the canons of reason, about the things that are justified and unjustified. Or it would involve a deliberation about the grounds on which we may rightly or wrongly remove a whole class of beings from the protection of the law.

Cox seemed to join a tendency, widespread among lawyers, to back away from this project in deliberation, because they would back away from the claims of reason. They are quick to disclaim that they are engaged, as lawyers, in moral reasoning, because they have become dubious about the notion of moral reasoning itself. They may engage in some rather convoluted forms of reasoning, which may resemble moral reasoning, but they are no longer persuaded that there are genuine moral truths, which can supply the substance of moral reasoning. As a consequence, arguments about "rights" must turn on some other considerations apart from the things that are truly rightful, for the commentators have lost their confidence that they can speak any longer about the things that are *truly* right.

The Founders, in the Declaration of Independence, wrote without embarrassment of self-evident moral truths—by which they did not mean truths evident to every self who happened down the street, but truths that had to be grasped, as the saying went, per se nota, as axioms in our reasoning. But by the time we reach Laurence Tribe, that professor will not claim that there are any moral truths that lie behind our rights or that the proposition "all men are created equal" has the standing of a truth. At most, he will allow, our moral sentiments merely indicate the convictions that are "powerfully held."[12] But of course the Founders did not say, in the declaration, that "all men are created equal" was merely a proposition they "powerfully held." And they did not suggest that the proposition would cease to be true if they ceased to hold to it quite as powerfully.

But that conviction has eroded from our public men and women, and in this respect, Cox and Tribe are hardly in a class by themselves. They are, in fact, representative among lawyers, right as well as left. The human life bill was opposed by Robert Bork and other conservative lawyers, but Bork has not joined with Tribe more recently on the freedom of choice bill. Over the interval of ten years, Tribe has preserved the same understanding of "rights," divorced from moral reasoning, and when the direction of the Court began to change, that understanding could move him, without wrenching, to do a turnabout on the authority of Congress to legislate on abortion.

For the question before the Congress now is not the move to protect the unborn child, but to protect the one who bears a right to an abortion. And the constitutional question has been rendered more awkward now for Tribe by the decision in the *Webster* case in 1989.[13] The Court decided in that case that the states may actually begin legislating to protect unborn children beyond the arbitrary divisions of trimesters in the pregnancy. As the chief justice suggested, the states might actually seek to protect children from the moment of conception. But with the freedom of choice bill, there has been a move in the Congress to override this authority on the part of the states. The bill would impose on the states a statute that incorporates those unrestricted rights of abortion that were articulated in *Roe v. Wade* and *Doe v. Bolton*. In other words, we may have a replay of the situation in *Katzenbach v. Morgan*: The Court has declared that it would be quite constitutional for the states to begin protecting unborn children. But now the Congress would seem to differ from the Court and revise the judgment that the Court has reached on a matter of constitutional authority.

The political situation has turned around, and so too have the people who opposed in the past the effort of the Congress to take up

---

12. See Laurence Tribe, *Constitutional Choices* (Cambridge: Harvard University Press, 1985), 5, 6, 8.

13. See Webster v. Reproductive Health Services, 106 L.Ed.2d 410 (1989).

this franchise from *Katzenbach v. Morgan* and legislate on abortion. Professor Tribe had thought, in 1981, that the Congress could not act through ordinary legislation to check, or alter, the judgment of the Court.[14] But now, of course, his mind has changed, though he does not supply an account of the reasons that justify his change. Tribe has testified more recently on behalf of the freedom of choice bill, but even he has had his artfulness strained by the need to show just what part of the Constitution would allow the federal government to pass by the authority of the states and legislate directly on the matter of abortion. Here he has been content to dip into Professor Cox's inventory of devices. Cox had been willing to invoke the commerce clause, in 1965, in *Katzenbach v. McClung* in support of the Civil Rights Act: If black people suffered discrimination in restaurants and inns, they might be discouraged from traveling in interstate commerce, and the result is that there would be fewer orders for meat, linen, silverware. And so, summing matters up, the wrong of discrimination against black people was that it would interfere with the interstate flow of meat.[15]

That was, of course, an implausible way of arguing the question, but some lawyers thought it was the main way they had to argue in order to bring in the commerce clause and allow the federal government to reach these private establishments. In the same spirit, Professor Tribe has been willing to make game use of an implausible mode of argument. And so, with a straight face, he was willing to tell a committee of the Senate in 1992 that restrictions on abortion in the separate states "would interfere with freedom of travel (which of course includes the freedom to decide whether and where to travel) and would generate significant burdens on interstate facilities":

> [L]ocal or statewide restrictions on reproductive freedom would likely force many women to travel from States that have chosen to erect legal barriers to contraception or to abortion, to States or foreign nations where safe and legal procedures are available. Indeed, the years preceding Roe and Doe saw precisely such a massive interstate migration, as hundreds of thousands of women travelled from restrictive States to those where abortions were

14. See Tribe's testimony in Senate Committee, *Hearings on S. 158*, 242–56, esp. 243, 250–51.

15. See Katzenbach v. McClung, 379 U.S. 294 (1965), at 299–300, 303–4.

more freely performed. In 1972, for example, almost 80 per cent of all legal abortions in this country took place in just two States: New York and California.[16]

Without the benefit of evidence, Tribe simply draws the inference that people were traveling from all over the country, filling the interstate highways. But the advent of the commerce clause was meant to mark a national community that found its real integration as a community precisely through the free movement of persons and goods across the lines of the states. This movement was taken then as a "good," or a sign of health. Why should it be construed then as a "problem" or an injury? Tribe suggests, largely through the coloring of his language, that this traffic might pose hazards to the public safety. He writes, darkly, of "the human toll taken by this highway of anguish and frustration"—though as far as we know, there is no higher volume of deaths on the highway attributable to the movement of people seeking abortions. But beyond that speculation of mortal danger on the highways, Tribe thought there was a serious prospect of a "distorting effect on interstate commerce" or a "dislocation" of medical services. There would be a massive shift to the clinics of those states that permitted a freer access to abortion, and the result would be a "severe impact on medical services" in those areas.[17]

But there is no principle that tells us just what is the right or correct distribution of these surgeries among the States. In the absence of that standard of judgment, it would appear that certain states would simply be doing a more thriving business in these kinds of operations. Hitherto, the report of these currents of business has often been taken as signs of local prosperity, not as a malady that calls for federal restraint: Factory outlets crop up in New Hampshire and bring a massive stream of traffic from Massachusetts. On the other hand, the absence of major-league baseball in northern New England causes a persistent flow of baseball fans to Boston. In the presence of these trends, no one suggested that there was a "dislocation" of business or threats of massive traffic. Nor did anyone draw the inference that the federal government ought to be

16. See Tribe's statement in Senate Committee on Labor and Human Resources, *Hearings on The Freedom of Choice Act of 1991*, 103d Cong., 1st sess., 13 May 1992, 31–36, at 31.

17. Ibid., 32.

reducing the pressure to travel through the handy device of encouraging more factory outlets or insuring the presence of major-league teams in the other states.

And yet, from these cryptic intimations about injuries or dislocations, Tribe would invoke the authority of the national government to rush to the rescue under the commerce clause. With that device, the federal government would vindicate the right to abortion as a right of national citizenship. But once again, the supposed "right to travel," or the concern for "interstate commerce," is offered as an implausible surrogate. For Tribe, they do not supply, even remotely, his sense of the "wrong" engaged in this problem. That wrong, for him, has ever been the restriction on the freedom to order an abortion. The rhetorical straining over the "right to travel" is something that becomes necessary for him only because of the need to find some familiar formula that might explain, even tenuously, just why this matter should come within the reach of the federal government.

But even with an argument put forth knowingly as a contrivance, Tribe reveals his understanding as unreflectively as Aunt Sally revealed hers, when she remarked, "Well, it's lucky; because sometimes people do get hurt" [when steam engines blow up]. Tribe assumes, once again, that the bearer of the right, the one who merits our concern and solicitude, is the person who is seeking to order an abortion. It never seems to occur to him that the bearer of the right could be the intended victim of the abortion. If we looked at the matter with that lens, the commerce clause could even be used more persuasively on the other side; for it could be contended now that an abortion threatens most emphatically to interfere with the right of the fetus to travel in interstate commerce! And indeed, if we invoked the kinds of arguments that became familiar in the cases on civil rights, the engagement of the commerce clause would become even deeper: For after all, if abortions did not remove, each year, 1.5 million births, those babies would be generating a substantial demand for goods and services. If discrimination against blacks was said to depress the volume of trade between the states, it should be even more evident, by the same measure, that the current policy on abortion would have the most depressing effect on the interstate business in bassinets, baby food, toys, first cars, college educations, weddings—to say nothing of the production and revenue lost from a cohort of over a million new taxpayers who would start to come on the scene, in waves, eighteen years hence.

Once again, an accomplished professor of law is pretending that the concepts in the Constitution actually supply his understanding of the rights and wrongs of the matter. But in fact, he is fitting the document to suit his own purposes, and he is filling in the blanks of the Constitution. The commerce clause would not work at all toward Tribe's ends if we merely started with the rival assumption: that it is the child in the womb, rather than the pregnant woman, who is the bearer of the right; that it is the child who stands to suffer an even more emphatic restriction of her freedom, including her freedom to move in interstate commerce. But the Constitution itself evidently does not supply to Tribe an understanding of who is in fact the true bearer of the right. That is not, however, the point on which he chose to concentrate his considerable wit in deliberating about the problem. And if we take him at his word, nothing in the Constitution alerts us to that question or suggests any canons of reason for deliberating on the problem.

I have sought to show, at length, in another work, that we are obliged, persistently, to move "beyond the Constitution," to the principles antecedent to the Constitution, for the sake of applying the text to the cases that arise in our law. And it becomes necessary for us to deliberate in that style even as we try to settle the meaning of the rights that are mentioned in the text.[18] In this vein, I have tried to restate some of the arguments posed by the Federalists against a Bill of Rights. Those criticisms were not launched by men who were hostile to the notion of rights but, quite the contrary, by men who saw the protection of natural rights as the principal, defining end of the government. Their main concern was that the Bill of Rights would actually narrow or truncate the range of our rights, largely because it would misinstruct the American people about the ground of their rights. The Bill of Rights threatened to obscure the difference between natural law and positive law as the source of our rights (as seen, for example, in that expression, quite familiar in our discourse, about the freedoms of speech we enjoy "through the First Amendment"—as though, in the absence of that amendment, we would not bear these rights). And that central confusion, between natural right and positive right, would be advanced through the more common device of confounding principles with the

18. See my book, *Beyond the Constitution* (Princeton: Princeton University Press, 1990), especially chapter four, "On the Dangers of a Bill of Rights: Restating the Federalist Argument."

instances in which principles are manifested. The Bill of Rights would offer an inventory of items touching on searches and seizures and the quartering of troops in private houses. A citizen could commit the list to memory without learning anything much deeper about the principles that stand behind the list; the principles that may cover, in their reach, items that were never written down. To the current provisions in the first eight amendments, we might as plausibly add a right not to have our automobiles searched *unreasonably*, to have our luggage inspected *without cause*, or to have blood removed from our arms, without a compelling reason, after an auto accident. We might add these provisions to the kinds of passages that bar, say, "unreasonable" searches and seizures. We could go on in this way, listing without limit the variety of cases in which our freedom could be restricted unjustly, and yet we may never get clear on the matter that is truly decisive in these cases: namely, the grounds on which we make these distinctions between the restrictions on freedom that are justified or unjustified, reasonable or unreasonable.

The meaning of our "rights" in any case must always pivot on that question, and it must persistently drive us then outside the text of the Constitution to the principles of judgment. On this matter, some of us have made a minor living in arranging an array of cases, from our law, that bear out this point. I would pick out only one here for a brief mention. In *Edwards v. California*,[19] the Supreme Court was faced with a statute that barred people or corporations from bringing into California "any indigent person who is not a resident of the state, knowing him to be an indigent person." The Court was unanimous in striking down the statute, but the judges split into three separate opinions as they argued with a curious tenacity about the precise ground, in the Constitution, for the holding. Justice Byrnes wrote for the majority in using the commerce clause. That is to say, he professed to find, in this statute, an interference with the movement of persons and goods in a national community, with transactions moving across the boundaries of the states. Justice Douglas was mildly offended by this willingness to use the commerce clause and liken the movement of persons to the commerce in "cattle, fruit, [and] steel." He and Justice Jackson preferred to find the ground of the judgment in the clause on privileges and immunities and the rights of citizen-

19. Edwards v. California, 314 U.S. 160 (1941).

ship. One might have used also the equal protection clause and claimed that the state was creating two tiers in the freedom to move across the lines of the state, with some people denied that freedom solely on the basis of their indigence. The judges seemed firmly persuaded that their colleagues had the matter emphatically wrong, and yet the striking point is that all three of these judges made their way in the end to precisely the same ground for the judgment.

For quite apart from whether the judges used the commerce clause or the privileges and immunities clause or invoked the equal protection of the laws, all these clauses admitted the same understandings: Even with the commerce clause it was understood that the states may interpose certain barriers to movement through inspections for health and safety. Even with the privileges and immunities clause, it was understood that a state may bar the movement of people fleeing from prosecution. Under all these provisions, it was understood that the states could restrict the movement of persons because of contagion or criminality, and so the case would have to pivot finally on the question of just why indigence or poverty was not the same as contagion and criminality: Why would "indigence" not supply, then, a comparable justification for restricting the freedom of people to move across the lines of a state?

The problem finally came down to the understanding of "determinism": Poverty or wealth could not "determine" the moral character of any person, or to put it another way, we could not plausibly draw any moral inferences about people on the basis of their poverty and wealth, and establish that people *deserve* to be restrained from entering a state. Through one route or another, each of the judges made his way to this ultimate ground of the judgment. Justice Byrnes put it this way: "Poverty and immorality are not synonymous."[20] Justice Jackson rearranged the same understanding in this manner:

> 'Indigence' in itself is neither a source of rights nor a basis for denying them. The mere state of being without funds is a neutral fact—constitutionally an irrelevance, like race, creed, or color. . . . I think California had no right to make the condition of Duncan's purse, with no evidence of violation by him of any

20. Ibid., 176–77.

law or social policy which caused it, the basis of excluding him or of punishing one who extended him aid.[21]

The clauses in the Constitution alerted the judges to certain presumptive freedoms, but those clauses could not supply the grounds of judgment about the restrictions that were justified and the claims of freedom then that were rightful. In order to arrive at the grounds of judgment, the judges were compelled to move to a structure of moral judgment outside the text, to the canons of reasoning that could finally explain the restrictions, or disabilities, that were justified or unjustified.[22]

I must quickly add that I do not claim any striking originality here; I would think that, by this time, in the seasons of our experience, these points would have been long understood. And for that reason, I would think that a seasoned lawyer such as Laurence Tribe or Archibald Cox would know that he could not simply invoke the commerce clause as though it could settle a national policy on abortion. He could not pretend that the commerce clause itself would establish that an unborn child cannot be the bearer of rights. I would expect him to acknowledge that this kind of conclusion cannot be drawn in some mechanical way from the text: The conclusion must really depend on layers of principled reasoning about the grounds on which we regard the unborn child as anything less than a human being, or even an animal, who can claim some protections under the law. But when a practiced lawyer affects not to understand something that a tutored undergraduate can grasp without strain, one must wonder whether there is some other purpose at work that cannot be disclosed. For one reason or another, it is evidently not politic for Tribe to acknowledge an understanding that would render complicated or equivocal a case for abortion that he simply does not care to render, at this time, more complicated or equivocal.

But for Tribe, the reluctance to enter into a discipline of justifying rights may cover an even deeper problem: namely, that he has cut the ground out from under any claim to take seriously a "moral" standing of rights. He has done that mainly through the insistence that there are no moral truths that can supply the substance and justification of

21. Ibid., 184–85.
22. For a fuller argument of this point, and an extended discussion of the Edwards case, see *Beyond the Constitution*, 82–89 and passim.

rights in that moral sense. But without that moral substance, as I have said, "rights" cease to name things that are "truly rightful." When the claim to moral substance is removed, rights would be reduced mainly to a set of conventions or the assignment of certain freedoms and franchises in a system of conventions or rules, much in the way that the rules of baseball would give us the "right" to go to first base after four balls wide of the strike zone. For Tribe has professed, after all, that the standards governing his judgment are nothing more than "subjective." And he has held to that premise even when he has been given to the most emphatic pronouncements that certain arguments in the law are "plainly wrong" or "plainly right." Tribe has recorded his disclaimer in this way:

> Even if we could settle on firm constitutional postulates, we would remain inescapably *subjective* in the application of those postulates to particular problems and issues. . . . For me [the hard cases of constitutional interpretation] seem basically unanswerable; theories that offer or presuppose answers to them—*any* answers—seem not worth pursuing with passion or even worth criticizing in great detail. . . . [W]henever I suggest . . . for want of space or of humility, that one or another decision [of the courts] seems to me 'plainly right' or 'plainly wrong,' or that some proposal or position is 'clearly' consistent (or inconsistent) with the Constitution, I hope my words will be understood as shorthand not for a conclusion I offer as indisputably 'correct' but solely for a conviction I put forward as powerfully held. . . . [23]

Tribe has been willing, at any rate, to put forth his arguments with conviction, and the conviction repels any impression that Tribe suffers the least doubts about the truth, or the commanding plausibility, of his own arguments. In fact, it would be hard to account for the advocacy that surrounds the argument over abortion without recognizing that the cause has been affected with a moral passion: The freedom to choose an abortion has been translated into nothing less than a fundamental, "constitutional right," and that "right" has been put forth now with all of the properties that attach to a right in its stricter, moral sense. The proponents of a right to abortion have not claimed that rather

---

23. Tribe, *Constitutional Choices* (emphasis added on *subjective*).

diminished "right" that simply arises out of a system of rules or conventions, arbitrarily fashioned. They would not suggest that the "right to an abortion" stands on the same plane as the right to have a "designated hitter" on the field; a right that may be dissolved as readily as it was created, without the sense of anything truly important at stake. The "right to an abortion" has been regarded as something that runs far deeper than that, as something planted in the deeper postulates of right and wrong that stand behind the Constitution.

This matter was brought home to me in a telling way several years ago at one of those conferences assembled to mark the bicentennial of the Constitution. One professor of political theory began his presentation by denying that there were any natural rights in the strict sense; rights that have an independent or objective standing, apart from the local ethos or the local culture in which they are created. He argued, in the style of communitarianism, that all rights were conventional, that they grew out of a local discourse. The object, then, was to encourage people to find their citizenship and their character by engaging in this discourse. (That recipe seemed to be happily suited to professors and writers, who find it easier than mechanics and grocery clerks to engage in "discourse" as a way of life.) I made the comment in response that the domain of that public discourse was often contracted and diminished when the courts removed certain subjects from the hands of local legislatures—as, for example, in matters of pornography or abortion. If there is nothing that people can practically do to legislate on the matter of abortion, they quickly lose any real incentive to expend their energies in discourse on the subject. The discourse that compels citizens is the discourse that is important precisely because it is bound up with the practical shaping of the laws. I suggested then to the speaker that he might find himself coinciding with some conservatives who would return more subjects to the domain of local legislation and local discourse by having the courts recede from these questions and return them to the political arena.

The speaker met my point at a tangent by remarking that he certainly agreed with me on the matter of pornography. I pressed the point and asked whether he would agree also on the matter of abortion. To that, he simply repeated the announcement that he agreed with me on the question of pornography. The audience could hardly fail to notice the omission, and so from different parts of the hall voices were heard pressing the question and asking, "But *what about* abortion?" To which the speaker, taken aback, finally shouted, "No." "Why not?" someone else called. Because, he said, "people do have *rights!*" They have rights, that is, that do not depend on local conventions or on the opinions that are molded in a local discourse.

That begins to sound rather like the rudiments or properties of "natural rights," and it is certainly closer to the logic that Chairman Biden was invoking when he opened the hearings over Robert Bork in 1987. What was at stake for Biden and his allies in these hearings was the jurisprudence that sustained *Roe v. Wade*, with its claims for privacy and abortion. And in laying out the ground for the defense of those rights, Biden staked out a strong natural rights position, as a way of forming a sharper contrast with the legal positivism of Robert Bork:

> As a child of God [said Biden], I believe my rights are not derived from the Constitution. My rights are not derived from any government. My rights are not derived from any majority. *My rights are because I exist.* They were given to me and each of my fellow citizens by our creator and they represent the essence of human dignity.[24]

The argument here was that we possessed rights quite apart from the rights that were "posited," or set down, in a statute or in the Constitution. Against those claims of "positive" law, there were rights that existed before the advent of any statutes or constitutions, "rights" that simply sprung from our natures as human beings. Cast in that form, the moral and juridical notion of rights would be anchored in an *objective fact*, namely, the fact of human nature and the actual existence of a discrete, real person. But in that construction, Biden's understanding would seem to cover the child in the womb, as soon as that being comes to "exist." Yet, Senator Biden would not accept that implication, for it would extend the protections of natural law to the fetus, or the unborn child. And that understanding would certainly impair the claim, made by a pregnant woman, of a "right to an abortion." Apparently, Biden would avert this unwelcome meaning in his words by holding that there is something more doubtful about the "facts"

---

24. Senate Committee on the Judiciary, *Hearings on the Nomination of Robert Bork,* 100th Cong., 1st sess., 1987, 97 (emphasis added).

concerning the child in the womb: He may profess to be an agnostic on the question of whether there are any facts we are obliged to respect, as "facts," to establish just when the child has come to "exist" and whether that being in the womb can be said yet to be human.

That may be intelligible, but it would also represent a radical shift in the understanding of "natural rights." The force of natural rights arose from the claim that those rights are grounded in certain "truths" about human nature. But those rights would be called into serious doubt if those "truths" concerning human nature were thought to be matters merely of belief now, rather than truths. As Lincoln explained, the right of the black man to govern himself "depends on whether a negro is *not* or *is* a man":

> If he is *not* a man, why in that case, he who *is* a man may, as a matter of self-government, do just as he pleases with him. . . . [But] if the negro is a *man*, why my ancient faith teaches me that 'all men are created equal;' and that there can be no moral right in connection with one man's making a slave of another.[25]

If the black man were a man, then he would have the right of any other human being to be governed by his own consent. But what, or who, determined whether he was a human being? Senator Biden declared, in explaining the logic of natural rights, that he had rights that did not depend on the will of any majority, rights that claimed their own, independent ground of truth. Presumably then, he would not argue that human beings have a right to be free from slavery—and yet hold, at the same time, that whether they are regarded as human would depend on the opinions held by those around them. Of what sense would it be to claim that we have rights that do not depend on the sufferance of a majority and then say that our very standing as humans—as rights-bearing beings—may depend on the opinions of the majority? Or, even worse, could it depend on the opinions of those, like the owners of slaves, who have a direct interest in denying these rights? How, then, could the "existence," or the "human" standing of the child in the womb, be made any more dependent on the opinions or "beliefs" of others? Or, even worse, how

---

25. Speech on the Kansas-Nebraska Act, 1854, in *The Works of Abraham Lincoln*, ed. Roy P. Basler (New Brunswick, N.J.: Rutgers University Press, 1953), vol. 2, 265–66 (emphases in the original).

dependent on the opinions of those people who think that their own interests would be advanced by "terminating" the child?

A construction of that kind would make a shambles of the argument against slavery; it would also be an incoherent rendering of any argument that claims to be built on the ground of "natural rights." The understanding of natural law depends on the assumption that there is nothing subjective about the state of being a human. As Harry Jaffa has remarked, on this head, the question of whether anyone is a human being cannot be a "value judgment"; it cannot hinge on the question of whether anyone else attaches a value to our lives and happens to regard us as humans. At the very least, it must be a matter that lends itself—once again—to the light that may be cast by principled reasoning. Hence, I must find, for myself, a rather melancholy reflection on our time when the member of the Supreme Court who has been the most reserved about abortion declares, in dissent in the recent *Casey* case, that the question of when human life begins must be a "value judgment." This from Justice Scalia, who went on to observe that "some societies have considered newborn children not yet human, or the incompetent elderly no longer so."[26]

Scalia has endorsed the position of conservative jurisprudence on the question of abortion, in returning the matter entirely to the jurisdiction of the states. He had remarked in the *Cruzan* case, in 1990, that the point at which life becomes worthless or open to protection is not "set forth in the Constitution"; nor is it "known to the nine Justices of this Court any better than . . . [to] nine people picked at random from the Kansas City telephone directory."[27] Just who is a human being, just when life begins, are questions best determined through the taking of evidence and the settling of judgments, and Scalia seems to assume that the principles of the Constitution would have no bearing on the problem: Apparently, the Constitution could not be the source of any principles of reasoning that could test the plausiblity, or the arbitrariness, of the judgments reached in the separate states.

Scalia takes it for granted that any state may plausibly enact the policy of *Roe v. Wade* and establish a regime of "abortion on demand" at any stage of pregnancy. That is to say, Scalia assumes that the unborn child may be withdrawn entirely from a class of beings who are given

---

26. Planned Parenthood v. Casey, 120 L.Ed.2d 674 (1992), at 784.

27. Cruzan v. Director, Missouri Health Department, 111 L.Ed.2d 224 (1990), at 251 (concurring).

some protection in the law—that it may be treated, in that respect, as a being with even less of a claim to protection than the spotted owl—and that none of this would raise the slightest constitutional question.

But let us approach this matter gently from another angle by bringing back the hypothetical case I had introduced earlier. I had suggested a situation in which governments in the South were standing back and permitting assaults on the lives of black people. When this policy of the state is challenged, the state admits the legal validity of the Thirteenth and Fourteenth Amendments, but it insists at the same time that the amendments could apply plausibly only to people who are human. And it avers now that certain people of a deep color are not actually human. In support of this position, the state produces, as I suggested, an authoritative color chart, to measure gradations in shading and we are simply told, with the voice of authority, that these shadings mark degrees of "humanness."

There cannot be much doubt as to how a court would deal with an argument of that kind. Even a court composed of judicial conservatives is likely to say that the law was passed in a manner that was formally legal, but that it lacked the substance of justice. In one way or another, the judges would explain that the policy of the state withdrew the protections of law from people on the strength of criteria that were finally arbitrary. I would expect no one to be sharper than Justice Scalia in focusing the burden of demonstration that would be placed upon the state: The authorities would be compelled to show that there was some ground of principle, or scientific evidence, to support the claim that steps along the color chart truly marked off degrees of humanity, or discontinuities in nature, so that as soon as we exceeded, say, Shade 11, and moved to 12, we were no longer dealing with a human being.

Nothing in this method, or in this style of argument, would be alien to Scalia. What is astonishing, rather, is that Scalia, with his rich imagination, has still not made the connection. With a logical tenacity he has resisted those facile efforts, on the part of local authorities, to disguise "takings of property" as mere "regulations."[28] And his colleagues have often encountered efforts in the past to remove rights in different ways by classifying people as "aliens" or "indigents." But he

---

28. See, for example, Scalia in Nollan v. California Coastal Commission, 97 L.Ed.2d 677 (1987).

would seem to suggest now that he cannot summon the same powers of reason in challenging the grounds on which local authorities may simply classify some beings as "nonhuman"—and remove them altogether from the protections of the law. When it comes to other cases involving the manipulation of labels or classifications, Scalia has not thought that judges were obliged to stand, witless and gullible. He has tended to assume that the judges have resources for deliberating on the plausibility of the classifications or on the question of whether any of them would justify a withdrawal of rights.

Why, then, would it require anything novel to raise the same questions if the states begin legislating again on the matter of abortion? If a legislature allowed abortions up to the third trimester, or if it permitted abortions in the case of children who were likely to be infirm or retarded, why would the same style of reasoning not come into play? Why would it not be quite as plausible for us to ask: What separates the child in the womb at six months from the child at six months and a day? How could that child have crossed a barrier between the nonhuman and the human? What attributes, necessary to her standing as a human being, did she not have the day before, at the age of twenty-four weeks?

The only conclusion I can draw is that Scalia does not see this identity in the style of deliberation because his understanding is indeed mirrored in his words when he says that the question of human life must be a "value judgment": This question is apparently affected, for him, with far more of the inscrutable than the question of when a regulation becomes a "taking" or whether an alien may be deprived of a college education at the expense of the state. The question of life seems to be immured, for him, in layers of mystery as thick as the layers that render this question mystical for Archibald Cox or Laurence Tribe. And for these scholars of the law, conservative as well as liberal, the problem seems to be delivered to a domain beyond the canons of reason.

But to believe that the question has been removed in that way, from the reach of reason, is to to believe that members of our political class can no longer reason in the style of Lincoln, in that famous fragment he wrote for himself, when he imagined himself engaged in a conversation with the owner of a slave. I have quoted and overquoted this fragment, but it is probably worth recalling yet again. Lincoln put the question of why the slaveholder was justified in holding a black man as property:

You say A. is white, and B. is black. It is color, then: the lighter having the right to enslave the darker? Take care. By this rule, you are to be slave to the first man you meet, with a fairer skin than your own.

You do not mean *color* exactly?—You mean the whites are *intellectually* the superiors of the blacks, and therefore have the right to enslave them? Take care again. By this rule, you are to be slave to the first man you meet, with an intellect superior to your own.[29]

Nowhere, in this chain of reasoning, is there an appeal to revelation or religious belief, or to any of those irreducible opinions that could compose a "value judgment." I cannot believe that even the current members of our political class would not understand this fragment, or that they have lost the capacity to reason in this manner on any matter of consequence. In that event, we may ask why the same kind of reasoning would not be applied quite as aptly to the question of why the unborn child should be regarded as anything less than a human being, a bearer of rights, with a claim to the protections of the law. Again, I do not ask today for anyone to share my judgment on this momentous question. I merely ask why so many accomplished jurists and professors of law should regard the question as nearly inscrutable. And why do they assume that, however we identify the rights and wrongs of abortion, those judgments will have almost nothing to do with this brand of principled reasoning?

Whether we are dealing, then, with the Left or the Right, with so-called liberals or conservatives, the malady I am attributing to the lawyers remains the same. The positivism of these lawyers seems to have taken hold at a level far deeper than the reflexes that separate these people in the politics of our day. In that respect, I have been tempted in the past to invoke Henry James, to suggest that liberalism and conservativism among the judges are but "different chapters of the same general subject." The positivism of the judges and lawyers may be deepened by the "skepticism" of the age, and it may be fed, for liberals or conservatives, from different sources. For the liberals, it may be a recoil from the claim to know moral truths. For the conservatives, it may be a dubiety about the claims of reason or a recoil from people, swollen with conceit and moralism, who have been all too

---

29. Lincoln, *Works of Abraham Lincoln*, vol. 2, 222–23 (italics in original).

cavalier in annexing the claims of reason to their partisan agendas. But in either event, the result is the same. There is, on both sides, a recoil from reason and from the prospect of identifying rights, not by stipulation or declaration, but by the discipline of deliberating in a principled way about the grounds of judgment.

Both liberals and conservatives have professed their dubiety about natural rights, and yet both of them end up, in practice, depending on the logic of natural rights and appealing to their maxims. It is arguable that every corruption of natural law finds its origin in the doctrines of natural law, and the vices of positivism may also find their sources in the confusions cast up by the teachings of natural right. The claim that justice means nothing more than the rule of the strong is an argument that takes on its bite only when we have an awareness of the argument that it is seeking to resist. In this vein, Thrasymachus can become interesting, in Plato's *Republic*, only when he is set off against Socrates. But that is to say, these confusions of our own age have an ancient source. And yet, the proper rejoinder to them is no less ancient. In the opening pages of that classic work *The Rights of War and Peace*, Grotius took note of those people who have "despised what has been done in this province of jurisprudence, so far as to hold that no such thing existed, except as a mere name." They would turn rights into wrongs, as though the conversion involved nothing more than the alteration of labels. Or they would transmute "right" into the mere rule of the strong. They would declare nothing wrong that is useful. As Grotius remarked, "Antigonus laughed at a man, who, when he was besieging his enemies' cities, brought to him a Dissertation on Justice. And Marius said that the din of arms prevented his hearing the laws."[30] But the study of law and jurisprudence could not begin until these common errors were refuted and set aside, for as Grotius observed, almost in passing, as a matter nearly too obvious to bear an extended commentary, "our discussion of Rights is worthless if there are no Rights."[31]

And if some of our most accomplished lawyers can manage to detach themselves from these venerable fallacies, from these long-settled ways of changing the subject and missing the point, we too may resume; we may begin, again, the work of jurisprudence.

---

30. Grotius, *De Jure Belli et Pacis*, trans. William Whewell (1625; reprint, Cambridge: John W. Parker, 1853), vol. 1, xxxviii–xxxix.

31. Ibid., xl.

Is the Idea of Human Rights Ineliminably Religious?

Michael J. Perry

> We almost all accept . . . that human life in all its forms is *sacred*. . . . For some of us, this is a matter of religious faith; for others, of secular but deep philosophical belief.
>
> —Ronald Dworkin

> The conception of human rights, based upon the assumed existence of a human being as such, broke down at the very moment when those who professed to believe in it were for the first time confronted with people who had indeed lost all other qualities and specific relationships—except that they were still human. *The world found nothing sacred in the abstract nakedness of being human.*
>
> —Hannah Arendt

The name of the state where I was born and raised—Kentucky—derives from a Native American word meaning "the dark and bloody ground." An apt name for this century in which we have been born and raised—this century now ending—is the dark and bloody time: The twentieth century has surely been as unrelentingly dark and bloody as any in human history. In the midst of the countless grotesque inhumanities of the twentieth century, however, there is a heartening story: the emergence in international law of the idea of human rights and the protection by international law of what many

---

Epigraphs from Ronald Dworkin, "Life is Sacred. That's the Easy Part," *New York Times Magazine*, 16 May 1993, 36; Hannah Arendt, *The Origins of Totalitarianism* (New York: Harcourt Brace, 1973), 299 (emphasis added).

consider to be basic human rights. (Not that the idea of human rights is new. In one form or another, the idea is very old.[1])

The protection of human rights by international law in the period since the end of World War II—what I, following many others, shall call the internationalization of human rights—is an important and hopeful story, amply recounted elsewhere.[2] But it is not a story that should dispel our skepticism about the extent to which many basic human rights, notwithstanding their protection by international law, are really any better off now than they were before 1945. (Even in this final decade of the twentieth century, the furious slaughter of innocents continues—most famously, perhaps, in the former Yugoslavia.) Neither that story nor that skepticism is the subject of this chapter, however. The internationalization of human rights—and the attendant rhetoric of human rights so pervasive in the world today, especially in the Western world—presents an important occasion, in my view, for addressing several fundamental questions about human rights, in particular about the idea of human rights.

The idea of human rights—the idea that has emerged in international law in the period since World War II—is complex. In a book of my own that will eventually include this essay, I mean to explore all the main constituents of the idea. Here, however, I am interested only in one constituent, albeit a foundational one: the conviction that every

---

1. See Leszek Kolakowski, *Modernity on Endless Trial* (Chicago: University of Chicago Press, 1990), 214:

> It is often stressed that the idea of human rights is of recent origin, and that this is enough to dismiss its claims to timeless validity. In its contemporary form, the doctrine is certainly new, though it is arguable that it is a modern version of the natural law theory, whose origins we can trace back at least to the Stoic philosophers and, of course, to the Judaic and Christian sources of European culture. There is no substantial difference between proclaiming "the right to life" and stating that natural law forbids killing. Much as the concept may have been elaborated in the philosophy of the Enlightenment in its conflict with Christianity, the notion of the immutable rights of individuals goes back to the Christian belief in the autonomous status and irreplaceable value of the human personality.

2. See, for example, Louis B. Sohn, "The New International Law: Protection of the Rights of Individuals Rather Than States," *American University Law Review* 32 (1982): 1; Robert Drinan, *Cry of the Oppressed: The History and Hope of the Human Rights Revolution* (San Francisco: Harper & Row, 1987).

There are many good studies of different aspects of the international law of human rights. See, for instance, Philip Alston, *The United Nations and Human Rights: A Critical Appraisal* (Oxford: Clarendon Press, 1992); Theodor Meron, ed., *Human Rights in International Law: Legal and Policy Issues*, 2 vols. (Oxford: Clarendon Press, 1984).

human being is sacred. Is that conviction inescapably religious—and the idea of human rights, therefore, ineliminably religious?

"The International Bill of Human Rights," as it is sometimes called, consists of three documents. The first of the these, the Universal Declaration of Human Rights (1948), speaks, in the preamble, of "the inherent dignity . . . of all members of the human family" and of "the dignity and worth of the human person." In Article 1, the declaration proclaims: "All human beings . . . should act towards one another in a spirit of brotherhood." The second and third documents are the International Covenant on Civil and Political Rights (1976) and the International Covenant on Economic, Social and Cultural Rights (1976). The preamble common to both covenants echoes the universal declaration in speaking of "the inherent dignity . . . of all members of the human family." The universal declaration's preamble then states: "[T]hese rights derive from the inherent dignity of the human person. . . . " The Vienna Declaration and Programme of Action, adopted on June 25, 1993, by the UN-sponsored World Conference on Human Rights,[3] reaffirms this language in insisting that "all human rights derive from the dignity and worth inherent in the human person . . . "

A regional human rights document, the American Declaration of the Rights and Duties of Man (1948), begins: "The American peoples have acknowledged the dignity of the individual. . . . The American states have on repeated occasions recognized that the essential rights of man are not derived from the fact that he is a national of a certain state, but are based upon attributes of his human personality. . . . " The preamble to the American declaration proclaims: "All men . . . should conduct themselves as brothers to one another." Another regional document, the American Convention on Human Rights (1978), echoes the American declaration in stating, in the preamble, that "the essential rights of man are not derived from one's being a national of a certain state, but are based upon attributes of the human personality. . . ." Similarly, the African [Banjul] Charter on Human and Peoples' Rights (1986) says, in its preamble, that "fundamental human rights stem from the attributes of human beings. . . . "

3. The representatives of 171 states adopted by consensus The Vienna Declaration and Programme of Action.

The idea of human rights that informs these various international human rights documents (and many others) is, then, in part, the idea that *there is something about each and every human being, simply as a human being, such that certain choices should be made and certain other choices rejected; in particular, certain things ought not to be done to any human being and certain other things ought to be done for every human being.*[4] The "every human being, simply as a human being," is represented in the Universal Declaration of Human Rights (Article 2) by this language: "Everyone is entitled to all the rights and freedoms set forth in this Declaration, without distinction of any kind, such as race, colour, sex, language, religion, political or other opinion, national or social origin, property, birth or other status."[5] Both the International Covenant on Economic, Social and Cultural Rights and the International Covenant on Civil and Political Rights contain identical language.

What, precisely, is that "something about each and every human being, simply as a human being"—what is it about us "simply as human beings"—such that, in particular, certain things ought not to be done to us and certain other things ought to be done for us? To ask the question in the words of the American declaration, the American convention, and the African charter, what are the relevant "attributes" of each and every human being—the attributes on which "the essential rights of man" are based? The principal such attribute, according to the documents of the International Bill of Human Rights, is "the inherent dignity of all members of the human family" (from which, according to the documents, human rights derive).

What are we to make of such talk: talk about "the inherent dignity" of all human beings—about all human beings as members of one "family"—and about the importance, therefore, of all human beings acting toward one another "in a spirit of brotherhood"? It is

4. At least, certain things ought not to be done to any human being *in particular circumstances* and certain other things ought to be done for every human being *in particular circumstances.*

For some of the things that ought or ought not to be done, it may be the case that only some human beings, not all human beings, ought or ought not to do them.

For some of the things that ought or ought not to be done, the "ought" or "ought not" may be presumptive rather than unconditional or absolute.

5. Article 2 continues: "Furthermore, no distinction shall be made on the basis of the political, jurisdictional or international status of the country or territory to which a person belongs, whether it be independent, trust, non-self-governing or under any other limitation of sovereignty."

easy enough to understand such talk as *religious* talk.[6] (More about
that later.) But is it possible, finally, to understand such talk in a
nonreligious ("secular") sense? Is there, at least, a nonreligious equivalent for such talk—and, if so, what is it? Or must we conclude that the
idea of human rights is indeed ineliminably religious, that a fundamental constituent of the idea, namely, *the conviction that every human
being is sacred—that every human being is "inviolable,"*[7] *has "inherent dignity," is "an end in himself," or the like*—is inescapably religious?[8]

---

6. But cf. Robert Ombres, "The Ethics of Human Rights," *Law & Justice* 114/115
(1992): 140: "[R]eferences to God, Nature and even Human Nature were deleted from the
drafts of the 1948 Universal Declaration of Human Rights shortly before its adoption."

7. Cf. Ronald Dworkin, *Life's Dominion: An Argument About Abortion, Euthanasia,
and Individual Freedom* (New York: Alfred A. Knopf, 1993), 25: "Some readers . . . will
take particular exception to the term 'sacred' because it will suggest to them that the
conviction I have in mind is necessarily a theistic one. I shall try to explain why it is not,
and how it may be, and commonly is, interpreted in a secular as well as in a conventionally religious way. But 'sacred' does have ineliminable religious connotations for many
people, and so I will sometimes use 'inviolable' instead to mean the same thing, in
order to emphasize the availability of that secular interpretation."

8. Nietzsche was unrelentingly contemptuous of the conviction that every human
being is sacred—as, for example, in this bleak and sobering passage from *The Will to
Power*:

> In moving the doctrine of selflessness and love into the foreground, Christianity
> was in no way establishing the interests of the species as of higher value than the
> interests of the individual. Its real *historical* effect, the fateful element in its effect,
> remains, on the contrary, in precisely the enhancement of egoism, of the egoism of
> the individual, to an extreme (—to the extreme of individual immortality). Through
> Christianity, the individual was made so important, so absolute, that he could no
> longer be sacrificed: but the species endures only through human sacrifice— All
> "souls" became equal before God: but this is precisely the most dangerous of all
> possible evaluations! If one regards individuals as equal, one calls the species into
> question, one encourages a way of life that leads to the ruin of the species: Christian-
> ity is the counterprinciple to the principle of *selection*. If the degenerate and sick
> ("the Christian") is to be accorded the same value as the healthy ("the pagan"), or
> even more value, as in Pascal's judgment concerning sickness and health, then
> unnaturalness becomes law—
> This universal love of men is in practice the *preference* for the suffering, under-
> privileged, degenerate: it has in fact lowered and weakened the strength, the
> responsibility, the lofty duty to sacrifice men. All that remains, according to the
> Christian scheme of values, is to sacrifice oneself: but this residue of human
> sacrifice that Christianity concedes and even advises has, from the standpoint of
> general breeding, no meaning at all. The prosperity of the species is unaffected by
> the self-sacrifice of this or that individual (—whether it be in the monkish and
> ascetic manner or, with the aid of crosses, pyres, and scaffolds, as "martyrs" of
> error). The species requires that the ill-constituted, weak, degenerate, perish: but
> it was precisely to them that Christianity turned as a conserving force; it further
> enhanced that instinct in the weak, already so powerful, to take care of and

What does it means to say that a conviction (belief, idea, worldview, etc.) is or is not "religious"?⁹

In *Sources of the Self: The Making of the Modern Identity*, Charles Taylor has observed that "[t]he problem of the meaning of life is . . . on our agenda, however much we may jibe at the phrase."¹⁰ The problem of the meaning of life does not arise for everyone, it is not on everyone's agenda (even if, as Taylor says, it is on "our" agenda). But it does arise for many. The problem can even arise *again* for someone, after it had been resolved, or repressed—someone who had been convinced of the meaningfulness of life, but whose conviction has gradually been eroded or has suddenly been shattered. A principal occasion of its arising (or arising again)—at least, of its arising in an existential, as distinct from merely intellectual, way—is a searing encounter with such a common but elemental event as sickness, old age, or death. Another principal occasion is an encounter, whether personal or vicarious, with evil and the terrible, primal suffering evil causes. Such experiences, and experiences of other kinds, can leave one with a feeling that one is, or might be, a stranger, an alien, an exile, homeless, anxious, vulnerable, threatened, in a world, a uni-

---

preserve themselves and to sustain one another. What is "virtue" and "charity" in Christianity if not just this mutual preservation, this solidarity of weak, this hampering of selection? What is Christian altruism if not the mass-egoism of the weak, which divines that if all care for one another each individual will be preserved as long as possible?—

If one does not feel such a disposition as an extreme immorality, as a crime against life, one belongs with the company of the sick and possesses its instincts oneself—

Genuine charity demands sacrifice for the good of the species—it is hard, it is full of self-overcoming, because it needs human sacrifice. And this pseudo humaneness called Christianity wants it established that no one should be sacrificed— Friedrich Nietzsche, *The Will to Power*, trans. Walter Kaufmann and R. J. Hollingdale; ed. Walter Kaufmann (New York: Random House, 1967), 141–42.

9. My discussion here is adapted from a longer discussion elsewhere. See Michael J. Perry, *Love and Power: The Role of Religion and Morality in American Politics* (New York: Oxford University Press, 1991), chap. 5.

10. Charles Taylor, *Sources of the Self: The Making of the Modern Identity* (Cambridge: Harvard University Press, 1989), 18. Taylor also observes that "those whose spiritual agenda is mainly defined in this way are in a fundamentally different existential predicament from that which dominated most previous cultures and still defines the lives of other people today" (ibid). On the "notorious vagueness" of the question "What is the Meaning of Life?" see W. D. Joske, "Philosophy and the Meaning of Life," in E. D. Klemke, ed., *The Meaning of Life* (New York: Oxford University Press, 1981), 248 ff. See also R. W. Hepburn, "Questions about the Meaning of Life," in *The Meaning of Life*, 209.

verse, that is, finally and radically, unfamiliar, hostile, perhaps even pointless, absurd. Albert Camus wrote: "What, then, is that incalculable feeling that deprives the mind of the sleep necessary to life? A world that can be explained even with bad reasons is a familiar world. But, . . . in a universe suddenly divested of illusions and lights, man feels an alien, a stranger. His exile is without remedy since he is deprived of the memory of a lost home or the hope of a promised land. This divorce between man and his life, the actor and his setting, is properly the feeling of absurdity."[11]

Because of its radically alienating character, any such experience can be an occasion of existential confrontation with the problem of meaning:

> Am I indeed an alien, an exile, homeless, in a world, a universe, that is strange, hostile, pointless, absurd? Or, instead, is the world, finally and radically, familiar, even gracious; does the world have a point, is it a project; is the world, in that sense, meaningful: meaning-full, full of meaning rather than bereft of it (and therefore meaning-less, absurd)? In particular, is the world hospitable to me in my deep yearning to be at home, rooted, connected?[12]

For the person deep in the grip of, the person claimed by, the problem of meaning, "[t]he cry for meaning is a cry for ultimate relationship, for ultimate belonging," wrote Abraham Heschel. "It is a cry in which all pretensions are abandoned. Are we alone in the wilderness of time, alone in the dreadfully marvelous universe, of which we are a part and where we feel forever like strangers? Is there a Presence to live by? A Presence worth living for, worth dying for? Is there a way

---

11. Albert Camus, *The Myth of Sisyphus and Other Essays* (New York: Vintage Books, 1955). See Leszek Kolakowski, *The Presence of Myth* (Chicago: University of Chicago Press, 1989), esp. chap. 8, "The Phenomenon of the World's Indifference." Cf. Blaise Pascal, *Pensees* (New York: Viking, 1966), 95: "The eternal silence of these infinite spaces fills me with dread."

12. See David Tracy, *Plurality and Ambiguity: Hermeneutics, Religion, Hope* (San Francisco: Harper & Row, 1987), 87: "Like strictly metaphysical questions, religious questions must be questions on the nature of Ultimate Reality. Unlike metaphysical questions, religious questions deliberately ask the question of the meaning and truth of Ultimate Reality not only as it is in itself *but as it is existentially related to us*. The religious classics are testimonies to the responses of the religions to those questions" (emphasis added).

of living in the Presence? Is there a way of living compatible with the Presence?"[13]

One fundamental response to the problem of meaning is "religious": the trust that the world is finally meaningful, meaningful in a way hospitable to our deepest yearnings. The word *religion* derives from the Latin verb *religare*, which means to bind together again that which was once bound but has since been torn or broken; to heal.[14] A "religious" vision, then, etymologically understood, is a vision of final and radical reconciliation, a set of beliefs about how one is or can be bound or connected to the world—to the "other" and to "nature"—and, above all, to Ultimate Reality in a profoundly intimate way. If a worldview is not grounded or embedded in a vision of the finally or ultimately meaningful nature of the world and of our place in it, it is a confusion, on the understanding of religion I'm presenting here, to think of that worldview as "religious"—even if the worldview, like Marxism, is all-encompassing.[15]

Throughout human history it has been the religious "mystics" who have trusted most deeply and affirmed most passionately the ultimate meaningfulness of reality.[16] Although such a person's experi-

---

13. Abraham Heschel, *Who Is Man?* (Stanford: Stanford University Press, 1965), 75. Cf. Fyodor Dostoevsky, *The Brothers Karamazov* (New York: Norton, 1976), 235: "For the secret of man's being is not only to live but to have something to live for. Without a stable conception of the object of life, man would not consent to go on living, and would rather destroy himself than remain on earth, though he had bread in abundance." (This is one of the Grand Inquisitor's statements in chapter 5 of Book Five.)

14. Cf. "Religion," *Oxford English Dictionary*, vol. 13 (Oxford: Oxford University Press, 1989), 568.

15. See David Braybrooke, "Ideology," in *Encyclopedia of Philosophy*, vol. 4, ed. Paul Edwards (New York: Macmillan, 1967), 124.

16. Harvey Egan has written that "there is a sense in which all great religions are mystical at heart and that mysticism is the full-flowering of any religious tradition." Harvey Egan, *What Are They Saying About Mysticism?* (New York: Paulist Press, 1982), 17. According to Wayne Proudfoot, the very ubiquity of mystical experience among the world religions suggests that mysticism may be regarded as "a *paradigm* of religious experience." Wayne Proudfoot, *Religious Experience* (Berkeley: University of California Press, 1985), xviii. Some commentators distinguish between two fundamental types of mystical experience, two kinds of experience of union with God or the Absolute: (1) the experience of union but not identity with God (as attested to by mystics in theistic traditions such as Christianity, Judaism, and Islam), and (2) the experience of complete absorption into the divine. Cf. Proudfoot, *Religious Experience*, 121: "The terms in which the subject understands what is happening to him are constitutive of the experience; consequently those in different traditions have different experiences. Jewish and Buddhist mystics [for example] bring entirely different doctrinal commitments, expecta-

ence that the world is ultimately meaningful is deeply personal, the religious mystic denies that the experience is reducible to an idiosyncratic, perhaps even pathological, psychological state. Notwithstanding its noetic quality, however, and for all its power, the mystical experience is often, if not invariably, transitory.[17] Moreover, not everyone is graced by such experience (or graced as often, or to the same degree). In the aftermath of mystical experience, therefore, or in its absence, fundamental questions about the meaningfulness of human existence—questions that so thoroughly pervade, and so relentlessly subvert, our lives—remain in need of answers that are intellectually satisfying and emotionally resonant. In Milan Kundera's *The Unbearable Lightness of Being*, the narrator, speaking of "the questions that had been going through Tereza's head since she was a child," says that "the only truly serious questions are ones that even a child can formulate. Only the most naive of questions are truly serious. They are the questions with no answers. A question with no answer is a barrier that cannot be breached. In other words, *it is questions with no answers that set the limits of human possibilities, describe the boundaries of human existence.*"[18] Communities, especially historically extended communities—"traditions"— are the principal matrices and repositories of religious answers to such questions:[19] Who

tions, and rules for identifying their mental and bodily states to their experiences, and thus *devekuth* and *nirvana* cannot be the same."

17. According to William James, "transience" is a third mark of mystical experience. Commenting on James, Proudfoot writes: "The two secondary marks by which James characterizes the mystical state, transience and passivity, are also related to the noetic quality of the experience. Passivity conveys the sense of being grasped and of being subject to some power beyond oneself. Both passivity and transience reflect the perception that the experience is not under the subject's voluntary control. It cannot be manipulated or guaranteed by the subject's decision or by causes that he might set in motion. He can prepare himself for it, but the experience is finally not subject to his control. The rules for the identification of an experience as mystical include the condition that he judge it to be something other than an artifact of his own thought and actions." Proudfoot, *Religious Experience*, 147–48.

18. Milan Kundera, *The Unbearable Lightness of Being* (New York: Harper & Row, 1984), 139 (emphasis added).

19. "Not the individual man nor a single generation by its own power, can erect the bridge that leads to God. Faith is the achievement of many generations, an effort accumulated over centuries. Many of its ideas are as the light of the star that left its source a long time ago. Many enigmatic songs, unfathomable today, are the resonance of voices of bygone times. There is a collective memory of God in the human spirit, and it is this memory which is the main source of our faith." From Abraham Heschel's two-part essay "Faith," first published in volume 10 of *The Reconstructionist*, Nov. 3 and 17,

are we? Where did we come from; what is our origin, our beginning? Where are we going; what is our destiny, our end?[20] What is the meaning of suffering? Of evil? Of death? And there is the cardinal question, the question that comprises many of the others: Is the world ultimately meaningful or, instead, ultimately bereft of meaning, meaning-less, absurd? If any questions are fundamental, *these* questions—"religious or limit questions"[21]—are fundamental. Such questions—"naive" questions, "questions with no answers," "barriers that cannot be breached"—are "the most serious and difficult . . . that any human being or society must face. . . . To formulate such questions honestly and well, to respond to them with passion and rigor, is the work of all theology. . . . Religions ask and respond to such fundamental questions. . . . Theologians, by definition, risk an intellectual life on the wager that religious traditions can be studied as authentic responses to just such questions."[22]

To say that a conviction is "religious," therefore, is to say that the conviction is embedded in a religious vision or cosmology, that it is an aspect, a constituent, of such a vision: a vision according to which the world is ultimately meaningful (in a way hospitable to our deepest yearnings). (Of course, not every religious tradition tells the same story about the way in which the world is ultimately meaningful; often the stories are different, even if sometimes the stories are quite similar.) To ask if the conviction that every human being is sacred—the conviction that every human being is "inviolable," has "inherent dignity," is "an end in himself," or the like—is inescapably religious is to ask if the conviction can be embedded in, if it can be supported by—or, at least, if it can cohere with—either a nonreligious cosmol-

1944. For a later statement on faith, incorporating some of the original essay, see Abraham Heschel, *Man Is Not Alone* (New York: Harper & Row, 1951), 159–76. On community/tradition as a principal matrix of moral beliefs, see Michael J. Perry, *Morality, Politics, and Law* (New York: Oxford University Press, 1988), 24–33.

  20. See Robert Coles, *The Spiritual Life of Children* (Boston: Houghton Mifflin, 1990), 37: "The questions Tolstoy asked, and Gauguin in, say, his great Tahiti triptych, completed just before he died ('Where Do We Come From? What Are We? Where Are We Going?'), are the eternal questions children ask more intensely, unremittingly, and subtly than we sometimes imagine." Cf. Heschel, *Who Is Man?*, 28: "In an old rabbinic text three other questions are suggested: '*Whence* did you come?' '*Whither* are you going?' 'Before *whom* are you destined to give account?' "

  21. Tracy, *Plurality and Ambiguity*, 86.

  22. David Tracy, *The Analogical Imagination* (New York: Crossroads, 1981), 4.

ogy, according to which the world is, at the end of the day, not mean-ingful but meaningless, or a cosmological agnosticism that neither affirms nor denies the ultimate meaningfulness of the world.

Real moralities—the moralities that various human communities have actually lived—have always been cosmologically embedded: In every human community across time and space, "moral norms are closely linked to beliefs about the facts of human life and the world in which human life is set. . . . To know what people find good in human action, we must know something about the powers and vulnerabilities they find characteristically human, and about how they explain the constraints that nature, power, finitude, and mortality impose on per-sons. . . . [W]hen they formulate moral norms and impose them on themselves and others, [persons] are trying to formulate relationships between realities and human purposes that allow them 'to live as [they] would in a world that is the way it is.'"[23] The conviction that every human being is sacred is cosmologically embedded; it is (as we will see) embedded in a religious cosmology.[24] Indeed, in one or another version the conviction is embedded in more than one religious cosmology.[25] The question before us is whether the conviction can be embedded in (or if it can cohere with) either a nonreligious cosmology or a cosmologi-cal agnosticism.

As I said, it is easy to understand talk about "the inherent dignity" of all human beings and related talk—for example, about all human beings as members of one "family"—as *religious* talk. But can we understand such talk in a secular sense? I now want to present a religious version of talk about the inherent dignity of all human be-ings; that is, I want to present a religious version—the Christian version, or at least *a* Christian version—of the conviction that every human being is sacred. We will then be in a better position to discern

---

23. Robin W. Lovin and Frank E. Reynolds, "Focus Introduction," *Journal of Reli-gious Ethics* 14 (1986): 48, 56–57. See id.; Robin W. Lovin and Frank E. Reynolds, "In the Beginning," in Robin W. Lovin and Frank E. Reynolds, eds., *Cosmogony and Ethical Order: New Studies in Comparative Ethics* (1985), 1.

24. Cf. Nietzsche, *Will to Power*, 184: "What is the *counterfeiting* aspect of morality?— It pretends to *know* something, namely what 'good and evil' is. That means wanting to know why mankind is here, its goal, its destiny. That means wanting to know that mankind *has* a goal, a destiny—" What was Nietzsche's teleology? See 544–50 ("The Eternal Recurrence").

25. See note 51 and accompanying text.

whether there is—indeed, whether there can be—an intelligible secular version of the conviction.

For Christians, the basic shape of the good life is indicated by the
instruction given by Jesus at a Passover seder on the eve of his execu-
tion: "I give you a new commandment: love one another; you must
love one another just as I have loved you."[26] The "one another" is
radically inclusive: "You have heard how it was said, You will love
your neighbor and hate your enemy. But I say this to you, love your
enemies and pray for those who persecute you; so that you may be
children of your Father in heaven, for he causes his sun to rise on the
bad as well as the good, and sends down rain to fall on the upright
and the wicked alike. For if you love those who love you, what re-
ward will you get? Do not even the tax collectors do as much? And if
you save your greetings for your brothers, are you doing anything
exceptional? Do not even the gentiles do as much? You must therefore
set no bounds to your love, just as your heavenly Father sets none to
his."[27]

    But *why* should we "love one another"? The answer, in the vision
of Judaism and Christianity, a vision nourished by what David Tracy
has called "the analogical imagination,"[28] is that the Other (the outsider, the stranger, the alien), too, no less than oneself and the mem-

    26. John 13:34. See John 15:12, 17. (This and the other translations in this chapter
are those of *The New Jerusalem Bible* [Garden City: Doubleday, 1985].) See generally
Edmun Santurri and William Werpehowski, eds., *The Love Commandments: Essays in
Christian Ethics and Moral Philosophy* (Washington, D.C.: Georgetown University Press,
1992). See also Garth L. Hallett, *Christian Neighbor-Love: An Assessment of Six Rival
Versions* (1989). (For a recent collection of secular philosophical essays on "altruism,"
see *Social Philosophy & Policy* 10 [1993]: 1–245.) On the relation between the commandment to "love God" and the commandment to "love one another," see note 44. Cf.
Nietzsche, *Will to Power,* 183: " '[L]ove': the ideal state of the herd animal that no longer
wants to have enemies."
    27. Matthew 5:43–48. See Luke 6:27–35. (Such a conception of the good is not
confined to semitic spiritualities: For Buddhists, for example, the good life centrally
involves compassion [*karuna*] for all sentient creatures and therefore for all human
beings.) Cf. Nietzsche, *Will to Power,* 120: "One drives nature out of morality when one
says 'Love your enemies': for then the natural 'Thou shalt love thy neighbor and hate
thy enemy' in the law (in instinct) has become meaningless; then this love of one's
neighbor must also find a new basis (as a kind of love of God). Everywhere, God is
inserted and utility withdrawn; everywhere the real origin of morality is denied: the
veneration of nature, which lies precisely in the recognition of a natural morality, is
destroyed at its roots—"
    28. See Tracy, *Analogical Imagination.*

bers of one's family or of one's tribe or nation or race or religion, is a "child" of God—God the creator and sustainer of the universe, imag-(in)ed, analogically, as loving "parent"[29]—and therefore a "sister" or "brother." As Hilary Putnam has written, the moral image central to what Putnam calls the Jerusalem-based religions "stresse[s] equality and also fraternity, as in the metaphor of the whole human race as One Family, of all women and men as sisters and brothers."[30] (At the beginning of its Pastoral Letter on Catholic Social Teaching and the U.S. Economy, titled *Economic Justice for All*, the National Conference of Catholic Bishops wrote: "This letter is a personal invitation to Catholics to use the resources of our faith, the strength of our econ-omy, and the opportunities of our democracy to shape a society that better protects the dignity and basic rights of our *sisters and brothers both in this land and around the world.*"[31]) In a recent essay on "The Spirituality of The Talmud," Ben Zion Bokser and Baruch M. Bokser state: "From this conception of man's place in the universe comes the sense of the supreme sanctity of all human life. 'He who destroys one person has dealt a blow at the entire universe, and he who sustains or saves one person has sustained the whole world.' "[32] They continue:

> The sanctity of life is not a function of national origin, religious affiliation, or social status. In the sight of God, the humble citizen is the equal of the person who occupies the highest office. As one talmudist put it: "Heaven and earth I call to witness, whether it be an Israelite or pagan, man or woman, slave or maidservant, according to the work of every human being doth the Holy Spirit rest upon him." . . . As the rabbis put it: "We are obligated to feed non-Jews residing among us even as we feed Jews; we are obligated to visit their sick even as we visit the Jewish sick; we are obligated to attend to the burial of their dead even as we attend to the burial of the Jewish dead."[33]

---

29. In the Bible, God—Ultimate Reality—is often imaged as "parent," sometimes as "father," sometimes as "mother." Cf. Eizabeth Johnson, *She Who Is: The Mystery of God in Feminist Theological Discourse* (New York: Crossroads, 1992).

30. Hilary Putnam, *The Many Faces of Realism* (LaSalle: Open Court, 1987), 60–61.

31. National Conference of Catholic Bishops, *Economic Justice for All* (1986), v (emphasis added).

32. Ben Zion Bokser and Baruch M. Bokser, "Introduction: The Spirituality of the Talmud," in *The Talmud: Selected Writings* (New York: Paulist Press, 1989), 7.

33. Ibid., 30–31.

Friedrich Nietzsche was relentlessly critical of what he called "the
concept of the 'equal value of men before God.'" That concept, he
wrote,

> is extraordinarily harmful; one forbade actions and attitudes that
> were in themselves among the prerogatives of the strongly
> constituted—as if they were in themselves unworthy of men.
> One brought the entire tendency of the strong into disrepute
> when one erected the protective measures of the weakest (those
> who were weakest also when confronting themselves) as a form
> of value.
>
> Confusion went so far that one branded the very virtuosi of life
> (whose autonomy offered the sharpest antithesis to the vicious
> and unbridled) with the most opprobrious names. Even now one
> believes one must disapprove of a Cesare Borgia; that is simply
> laughable. The church has excommunicated German emperors
> on account of their vices: as if a monk or priest had any right to
> join in a discussion about what a Frederick II may demand of
> himself. A Don Juan is sent to hell: that is very naive. Has it been
> noticed that in heaven all interesting men are missing?—Just a
> hint to the girls as to where they can best find their salvation.—If
> one reflects with some consistency, and moreover with a deep-
> ened insight into what a "great man" is, no doubt remains that
> the church sends all "great men" to hell—it fights *against* all
> "greatness of man." . . .
>
> The degeneration of the rulers and the ruling classes has been
> the cause of the greatest mischief in history! Without the Roman
> Caesars and Roman society, the insanity of Christianity would
> never have come to power.
>
> When lesser men begin to doubt whether higher men exist,
> then the danger is great! And one ends by discovering that there
> is *virtue* also among the lowly and subjugated, the poor in spirit,
> and that *before God* men are equal—which has so far been the *non
> plus ultra* of nonsense on earth! For ultimately, the higher men
> measured themselves according to the standard of virtue of
> slaves—found they were "proud," etc., found all their higher
> qualities reprehensible.
>
> When Nero and Caracalla sat up there, the paradox arose: "the
> lowest man is worth more than the man up there!" And the way

was prepared for an image of God that was as remote as possible from the image of the most powerful—the god on the cross![34]

One might respond to the religious vision sketched here, if not like Nietzsche, then this way: "Even if I assume, for the sake of argument, that the Other is a 'child' of God and therefore my 'sister' or 'brother,' still, why should I love the Other? In particular, why should I give a damn about the well-being of her or him who is, in some deep sense, my sister or my brother?" For us—or, at least, for most of us—it is a fundamental conviction, born not merely of our own experience, but of the experience of the historically extended communities ("traditions") that for many of us have been formative, that an important constituent of one's own well-being—of one's authentic flourishing as a human being—is concern for the well-being of one's sisters and brothers. We believe, based on that experience, that a life of loving connection to one's sisters and brothers is, to that extent, a flourishing life and that a life of unloving—uncaring—alienation from one's sisters and brothers is, to that extent, a withering life. This fundamental conviction about human good—about what it means to be (truly, fully) human, about what is of real and ultimate value in life, about what makes a life most deeply meaningful[35]—is, for us, bedrock; this is where our spade is turned.[36] There may be little of resonance for us to say, if indeed there is anything, *to* one who rejects the conviction—which, it bears emphasis, is not necessarily, for a person whose conviction it is, a religious conviction. But there is this to say *about* one who rejects it: He or she is, by our lights, no less in the grip of a pathology of estrangement than if he or she were to reject that an important constituent of one's own well-being is concern for the well-being of one's child, or spouse, or parent.[37] (" . . . Plato got moral philosophy off on the wrong foot. He led

34. Nietzsche, *Will to Power*, 466–68.

35. See Martha Nussbaum, *Aristotle on Human Nature and the Foundations of Ethics* (St. Lawrence: St. Lawrence University, 1990), 22: "[T]o find out what our nature is seems to be one and the same thing as to find out what we deeply believe to be most important and indispensable [in a human life]."

36. See Ludwig Wittgenstein, *Philosophical Investigations* (Oxford: Basil Blackwell, 1953), sec. 217, "I have reached bedrock, and this is where my spade is turned."

37. Cf. Robert Nozick, *Philosophical Explanations* (Cambridge: Harvard University Press, 1981), 403:

Recall Glaucon's challenge to Socrates in Plato's *Republic*: show that being moral is better for the agent, apart from its external consequences. To isolate these consequences, Glaucon imagines a ring that makes someone invisible. With this

moral philosophers to concentrate on the rather rare figure of the psychopath, the person who has no concern for any human being other
than himself. Moral philosophy has systematically neglected the much
more common case: the person whose treatment of a rather narrow
range of featherless bipeds is morally impeccable, but who remains
indifferent to the suffering of those outside this range, the ones he or
she thinks of as pseudohumans."[38]) The serious question among us—
some of whom count ourselves religious, but others of whom do not—
is not whether a life of loving connection to our sisters and brothers is
(to that extent) a flourishing life, but this: "Who is my sister? Who is my
brother?"[39] Or, in a different but spiritually equivalent terminology:

---

ring he is able to act immorally with no external penalty: he can rob, murder, and
rape without being caught or punished. Is there any reason why he should not do
this? Glaucon sharpens the issue by imagining that the immoral man has the
reputation of being moral, he is honored and praised as moral, while another man
is thought to be immoral and so is condemned and shunned. Glaucon asks Socrates to show, despite this, that the second moral person is better off than the first
immoral one, that we would be better off being that second than the first.
"[T]he answer that [Plato] puts into the mouth of Socrates is that the just man is happy
because his soul is harmoniously ordered, because, as we would say, he has an integrated personality, whereas the unjust man's personality is disintegrated, and the man
who represents the extreme of injustice is psychotic, his soul is a chaos of internal
strife." John Mackie, *Ethics: Inventing Right and Wrong* (New York: Penguin Press, 1977),
190–91. Should we take Socrates' response seriously? See Bernard Williams, *Ethics and
the Limits of Philosophy* (Cambridge: Harvard University Press, 1985), 46:

> There is also the figure, rarer perhaps than Callicles supposed, but real, who is
> horrible enough and not miserable at all but, by any ethological standard of the
> bright eye and the gleaming coat, dangerously flourishing. For those who want to
> ground the ethical life in psychological health, it is something of a problem that
> there can be such people at all. But it is a significant question, how far their
> existence, indeed the thought of their existence, is a cultural phenomenon. They
> seem sleeker and finer at a distance. Some Renaissance grandee fills such a role
> with more style than the tawdry fascist bosses, gangsters, or tycoons who seem,
> even as objects of fantasy, to be their chief contemporary instances. Perhaps we
> deceive ourselves about the past.

38. Richard Rorty, "Human Rights, Rationality, and Sentimentality," in *On Human
Rights*, ed. Stephen Shute and Susan Hurley (New York: Basic, 1993), 111, 123–24.
39. See James Burtchaell, "The Source of Conscience," *Notre Dame Magazine* 13
(winter 1984–85): 20, 20–21:

> The Catholic tradition embraces a long effort to uncover the truth about human
> behavior and experience. Our judgments of good and evil focus on whether a
> certain course of action will make a human being grow and mature and flourish, or
> whether it will make a person withered, estranged and indifferent. In making our
> evaluations, we have little to draw on except our own and our forebears' experi-
> ence, and whatever wisdom we can wring from our debate with others. . . .
> What we are trying to unpuzzle are things like childbearing and immigration

"Who is my neighbor?"[40]—which is the very question to which, according to Luke's Gospel, Jesus responded with the parable of the Good Samaritan.[41]

---

and economic policy and infant mortality and drug use and family fidelity and so much else about which we must frame moral judgments. With our fellow communicants we share commitments and assumptions: that we are happier giving than getting, that there is no greater love than to put down your life for your neighbor, and that your neighbor always turns out to be the most unlikely person.
On our neighbor always turning out to be the most unlikely person, see note 41 and accompanying text (parable of the Good Samaritan). (For a revised version of Burtchaell's essay, and for several other illuminating essays by Father Burtchaell, see James Burtchaell, *The Giving and Taking of Life* [Notre Dame: University of Notre Dame Press, 1989].)

40. See Matthew 22:34–40: "But when the Pharisees heard that he had silenced the Sadducees they got together and, to put him to the test, one of them put a further question, 'Master, which is the greatest commandment of the Law?' Jesus said to him, 'You must love the Lord your God with all your heart, with all your soul, and with all your mind. This is the greatest and the first commandment. The second resembles it: You must love your neighbor as yourself. On these two commandments hang the whole Law, and the Prophets too." See also Mark 12:28–34; Luke 10:25–28. (On the relation between the two commandments, see note 44.) Cf. Mackie, *Ethics*, 243: "D. D. Raphael, in 'The Standard of Morals', in Proceedings of the Aristotelian Society 75 (1974–75) follows Edward Ullendorff in pointing out that whereas 'Thou shalt love thy neighbor as thyself' represents the Greek of the Septuagint (Leviticus 19:18) and of the New Testament, the Hebrew from which the former is derived means rather 'You shall treat your neighbor lovingly, for he is like yourself.' " (Thus, Bruce Ackerman need not worry that he is being asked to love the "stranger" as himself. *That*, protests Ackerman, "[o]nly a God could do . . . : there are too many strangers with too many strangenesses." Bruce Ackerman, *The Future of Liberal Revolution* [New Haven: Yale University Press, 1992], 21.)

41. See Luke 10:29–37:
But the man was anxious to justify himself and said to Jesus, "And who is my neighbour?" In answer Jesus said, "A man was once on his way down from Jerusalem to Jericho and fell into the hands of bandits; they stripped him, beat him and then made off, leaving him half dead. Now a priest happened to be travelling down the same road, but when he saw the man, he passed by on the other side. In the same way a Levite who came to the place saw him, and passed by on the other side. But a Samaritan traveller who came on him was moved with compassion when he saw him. He went up to him and bandaged his wounds, pouring oil and wine on them. He then lifted him onto his own mount and took him to an inn and looked after him. Next day, he took out two denarii and handed them to the innkeeper and said, 'Look after him, and on my way back I will make good any extra expense you have.' Which of these three, do you think, proved himself a neighbour to the man who fell into the bandits' hands?" [The man] replied, "The one who showed pity towards him." Jesus said to him, "Go, and do the same yourself."
In the annotation of *The New Jerusalem Bible*, a footnote appended to "Samaritan" says that "[t]he contrast is between the element in Israel most strictly bound to the law of

One response to the question, a religious response, is that the Other, too, is, in the deepest possible sense—that is, as a child of God—your sister or brother. To fail to "see" the Other as sister or brother is (according to this religious response) to succumb to a kind of blindness: blindness to the true nature or being both of the Other and of oneself, which nature/being consists partly in a profound kinship (connection, relatedness) between self and Other. And to fail to love the Other as sister or brother—worse, to hate the Other—is to succumb to the pathology of estrangement; it is, to that extent, to wither as a human being rather than to flourish.[42] That the estrangement is radical—indeed, that it is estrangement even from "the Lord your God"[43]—and involves the most fundamental and enduring failure to achieve human well-being, is emphasized in the searing "Last Judgment" passage of Matthew:

> When the Son of man comes in his glory, escorted by all the angels, then he will take his seat on his throne of glory. All nations will be assembled before him and he will separate people from one another as the shepherd separates sheep from goats. He will place the sheep on his right hand and the goats on his left. Then the King will say to those on his right hand, "Come, you whom my Father has blessed, take as your heritage the kingdom prepared for you since the foundation of the world. For I was hungry and you gave me food, I was thirsty and you gave me drink, I was a stranger and you made me welcome, lacking clothes and you clothed me, sick and you visited me, in prison and you came to see me." Then the upright will say to him in reply, "Lord, when did we see you hungry and feed you, or thirsty and give you drink? When did we see you a stranger and make you welcome, lacking clothes and clothe you? When did we find you sick or in prison and go to see you?" And the King will answer, "In truth I tell you, in so far as you did this to one of the least of these brothers of mine, you did it to me." Then he will

love, and the heretic and stranger, . . . from whom normally only hate could be expected."

42. I may love the Other even if I do not understand that the Other is my sister or brother. And I may understand that the Other is my sister or brother and yet fail to love the Other.

43. See note 40.

say to those on his left hand, "Go away from me, with your curse upon you, to the eternal fire prepared for the devil and his angels. For I was hungry and you never gave me food, I was thirsty and you never gave me anything to drink, I was a stranger and you never made me welcome, lacking clothes and you never clothed me, sick and in prison and you never visited me." Then it will be their turn to ask, "Lord, when did we see you hungry or thirsty, a stranger or lacking clothes, sick or in prison, and did not come to your help?" Then he will answer, "In truth I tell you, in so far as you neglected to do this to one of the least of these, you neglected to do it to me." And they will go away to eternal punishment, and the upright to eternal life.[44]

---

44. Matthew 25:31–46. In Matthew's Gospel, these are Jesus' final words to his disciples before the beginning of the passion narrative. Matthew 26:1–2 states: "Jesus had now finished all he wanted to say, and he told his disciples, 'It will be Passover, as you know, in two days' time, and the Son of Man will be handed over to be crucified.' "
In the view of great German Catholic theologian Karl Rahner—a view consistent with the eschatology of the Last Judgment passage—not only is there no tension between the commandment to love God and the commandment to love one another, there is "a radical identity of the two loves." Karl Rahner, *Theological Investigations*, vol. 6 (Baltimore: Helicon Press, 1969), 231, 236. In his "Reflections on the Unity of the Love of Neighbor and the Love of God," Rahner wrote: "It is radically true, i.e. by an ontological and not merely 'moral' or psychological necessity, that whoever does not love the brother whom he sees, also cannot love God whom he does not see, and that one can love God whom one does not see only *by* loving one's visible brother lovingly" (ibid, 247). Rahner's reference is to a passage in John's first letter in which it is written: "Anyone who says 'I love God' and hates his brother, is a liar, since whoever does not love the brother whom he can see cannot love God whom he has not seen" (John 4:20). See note 41 and accompanying text (parable of the Good Samaritan). In Rahner's view, the two great commandments are really one. See Rahner, *Theological Investigations*, 232. Rahner argued that if and to the extent one loves one's neighbor, one has achieved the ontological/existential state of being/consciousness that constitutes "love of God" even if one does not "believe in God" (238–39). If Rahner is right, then it is a mistake, a confusion, to say that one should love the Other *because* we love, or should love, God and God wants us to—or *because* we fear, or should fear, God and God wants us to. We may say, instead, that to love the Other (who is "sister" or "brother") just is to love God (who is "parent")—and that we should achieve the ontological/existential state of being/consciousness that constitutes "love of the Other" (= "love of God") because that state is the highest human good; to have achieved that radically unalienated condition is to have become "truly, fully" human. "We are well aware that we have passed over from death to life because we love our brothers. Whoever does not love, remains in death." (John 3:14).
Has Rahner pushed a good idea—that no one can be judged to love God who fails to love his or her neighbor—too far? One can accept that idea while rejecting Rahner's identification of love of God with love of neighbor. Tim Jackson has suggested, in

The response of the Gospel to "Who is my sister/brother/neigh-bor?"— and kindred responses—is religious in the fundamental sense that such a response is embedded in a religious vision of the world and of our place in it. Of course, there are differences among religious visions within the relevant range—sometimes large differences, some-times small. The analogical imagination does not yield precisely the same vision in every time or in every place. How a person or a commu-nity arrives at a religious vision is a difficult question—as is the ques-tion how one brings another to such a vision. Moreover, different religious traditions, and even different theologies within the same broad religious tradition, proffer different answers to such questions.

It bears emphasis that a theistic religious vision does not necessar-ily include (though, of course, some conventional theistic religious visions do include) a conception of "God" as a kind of divine legislator, issuing directives for human conduct.[45] Indeed, a religious person may well believe that such a "God"—such an idol—is dead.[46] The impera-tive to "love one another as I have loved you" can be understood (and in my view should be understood) not as a piece of divine legislation, but as a (truly, fully) human response to the question of how to live. However, to say that the response is a human one does not entail that it is not also a religious response. What makes the imperative a *religious* human response and not merely a secular one is that the response is the existential yield of a religious conviction about how the world (includ-ing we-in-the-world) hangs together: in particular, the conviction that

correspondence, that "surely there is such a thing as the *direct* love of God, as for instance in the ecstatic prayer of some mystics or in Holy Communion. Human beings are social animals, no doubt, but they are also born for a vertical relation to the Super-natural." Cf. Jean Porter, "Salvific Love and Charity: A Comparison of the Thought of Karl Rahner and Thomas Aquinas," in *The Love Commandments: Essays in Christian Ethics and Moral Philosophy,* ed. Edmund Santurri and William Werpehowski (Washington, D.C.: Georgetown University Press, 1992), 240.

    45. I can't tell whether Martha Nussbaum understands this. See Martha Nuss-baum, "Skepticism about Practical Reason in Literature and the Law," *Harvard Law Review* 107 (1994): 714, 739–40.

    46. On the death of such a "God," see Charles Larmore, "Beyond Religion and Enlightenment," *San Diego Law Review* 30 (1993): 799, 799–802.

    Indeed, as my footnote references to Buddhism—whose "theological" discourse is, in the main, nontheistic—suggest, the vision is not necessarily even theistic *in any conventional sense.* Whether mainline Buddhism is theistic in an unconventional sense is a difficult question. See David Tracy, "Kenosis, Sunyata, and Trinity: A Dialogue With Masao Abe," in *The Emptying God: A Buddhist-Jewish-Christian Conversation,* ed. John B. Cobb Jr. and Christopher Ives (Maryknoll: Orbis Books, 1990), 135.

the Other is, finally, one's own sister or brother—and should receive, therefore, the gift of one's loving concern.[47]

Indeed, a theistic religious vision is not necessarily attended by confident, much less dogmatic, God talk. (I have developed the point elsewhere.[48]) If that statement seems strange, consider what one scholar has recently stressed about Thomas Aquinas, perhaps the greatest Christian theologian: "[M]uch of [Aquinas's] doctrine about talking about God is in truth a carefully qualified *via negativa*. . . . Aquinas would simply agree with modern antitheists that we cannot say what God is; and that human language is inadequate to the claimed reality of God; and that there is something improper even in saying that God is a being. But not only does Aquinas think that none of these admissions disqualifies him from theism; he actually thinks that the theist should make these admissions."[49] Of course, and as Aquinas understood, to insist that we cannot say what God is—that we can only follow a *via negativa* and say what God is not—is not to deny that we can try to mediate our experience of Ultimate Reality analogically—for example, by speaking of God as *like* a loving "parent," and of the Other as *like* a "sister" or "brother." In addition to his "carefully qualified *via negativa* . . . Aquinas also has, of course, a *via positiva* about God-talk, namely, the 'doctrine of analogy.' . . . "[50] However, to insist, with Aquinas, that in talking about God we must either follow a *via negativa* or speak analogically is *not* to say that God talk is merely metaphorical or figurative or poetic. Aquinas was, after all, a committed theological realist.

To forestall predictable misunderstanding, let me make two points. First, in sketching a religious version of the conviction that every

---

47. In Buddhism, the relevant conviction is that the Other—who, appearances (illusions) to the contrary notwithstanding, is not really other at all, not, at any rate, in any deep sense—is an object of infinite compassion. (The Buddhist greeting "Namasté" means, roughly, "I greet the place within you where we are one.")

48. See Perry, *Morality, Politics, and Law*, 72–73. Nor is such a vision necessarily attended by belief in an afterlife. Cf. Timothy Jackson, "The Disconsolation of Theology: Irony, Cruelty, and Putting Charity First," *Journal of Religious Ethics* 20 (1992): 1, 19 (arguing that "a future heaven and/or hell ought not to play much of a role in [Christian] ethics, whatever role they may play in cosmology").

49. T. D. J. Chappell, "Why Read Aquinas?," *Times Literary Supplement*, 1 May 1992, 25 (reviewing Brian Davies, *The Thought of Thomas Aquinas* [Oxford: Clarendon Press, 1992]).

50. Ibid., 25.

human being is sacred, I have relied on the religious materials I know best. In relying primarily on Christian materials, however, I do not mean to suggest that there are not ample materials in other religious traditions out of which one can construct, or reconstruct, a relevantly similar version of the conviction. Of course, just as there are differences among the precise religious visions adhered to by different sects within Christianity, there are differences among the precise visions adhered to by different world religions. (Again, the analogical imagination does not yield precisely the same vision in every time or place.) But such differences as there are ought not to obscure the fact that the experience of all human beings as sacred is widely shared among different sects and religions, albeit expressed—mediated—differently in different traditions. And that common ("ecumenical") ground helps explain the emergence of the idea of human rights as a point of convergence among peoples from different religious traditions.[51]

Second, in presenting a religious version of the conviction that every human being is sacred, and in relying primarily on Christian materials in doing so, I do not mean to deny that the lived practice, as distinct from the professed ideals, of every religious tradition, including Christianity, offers at best equivocal support for what many of us consider to be basic human rights. Indeed, I do not mean to deny even that the professed ideals of religious traditions—at least on some quite plausible construals of those ideals—fail to support, and may even oppose, some such rights. Christianity is a conspicuous example.[52] There has been an obvious tendency on the part even of the

51. See David Cohn-Sherbok, ed., *World Religions and Human Liberation* (Maryknoll: Orbis Books, 1992); Hans Küng and Jürgen Moltmann, eds., *The Ethics of World Religions and Human Rights* (Philadelphia: Trinity Press International, 1990); Leroy Rouner, ed., *Human Rights and the World's Religions* (Notre Dame: University of Notre Dame Press, 1988); Arlene Swidler, ed., *Human Rights in Religious Traditions* (New York: Pilgrim Press, 1982); Robert Traer, *Faith in Human Rights: Support in Religious Traditions for a Global Struggle* (Washington: Georgetown University Press, 1991).

52. See Sandra Schneiders, "Does The Bible Have a Postmodern Message?" in *Postmodern Theology: Christian Faith in a Pluralist World*, ed. Frederic Burnham (San Francisco: Harper & Row, 1989), 56, 64–65:

[There are] two problems: the ideological *use* of Scripture, which is, if you will, an exterior problem; and the ideological *content* of Scripture, which is intrinsic to the text.

The question of the *use* of Scripture for purposes of oppression is being focused in the third-world struggle of the poor from domination by the rich and for participation in the societies and cultures which have been, for so long, controlled by the economically powerful for their own advantage. The struggle involves

world's "great" religious traditions to tribalism, racism, and sexism—
and worse. ("[T]he great religious ages were notable for their indifference to human rights in the contemporary sense. They were notorious not only for acquiescence in poverty, inequality, exploitation and
oppression but for enthusiastic justifications of slavery, persecution,
abandonment of small children, torture, genocide."[53]) No person who
takes seriously the resources of one or another religious tradition
should deny "the brokenness and ambiguity of every tradition" or
repress "one's own inevitably ambivalent relationship to [the tradi-
tion]."[54] A self-critical attitude toward one's own tradition is "the
route to liberation from the negative realities of [the] tradition."[55]

> For believers to be unable to learn from secular feminists on the
> patriarchal nature of most religions or to be unwilling to be
> challenged by Feuerbach, Darwin, Marx, Freud, or Nietzsche is to
> refuse to take seriously the religion's own suspicions on the
> existence of those fundamental distortions named sin, ignorance,
> or illusion. The interpretations of believers will, of course, be
> grounded in some fundamental trust in, and loyalty to, the Ulti-
> mate Reality both disclosed and concealed in one's own religious
> tradition. But fundamental trust, as any experience of friendship
> can teach, is not immune to either criticism or suspicion. A reli-
> gious person will ordinarily fashion some hermeneutics of trust,

wresting the sacred text from those who have used it to legitimate their oppressive regimes and strategies and delivering it into the hands of the oppressed as a
resource for liberation. . . . The problem of the ideological use of scripture is
soluble and is slowly being solved.

The second problem . . . , that of the ideological *content* of Scripture, is much
more complicated. It is being focused in the struggle of women for liberation from
patriarchal oppression in family, society, and church, and in the struggle of femi-
nists, both men and women, to destroy the patriarchal ideology which grounds
not only sexism but racism, classism, clericalism, and all the other forms of dualis-
tic hierarchy in which the powerful dominate the weak in the name of God. Here
the problem is not that the Scripture has been *used* to legitimate oppression
(although this is a continuing problem) but that the Bible itself is both a product
and a producer of oppression, that some of its *content* is oppressive.

Schneiders's elaboration of the problem and her overview of the various responses of
women (especially feminist theologians) and others to it (63–71) are excellent. (Schneiders
is a Catholic theologian.)

53. Arthur M. Schlesinger Jr., "The Opening of the American Mind," *New York
Times Book Review,* 23 July 1989, 26.

54. Tracy, *The Audilogical Imagination,* 105.

55. Ibid., 100.

even one of friendship and love, for the religious classics of her or his tradition. But, as any genuine understanding of friendship shows, friendship often demands both critique and suspicion. A belief in a pure and innocent love is one of the less happy inventions of the romantics. A friendship that never includes critique and even, when appropriate, suspicion is a friendship barely removed from the polite and wary communication of strangers. As Buber showed, in every I-Thou encounter, however transient, we encounter some new dimension of reality. But if that encounter is to prove more than transitory, the difficult ways of friendship need a trust powerful enough to risk itself in critique and suspicion. To claim that this may be true of all our other loves but not true of our love for, and trust in, our religious tradition makes very little sense either hermeneutically or religiously.[56]

The religious-cosmological context of the conviction that every human is sacred—the context I sketched in the preceding section—is not appealing to everyone. It was very unappealing to Nietzsche. And even for one to whom it is greatly appealing, it may not be credible. It is not credible, for example, to Jürgen Habermas, who has written: "[By confronting] the conscientious question about deliverance for the annihilated victims[,] we become aware of the limits of that transcendence from within which is directed to this world. But this does not enable us to ascertain the *countermovement* of a compensating transcendence from beyond. That the universal covenant of fellowship would be able to be effective retroactively, toward the past, only in the weak medium of our memory . . . falls short of our moral need. But the painful experience of a deficit is still not a sufficient argument for the assumption of an 'absolute freedom which saves in death.' "[57]

Even if one finds incredible the religious-cosmological context of the conviction that every human being is sacred, the question persists whether the religious version of the conviction isn't finally the only intelligible version. Can there be an intelligible secular version—an intelligible version not finally rooted in a religious vision of the world

56. Tracy, *Philosophy and Antiquity,* 84–85, 86, 97–98, 112.
57. Jürgen Habermas, "Transcendence from Within, Transcendence in this World," in *Habermas, Modernity, and Public Theology,* ed. Don S. Browning and Francis Fiorenza (New York: Crossroads, 1992), 226, 238.

and of our place in it? Can the conviction be embedded either in a nonreligious cosmology or in cosmological agnosticism? Consider Glenn Tinder's statement:

> Nietzsche's stature is owing to the courage and profundity that enabled him to make all this unmistakably clear. He delineated with overpowering eloquence the consequences of giving up Christianity, *and every like view of the universe and humanity*. His approval of those consequences and his hatred of Christianity give force to his argument. Many would like to think that there are no consequences—that we can continue treasuring the life and welfare, the civil rights and political authority, of every person without believing in a God who renders such attitudes and conduct compelling. Nietzsche shows that we cannot. We cannot give up the Christian God—*and the transcendence given other names in other faiths*—and go on as before. We must give up Christian morality too. If the God-man is nothing more than an illusion, the same thing is true of the idea that every individual possesses incalculable worth. The standard of *agape* collapses. It becomes explicable only on Nietzsche's terms: as a device by which the weak and failing exact from the strong and distinguished a deference they do not deserve. Thus the spiritual center of Western politics fades and vanishes.[58]

(Tinder's emphasis on the Christian tradition will surely and understandably be, for some non-Christians, a provocative distraction from his fundamental point. Tinder's [and Nietzsche's] point loses nothing, however, if the emphasis is placed not on the Christian tradition, but on the Jewish, for example. Recall the comment on the Talmud quoted earlier in this chapter.[59])

Is Tinder right? We may agree with Charles Larmore that morality is now widely understood (or, at least, understood by many of us, religious or not, who read essays like this one) to be independent of

---

58. Glenn Tinder, "Can We Be Good without God: The Political Meaning of Christianity," *Atlantic*, December 1989, 69, 80 (passages rearranged and emphasis added).

59. Nor does the point lose anything if the emphasis is put, for example, on the (Mahayana) Buddhist tradition, with its insistence on compassion for all sentient creatures as the fitting response to the true—as distinct from the illusory—nature of the world.

God conceived of as the supreme moral legislator.[60] But is it plausible to think that morality can be independent of *any* cosmological convictions— any convictions about how the world (including we-in-the-world) hangs together. After Nietzsche, is it plausible to think that a morality embedded in religious convictions about how the world hangs together can be more or less equivalent to a morality embedded in the conviction that the world is nothing but a great cosmic process utterly bereft of ultimate meaning and therefore, from a human point of view, absurd.[61] ("There is no meaning in the bowels of the universe."[62]) Nietzsche declared: " 'Naiveté: as if morality could survive when the *God* who sanctions it is missing! The 'beyond' absolutely necessary if faith in morality is to be maintained."[63] Writing recently of "anthropocentrism, [which] by abolishing all horizons of significance, threatens us with a loss of meaning and hence a trivialization of our predicament," Charles Taylor has said: "At one moment, we understand our situation as one of high tragedy, alone in a silent universe, without intrinsic meaning, condemned to create value. But at a later moment, the same doctrine, by its own inherent bent, yields a flattened world, in which there aren't very meaningful choices because there aren't any crucial issues."[64]

Consider a cosmology according to which the world is, finally and radically, meaningless—or, even if meaningful in some sense, not meaningful in a way hospitable to our deepest yearnings for what Heschel called "ultimate relationship, ultimate belonging."[65] Con-

---

60. See Larmore, "Beyond Religion and Enlightenment."

61. Cf. Nietzsche, *Will to Power*, 169:

Man a little, eccentric species of animal, which—fortunately—has its day; all on earth a mere moment, an incident, an exception without consequences, something of no importance to the general character of the earth; the earth itself, like every star, a hiatus between two nothingness, an event without plan, reason, will, self-consciousness, the worst kind of necessity, *stupid* necessity— Something in us rebels against this view; the serpent vanity says to us: "all that *must* be false, *for* it arouses indignation— Could all that not be merely appearance? And man, in spite of all, as Kant says—"

62. Bruce Ackerman, *Social Justice in the Liberal State* (New Haven: Yale University Press, 1980), 368.

63. Nietzsche, *Will to Power*, 147.

64. Charles Taylor, *The Ethics of Authenticity* (Cambridge: Harvard University Press, 1991), 68.

65. See Joske, "Philosophy and the Meaning of Life," 250: "If, as Kurt Vonnegut speculates in *The Sirens of Titan*, the ultimate end of human activity is the delivery of a small piece of steel to a wrecked space ship wanting to continue a journey of no

sider, for example, Clarence Darrow's bleak vision (as recounted by Paul Edwards):

> Darrow, one of the most compassionate men who ever lived, . . . concluded that life was an "awful joke." . . . Darrow offered as one of his reasons the apparent aimlessness of all that happens. "This weary old world goes on, begetting, with birth and with living and with death," he remarked in his moving plea for the boy-murderers Loeb and Leopold, "and all of it is blind from the beginning to the end." Elsewhere he wrote: "Life is like a ship on the sea, tossed by every wave and by every wind; a ship headed for no port and no harbor, with no rudder, no compass, no pilot; simply floating for a time, then lost in the waves." In addition to the aimlessness of life and the universe, there is the fact of death. "I love my friends," wrote Darrow, "but they all must come to a tragic end." Death is more terrible the more one is attached to things in the world. Life, he concludes, is "not worthwhile," and he adds . . . that "it is an unpleasant interruption of nothing, and the best thing you can say of it is that it does not last long."[66]

One prominent contemporary proponent of a Darrowian cosmology, the physicist (and Nobel laureate) Steven Weinberg, "finds his own world-view 'chilling and impersonal.' He cannot understand people who treat the absence of God and of God's heaven as unimportant."[67]

---

importance whatsoever, the end would be too trivial to justify the means." See also Nozick, *Philosophical Explanations*, 586: "If the cosmic role of human beings was to provide a negative lesson to some others ('don't act like them') or to provide needed food to passing intergalactic travelers who *were* important, this would not suit our aspirations—not even if afterwards the intergalactic travelers smacked their lips and said that we tasted good."

66. Paul Edwards, "Life, Meaning and Value of," *Encyclopedia of Philosophy*, vol. 4, ed. Paul Edwards (New York: Macmillan, 1967), 467, 470. Whether Clarence Darrow was in fact "one of the most compassionate men who ever lived" is open to serious question. For a revisionist view of Darrow, see Gary Wills, *Under God: Religion and American Politics* (New York: Simon & Schuster, 1990), chaps. 8–9.

67. John Leslie, "Is It All Quite Simple? The Physicist's Search for a Theory of Everything," *Times Literary Supplement*, 29 January 1993, 3 (reviewing, inter alia, Steven Weinberg, *Dreams of a Final Theory* [New York: Pantheon Books, 1992]). Cf. Paul Davies, "The Holy Grail of Physics," *New York Times Book Review*, 7 March 1993, 11 (reviewing, inter alia, Weinberg's book): "Reductionism [in physics] may be a fruitful research method, but it is a bleak philosophy. . . . If the world is but a collection of inert atoms interacting through blind and purposeless forces, what happens to . . . the meaning of

Where is the place in a cosmological view like Weinberg's for the
conviction that every human being is sacred—the conviction that every human being is inviolable, has inherent dignity, is an end in
himself or herself, and so on—to gain a foothold? Indeed, embedded
in the view that the world is merely a process devoid of ultimate
meaning, what would the conviction that every human being is sacred even mean? If the only intelligible version of the conviction is
religious, then cosmological agnosticism, which neither affirms nor
denies the ultimate meaningfulness of the world, entails agnosticism
about the sacredness *vel non* of human beings.

In writing recently about abortion and euthanasia, Ronald Dworkin
has asserted that "[w]e almost all accept, as the inarticulate assumption behind much of our experience and conviction, that human life in
all its forms is *sacred*. . . ."[68] Dworkin then observes that "[f]or some
of us, [the sacredness of human life] is a matter of religious faith; for
others, of secular but deep philosophical belief."[69] Now, many folks
who believe that every human being is sacred do not count themselves religious; some of them even embrace nonreligious views like
Weinberg's. The question nonetheless persists whether there is an
intelligible secular version of the conviction about the sacredness of
every human being. Imagine a nonreligious person saying: "That every human being is sacred is not, for me, a religious tenet; it is a
secular but deep philosophical belief." We may ask: "Please tell us
something about the constellation of views—views about how the
world, including we-in-the-world, hangs together—in which, for

life?" For a controversial critique of such scientific reductionism, see Brian Appleyard,
Understanding the Present: Science and the Soul of Modern Man (New York: Doubleday,
1992). On philosophical inquiry into cosmology, see Derek Parfit, "The Puzzle of Reality," *Times Literary Supplement*, 3 July 1992, 3.

Several recent papers in a fierce and ongoing debate about the consistency or
inconsistency of claims made in evolutionary biology with Christian claims are relevant
here. All the papers are by persons who identify themselves as Christians. In the
September 1991 issue of *Christian Scholar's Review*, see Alvin Platinga, "When Faith and
Reason Clash: Evolution and the Bible"; Howard Van Till, "When Faith and Reason
Cooperate"; Ernan McMullin, "Platinga's Defense of Special Creation"; Alvin Platinga,
"Evolution, Neutrality, and Antecedent Probability: A Reply to McMullin and Van Till."
In the June/July 1993 issue of *First Things*, see Howard Van Till and Philip Johnson,
"God and Evolution: An Exchange."

68. Dworkin, "Life is Sacred," 36.
69. Ibid., 36.

you, that philosophical belief is embedded." Imagine this answer: "For me the conviction that every human being is sacred is not only axiomatic; it is unconnected to any of my views about how the world hangs together." (Perhaps the answer includes this statement: "I have no confident views about how the world hangs together. I'm agnostic about all such 'religious' or 'cosmological' matters.") It seems, then, that the premise that every human being is sacred is, for our nonreligious interlocutor, less a conviction about (a part of) the world than a kind of free-floating aesthetic preference. In Dworkin's view, however, the premise is, even for most nonreligious persons who hold it, much more than an aesthetic preference.

In his book on abortion and euthanasia, Dworkin writes that "one of [his] main claims [is] that there is a secular as well as a religious interpretation of the idea that human life is sacred."[70] Dworkin purports to explain, in his book, how the conviction that every human being (or, as Dworkin says, "life") is sacred "may be, and commonly is, interpreted in a secular as well as in a conventionally religious way."[71] To say that a human life is sacred is partly to say, according to Dworkin, "that it has *intrinsic* and *objective* value quite apart from any value it might have to the person whose life it is."[72] Emphasizing in particular the notion of "intrinsic" value, Dworkin writes: "[M]uch of our life is

---

70. Dworkin, *Life's Dominion*, 195.

71. Ibid., 25. Curiously, elsewhere in his book Dworkin writes that that he "can think of no plausible account of the content that a belief must have in order to be deemed religious that would rule out convictions about why and how human life [is sacred], except the abandoned notion that religious belief must presuppose a god" (163). He also says that "why and how human life is sacred" is an "essentially religious issue" (165). It is not obvious why, if (as Dworkin insists) there is a secular interpretation or version of the idea that human life is sacred, the issue of why and how human life is sacred is *essentially* religious. If the idea that human life is sacred is *not* essentially religious, why is the issue of why and how human life is sacred essentially religious? Dworkin's principal incentive to claim that the idea that human life is sacred can be interpreted in a secular as well as in a religious way is that, for purposes of his characterization of the abortion controversy, he wants to be able to attribute the idea (in its secular version) to secular folks as well as (in its religious version) to religious ones. His principal incentive to claim that the issue of why and how human life is sacred is essentially religious is that, for purposes of his argument about the (un)constitutionality of restrictive abortion legislation, Dworkin wants to be able to rely on a constitutional premise according to which government may not take coercive action predicated on nothing more than a contested position on an essentially religious issue (see 160–68). (That there is such a constitutional premise is open to question. Cf. Michael Perry, "Religious Morality and Political Choice: Further Thoughts—and Second Thoughts—on *Love and Power*," *San Diego Law Review* 30 [1993]: 703.)

72. Dworkin, "Life is Sacred," 36 (emphasis added).

based on the idea that objects or events can be valuable in themselves. . . . [T]he idea that some events or objects are valuable in and of
themselves . . . is . . . a familiar part of our experience. . . . The idea
of intrinsic value is commonplace, and it has a central place in our
shared scheme of values and opinions. . . . Something is intrinsically
valuable . . . if its value is *independent* of what people happen to enjoy
or want or need or what is good for them."[73]

Dworkin's comments about "intrinsic" value obscure rather than
clarify that value is always and everywhere value *for* someone(s) or
something(s). The notion of something being valuable independently
of a beneficial relation to anyone or anything—whether a human
being, a nonhuman but living entity, or God—is perfectly opaque.
Putting aside things that are values either for nonhuman entities or
for God, we may say that "the category of values is anthropocentric,
in that it corresponds to interests which can only take root in creatures
with something approaching our own affective make-up. . . . [V]al-
ues are only ascribable from points of view constituted by human
patterns of affective response. A wholly dispassionate eye would be
as blind to them as a black-and-white camera to chromatic colors."[74]

---

73. Dworkin, *Life's Dominion*, 69–71.
74. A. W. Price, "Varieties of Objectivity and Values," *Proceedings of the Aristotelian
Society* 83 (1983): 103, 106. See David Hume, *A Treatise of Human Nature*, ed. L. Selby-
Bigge (Oxford: Clarendon Press, 1973), 469: "Vice and virtue, therefore, may be
compar'd to sounds, colours, heat and cold, which, according to modern philosophy,
are not qualities in objects, but perceptions in the mind: And this discovery in morals,
like that other in physics, is to be regarded as a considerable advancement of the
speculative sciences; tho', like that, too, it has little or no influence on practice." See
also Anthony Kronman, "A Comment on Dean Clark," *Columbia Law Review* 89 (1989):
1748, 1755: "[The view] that there are goods which are not the goods of any human
beings at all, is likely to appear . . . wholly unintelligible, for it conflicts with what is
perhaps the deepest and most widely shared orthodoxy of modern moral thought—the
assumption that only the goods of human beings (or perhaps sentient beings) count in
assessing different practices and institutions." Cf. Robin W. Lovin, "Empiricism and
Christian Social Thought," *Annual of Society of Christian Ethics* (1982): 25, 41: "Ethics will
never be like physics, chemistry, or certain types of sociology, because it understands
the moral reality to be about an interaction between persons and the world which can
only be known from the reports of those who experience that interaction."
    Does Dworkin disagree? It's difficult to tell. Cf. Dworkin, *Life's Dominion*, 248 n. 1:
"I do not mean to take any position on a further, very abstract philosophical issue not
pertinent to this discussion: whether great paintings would still be valuable if intelligent life were altogether destroyed forever so that no one could ever have the experience of regarding paintings again. There is no inconsistency in denying that they would
have value then, because the value of a painting lies in the kind of experience it makes

The relevant distinction here is between "intrinsic" value and "instrumental" value. To say that something has intrinsic value is to say, not that something has value even if it has no value for anyone (not even God) or anything—what would *that* mean?—but that something has value for someone (or something) *not merely as a means to an end but as an end in itself.* And to say that something has "objective" value and not (or not merely) "subjective" value is to say that something has value for someone (for example, that it is good for one, that it is conducive to or perhaps even constitutive of one's flourishing) *even if one is unaware that it has value for one—indeed, even if one believes that it has disvalue for one.*[75] Now, that something has both objective and intrinsic value for someone does not mean that it is sacred. An end to my itch has both objective and intrinsic value for me (or so we may assume), but it is not thereby sacred. For some persons who count themselves religious, to say that every human being is sacred is to say (speaking analogically) that every human being is the beloved child of God (God who is love). For persons who do not count themselves religious, what does it mean to say that every human being is sacred?

According to Dworkin, "[T]he nerve of the sacred lies in the value we attach to a process or enterprise or project rather than to its results considered independently from how they were produced."[76] The sacredness of human beings is rooted, for nonreligious persons,

---

available, while still insisting that this value is intrinsic because it does not depend on any creatures' actually wanting that kind of experience."

At one point in his discussion of "intrinsic" value, Dworkin writes: "David Hume and many other philosophers insisted that objects or events can be valuable only when and because they serve someone's or something's interests. On this view, nothing is valuable unless someone wants it or unless it helps someone get what he does want" (69). The second sentence here is a glaring non sequitur. It does not follow, from the Humean view, that nothing is valuable unless someone wants it or unless it helps someone get what he or she does want. It follows only that nothing is valuable unless it serves someone's or something's interests. That something serves my interests does not entail that I want it (or that it helps me get what I do want). After all, I may not know that something serves my interests, or I may not know what my real interests are. Indeed, that I want something (or that it helps me get what I do want) does not entail that it serves my interests: I may want things that are not good for me—indeed, that are bad for me.

75. To say that something has *merely* subjective value for someone is to say that the person believes it to have value for her or him even though it does not. Considered in isolation, something may have (objective and/or subjective) value for someone, even if considered in context it does not: One thing that has value for someone may crowd out or preclude another thing that has even greater value for that person.

76. Dworkin, *Life's Dominion*, 78.

in two basic facts about human beings (argues Dworkin). First, every human being is "the highest product of natural creation. . . . [T]he idea that human beings are special among natural creations is offered to explain why it is horrible that even a single human individual life should be extinguished."[77] Second, "each developed human being is the product not just of natural creation, but also of the kind of deliberative human creative force that we honor in honoring art."[78] "The idea that each individual human life is inviolable is therefore rooted . . . in two combined and intersecting bases of the sacred: natural *and* human creation."[79]

> The life of a single human organism commands respect and protection, then, no matter in what form or shape, because of the complex creative investment it represents and because of our wonder at the . . . processes that produce new lives from old ones, at the processes of nation and community and language through which a human being will come to absorb and continue hundreds of generations of cultures and forms of life and value, and, finally, when mental life has begun and flourishes, at the process of internal personal creation and judgment by which a person will make and remake himself, a mysterious, inescapable process in which we each participate, and which is therefore the most powerful and inevitable source of empathy and communion we have with every other creature who faces the same frightening challenge. The horror we feel in the willful destruction of a human life reflects our shared inarticulate sense of the intrinsic importance of each of these dimensions of investment.[80]

This, then, is Dworkin's rendering of a secular version of the conviction that every human being is sacred. Even if in truth the world is nothing but a process bereft of ultimate meaning, every human being is nonetheless sacred, according to Dworkin, because "each human being . . . is a creative masterpiece"[81]—a masterpiece of "natural *and* human creation."[82]

---

77. Ibid., 82. See 81–84.
78. Ibid., 82.
79. Ibid., 83.
80. Ibid., 84.
81. Ibid., 82.
82. Ibid., 83.

Does Dworkin succeed in portraying an intelligible secular version of the conviction that every human being is sacred? Important questions need to be answered—or so it seems to me. How does the fact that something is a masterpiece of natural and human creation make that something not merely a creative masterpiece but sacred? What is the precise sense of "sacred" in play in Dworkin's portrayal? Let us agree that every human being is a creative masterpiece and, as such, inspires (or should inspire) awe in us. That something justifiably inspires awe in us, however—James Joyce's *Ulysses*, for example—entails neither that we believe it to be sacred nor that it is sacred.

To say that every human being is sacred is ordinarily to say something about (what is believed to be) the true nature of every human being. Of course, something may inspire awe in us, and we may therefore value it—it may have value for us, both objective value and intrinsic value—because it is sacred (or, at least, because we believe it to be sacred). But to suggest, as in his book Dworkin at least sometimes does, that something is sacred *because* it inspires awe in us, because we value it, is to reverse the ordinary order of things. (Recall, for example, Dworkin's statement that "the nerve of the sacred lies in the value we attach to a process or enterprise or project rather than to its results considered independently from how they were produced."[83] Or his statement that "[t]he life of a single human organism commands respect and protection . . . because of our wonder at the . . . processes that produce new lives from old ones . . . "[84]) Dworkin seems to be using *sacred* in what we may call a weak, or "subjective," sense—something (e.g., a human life) is sacred *because*, or *in the sense that*, it inspires awe in us and we attach great value to it—rather than in the strong, or "objective," sense—something is sacred and *therefore* it inspires awe in us and we attach great value to it. Moreover, in using *sacred* in the weak or subjective sense, Dworkin is trading on the greater strength of the objective sense in which the word is ordinarily used.

That rhetorical strategy, however, is problematic. The premise that every human being is sacred-in-the-subjective-sense cannot begin to bear the weight of the premise that every human being is sacred-in-the-objective-sense. Imagine someone saying to a Bosnian Serb: "The Bosnian Muslim, too, no less than you, is sacred. It is

83. Ibid., 78.
84. Ibid., 71.

wrong for you to rape her." If *sacred* is meant in the subjective sense, the Bosnian Serb may reply: "Sacred to you and yours, perhaps, but not to me and mine. In the scheme of things, we happen not to attach much value to her life." By contrast, *sacred* in the objective sense is not fundamentally a matter of "sacred to you" or "sacred to me"; it is, rather, a matter of how things really are. (Of course, one may disbelieve the ontology, but that's a different problem.) If every human being is sacred in the objective sense, then, in violating the Bosnian Muslim, the Bosnian Serb does not merely violate what some of us attach great value to; he violates the very order of creation.

Now, Dworkin may insist that he's been misunderstood. He may insist that he means *sacred* in the objective sense, and that on his account of *sacred* the Bosnian Serb is indeed violating the very order of creation. He may say that the Bosnian Muslim has intrinsic value even for the Bosnian Serb—and objective value, too: that the welfare of the Bosnian Muslim is an intrinsic good for the Bosnian Serb even if the Bosnian Serb will remain forever unaware of that fact. But if Dworkin wants to respond in some such way, then he must forswear any explanation of the sacredness of someone or something in terms of, or by reference to, "the value we attach to" that someone or something. He must explain it solely in other terms. It is not clear, however, what that other explanation might be; in particular, it is not obvious that either a secular cosmology or cosmological agnosticism can yield the requisite conviction about how things really are. How do we get from "the universe is (or might be) nothing but a cosmic process bereft of ultimate meaning" to "every human being is nonetheless sacred (in the strong or objective sense)"? Of course, even in an absurd universe, a universe bereft of transcendent meaning, there can be creative masterpieces. But, again, that something is a creative masterpiece and understandably inspires awe in us entails neither that it is sacred nor even that we believe it to be sacred (in the strong sense).

Has Dworkin identified an intelligible secular version of the conviction that every human being is sacred? It seems not, if *sacred* is meant in the objective sense. If, however, *sacred* is meant in the subjective sense, perhaps Dworkin has identified an intelligible secular version. But if he has, Dworkin's secularized claim that every human being is sacred is a substantially weaker claim—it claims much less—than the paradigmatic claim about the sacredness of all human beings. In any event, Dworkin has said nothing to diminish suspicion that the conviction that every human being is sacred—*sacred in the strong/objective sense, sacred because of how the world really is, and not because of what we attach value to in the world*—is inescapably religious. The challenge is to identify an intelligible secular version of *that* conviction. In his review of Dworkin's book for the London *Times Literary Supplement*, Robert Grant concluded that "[i]n *Life's Dominion*, Professor Dworkin makes considerable play with, indeed frankly exploits, the idea of the sacred, but shows no understanding of it."[85]

In a recent essay critiquing "skepticism about practical reason in literature and in the law," Nussbaum asserts that "the good of other human beings is an end worth pursuing in its own right, apart from its effect on [one's] own pleasure or happiness."[86] (It is clear that by "other human beings" Nussbaum is referring not just to *some* other human beings but to *all* other human beings.) But *why* is the good of every human being an end worth pursuing in its own right? Nussbaum doesn't say. She merely reports, in the final paragraph of her essay, that "it seems to be a mark of the human being to care for others and feel disturbance when bad things happen to them."[87] Now, few will deny that it seems to be a mark of the human being to care for *some* other human beings—the members of one's family, say, or even of one's tribe or nation or race or religion. But it is not a mark of all human beings—it is not a mark of "the human being" as such—to care for *all* other human beings.[88] Recall Rorty's comparison of "the rather rare figure of the psychopath, the person who has no concern for any human being other than himself" to "the much more common case: the person whose treatment of a rather narrow range of featherless bipeds is morally impeccable, but who remains indifferent to the suffering of those outside this range, the ones he or she thinks of as pseudohumans."[89]) Rorty's "much more common case" is also much more common than the person at the other extreme from the

---

85. Robert Grant, "Abortion and the Idea of the Sacred," *Times Literary Supplement*, 18 June 1993, 11.

86. Nussbaum, *Aristotle on Human Nature*, 718.

87. Ibid., 744.

88. See the text referred to by note 99 regarding Primo Levi's description of "us-ism."

89. See Rorty, "Human Rights, Rationality, and Sentimentality."

psychopath: someone who, like Mother Teresa, cares deeply about the authentic well-being of every human being. We sometimes mark just how *uncommon* such persons are, in the real world, by calling them "saints."

If it were a mark of every human being to care for every other human being (and to feel disturbance when bad things happen to any other human being), the "why" question would be merely academic. But because very many human beings—indeed, perhaps most human beings—have not in the past cared for, nor do they today care for, every human being, the question is both practical and urgent: Why is the good of every human being an end worth pursuing in its own right? In her essay, Nussbaum stands mute before that question. One answer—the answer that informs the international law of human rights—is that the good of every human being is an end worth pursuing in its own right *because every human being is sacred*. I am suggesting, in this chapter, that there may be no intelligible secular version of that answer—no intelligible secular version of the conviction that every human being is sacred.

If—*if*—the conviction that every human being is sacred is inescapably religious, it follows that the idea of human rights is ineliminably religious, because the conviction is an essential, even foundational, constituent of the idea. The possibility that the idea of human rights is ineliminably religious poses a problem for the secular or agnostic enthusiast of human rights. One response to the problem is to try to defend human rights claims, not by relying on the conviction that every human being is sacred, but by means of a justificatory strategy that avoids reliance on that conviction—that avoids reliance, therefore, on "the idea of human rights." I now want to identify and comment briefly on two such strategies.[90]

---

90. There are, of course, others. (See note 101 mentioning the work of John Finnis and that of Jürgen Habermas.) A prominent secular argument for human rights—that is, a prominent secular argument that does not rely on the (ineliminably religious?) idea of human rights—is Alan Gewirth's. See Alan Gewirth, *Reason and Morality* (Chicago: University of Chicago Press, 1978), chaps. 1–2; Alan Gewirth, *Human Rights: Essays on Justification and Applications* (Chicago: University of Chicago Press, 1982), 41–78; Alan Gewirth, "The Epistemology of Human Rights," *Social Philosophy & Policy* 1 (1984): 1. For one of Gewirth's most recent statements, see Alan Gewirth, "Human Dignity as the Basis of Rights," in *The Constitution of Rights: Human Dignity and American Values*, ed. Michael Meyer and William Parent (Ithaca: Cornell University Press, 1992), 10. Gewirth's argu-

The Definitional Strategy

[T]here is today no way of "proving" that napalming babies is bad except by asserting it (in a louder and louder voice), *or by defining it as so, early in one's game, and then later slipping it through, in a whisper, as a conclusion.*[91]

The idea of human rights, again, is that because every human being is, simply as a human being, sacred, certain choices should be made and certain other choices rejected; in particular, certain things ought not to be done to any human being and certain other things ought to be done for every human being. The definitional strategy is a different way of trying to defend human rights claims—especially claims about what ought not to be done to any human being or about what ought to be done for every human being (or about both)—in particular, a way that does not rely on the premise that human beings are sacred. According to the definitional strategy, certain things ought not to be done to any human being and certain other things ought to be done for every human being simply because "the moral point of view"— understood as the "impartial" or "universal" point of view—requires it. In commenting on "that sort of impartiality that constitutes the moral point of view," James Griffin has written that "[w]e all agree that to look at things morally is to look at them, in some sense or other, impartially, granting every person some sort of equal status. Of course, we should have to make this notion of equal status more determinate—say through one interpretation or other of the Ideal Observer or Ideal Contractor. In any case, principles of equality can be principles of impartiality in this sense: they can express the spirit with which one will, if one is moral, consider the facts of the matter."[92]

ment has been extremely controversial, to say the least. Indeed, I am tempted to say that there is as close to a consensus as one gets in serious moral philosophy that Gewirth's argument simply doesn't work. See, for example, Edward Regis, ed., *Gewirth's Ethical Rationalism* (Chicago: University of Chicago Press, 1984); Brian M. Barry, *Theories of Justice* (Berkeley: University of California Press, 1989), 285–88. For a careful restatement and defense of Gewirth's argument, see Derek Beyleveld, *The Dialectical Necessity of Morality: An Analysis and Defense of Alan Gewirth's Argument for the Principle of Generic Consistency* (Chicago: University of Chicago Press, 1991). For a skeptical review of Beyleveld's book, see Nick Fotion, *Ethics* 101 (1993): 579.

91. Arthur A. Leff, "Economic Analysis of Law: Some Realism about Nominalism," *Virginia Law Review* 60 (1974): 451, 454 (emphasis added).

92. James Griffin, *Well-Being* (Oxford: Clarendon Press, 1987), 239.

The definitional strategy is deeply problematic, because it fails even to address what David Tracy has called the "limit-question" of morality: "Why be moral at all?"[93] (Richard Rorty has contrasted "the rational egoist's question 'Why should I be moral?'" to "the much more frequently posed question 'Why should I care about a stranger, a person who is no kin to me, a person whose habits I find disgusting?'"[94] But, given the conventional understanding of the "moral" point of view as the "impartial" or "universal" point of view, the question "Why should I be moral?" just *is* the question "Why should I care about a stranger . . . ?"). The definitional strategy fails to respond to this fundamental challenge:

> You claim that we ought not to do certain things to any human being, and that we ought to do certain other things for every human being. We ask why. You say that the moral (impartial, universal) point of view requires it. For the sake of argument we will stipulate to your definition of "moral." Our challenge remains, but now we'll express it this way: Why ought we to adopt "the moral point of view"; why ought we to be "moral" in the stipulated sense? Why ought we to give a damn about being "moral" or doing the "moral" thing? We are right back where we started: What reasons—what real-world, flesh-and-blood reasons—are there for doing for every human being those certain things that the moral point of view requires be done for every human being and for not doing to any human being those certain other things that the moral point of view forbids be done to any human being?

The fundamental challenge to each and every human rights claim— in particular, to each and every claim about what ought not to be done to any human being or what ought to be done for every human being—is a demand for reasons. James Nickel has distinguished between two different interpretations of the demand: one according to which it is "a demand for prudential reasons" and another accord-

---

93. David Tracy, "Theology, Critical Social Theory, and the Public Realm," in *Habermas, Modernity, and Public Theology*, ed. Don S. Browning and Francis Fiorenza (New York: Crossroads, 1992), 19, 37.
94. Rorty, "Human Rights, Rationality, and Sentimentality," 133.

ing to which it is "a request for moral reasons."[95] (The distinction between "prudential" and "moral" is deeply problematic, at least for anyone with an Aristotelian understanding of morality.[96] But let's move on.) The second interpretation, Nickel suggests, "assumes that one's audience has transcended egoism and is prepared to accept arguments that appeal directly to what is reasonable from the moral point of view, whether or not it can be shown that adopting this perspective is likely to promote the long-term interests of the individual."[97] But the problem is larger, much larger, than "egoism": One may favor, not just oneself, or even just one's family, but just one's tribe or nation or race or religion. The assumption that those to whom human rights claims are addressed have "transcended" such favoritism is wildly implausible.[98] The fundamental challenge to human rights claims is a real-world challenge: Many to whom such claims are addressed have conspicuously not adopted anything like "the moral (impartial, universal) point of view." The moral point of view is not a justificatory basis for human rights claims—at least, not a fundamental basis. The moral point of view is itself in dire need of justification, especially in a world—*our* world, the *real* world—that is often fiercely partial/local rather than impartial/universal. The real world is full of what Primo Levi called "us-ism": "Those on the Rosenstrasse who risked their lives for Jews did not express opposition

---

95. James Nickel, *Making Sense of Human Rights: Philosophical Reflections on the Universal Declaration of Human Rights* (Berkeley: University of California Press, 1987), 91.

96. See Stephen Scott, "Motive and Justification," *Journal of Philosophy* 85 (1988): 479, 499: "When he was deliberating about how to live, St. Augustine asked, 'What does anything matter, if it does not have to do with happiness?' His question requires explanation, because he is not advising selfishness nor the reduction of other people to utilities, and even qualification, because other things can have some weight. All the same, the answer he expects is obviously right: only a happy life matters conclusively. If I had a clear view of it, I could have no motive to decline it, I could regret nothing by accepting it, I would have nothing about which to deliberate further." Cf. Richard Taylor, "Ancient Wisdom and Modern Folly," *Midwest Studies in Philosophy* 13 (1988): 54, 57, 58: "The Greek *eudaimonia* is always translated 'happiness,' which is unfortunate, for the meaning we attach to the word *happiness* is thin indeed compared to what the ancients meant by *eudaimonia*. *Fulfillment* might be a better term, though this, too, fails to capture the richness of the original term. . . . The concept of happiness in modern philosophy, as well as in popular thinking, is superficial indeed in comparison." For an extended discussion of the "Why be moral?" problem from a neo-Aristotelian perspective, see Rudolph Bittner, *What Reason Demands* (New York: Cambridge University Press, 1989).

97. Nickel, *Making Sense of Human Rights*, 91.

98. See text accompanying note 89.

to anti-semitic policies per se. They displayed primarily what the late Primo Levi, a survivor of Auschwitz, called 'selfishness extended to the person closest to you . . . us-ism.' In most of the stories that I have heard of Aryans who risked their lives for Jews to whom they were married, they withdrew to safety, one by one, the moment their loved ones were released. Their protests bring home to us the iron limits, the tragically narrow borders, of us-ism."[99]

The question remains: What reasons are there for adopting "the moral point of view"? Charles Taylor, commenting critically on moral theories that are variations on the definitional strategy—in particular, theories that exclude discourse about human well-being—has put the point this way: "[Such theories] leave us with nothing to say to someone who asks why he should be moral. . . . But this could be misleading, if we seemed to be asking how we could convince someone who saw none of the point of our moral beliefs. There is nothing we can do to 'prove' we are right to such a person. But imagine him to be asking another question: he could be asking us to make plain the point of our moral code, in articulating what's uniquely valuable in cleaving to these injunctions [e.g., act 'impartially']. Then the implication of these theories is that we have nothing to say which can impart insight. We can wax rhetorical and propagandize, but we can't say what's good or valuable about [the injunctions], or why they command assent."[100]

---

99. Nathan Stoltzfus, "Dissent in Nazi Germany," *Atlantic*, September 1992, 87, 94.

100. C. Taylor, *Sources of the Self*, 87. See also p. 3: "Much contemporary moral philosophy, particularly but not only in the English-speaking world, has given such a narrow focus to morality . . . This moral philosophy has tended to focus on what it is right to do rather than on what it is good to be, on defining the content of obligation rather than the nature of the good life . . . This philosophy has accredited a cramped and truncated view of morality in a narrow sense, as well as of the whole range of issues involved in the attempt to live the best possible life, and this not only among professional philosophers, but with a wider public." (Taylor's book is, among other things, a powerful argument for a different, larger understanding of "moral," an Aristotelian rather than a Kantian understanding. See 4, 14–15, 63–64, 79, 87.)

The effort to evade the why-be-moral question by distinguishing between "reasons" and "motives" is unavailing—as, indeed, is implicit in Taylor's comments. See Henry Veatch, "Modern Ethics, Teleology, and Love of Self," *Monist* 75 (1992): 52, 60:

[T]he stock answer given to this question has long been one of trying to distinguish between a *reason* and a *motive* for being moral. For surely, it is argued, if I recognize something to be my duty, then surely I have a reason to perform the required action, even though I have no motive for performing it. In fact, even to

The definitional strategy is unavailing. Of course, a strategy is not definitional if it explains "the moral point of view" on the basis of a cosmological vision that yields something like the premise that every human being is sacred. But then we're back to the question whether such a premise isn't inescapably religious.[101]

ask for a motive for doing something, when one already has a reason for doing it, would seem to be at once gratuitous and unnecessary—at least so it is argued. Unhappily, though, the argument has a dubious air about it at best. For does it amount to anything more than trying to prove a point by first attempting to make a distinction, implying that the distinction is no mere distinction, but a distinction with a difference—viz. the distinction between a reason and a motive. But then, having exploited the distinction, and yet at the same time insinuating that one might conceivably have a reason for doing something, but no motive for doing it, the argument draws to its conclusion by surreptitiously taking advantage of the fact that there possibly is no real distinction between a reason and a motive after all, so that if one has a reason for doing a thing, then one has a motive for doing it as well. In other words, it's as if the argument only succeeds by taking back with its left hand what it had originally given with its right.

101. John Finnis's argument in defense of a requirement "of fundamental impartiality among the human subjects who are or may be partakers of [basic human goods]" is simply unavailing. For the argument, see John Finnis, *Natural Law and Natural Rights* (Oxford: Clarendon Press, 1980), 106–8: "[John] Finnis has tried to do in two pages what . . . others have devoted entire books to: . . . show that egoism is inherently self-contradictory or irrational. All of these attempts have failed. It is surprising that Finnis deals with such a problematic and contentious issue in such a brief and casual fashion." J. D. Goldsworthy, "God or Mackie: The Dilemma of Secular Moral Philosophy," *American Journal of Jurisprudence* (1985): 43, 75; see also 73–77. One of Finnis's most recent writings fares no better: John Finnis, "Natural Law and Legal Reasoning," in *Natural Law Theory: Contemporary Essays*, ed. Robert P. George (Oxford: Clarendon Press, 1992), 134.
    Given the current prominence in some circles of Habermasian "discourse ethics," this recent statement by Jürgen Habermas is worth reporting—a statement that should be very sobering for anyone tempted to believe that discourse ethics might supply an effective secular argument for human rights: "It is true that a philosophy that thinks postmetaphysically cannot answer the question that [David] Tracy . . . calls attention to: why be moral [i.e., impartial] at all?" Habermas, "Transcendence," 239.
    What Habermas then goes on to say is really quite remarkable, if not incredible: At the same time, however, this philosophy can show why this question does not arise meaningfully for communicatively socialized individuals. We acquire our moral intuitions in our parents' home, not in school. And moral insights tell us that we do not have any good reasons for behaving otherwise: for this, no self-surpassing of morality is necessary. It is true that we often behave otherwise, but we do so with a bad conscience. The first half of the sentence attests to the weakness of the motivational power of good reasons; the second half attests that rational motivation by reasons is more than nothing [*auch nicht nichts ist*]—moral convictions do not allow themselves to be overridden without resistance. (239)
Let's put aside the fact that "we" acquire our moral "intuitions" in many places besides (or in addition to) our parents' home—in the streets, for example. The more important

The Self-Regarding Strategy

The self-regarding strategy is yet another way—a way that does not rely on anything like the premise that human beings are sacred—of trying to defend human rights claims. According to the self-regarding strategy, it is good for oneself or for one's family/tribe/nation/race/religion that certain things not be done to any human being and certain other things be done for every human being. This strategy needs to be distinguished from (lest it collapse into) the different (and inescapably religious?) strategy according to which every human being is sacred and it is good for everyone to recognize that fact and act accordingly. According to the self-regarding strategy, it is good for oneself or for one's nation or other group that certain things not be done and certain other things be done even if it is not the case that every human being is sacred.

The fundamental problem with the self-regarding strategy, *as a strategy for defending human rights claims*, is twofold. First, it is not clear how much more than "a mere nonagression treaty"[102]—a treaty among persons who either fear one another or, at least, think that one day they may have reason to fear one another—the self-regarding strategy can support. A recent, prominent self-regarding strategy is David Gauthier's contractarian argument. Let's put aside the question whether the argument works[103] and look simply at the aim of the argument, which, according to Gauthier, is to show "that rational persons will recognize a role for constraints, both unilateral and mutual, in their choices and decisions, that rational persons would agree ex ante on certain mutual constraints were they able to do so, and that rational persons will frequently comply with those mutual constraints in their

---

point, for present purposes, is that we do not all acquire the same moral intuitions. Some of us acquire moral intuitions that enable us to ignore, and perhaps even to brutalize, the Other without any pangs of "conscience." It is incredible that in the waning days of this unbearably brutal century, Habermas—writing in Germany, of all places—could suggest otherwise. We need not even look at the oppressors themselves; we need look only at those whose passivity makes them complicitors—as the quotation in the text accompanying note 99 confirms.

102. See Williams, *Ethics and the Limits of Philosophy*, 103–4.

103. See Peter Vallentyne, ed., *Contractarianism and Rational Choice: Essays on David Gauthier's "Morals By Agreement"* (New York: Oxford University Press, 1991); David Gauthier and Robert Sugden, eds., *Rationality, Justice and the Social Contract* (Ann Arbor: University of Michigan, 1993).

interactions."[104] In particular, Gauthier's self-regarding argument does not aim to justify anything close to the range of rights established in international law—in the International Bill of Human Rights, for example. As one commentator has observed, "[Gauthier's] main interest is to give an account of rational and impartial constraints on conduct. If this does not capture the traditional conception of morality, so much the worse for the traditional conception. Rationality—not morality—is the important notion for him."[105]

Second, whatever rights beyond "a mere nonaggression treaty" a strategy like Gauthier's can support, it is not clear that such a strategy can support them as *human* rights—as rights of every human being. It may be able to support them only as rights among persons who fear one another (or think that one day they may have reason to fear one another) or who need one another's cooperation (or think that one day they may need one another's cooperation). Nietzsche wrote: "Justice (fairness) originates among those who are approximately *equally powerful*, as Thucydides . . . comprehended correctly. . . . [J]ustice is repayment and exchange on the assumption of an approximately equal power position. . . . Justice naturally derives from prudent concern with self-preservation; that means, from the egoism of the consideration: 'Why should I harm myself uselessly and perhaps not attain my goal anyway?'"[106] Even if you are not within the circle of those I happen to respect and for whom I happen to have concern, if you are my neighbor I may fear your aggression or need your cooperation. But if you are a Somalian, or a Bosnian Muslim, we (as North Americans) may not fear *your* aggression or even think that one day we may have reason to fear your

104. David Gauthier, "Rational Constraint: Some Last Words," in *Contractarianism and Rational Choice*, ed. Peter Vallentyne (New York: Oxford University Press, 1991), 323, 330.

105. Peter Vallentyne, "Gauthier's Three Projects," in *Contractarianism and Rational Choice*, ed. Peter Vallentyne (New York: Oxford University Press, 1991), 1, 2. Cf. Robert Sugden, "The Contractarian Enterprise," in *Rationality, Justice and the Social Contract*, ed. David Gauthier and Robert Sugden (Ann Arbor: University of Michigan, 1993), 1, 8: "At the core of [Gauthier's project] is the thought that traditional moral theory relies on the supposed existence of entities, such as God or goodness, which are external to human life yet somehow matter. A defensible morality should dispense with such mysterious entities, and accept that life has no meaning outside itself."

106. Friedrich Nietzsche, "All Too Human," in *Basic Writings of Nietzsche*, trans. Walter Kaufmann (New York: Modern Library, 1973), 148. See note 142 and accompanying text.

aggression; and we may not need *your* cooperation or even think that one day we may need your cooperation. Indeed, even if you live among us but are, say, severely handicapped, we may not think that you have anything to offer us.

> [Gauthier's contractarian] view of the relationship between the individual and society has some implications about which even the most committed contractarians are uneasy. If justice is wholly a matter of reciprocity, do we have any obligation to support people who are so severely handicapped that they can offer us nothing in return? . . . Gauthier has to concede that the handicapped lie "beyond the pale of morality tied to mutuality"; if we have moral duties in these cases, [Gauthier's] theory cannot account for them. Each of us may feel *sympathy* for the handicapped, and if so, the welfare of the handicapped will be among the ends we pursue; but this is a matter of preference, not moral obligation.[107]

Perhaps it is the case, however, that even if you are only a lowly inhabitant of an alien, distant, and weak community, we or some of those who happen to be within the circle of our respect and concern may eventually suffer in ways not always easy to predict or even foresee if we fail to act toward you as if you, too, were within the circle of our respect and concern—if, in that sense, we fail to take you into the circle of our respect and concern. Although, again, their principal justificatory reliance is on the idea of human rights—although, that is, their principal argument is other-regarding—even the Universal Declaration of Human Rights and the other documents of the International Bill of Human Rights contain at least a hint of a self-regarding argument, namely: If you want to enjoy the fruits of peace in the world, you must extend your respect and concern to all human beings. The Univer-

---

107. Sugden, "Contractarian Enterprise," 5. Gauthier has written that *Morals By Agreement*

is an attempt to challenge Nietzsche's prescient remark, "As the will to truth . . . gains self-consciousness . . . morality will gradually perish." It is an attempt to write moral theory for adults, for persons who live consciously in a post-anthropomorphic, post-theocentric, post-technocratic world. It is an attempt to allay the fear, or suspicion, or hope, that without a foundation in objective value or objective reason, in sympathy or in sociality, the moral enterprise must fail.

David Gauthier, "Moral Artifice," *Canadian Journal of Philosophy* 18 (1988): 385. In the end, however, as the text accompanying this note confirms, Gauthier does not challenge Nietzsche so much as he embraces a Nietzschean conception of justice.

sal Declaration of Human Rights, the International Covenant on Economic, Social and Cultural Rights, and the International Covenant on Civil and Political Rights all state, in their preambles, that "recognition . . . of the equal and inalienable rights of all members of the human family is the foundation of freedom, justice *and peace* in the world" (emphasis added). Similarly, the European Convention for the Protection of Human Rights and Fundamental Freedoms (1953) states that the "Fundamental Freedoms" it affirms "are the foundation of justice *and peace* in the world" (emphasis added).

As a matter of domestic political debate—as a matter of domestic realpolitik—plausible self-regarding ("pragmatic") reasons for our nation taking even the lowliest of the low into the circle of those it happens to respect and for whom it happens to have concern are undoubtedly an important complement to the other-regarding argument (i.e., the idea of human rights) for our nation doing so.[108] Addressing the World Conference on Human Rights in June 1993, U.S. Secretary of State Warren Christopher included self-regarding reasons in his argument that the nations of the world should take seriously the cause of human rights, including the cause of democracy: "A world of democracies would be a safer world. . . . States that respect human rights and operate on democratic principles tend to be the world's most peaceful and stable. On the other hand, the worst violators of human rights tend to be the world's aggressors and proliferators. These states export threats to global security, whether in the shape of terrorism, massive refugee flows, or environmental pollution. Denying human rights not only lays waste to human lives; it creates instability that travels across borders."[109]

It seems quite doubtful, however, that self-regarding reasons can by themselves bear all the weight. Put another way, it seems doubtful that any domestic political argument that is not at least

108. Cf. Henry Kissinger, "Continuity and Change in American Foreign Policy," *Society* 15 (1977): 97, 99: "[O]ne of the basic challenges of foreign policy [is] the perennial tension between morality and pragmatism. Whenever it has been forced to wield its great power, the United States has also been driven to search its conscience. How does our foreign policy serve moral ends? How can the United States carry out its role as human example and champion of justice in a world in which power is still often the final arbiter? How do we reconcile ends and means, principle and survival? How do we keep secure both our existence *and* our values? These have been the moral and intellectual dilemmas of the United States for two hundred years."

109. Warren Christopher, "Democracy and Human Rights: Where America Stands," *U.S. Department of State Dispatch* 4 (1993): 441, 442.

partly other-regarding—that does not appeal at least in part to the conviction that every human being is sacred—can do the required work. The self-regarding reasons are, after all, abstract and highly speculative; their applicability to many concrete contexts is either just barely plausible or not plausible at all. Consider, in that regard, Jerome Shestack's catalog of such reasons, which I quote in the footnote.[110] As one human rights scholar has concluded, self-regarding

110. See James Shestack, "An Unsteady Focus: The Vulnerabilities of the Reagan Administration's Human Rights Policy," *Harvard Human Rights Yearbook* 2 (1989): 25, 49–50 (footnotes omitted):

What reasons should motivate an administration to afford human rights a central role in United States foreign policy as a matter of national interest? I believe that there are at least the following compelling motivations:

1. Human rights values advance national security. Nations that accept human rights are likely to be more stable and make better allies. Repression of human rights invites interventions and endangers stability. Conversely, human rights include responsiveness to the will of the people and restraints on aggressive action.

2. Human rights and world peace are interrelated. Peace and stability cannot be maintained in a world in which people are repressed and impelled to rise up against their oppressors. Afghanistan, Armenia, Burundi, Bangladesh, Haiti, the Philippines and many other places are stark examples.

3. Human rights are premised on the observance of rules of international law. Acceptance of the rule of law is a condition for a system of world order which, in turn, promotes world peace.

4. Human rights have become a central item on the global agenda, appealing to the expectations of people on every continent. The United States is perceived as having an immense potential to further human dignity and freedom. Championing human rights affords the United States the opportunity to be relevant to that agenda and responsive to the aspirations of peoples around the world.

5. Advancing economic and social human rights removes causes of tension and instability among less developed nations and promotes an equitable world order.

6. Human rights endeavors offer the United States the opportunity to act in concert with other nations to generate "coalitions of shared purposes."

7. Human rights address one of the world's most pressing problems: the enormous increase of refugees. The plight of refugees contributes to international tensions, and refugees impose huge burdens on nations to which they flee. Enforcing human rights will alleviate the suffering and number of refugees.

8. Including human rights in foreign policy formulation is favored by Congress. Without accommodation to this concern, the executive branch faces a polarized foreign policy marked by continuing disputes with Congress. A consensus with Congress on human rights issues advances the effectiveness and reliability of United States foreign policy initiatives.

"arguments are hard to prove and not fully persuasive. Despite considerable effort, it has been difficult to construct a wholly convincing 'selfish' rationale for major U.S. national commitments to promote the human rights of foreigners."[111] How confident are we that we Americans will eventually suffer if we fail to take the Bosnian Muslims, for example, or the Tibetan Buddhists, into the circle of our respect and concern? Confident enough to incur the costs of taking them in (if we do not also believe that they and all human beings are sacred)? In any event, no political argument for our nation taking the human rights of distant peoples seriously will begin to have the power of an argument that appeals at least in part to the conviction that all human beings are sacred. That conviction, after all, is partly constitutive of the American identity.[112]

Moreover, in the Declaration of Independence, the conviction is presented in a religious version: "We hold these truths to be self-evident, that all men are created equal, that they are endowed by their Creator with certain inalienable Rights, that among these are Life, Liberty and the pursuit of Happiness." What becomes of that proclamation—a proclamation that has been formative of our national identity[113]—if we abandon our belief in the "Creator"? Is there

9. Human rights policies command respect and support from this nation's citizenry. Conversely, foreign policies which ignore human rights are likely to be self-defeating by failing to sustain popular support.

10. Finally, advancing human rights reinforces this nation's own cohesion, its moral purpose and its appreciation of its own domestic liberties. Human rights have long been a focus for shared purpose in this nation's tradition, and a sense of shared purpose among its people is in the national interest.

111. Richard Bilder, "Human Rights and U.S. Foreign Policy: Short-Term Prospects," *Virginia Journal of International Law* 14 (1974): 597, 608. See also Richard Bilder, "Rethinking International Human Rights: Some Basic Questions," *Wisconsin Law Review* (1969): 171, 187–91.

112. Cf. Bilder, "Human Rights and U.S. Foreign Policy," 608–9: "Moral compromises . . . may have real costs in terms of the way Americans view their own country and its role in the world. We are coming to see that national pride, self-respect, cohesion, and purpose are meaningful elements of both national power and domestic tranquility. It is true that there are practical limits to what the United States can reasonably attempt to accomplish in promoting the human rights of other peoples. But, in a period following Vietnam and Watergate, it may be worth some foreign policy risks to reassert historic American commitments to human worth and dignity."

113. See Christopher, "Democracy and Human Rights," 441: "America's identity as a nation derives from our dedication to the proposition 'that all Men are created equal and endowed by their Creator with certain unalienable rights.'"

an intelligible secular version of the proclamation? Whatever the answer, for most Americans the power of the conviction that all human beings are sacred and the power of an argument that appeals to that conviction derive substantially from the fact that for them, the conviction that human beings are sacred is a religious conviction, even if for others the conviction is not religious—indeed, even if the conviction is not inescapably religious. For most Americans, the religious language of the Declaration ("all men are *created* equal, . . . they are endowed by their *Creator*") remains a resonant language, even if for others it is an antique language from an irretrievable past.

Unlike the definitional strategy, the self-regarding strategy for insisting that certain things not be done to any human being and that certain other things be done for every human being should not be dismissed. But the self-regarding strategy is probably availing only or mainly as a buttress, a complement, to the strategy that relies on the idea of human rights—on the conviction that every human being, even the lowliest inhabitant of the most alien, distant, and weak community, is sacred. Significantly, neither individually nor even cumulatively can self-regarding reasons by themselves begin to account for the passionate other-regarding character of most discourse in support of human rights claims.

To suggest that the idea of human rights is ineliminably religious—that there is, finally, no intelligible secular version of the idea of human rights, that the conviction that human beings are sacred is inescapably religious—is *not* to deny that one can take human rights very seriously indeed without being religious, that agnostics, too, even atheists, can be take human rights seriously, that they, too, can love the Other.[114] *Of course* atheists—like Albert Camus[115]—can take human rights seriously, *of course* they and other nonreligious persons can love the Other. Indeed, if the Other really is, in some deep sense, one's sister or brother, then it would be surprising if every nonreligious person were existentially disconnected from that truth.[116] But, of course, as the

---

114. In his review of my book *Love and Power*, Ned Foley thought that I was denying that one can be moral without being religious. See Edmund Foley, "Tillich and Camus, Talking Politics," *Columbia Law Review* 92 (1992): 954, 964–77.

115. See ibid.

116. Cf. Kristen Monroe, Michael Barton, and Ute Klingeman, "Altruism and the Theory of Rational Action: Rescuers of Jews in Nazi Europe," *Ethics* 101 (1990): 103;

example of Camus attests, to be connected to that truth existentially, as Camus certainly was, is not necessarily to affirm it intellectually.

(And, alas, as countless depressing examples illustrate, to affirm intellectually the truth—if it is a truth—that the Other is sister or brother is not necessarily to be connected to the truth existentially: To believe that the Other is sister or brother is not necessarily to experience any love for the Other; indeed, thanks to weakness of will or some pathology, one can believe that the Other is sister or brother *while standing on the Other's neck.*)

However, as the Polish philosopher Leszek Kolakowski has written: "When Pierre Bayle argued that morality does not depend on religion, he was speaking mainly of psychological independence; he pointed out that atheists are capable of achieving the highest moral standards . . . and of putting to shame most of the faithful Christians. That is obviously true as far as it goes, *but this matter-of-fact argument leaves the question of validity intact; neither does it solve the question of the effective sources of the moral strength and moral convictions of those 'virtuous pagans.'* "[117] That Camus achieved the highest moral standards, that he loved the Other, even that in doing so he understood himself to be engaged in a profound act of resistance and rebellion—resisting and rebelling against what he believed to be the ultimate absurdity, or meaninglessness, of the universe[118]—"leaves the question of validity intact." In particular, and as Nietzsche saw clearly, it leaves intact the question: Why should we give a damn about the well-being of all human beings, including the weak and

---

Neera Badhwar, "Altruism v. Self-Interest: Sometimes a False Dichotomy," *Social Philosophy & Policy* 10 (1993): 90.

117. Leszek Kolakowski, *Religion* (New York: Oxford University Press, 1982), 191 (emphasis added).

118. But cf. Jackson, "Disconsolation of Theology," 9 ("Promethean self-creation and utterly gratuitous care for others risks collapsing into its (putative) opposite, a self-destructive and domineering hubris"); Fred Dallmayr, "Critical Theory and Reconciliation," in *Habermas, Modernity, and Public Theology*, ed. Don S. Browning and Francis Fiorenza (New York: Crossroads, 1992), 119, 139:

> If the world is totally corrupt and perverse, then this world must be destroyed and replaced by a completely new one through some kind of *creatio ex nihilo*; moreover, given the removal of absolutes, such creation can only be the work of human agents or producers. In this manner, reconciliation and redemption become the targets of goal-directed activity, that is, or purposive fabrication. . . . At the same time, being themselves part of the corrupt world, human agents can only perpetuate or re-create the state of corruption; thus, instrumentalism becomes inescapable and self-destructive.

the powerless—those whom Matthew's Gospel calls "the least of these brothers of mine"?[119]

Now, "the question of validity" (as Kolakowski calls it) is not always at issue, it is not always on the table. As I said, one can, like Camus, love the Other without being religious.[120] If two citizens, one of them religious, the other not, happen to agree that the Other is sacred, or at least that the well-being of the Other is of fundamental importance, the question of validity does not arise *between them*.[121] But that the question does not arise between them does not mean that it does not arise between or among others. After all, not everyone in the United States does, like Camus, love the Other; not everyone does agree that the well-being of all human beings—including the weak and the powerless—is of fundamental importance; not everyone agrees that he or she owes every human being respect or concern. The question of validity is often on the table—though often not explicitly—in the public square, as, for example, when redistributive issues are being debated.[122] ("Why should *we* be taxed to support *them*? Frankly, I don't give a damn about them. And even if I did, I've worked hard for my money and it's all I can do to take care of my own.") The mere fact that one can love the Other without being religious does not begin to respond to the question of validity when the question does arise, when it is at issue.

There is not only the question of validity. There is also, as Kolakowski said, "the question of the effective sources of the moral strength and moral convictions of those 'virtuous pagans.' " Habermas is frank in acknowledging the problem—and bleak in what he has to say about it: "Who or what gives us the courage for such a total engagement that in situations of degradation and deprivation is already being expressed when the destitute and deprived summon the energy each

---

119. Matthew 25:40.

120. For a series of meditations on Camus's work by one of the most important Christian (Catholic) writers of the late twentieth century—a writer who did not pretend that Camus was in any way an "anonymous" Christian—see Thomas Merton, "Seven Essays on Albert Camus (1966–68)," in *The Literary Essays of Thomas Merton*, ed. Patrick Hart (New York: New Directions, 1981), 179–301.

121. Foley suggests that it would not have arisen as between Paul Tillich and Albert Camus. He also explains that it need not arise as between someone who is "pro-choice" on the issue of abortion and someone who is "pro-life." See Foley, "Tillich and Camus," 973–75.

122. Cf. note 139.

morning to carry on anew? The question about the meaning of life is not meaningless. Nevertheless, the circumstance that penultimate arguments inspire no great confidence is not enough for the grounding of a hope that can be kept alive only in a religious language. The thoughts and expectations directed toward the common good have, after metaphysics has collapsed, only an unstable status."[123] Consider, with respect to the problem of the adequacy of any nonreligious response to the "effective sources" question, the relevance of what Timothy Jackson has said about antirealism: "[L]etting go of realism will in all probability leave a society without the wherewithal to found or sustain a commitment to liberty, equality, or fraternity—much less sorority. Such a society may live for a time on past cultural capital embodied in liberal institutions and traditions, but a purely conventional virtue will not last long. The issue is one of motivation and consistency."[124] The bleakness of Habermas's statement—about the "unstable status" that "thoughts and expectations directed toward the common good have after metaphysics has collapsed"—lends weight to Jackson's.

Of course, many persons will have an understandable incentive to reject the possibility that the idea of human rights is ineliminably religious: persons who do not count themselves religious, including some who count themselves antireligious but who embrace the idea of human rights—who embrace, in particular, the conviction that every human being is sacred. They will think: "The conviction that every human being is sacred cannot be inescapably religious, for if it were, how could we—we who are not religious and who may even look at religion as always and everywhere little more than a childish superstition—defend the idea of human rights?" How indeed?

Richard Rorty has recommended that we simply stop trying to defend the idea of human rights; in particular, he has recommended that we abandon what he calls our "human rights foundationalism",[125] which, in Rorty's view, has proven a futile project. For example, "Kant's account of the respect due to rational agents tells you that you should extend the respect you feel for people like yourself to all featherless bipeds. That is an excellent suggestion, a good formula for secularizing the Christian doctrine of the brotherhood of man. But it

---

123. Habermas, "Transcendence," 239.

124. Timothy Jackson, "The Theory and Practice of Discomfort: Richard Rorty and Pragmatism," *Thomist* 51 (1987): 270, 289.

125. Rorty, "Human Rights, Rationality, and Sentimentality," 116.

has never been backed up by an argument based on neutral premises, and it never will be."[126] Human rights foundationalism is not merely futile; it is, according to Rorty, "outmoded."[127] There is, says Rorty, a better project for us (i.e., for those of us who embrace the cause of human rights): "We see our task as a matter of making our own culture—the human rights culture—more self-conscious and more powerful, rather than demonstrating its superiority to other cultures by an appeal to something transcultural" (like the putative sacredness/inviolability/etc. of every human being).[128]

But is it really enough, when confronted by intellectual or, worse, existential repudiations of human rights, to retreat, pace Rorty, into a kind of ethnocentrism—at one point Rorty refers to "our Eurocentric human rights culture"[129]—proclaiming proudly and loudly that although among us late-twentieth-century North Americans and Western Europeans (and perhaps a few others), a great fondness for human rights, or for "the moral point of view," is nothing more a culturally acquired taste, it is *our* acquired taste,[130] and we are willing, if necessary, to fight and even die for it? Not even among all of us late-twentieth-century North Americans et al. has the taste—the cultural preference—for human rights been acquired. Recall, for example, Gauthier's Nietzschean "morality."[131] Moreover, why shouldn't those of us who have acquired a fondness for human rights try to disabuse ourselves of that fondness (if it is only an acquired taste)—at least, why shouldn't we try to moderate that fondness—once it becomes clear that

126. Ibid., 124–25. Rorty is far from alone in reaching that conclusion. See, for example, Jeffrie Murphy, "Afterword: Constitutionalism, Moral Skepticism, and Religious Belief," in ed. Alan S. Rosenbaum, *Constitutionalism: The Philosophical Dimension* (New York: Greenwood Press, 1988), 239, 243–45 (arguing that Kant failed in his effort to provide a secular foundation for the morality he wanted to defend).

127. Rorty, "Human Rights, Rationality, and Sentimentality," 116.

128. Ibid., 117. See also 117–18.

129. Ibid., 126.

130. See Bernard Williams, "Auto-da-Fé," *New York Review*, 28 April 1983, 33: "Rorty is so insistent that we cannot, in philosophy, simply be talking about human beings, as opposed to human beings at a given time. . . . Rorty . . . contrasts the approach of taking some philosophical problem and asking . . . 'What does it show us about *being human?*' and asking, on the other hand, 'What does the persistence of such problems show us about *being twentieth-century Europeans?*" (Emphasis in original.) See (in addition to Rorty, "Human Rights, Rationality, and Sentimentality") Richard Rorty, *Contingency, Irony, and Solidarity* (Cambridge and New York: Cambridge University Press, 1989), chap. 9, "Solidarity."

131. See notes 103–7 and accompanying text.

indulging a fondness for human rights can be, politically, economically, militarily, and in other ways a rather costly proposition? (I commented earlier on the imitations of a self-regarding strategy for supporting human rights claims.) Most importantly, if the fondness for human rights some of us have is, at bottom, nothing more than an acquired taste, what is there to say to those who have not acquired the taste—and who may even have acquired a taste for violating (what we call) human rights—other than, perhaps, "Try it, you'll like it (maybe)"?

Rorty suggests that we try to convert others to our human rights culture partly through a process of "manipulating sentiments, [of] sentimental education,"[132] a process in which we tell "sad and sentimental stories."[133] (Rorty refers to Aeschylus's *The Persians* and Harriet Beecher Stowe's *Uncle Tom's Cabin*.[134]) I don't mean to deny the importance of such stories in effecting "a progress of sentiments," as Rorty calls it.[135] (Jesus, too, told stories: parables.) But in what sense is it a *progress*, and not merely a *change*, of sentiments, if the new sentiments don't more accurately reflect a *truth* about the Other, namely, that the Other is—*really* is—sacred, that the Other is, somehow, sister or brother? In any event, in the view of most of us who embrace the cause of human rights, the fundamental wrong done, when human rights are violated, is not that our sentiments—the sentiments of "our Eurocentric human rights culture"—are offended. The fundamental wrong done is much deeper than that: It is that, somehow, the very order of the world—the *normative* order of the world—is transgressed.

Of course, we may be quite wrong to believe—it may be false to believe—that the world has a normative order that is transgressed by violations of human rights. But Rorty does not argue that it is a false belief that the normative order of the world is transgressed by violations of human rights. Whether or not it is a false belief is not the sort of issue the "pragmatist" Rorty finds it useful to address; indeed, it is the sort of issue he finds it useful to marginalize.[136] (If the idea of human rights is ineliminably religious, then human rights foundationalism is,

---

132. Rorty, 122.
133. Ibid., 119.
134. Ibid., 128.
135. Ibid., 129 (referring to Annette Baier, *A Progress of Sentiments: Reflections on Hume's Treatise* [Cambridge: Harvard University Press, 1991]).
136. See Rorty, 119.

finally, a theological project. In Rorty's view, however, theology is not a useful conversation.)

I am skeptical, however, that we can, without serious costs, marginalize the issue. There is not only the question I have already posed: In what sense is it a progress of sentiments, and not merely a change? There are other important problems. For example: If we have no reason to believe that the world has a normative order that is transgressed by violations of human rights—at least, if we have no reason to be other than agnostic about the issue—and if we nonetheless coerce others, and perhaps even, at the limit, kill others, in the name of protecting human rights, then are we coercing and killing in the name of nothing but our sentiments, our preferences? Does Rorty want to deny that it would be deeply problematic for us to coerce and kill in the name of nothing but our sentiments or preferences? (Tim Jackson has asked, in connection with Rorty's views: "Can one imagine dying for irony's sake?"[137] I want to ask: Can one imagine killing for irony's sake?) Does Rorty want to say something like this: "It's a brutal world out there. It's either them or us. It's either their culture or ours, either their sentiments/preferences or ours. It's not that might makes right. It's just that there is no right, only might. May our might, not theirs, prevail!" Rorty did once say something fully congruent with that position: "[W]hen the secret police come, when the torturers violate the innocent, there is nothing to be said to them of the form 'There is something within you which you are betraying. Though you embody the practices of a totalitarian society which will endure forever, there is something beyond those practices which condemns you.' "[138]

Although in my view, then, we should be wary about following Rorty's recommendation to abandon "human rights foundationalism," my aim in this chapter has not been to defend the (general) claim that the world has a normative order, much less the (particular) claim that every human being is sacred and therefore one attacks the normative order of the world—including one's own deepest nature—when one violates human rights. (The latter is the claim that, contra Rorty, there *is* "something within you which you are betraying.") My aim here—a much less ambitious and certainly more manageable aim—has been

137. Jackson, "Disconsolation of Theology," 10.
138. Richard Rorty, *Consequences of Pragmatism* (Minnesota: University of Minnesota Press, 1982), xlii.

only to inquire whether there is an intelligible secular version of the claim, the *foundational* claim, that every human being is sacred, or whether, instead, the claim is inescapably religious.

For many religious persons, certainly, the idea of human rights simply does not make sense, it does not exert a claim, apart from, cut off from, the Gospel vision of the world and of our place in it—or from some equivalent religious vision.[139] (Simone Weil wrote: "The Gospel makes no distinction between the love of our neighbor and justice. . . . The supernatural virtue of justice consists in behaving exactly as though there were equality when one is stronger in an unequal relationship."[140]) Some even fear that the only conception of justice likely to flourish apart from the Gospel (or some equivalent) vision, once we have exhausted our "past cultural capital,"[141] is the

---

139. See Jeremy Waldron, "Religious Contributions in Public Deliberation," *San Diego Law Review* 30 (1993): 817, 844–45:

> Consider, for example, the issue of whether property owners are obliged by natural law to share their wealth with the poor. Locke's position on this is well known:
>
>> [W]e know God hath not left one Man so to the Mercy of another, that he may starve him if he please: God the Lord and Father of all, has given no one of his Children such a Property, in his peculiar Portion of the things of this World, but that he has given his needy Brother a Right to the Surplusage of his Goods; so that it cannot justly be denied him, when his pressings Wants call for it.
>
> We might rephrase this as follows: "A needy person has a right to the surplus goods of a rich person if they are necessary to keep him from perishing." If we do, however, someone is likely to ask us for an *argument* to support this controversial proposition. In Locke, the argument is based on the seminal fact of God's creating the world for the sustenance of all men:
>
>> God made Man, and planted in him, as in all other Animals, a strong desire of Self-preservation, and furnished the World with things fit for Food and Rayment and other Necessaries of Life, Subservient to his design, that Man should live and abide for some time upon the Face of the Earth, and not that so curious and wonderful a piece of Workmanship by its own Negligence, or want of Necessaries, should perish again presently after a few moments continuance. . . .
>
> Once again, we might, at a pinch translate *that* into secular language: "That people have a right to make use of the goods that may help them to survive is common sense." It loses a little in the translation, though. Keeping hold of the idea that we were *meant* to survive, and that being denied access to the naturally available resources that we need is offensive to the fact of our existence is difficult in a secular tradition.

140. Simone Weil, *Waiting for God*, trans. Emma Crauford (New York: Capricorn Books, 1973), 139, 143 (quoted at the beginning of Jackson, "Disconsolation of Theology").

141. See text accompanying note 124.

dispiriting conception implicit in Nietzsche's genealogy of justice—
his genealogy, that is, of a kind of justice (a Gauthierian kind[142]):

> My dear Sir Long-Ears-and-Virtuous, we have no desire whatever
> to be better, we are very contented with ourselves, all we desire is
> not to harm one another—and therefore we forbid certain actions
> when they are directed in a certain way, namely against us, while
> we cannot sufficiently honor these same actions provided they are
> directed against enemies of the community—against you, for in-
> stance. We educate our children in them; we cultivate them— If
> we shared that "God-pleasing" radicalism that your holy madness
> recommends, if we were fools enough to condemn together with
> those actions the source of them, the "heart," the "disposition,"
> that would mean condemning our own existence and with it its
> supreme prerequisite—a disposition, a heart, a passion we honor
> with the highest honors. By our decrees, we prevent this disposi-
> tion from breaking out and expressing itself in an inexpedient
> way—we are prudent when we make such law for ourselves, we
> are also moral— Have you no suspicion, however faint, what
> sacrifice it is costing us, how much taming, self-overcoming, sever-
> ity toward ourselves it requires? We are vehement in our desires,
> there are times when we would like to devour each other— But the
> "sense of community" masters us: please note that this is almost a
> definition of morality.[143]

Let me emphasize that nothing in this chapter—nothing at all—is
meant to defend, as credible or even as appealing, any religious-
cosmological beliefs or any religious-moral beliefs, much less to com-
mend any such beliefs to anyone.[144] One certainly need not count
oneself a religious person in order to wonder—indeed, one can be one
of those "good many professors and other intellectuals [who] display
a hostility or skeptical indifference to religion that amounts to a thinly
disguised contempt for belief in any reality beyond that discoverable

---

142. See note 107 and accompanying text.
143. Nietzsche, "The Will to Power," 159–60.
144. Cf. Thomas Nagel, "A Faith of the Enlightenment," *Times Literary Supplement*, 14 December 1990 ("a religious answer stands as much in need of defence and
explanation as does a secular one").

by scientific inquiry and ordinary human experience"[145] and *nonetheless* wonder—whether the idea of human rights isn't ineliminably religious. One need not count oneself religious in order to wonder whether much secular moral-philosophizing hasn't been, for a very long time now, a kind of whistling in the dark.[146] (Recall, in that regard, Rorty's claim that the Kantian project has failed.[147]) Jeffrie Murphy, for example, insists that it is, for him, "very difficult—perhaps impossible—to embrace religious convictions," but he nonetheless claims that "the liberal theory of rights requires a doctrine of human dignity, preciousness and sacredness that cannot be utterly detached from a belief in God or at least from a world view that would be properly called religious in some metaphysically profound sense." Murphy continues: "[T]he idea that fundamental moral values may require [religious] convictions is not one to be welcomed with joy [by nonreligious enthusiasts of the liberal theory of rights]. This idea generates tensions and appears to force choices that some of us would prefer not to make. *But it still might be true for all of that.*"[148]

Nietzsche asked: "Now suppose that belief in God has vanished: the question presents itself anew: 'who speaks?' "[149] Echoing Nietzsche's question a brutal century later, Arthur Leff wrote:

Napalming babies is bad.
Starving the poor is wicked.
Buying and selling each other is depraved.
Those who stood up to and died resisting Hitler, Stalin, Amin, and Pol Pot—and General Custer too—have earned salvation.

---

145. Kent Greenawalt, *Religious Convictions and Political Choice* (New York: Oxford University Press, 1988), 6. See Perry, *Love and Power*, 67, 173 n.1. Cf. Richard John Neuhaus, *The Naked Public Square: Religion and Democracy in America* (Grand Rapids: W. B. Eerdmans, 1984), 86: "In the minds of some secularists the naked public square [i.e., neutral/impartial political discourse] is a desirable goal. They subscribe to the dogma of the secular Enlightenment that, as people become more enlightened (educated), religion will wither away; or, if it does not wither away, it can be safely sealed off from public consideration, reduced to a private eccentricity."

146. See Goldsworthy, "God or Mackie"; Arthur Alan Leff, "Unspeakable Ethics, Unnatural Law," *Duke Law Journal* (1979): 1229; Murphy, "Afterword." See also Philip Johnson, "Nihilism and the End of Law," *First Things* (March 1993): 19.

147. See text accompanying note 126.

148. Murphy, "Afterword," 248 (emphasis added).

149. Nietzsche, "The Will to Power," 157.

Those who acquiesced deserve to be damned.
There is in the world such a thing as evil.
[All together now:] Sez who?
God help us.[150]

---

150. Leff, "Unspeakable Ethics, Unnatural Law," 1249.

Rights in the Postmodern Condition

Pierre Schlag

Even within ordinary legal or political discourse, "rights" defy easy identification. Thus, rights are sometimes treated as concepts,[1] as argumentative trumps,[2] as factors of production,[3] as preconditions to bargaining,[4] as bearer-enabling entitlements,[5] as bearer-disabling entitlements,[6] as totems,[7] as sources of social solidarity,[8] as legitimation devices,[9] and so on.

A previous version of this chapter was presented at a legal theory workshop of the Columbia Law School. I thank the participants, as well as Paul Campos, Gary Minda, Steve Smith, and Steven Winter, for their helpful comments.

1. Geoffrey Marshall, "Rights, Options, and Entitlements," in *Oxford Essays in Jurisprudence*, ed. A. W. B. Simpson, 2d ser. (Oxford: Clarendon Press, 1973), 228.

2. Ronald Dworkin, *Taking Rights Seriously* (Cambridge: Harvard University Press, 1977), xi.

3. Ronald Coase, "The Problem of Social Cost," *Journal of Law & Economics* 3 (1960): 1, 43–44 ("A final reason for the failure to develop a theory adequate to handle the problem of harmful effects stems from a faulty concept of a factor of production. This is usually thought of as a physical entity which the businessman acquires and uses . . . instead of a right to perform certain [physical] actions.").

4. Robert Hale, "Coercion and Distribution in a Supposedly Non-Coercive State," *Political Science Quarterly* 38 (1923): 470–78; Coase, "Problem of Social Cost," 8 ("without this initial delimitation of rights there can be no market transactions").

5. Julius Stone, *The Province and Function of Law* (Cambridge: Harvard University Press, 1950), 118.

6. See Jeremy Paul, "The Hidden Structure of Takings Law," *Southern California Law Review* 64 (1991): 1393, 1438–41.

7. U.S. Constitution, amend. 1.

8. Staughton Lynd, "Communal Rights," *Texas Law Review* 62 (1984): 1417, 1440–41.

9. Allan C. Hutchinson and Patrick J. Monahan, "The 'Rights' Stuff: Roberto Unger and Beyond," *Texas Law Review* 62 (1984): 1477, 1486.

Indeed, to say, "I have a right," can mean any number of things, including: "I can do this." "Give me your money." "You can't do that." "The state should intercede on my behalf." "This is mine." "This is not yours." "You are a really bad person." "Stop what you're doing." "You're in trouble now." "Go to hell." It can also mean any combination of the above (and much more).

Rights are cast as substantialities, as relations, as frames. Rights are also cast as grounds for political redress or for legal action, as the mechanisms through which conflicts are resolved or mediated, as the endpoints in political and legal struggles.[10] They are cast as acts, scenes, agents, agencies, and purposes.[11] In short, rights can register on all sorts of different matrices and networks—everything from the rigorously charted moral space of the analytical philosophers, through the idolatrous discourse of the prototypical law review article, to material instantiation in residential architecture and capital investment.[12] Rights thus register in many different ways in many different kinds of modalities—modalities organized in terms of their own peculiar "logics": representational, symbolic, causal, logical, rhetorical, affective, material, economic, metaphysical, mythical, and so on.

Among American legal thinkers, however, the one unifying aspect of "rights" is that they are the object of sustained normative disputation. Indeed, much of American legal thought on rights consists precisely in the normative celebration, condemnation, or elaboration of "rights." Amid all this passionate normative contestation of rights, it is, of course, easy to believe that something very important must be at stake. One can easily begin to think that it is important to ask whether rights are normatively valuable and, if so, when and how, to whom, and so on.

But as one listens closely to all this passionate normative conversation, it is also possible to have a completely different experience and to pose a very different question. The experience is that of incredulity and the question is: "*What* are all these conversants talking about?"

10. For elaboration of this source-path-goal schema, see Steven Winter, "Transcendental Nonsense, Metaphoric Reasoning and the Cognitive Stakes for Law," *University of Pennsylvania Law Review* 137 (1989): 1105, 1214–20.

11. These are the main terms of Kenneth Burke's dramatistic ratios. Kenneth Burke, *On Symbols and Society* (Chicago: University of Chicago Press, 1989), 139–40.

12. For a provocative discussion of the imbrication of law and culture in landscape, see Steven Winter, "An Upside/Down View of the Countermajoritarian Difficulty," *Texas Law Review* 69 (1991): 1881, 1883–1919.

Indeed, in the midst of all the passionate normative, political, and philosophical claims made for, against, and about rights, one might begin to wonder: just what is the ontological identity of "rights?" When scholars present their celebrations and indictments of "rights," just what is it that is being celebrated or indicted? The answer, of course, is "rights." But this answer is just a reiteration of the problem: what are the conversants talking about? Are they talking about a philosophical concept, a juridical artifact fashioned by courts, an ethical imperative, a conjecture, a kind of socially sedimented ritual for the framing and dispositions of claims, a re-presentation of the social and economic power held by various subjects and backed up by state force? Which of these is the ontological identity of the referent "rights"? Or is it all these things (and many more) in various states of fusion—states of fusion whose actual composition might well differ from situation to situation, subject to subject, right to right?

It would be interesting to pursue this ontological question. Moreover, one would think that addressing this question would itself be a predicate for any intellectually serious discussion about the normative or political value of rights. For American legal thought, however, it is extremely important that this question be avoided. Indeed, it is the avoidance of the ontological question that allows all the passionate academic normative talk for, against, and about "rights" to get off the ground in the first place.

It is precisely the failure to ask the question of ontological identity that enables the participants in American legal thought to believe that "rights" have (1) a fairly robust ontological identity that is (2) generally recognized by the relevant conversants. It is this belief that allows the various participants in the "legal conversation" to think that when they are arguing for, against, or about rights, they are disagreeing over something, the same thing—namely, what they all call "rights." In turn, this belief that they are disagreeing over the same thing—what they all call "rights"—is absolutely essential to the intellectual cogency of all the passionate arguments for, against, and about rights.

The point becomes obvious if one considers the obverse situation. Suppose that "rights" were lacking any sort of robust ontological identity. Suppose, that "rights" were simply a floating signifier into which each subject projects his or her own socially individualized fears or hopes. If this were the case, there would be no *intellectual* point in making any sort of normative claims for or against "rights."

"R-i-g-h-t-s" by definition would be a jurisprudential equivalent of a Rorschach test. And if "r-i-g-h-t-s" were a kind of Rorschach test, then sustained and repeated *intellectual* inquiries into whether "r-i-g-h-t-s" should be condemned or celebrated would be a curious kind of category mistake.

Now the point here is not that rights are a kind of Rorschach test (though there is much to be said for this view). Rather, the point here is that the *intellectual* meaningfulness of normative and political arguments about rights depends upon the presumption that rights do have a robust and generally recognized ontological identity.[13] It is this presumption that provides the sense that the conversants are all talking about the same thing—namely, "rights"—and thus enables the normative conversation to get started. Without that presumption, it is hard to understand why anyone would have any intellectual interest in participating in the normative conversation. Indeed, once one drops the assumption that there is a robust referent that is generally recognized, the various competing arguments lose their intellectual interest. Indeed, they lose their identity as competing arguments altogether. They are neither competing nor arguments.

Not only does the presumption enable all the passionate normative and political conversation about rights to get started, but it allows this conversation to proliferate—virtually without any intellectual checks. Insofar as the presumption eclipses the need for any of the participants to actually articulate the ontological identity of rights, there are no serious intellectual restraints on what might be said for, against, or about rights. There is quite literally nothing of any intellectual character that claims for, against, or about rights can run up against. The only serious restraints on rights claims tend to be nonintellectual ones—restraints that issue from the nodding heads of disciplinary authority who point to the ostensible sources of their own authority and either nod approvingly ("Yes, this is what we mean by 'rights'") or disapprovingly ("No, this is not what we mean by 'rights'").

All of this raises a question: If there is no serious articulate account of a generally recognized robust ontology for rights, then what is it that sustains the belief that rights do have such an identity? In a

13. Paul Campos makes precisely this argument with respect to the status and role of "the text" in legal "interpretation." Paul Campos, "Against Constitutional Theory," *Yale Journal of Law & Humanities* 4 (1992): 279.

sense, this question has already been answered. Not only do the passionate normative arguments for and against rights depend upon such a generally recognized robust ontology, but the relentless practice of normative argumentation for, against, and about rights succeeds in establishing the presumption that rights do have such a robust ontology.

Indeed, the fervent desire among American legal thinkers to pursue their normative and political agendas succeeds in positing into existence whatever fundamental ontological forms are necessary to carry on such a conversation—not only "rights" but also other common items known variously as "rules," "doctrine," "principles," "values," and so on.[14] If the participants in this normative conversation of American legal thought have been unwilling to question the ontological identity of "rights," or indeed the ontological identity of any other fundamental ontological form, it is precisely because they wish to retain these fundamental ontological forms for use in their normative or political agendas.

In this chapter, I want to refine this argument by showing in some detail how two dominant aesthetics of American legal thought have enabled legal thinkers to believe that rights do have a robust and generally recognized ontology. Both of these dominant aesthetics—the analytic and the instrumental—are radically reductionist. And it is their radical reductionism that has enabled American legal thinkers to simply presume that rights have a robust ontology that is generally recognized. To the extent it is possible for American legal thinkers to escape the hold of these aesthetics and to perceive their radically reductionist effects—questions of possible relevance for both the reader and the author of this chapter—it is precisely because these aesthetics are unraveling.

Order and Progress—The Analytic and the Instrumental

The analytic aesthetic enacts a rhetoric of order—a rhetoric where the complexities and complications of life are subordinated to a rigorous, well-charted matrix of legal conceptions such as rights, duties, powers, and so on. In the analytic aesthetic, every legal conception

---

14. For elaboration, see Pierre Schlag, "Normativity and the Politics of Form," *University of Pennsylvania Law Review* 139 (1991): 801.

has its proper place. The instrumental aesthetic, by contrast, enacts a rhetoric of progress—a rhetoric where the shortfalls and inadequacies of a deficient present can be redressed through "change," "reform," "progress," "progressive legal change," or "transformative action."

A series of prototypical homologies are loosely associated, in the mode of *aesthetic affinity*, with the analytic and the instrumental aesthetic:

Analytic	Instrumental
Formalism	Realism
Rules	Standards
Order	Progress
Doctrine	Policy
Entity	Energy
Location	Direction
Authority	Value
Law	Equity
Past	Future
Security	Change
Object	Subject
Reification	Animism

The relations of these two aesthetics are multiple. Potential relations include not only opposition, but combination, appropriation, subordination, nesting, and mutual dependence.[15] The analytic and the instrumental aesthetic are not models, theories, or ideal types. They have no obvious borders or boundaries that would determinately help identify their own instantiations. And they are seldom found in a pure form. To the extent that it is possible to identify instantiations of

---

15. Moreover, the instrumental and the analytic do not exhaust the aesthetics of American legal thought. They have, however, been dominant in American legal thought since the late nineteenth century.

Some American legal thinkers have conceptualized rights in other aesthetics, most notably the holistic aesthetic. One of the most appealing holistic representations of legal concepts (including rights) was articulated by Felix Cohen: Felix Cohen, "Transcendental Nonsense and the Functional Approach," *Columbia Law Review* 35 (1935): 809. Despite its considerable intellectual appeal, Cohen's account of legal concepts has received very little recognition in the legal academy. Most recently, Cohen's account has been refined and elaborated by Steven Winter; see Winter, "Transcendental Nonsense."

these aesthetics, it is not because the instantiations meet a certain set of necessary and sufficient conditions, but because the instantiations fit in the manner of a gestalt or a family resemblance. The point is that the recognition of these two aesthetics is less a matter of model application than it is one of aesthetic sensibility.

The two aesthetics are described here as constitutive of the dominant conceptualizations of rights among American legal thinkers. It is important to keep in mind that the analytic and the instrumental aesthetic are instantiated in many of the concepts and artifacts of American legal thought—not just rights, but duties, immunities, powers, and so on. Some aspects of the two aesthetics described here will be generic, but other aspects will be peculiar to rights.

Because these aesthetics prefigure the rhetorical practices of American legal thinkers, the aesthetics themselves remain largely unseen and unnoticed. Indeed, American legal thinkers are often so passionately in thrall to the arguments and positions enabled by these aesthetics that they remain oblivious to the aesthetic character of their own legal arguments.

Each of these two aesthetics has a historical prototype. In other words, each aesthetic can be associated with a historical period and a historical form in which that aesthetic flourished. Thus, the analytic aesthetic flourished in the late-nineteenth-century thought of the legal academy—in the attempts by legal formalists, doctrinalists, analytical positivists, and proponents of scientific jurisprudence to systematize law into an orderly "science."[16] The confident and largely unquestioned dominance of this aesthetic as *the* form of law began to unravel in the early twentieth century. But despite this gradual unraveling, the analytic aesthetic has continued to shape—albeit in nonsystematic and somewhat haphazard ways—much of contemporary American legal thought.

The instrumentalist aesthetic flourished in mid- to late-twentieth-century American legal thought. Its most perfected expression was achieved through the moralist legal thought that dominated the legal academy after the advent of the Warren Court and the civil

---

16. The analytic aesthetic is not a complete account of late-nineteenth-century legal aesthetics. Indeed, one could easily identify aspects of late-nineteenth-century American legal thought that partake in the instrumentalist aesthetic. See Pierre Schlag, "The Problem of the Subject," *Texas Law Review* 69 (1991): 1627, 1632–62.

rights movements of the early 1960s.[17] Again, it is important to understand that the instrumentalist aesthetic does not exhaust the aesthetics of that period. Rather, the point is that mid- to late-twentieth-century legal thought presents and enacts the instrumentalist aesthetic in one of its most perfected forms. This aesthetic began to unravel in the late 1980s and early 1990s. But even as it unraveled (and continues to unravel to this day), the instrumentalist aesthetic continues to shape much of contemporary American legal thought.

The Analytic Aesthetic

The analytic aesthetic encompassed all manner of legal thought in late-nineteenth-century American legal thought—including the thematizations presently known as "legal formalism,"[18] "Langdellianism," "juristic science," "classical legal thought,"[19] and "analytical jurisprudence."[20] The analytic aesthetic creates order through a series of stabilizing metaphors and images: territorial spatialization/object/property/owner. The prototypical, indeed emblematic, artifact of this aesthetic in the late nineteenth century is the legal treatise, the learned tome, which lays out the form and content of the "law" in an orderly and purportedly comprehensive manner.

---

17. For various critiques of normativity in law, see Symposium, "The Critique of Normativity," *University of Pennsylvania Law Review* 139 (1991): 801–1075.

18. Thomas C. Grey, "Langdell's Orthodoxy," *University of Pittsburgh Law Review* 45 (1983): 1.

19. "Classical legal thought" is Duncan Kennedy's thematization of late-nineteenth-century legal thought. It has been elaborated recently by Morton Horwitz. The rise of classical legal thought coincides with the professionalization of American law schools in the second half of the nineteenth century. Classical legal thought reached its most confident and secure expression during that period of time. In significant respects, classical legal thought seems to overlap with what is frequently referred to as "legal formalism," "Langdellianism," "juristic science," and "analytic jurisprudence." Duncan Kennedy, "Towards an Historical Understanding of Legal Consciousness: The Case of Classical Legal Thought in America, 1850–1940," *Research in Law and Sociology* 3 (1980): 3; Morton Horwitz, *The Transformation of American Law 1870–1960* (New York: Oxford University Press, 1992), 9–32.

20. Analytical jurisprudence, stemming from John Austin, is positivist, while classical legal thought, as thematized by Kennedy and Horwitz, appears to be grounded in natural rights jurisprudence (Horwitz, *Transformation*). From a conventional jurisprudential standpoint, this difference is of major import. From the aesthetic perspective offered here, this "substantive" difference turns out to be insignificant.

The Territorialization of Law and
the Subdivision of Juridical Space

In the analytic aesthetic, law is spatialized; more specifically, it is territorialized. Law is framed as a field, a territory, a two-dimensional space that can be mapped and charted. This jurisprudential mapping occurs through the subdivision of the territorial space of law into various subparts, such as contract and torts or rights and duties. Each subpart is in turn subdivided into further subparts, such as negligence and intentional torts or rights in personam and rights in rem. These in turn are subdivided into even smaller subparts, and so on.

In late-nineteenth-century American legal thought, this analytical subpartitioning is relentless—verging on the obsessional. The first page of Christopher Columbus Langdell's notorious six-part article (ironically) entitled "A Brief Survey of Equity Jurisdiction" is exemplary. Langdell wrote:

> Rights are either absolute or relative. Absolute rights are such as do not imply any correlative duties. Relative rights are such as do imply correlative duties. . . . Relative rights, as well as their correlative duties, are called obligations; [and so on.][21]

This kind of acute subpartitioning was often sustained throughout entire treatises and throughout the excruciatingly detailed outlines that often served as their tables of contents.[22] At times, this analytical subpartitioning attained a kind of hypertrophic self-referentiality. Wigmore's programmatic (and unsuccessful) attempt to subdivide the science of law is emblematic:

> The Science of Law as a whole may be termed *Nomology.*
> The Science may be classified according to the different activities of thought which deal with the fact of law. These are four:

---

21. Christopher Langdell, "A Brief Survey of Equity Jurisdiction," *Harvard Law Review* 1 (1887): 1, 55.

22. The jurisprudence treatises of Austin, Salmond, and Gray, but not Holland, have such exquisitely detailed outlines. John Austin, *Lectures on Jurisprudence*, 5th ed., ed. Robert Campbell (London: J. Murray, 1885); John W. Salmond, *Jurisprudence*, 5th ed. (London: Stevens & Haynes, 1916); John Chipman Gray, *The Nature and Sources of the Law*, 2d ed., ed. Roland Gray (New York: Macmillan, 1948); T. E. Holland, *The Elements of Jurisprudence*, 5th ed. (Oxford: Clarendon Press, 1890).

Law may be conceived of as

    (1) A thing to be *ascertained* as a fact of human conduct; this branch to be termed *Nomo-scopy*.

    (2) A thing to be *questioned* and debated as a rule which by some standard might be different from what it is; this branch to be termed *Nomo-sophy*.

    (3) A thing to be *taught* as a subject of education; this to be termed *Nomo-didactics*.

    (4) A thing to be *made* and *enforced* by the state organs; this to be termed *Nomo-practics*.

  1. *Nomo-scopy* has three branches of activity:

    (a) It may concern itself with . . . this to be termed *Nomo-statics*.

    (b) It may concern itself with . . . this to be termed *Nomo-genetics*.

    (c) It may concern itself with . . . this to be termed *Nomo-physis*.

[And so on.][23]

One effect of this territorial spatialization and this relentless sub-partitioning is that law is stabilized and objectified into an orderly field of clearly delineated, bounded, perfectly contiguous, and perfectly nonoverlapping legal conceptions and propositions. Law is conceptualized as a chessboard—an image that was in fact used explicitly by the late-nineteenth-century analytical positivist, T. E. Holland:

> A Right varies with a variation in any one of the series of its constituent elements. . . . Thus the aggregate of rights may be likened *to a figure of two dimensions*: the shorter of these dimensions representing the law of persons; the longer the Law of Things. And the figure may be supposed to be marked off into squares, *like a chessboard*, ...[24]

Even today this subpartitioning aesthetic continues to organize much of American legal thought. The typical legal treatise and the typical law school casebook still exemplify this aesthetic. Correspondingly,

---

23. John H. Wigmore, "The Terminology of Legal Science (With a Plea for the Science of Nomo-Thetics)," *Harvard Law Review* 28 (1914): 1, 3.

24. Holland, *Elements of Jurisprudence*, 120.

TABLE *a*.   T. E. Holland's Conceptualization

	Law of Things					
	Shipping	Banking	Torts	Family	Succession	Etc.
Law of Persons						
Normal						
Lunatic						
Alien						
Covert						
Infant						
Etc.						

Source: T. E. Holland, *The Elements of Jurisprudence*, 5th ed. (Oxford: Clarendon Press, 1890), 121.

the typical law student still prepares for his or her exams by organizing each law school course into an *outline* form—self-created or commercial. Likewise, the aesthetic structure of most law review articles still exhibits this outline form. And even where the analytic aesthetic has collapsed—through the recognition of overlap, gaps, and indeterminacies—it nonetheless continues to haunt the legal mind as a kind of nostalgic aesthetic aspiration.

The recursive spatialization and compartmentalization of the analytic aesthetic already prefigures a certain *distinct* and *bounded* place for legal concepts, including rights.[25] Thus, in the great works of analytic jurisprudence, rights are typically accorded their own separate and discrete chapter.[26] This aesthetic territorialization and

25. On the image of rights as stable, bounded distinct entities, see Kennedy, "Understanding Legal Consciousness," 19; Jennifer Nedelsky, "Law, Boundaries, and the Bounded Self," *Representations* 30 (1990): 167; Mary Ann Glendon, *Rights Talk: The Impoverishment of Political Discourse* (New York: Maxwell Macmillan, 1991).

26. In the great works of nineteenth-century jurisprudence, rights are typically accorded a lexically and conceptually significant place—usually after the general discussion of law, its objects, and its study, but often before other arguably important legal conceptions such as duty, liability, intention, will, and so on. For instance, in the treatises of Austin, Salmond, and Gray, the discussion of rights is preceded only, if at all, by a general discussion of law, its sources, and the nature of its study. Some of the analytical positivists, students of Austin, explicitly emphasized the critical importance of rights in law. Holland, *Elements of Jurisprudence*, 69; Salmond, *Jurisprudence*, 179. John

compartmentalization establishes rights as distinct entities related to
other legal concepts such as duties, powers, and so on by means of
external relations. Indeed, it is this stabilization and objectification of
rights and other legal concepts in two-dimensional space that enabled the more sophisticated analytical thinkers such as Hohfeld to
specify and formalize the relations that obtain among the various
jural concepts.[27]

The "logic" of the analytic aesthetic is to produce juridical order
by perfecting and policing the analytical addresses of legal concepts
such as rights—by determining "precisely" or "scientifically" where
legal concepts are located within the juridical subdivisions.[28] Various
recurrent jurisprudential axes map out the terrain. Hence, in late-
nineteenth-century thought, the properties of specific rights—their
characteristics—often depend upon their location relative to fundamental jurisprudential axes, such as

moral/legal[29]
private/public[30]
in rem/in personam[31]

Chipman Gray, who claimed that it "is unimportant in theory whether a system of law
starts with a consideration of rights or of duties," nonetheless treated rights first in his
jurisprudence treatise. Gray, *Nature and Sources*, 73.

27. Notice Hohfeld's deployment of two-dimensional space to present his jural
opposites and jural correlatives:

Jural	rights	privilege	power	immunity
Opposites	no-rights	duty	disability	liability
Jural	right	privilege	power	immunity
Correlatives	duty	no-right	liability	disability

If it appears adequate to lay out jural correlatives and jural opposites in this way, it is
precisely because the jurisprudential world has already been reduced to a two-
dimensional space all ready for compartmentalization. Newcomb Hohfeld, "Some Fundamental Legal Conceptions As Applied in Judicial Reasoning," *Yale Law Journal* 23
(1913): 16, 30.

28. Duncan Kennedy describes this as a key feature of classical legal thought.
Kennedy, "Understanding Legal Consciousness."

29. William Edward Hearn, *The Theory of Legal Duties and Rights*, 3d ed. (Mel-
bourne: John Ferres, 1886), 143–44; Holland, *Elements of Jurisprudence*, 73–74; Gray,
Nature and Sources, 13.

30. Holland, *Elements of Jurisprudence*, 108–9.

31. Austin, *Lectures on Jurisprudence*, 394; Holland, *Elements of Jurisprudence*,
126–28.

negative/positive[32]
law/equity[33]

and so on.

The subpartitioning of the analytic occurs not just on the "outside" of rights, but within the "inside" as well. In the analytical jurisprudence of the late nineteenth century, rights are thus subpartitioned internally into prototypical elements:

The person entitled
The object
The act or forbearance
The person obliged[34]

The Right's Thing

Consonant with the objectifying effects of the analytic aesthetic, the late-nineteenth-century thinkers conceptualized rights as bestowing control over "objects" or "things." In the thought of the analytical positivists, the term *object* or *thing* thus became a context-transcendent category enabling them to write about all manner of things—including not just the usual physical things, but "immaterial things," "intangible things," and so on. All rights became rights over "objects" and "things." Holland, for instance, wrote that "a 'Thing' is what the law regards as the Object of Rights and Duties, irrespectively of that object being, as it usually is, a material object."[35] This fixation on the right's

---

32. Austin, *Lectures on Jurisprudence*, 394.

33. Christopher Columbus Langdell, "Classification of Rights and Wrongs," *Harvard Law Review* 13 (1900): 673, 677.

34. Holland, *Elements of Jurisprudence*, 79. Holland's more complete formulation: We have next to consider more particularly what is the character of those elements from which a Right results. They are

    (1) A person 'in whom the right resides' or who is 'clothed with the right,' or who is benefited by its existence.

    (2) In many cases, an object over which the right is exercised.

    (3) Acts of forbearances which the person in whom the right resides is entitled to exact.

    (4) A person from whom these acts or forbearances can be exected; in other words, against whom the right is available; in other words, whose duty it is to act or forbear for the benefit of the subject of the right. (78)

35. Ibid., 86.

thing enabled the a priori conceptual objectification of all kinds of rights—everything from the husband's marital rights over his wife to contract rights over employees.

Even when the late-nineteenth-century thinkers recognized the contrived or constructed character of this objectification, they deemed it nonproblematic. For instance, Holland declared that, "The fiction by which patents, bankrupts' estates, or easements are regarded as 'Things' is indeed not only harmless, but almost indispensable."[36]

The spatial and object imagery in rights (and indeed in jural relations generally) was so dominant among the late-nineteenth-century legal thinkers that the attempts to dispel the hold of this imagery required elaborate argument. Albert Kocourek, for instance, devoted an entire painstaking chapter of his jurisprudence treatise to convince his readers that legal conceptions ought not to be treated as real objects located in space. As Kocourek tactfully put it,

> Where does a concept exist? That answer seems to be plain enough—a concept can have no unique position in space; *it is not even clear* that it has any spatial limits, or indeed, any connection with space at all. . . . That a legal relation considered as a concept has no unique position in space may be accepted in practical reasoning when once *the unavoidable novelty is made familiar that juridical law is entirely a matter of concepts and not of material objects.*[37]

But for those who, unlike Kocourek, held fast to the territorial spatialization of law, the subdivision of juridical space, and the objectification of legal conceptions, rights appeared to be solid, substantial, and distinct. Even today, Holland's description of rights can still convey a sense of conceptual stability and analytical clarity:

---

36. Ibid., 86. Holland also defended the objectification of rights, tracing this objectification back to Cicero and Gaius.

The influence of the Institutes of Gaius and Justinian on the structure of Blackstone's commentaries (which in turn influenced the structure of the great works of nineteenth-century jurisprudence) is discussed in Alan Watson, "The Structure of Blackstone's Commentaries," *Yale Law Journal* 97 (1988): 795.

37. Albert Kocourek, *Jural Relations* (Indianapolis: Bobbs-Merrill, 1927), 234, 227–57 (emphasis added) (discussing attribution of physical qualities such as position, mobility, and partibility to legal relations). See also Albert Kocourek, "Attribution of Physical Qualities to Legal Relations," *Illinois Law Review* 19 (1925): 542; Albert Kocourek, "Basic Jural Relations," *Illinois Law Review* 17 (1923): 515.

A right which is at rest requires to be studied with reference to its "orbit" and its "infringement." By orbit we mean the sum, or extent, of the advantages which are conferred by its enjoyment. By its "infringement" we mean an act, in the strict sense of the term, which interferes with the enjoyment of these advantages. A knowledge of the former necessarily implies a knowledge of the latter, and *vice versa*, since the one is always precisely correlative with the other.[38]

Rights as Property

Consonant with the territorial spatialization of law, the subdivision of juridical space, and the objectification of rights, nineteenth-century legal thinkers often conceptualized rights in terms of property imagery and metaphors.[39] The great treatises of late-nineteenth-century analytic jurisprudence typically accorded conceptual and lexical priority[40] to property entitlements. Hence, Salmond, the analytical positivist, began his list of important rights by putting property rights first:

> *Rights over material things*—In respect of their number and variety, and of the great mass of legal rules relating to them, *these are by far the most important of legal rights*. Their nature is too familiar to require illustration.[41]

The priority of property entitlements was not simply conceptual and lexical, but cognitive as well: The nineteenth-century legal thinkers would routinely use property transactions or property law as a source of concrete illustrations for abstract discussions of the internal structure of rights.

Not surprisingly, all manner of rights were defined and conceptualized in terms of property images and metaphors. For instance,

---

38. Holland, *Elements of Jurisprudence*, 131.

39. Kennedy, "Understanding Legal Consciousness"; Horwitz, *Transformation*.

40. The analytical thinkers frequently used property law and property transactions as the first (when not the only) example to concretize abstract discussions of rights. Indeed, Salmond's first example in his general discussion of rights concerns the sale of land. Salmond, *Jurisprudence*, 185. Likewise, in explaining the structure of a right, Holland turns to a property example, a devise, to illustrate the main elements. Holland, *Elements of Jurisprudence*, 79.

41. Salmond, *Jurisprudence*, 187 (emphasis added).

rights having to do with personal reputation, domestic relations, and services were often cast in terms of property.[42] The conceptualization of rights as property enabled easy transposition of legal reasoning about property or market transactions to other aspects of human relations. Hence, with regard to the husband's rights in cases of seduction, for example, Salmond wrote,

> Every man has an interest and a right in the society, affections, and security of his wife and children. . . . Any wrongdoer has deprived him of something which was his, no less than if he had *robbed him of his purse.*[43]

Salmond also wrote:

> If I hire a physician, I obtain thereby a right to the use and benefit of his skill and knowledge, *just as,* when I hire a horse, I acquire a right to the use and benefit of his strength and speed.[44]

And more generally:

> A man may be the subject-matter of rights as well as the subject of them. His mind and body constitute an instrument which is capable of certain uses, just as a horse or a steam-engine is.[45]

The Right's Owner

Consonant with the conceptualization of rights as property, the relation of rights claimant to right was often conceptualized in much the same way as the relation of owner to property. Austin, for instance, spoke of "persons as *invested* with rights,"[46] of rights that *"reside* in

---

42. Ibid., 188–89.
43. Ibid., 188. Austin reached the same results earlier in connection with father-child, husband-wife relations, but, in contrast to Salmond, who seemed oblivious to his own reifications, Austin placed great emphasis on the fact that the juridical conceptualization of the wife, the child, or the slave as a thing was *analogical* only. Austin, *Lectures on Jurisprudence,* 385–88.
44. Salmond, *Jurisprudence,* 189.
45. Ibid., 189–90.
46. Austin, *Lectures on Jurisprudence,* 393 (emphasis added).

persons,"[47] and to persons "as *bearing* rights."[48] Salmond declared that "An *ownerless* right is an impossibility."[49] As he put it, "A right is . . . a legally protected interest; and *the object* of the right is *the thing* in which *the owner* has this interest."[50] Typically, the owner of the right was understood as an owner with complete dominion and control within the scope of his right.[51] Dominion and control in turn depended upon the endowment of the rights owner with free will.

Among the late-nineteenth-century legal thinkers, the conceptualization of the rights owner as a free-willed subject was critical to the entire conceptualization of rights. The free-willed subject served to generate the freely chosen subjective ends for which the right might be used—anything from "ownership or possession of a corporeal thing" to "the eating of shrimp salad."[52] Similarly, the free-willed subject was thought to be necessary to activate the assertion of the right.[53]

Indeed, much of the appeal of the analytic conceptualization of rights depended precisely upon the presence of a free-willed subject who would in virtue of the possession of rights be authorized to pursue his own freely chosen ends. Without a free-willed subject, there could be no pursuit of freely chosen ends, and thus the right would become quite literally aimless and worthless.[54] It was the free-willed subject

---

47. Ibid., 347 (emphasis added).

48. Ibid., 407 (emphasis added).

49. Salmond, *Jurisprudence*, 186 (emphasis added).

50. Ibid., 187 (emphasis added).

51. As Duncan Kennedy noted, the dominance of this property metaphor extended throughout classical legal thought:

The premise of Classicism was that the legal system consisted of a set of institutions, each of which had the traits of a legal actor. Each institution had been delegated by the sovereign people a power to carry out its will, which was absolute within but void without its sphere. The justification of this judicial role was the existence of a peculiar legal technique rendering the task of policing the boundaries of spheres an objective, quasi-scientific one.

Kennedy, "Understanding Legal Consciousness," 7.

52. Gray, *Nature and Sources*, 19.

53. As Gray put it: "The legal rights of a man are the rights which are exercisable on his own motion" (ibid). Moreover:

To give effect to a man's right, an exercise of free will on his part is necessary. No legal compulsion is laid on anyone to enforce his right as such. . . . It is of the nature of a man's right as such, that to seek or to abstain from seeking the aid of society for the protection of his interest is a matter of his own free will. (23)

54. There are, of course, other ways to legitimate rights, including the instrumentalist view that rights advance important social interests. John Chipman Gray mischaracterizes this social interest view and rejects it (ibid., 18).

with his own private ends who supplied the meaningful end for the exercise of the right.[55] The crucial import of the free-willed subject was very much on display in John Chipman Gray's jurisprudence treatise, which insisted in a sustained (and somewhat anxious) manner that the rights holder be endowed with free will[56]—either *"real"* free will in the case of "normal human beings,"[57] as Gray put it, or a *"fictitious"* free will in the case of "abnormal human beings" such as "babies," "idiots"[58] as well as animals. As Gray put it:

> It is quite conceivable, however, that there may have been, or indeed, may still be, systems of Law in which animals have legal rights—for instance, cats in ancient Egypt, or white elephants in Siam. When, if ever, this is the case, the wills of human beings must be attributed to the animals. There seems to be no essential difference between the fiction in such cases and in those where, to a human being wanting in legal will, the will of another is attributed.[59]

The Aesthetic Coherence of
the Analytic Description of Rights

It is easy enough to criticize the analytic conceptualization of rights. But for now, the point is to appreciate the security, the coherence, and even the appeal of this aesthetic (all, of course, from a certain point of view). Not only can the analytic aesthetic seem coherent, but it turns out that there is a resonance between the "form" of late-nineteenth-century legal thought and its representations of the "substantive" law.

The various metaphors and images that constitute the analytic aesthetic—territorial spatialization, object-forms, property and owner—are all mutually entailed and mutually reinforcing. Thus, as we have

---

55. For a discussion of the critical importance of "free will" as the key concept for the definition of legal doctrine in the latter part of the nineteenth century, see Duncan Kennedy, "Form and Substance in Private Law Adjudication," *Harvard Law Review* 89 (1976): 1685, 1728–30 ("[A]ll of the doctrines were recast as implications of the fundamental idea that private law rules protect individual free will" [1730; emphasis in original]).

56. Gray, *Nature and Sources,* 19, 23, 24, 27.

57. Ibid., 29, 53.

58. Ibid., 38, 52.

59. Gray, *Nature and Sources,* 43.

seen, the spatialization of the law enabled the subpartitioning of juridical space (and vice versa). In turn, the subpartitioning of juridical space enabled the objectification of the elements in that space—namely, legal conceptions such as rights. In turn, the objectification of rights and their conceptualization as "things" with "orbits" enabled rights to be conceptualized in terms of the metaphors and images of property.

The aesthetic coherence of this territorial spatialization/object/property/owner schema is also evident if one starts with property and proceeds toward the territorial spatialization of late-nineteenth-century thought. Thus, the dominance of property in the late nineteenth century (and before) can yield a property conception of law in which law's various subdivisions are all shaped through the metaphors and images of property. In turn, this subdivision of law easily yields the conceptualization of law as a vast territorial space. All these "substantive" representations, in turn, are consonant with an aesthetic of legal thought that depicts law as a vast field of contiguous and discrete sectors—precisely the aesthetic found in the great works of late-nineteenth-century thought.

In other words, the *very aesthetic form* of the legal treatises of the late nineteenth century can be understood as an introjection of the substantive conception of property into the very aesthetic of the late-nineteenth-century jurisprudential text. Viewed in this way, the entire deductive/inductive method of late-nineteenth-century juristic science is homologous with the establishment of "dominion and control" by the "free-willed owner."[60] The critical question is: Which classificatory category or scheme has "control and dominion" over which legal concept? Viewed this way, the intellectual method of late-nineteenth-century thought *is* the method of establishing dominion and control. Hence, through a process of metaphorical and imagistic transposition, the "dominion and control" of the free-willed property owner becomes *the order* of law.

Once in place, the analytic aesthetic can seem very stable. The analytic aesthetic is objectivist in character, and thus the legal ontology it establishes is cast in the image of objects: legal conceptions, including rights, appear to have solidity, permanence, substantiality,

---

60. For a description of this kind of sublimation, see Schlag, "Problem of the Subject," 1646–56.

boundedness, fixity, and determinacy. The appeal of this aesthetic lies precisely in the sense of *order* and *clarity* it brings to the legal materials. It is this desire for order and clarity that Christopher Columbus Langdell at once elicits and promises to fulfill in his famous preface to his first contracts casebook, *A Selection of Cases on the Law of Contracts*:

> [T]he number of fundamental legal doctrines is much less than is commonly supposed; the many different guises in which the same doctrine is constantly making its appearance, and the great extent to which legal treatises are a repetition of each other, being the cause of much misapprehension. If these doctrines could be so *classified* and *arranged* that each should be found *in its proper place*, and *nowhere else, they* would cease to be so formidable in number.[61]

The orderly classification desired by Langdell was precisely what the "science" of law would accomplish: As one commentator put it:

> The creation of a system properly designated as scientific requires: (a) the expression of all the component elements or constituents of the whole subject; (b) a classification of these in accordance with an appreciable principle which constitutes a guide to the arrangement. The result is necessarily a formal and visible picture displaying the whole as an articulate or coordinate body in which each part is seen in relation to the whole and the parts appear in reciprocal relation to each other—this is a system. There is no isolation; there is organization. *In a system of law subjected to such treatment there can be no real conflicts as to identical matter, . . .* [62]

At times, the analytic aesthetic did succeed in producing just this sense of confidence. But the confidence did not last.

---

61. Christopher Columbus Langdell, *A Selection of Cases on the Law of Contracts*, 2d ed. (Boston: Little, Brown, 1879), ix (emphasis added).
62. James Dewitt Andrews, "Jurisprudence: Development and Practical Vocation," *Yale Law Journal* 25 (1916): 306, 307 (emphasis added).

The Unraveling of the
Late-Nineteenth-Century Systematizations

"Conflicts as to identical matter" did occur—repeatedly. When Hohfeld argued in 1913 that there were eight basic fundamental legal conceptions, a number of commentators wondered with great seriousness whether this was the right number.[63] Roscoe Pound argued that eight terms were too many.[64] Albert Kocourek argued that there were (really) twenty-four.[65] And so on. By 1935, Joseph Beale wrote in his famous *Treatise on the Conflict of Laws* that

> Many methods might be devised of analyzing and classifying rights; and one would be bold indeed who should claim his own method to be the best. Nor is it possible to find in the authorities to which we turn for knowledge of law any classification of rights to which we may assent. Such essays in this direction as have been made by courts and by the authoritative writers on law have been little considered by the authors themselves and little regarded by their successors. In fact, the law is on its face an amorphous body of principles, and it can be analyzed only by going below the surface; nor is there any received method of proceeding. The classification indicated by its division into currently received topics—Contracts, Torts, Property, Procedure, Equity, and the like—is purely unscientific and unhelpful; it is useful only as furnishing labeled compartments into which the multitude of decisions may for convenience of study be sorted.[66]

As this statement reveals, the faith remained. But it was a much subdued and chastened faith. And as Beale's statement indicates, everything had to be redone.

---

63. Joe Singer recounts this aspect of the Hohfeld debate. Joseph William Singer, "The Legal Rights Debate in Analytical Jurisprudence from Bentham to Hohfeld," *Wisconsin Law Review* 1982: 975, 989–92.

64. Roscoe Pound, "Legal Rights," *International Journal of Ethics* 26 (1915): 92, 96, 97, 100.

65. Albert Kocourek, "Plurality of Advantage and Disadvantage in Jural Relation," *Michigan Law Review* 19 (1920): 47; Albert Kocourek, "Tabulae Minores Jurisprudentiae," *Yale Law Journal* 30 (1921): 215, 222–25.

66. Joseph Beale, *Treatise on the Conflict of Laws*, 2d ed. (New York: Baker, Voorhis & Co., 1935), 66.

The great late-nineteenth-century systematizations of law and rights have all unraveled. The confidence and belief in the system have vanished. The shell, the debris, and the aspirations, however, have remained. The late-nineteenth-century classifications have been left to "half survive in the back of lawyers' minds and the front of the law school curriculum," where they continue to shape legal thought.[67]

Significantly, the analytic aesthetic, its territorial spatialization of law, its objectification of legal concepts, its property imagery, and its free-willed owners have continued to shape much of the conceptualization of rights of the mid- to late-twentieth century. Indeed, the analytic aesthetic has continued to shape the conceptualizations and arguments of both the champions[68] and the critics[69] of rights and rights talk.

The Instrumentalist Aesthetic

The instrumentalist aesthetic is perhaps most perfectly exhibited in the confident aspirations for law of the mid- to late-twentieth-century American legal thinkers.[70] Indeed, the instrumentalist aesthetic was

---

67. Grey, "Langdell's Orthodoxy," 50.

68. Indeed, one of the most revered articles in the American legal academy of the late twentieth century, "The New Property," written by Charles Reich in 1964, uses an analytic conceptualization of rights to argue for new rights against the welfare state:

First the growth of government power based on the dispensing of wealth *must be kept within bounds*. Second, there must be *a zone of privacy* for each individual beyond which neither government nor private power can push—a hiding place from the all-pervasive system of regulation and control. Finally, . . . those forms of largess which are closely linked to status must be deemed *to be held as of right*.

Charles Reich, "The New Property," *Yale Law Journal* 73 (1964): 733, 785 (emphasis added).

69. Jennifer Nedelsky's argument that rights tend to promote a false picture of human autonomy depends upon the conception of "rights as boundaries"—or as described here, the analytical conceptualization of rights. Nedelsky, "Law, Boundaries."

The autonomy the American system is designed to protect can be achieved by erecting a wall of rights around the individual. Property provided an ideal symbol for this vision of autonomy, for it could both literally and figuratively provide the necessary walls. . . . Everyone is familiar with, or at least would immediately recognize as intelligible, the image of rights as boundaries defining the sphere within which human autonomy (or freedom or privacy) resides. (167)

70. Robert Summers identifies the American jurisprudential origins of what he calls "pragmatic instrumentalism" in the thought of leading intellectuals of the early twentieth century—persons who would typically be identified as "legal realists" and "philosophical pragmatists." Robert Summers, *Instrumentalism and American Legal Theory* (Ithaca, N.Y.: Cornell University Press, 1982).

so dominant in the mid- to late-twentieth-century American legal thought that it shaped all manner of thinking in that period, including the thematizations generally known as grand normative theory, law and economics, ad hoc policy analysis, orthodox doctrinalism, and even much critical legal studies (CLS) thought.

The rhetorical appeal and the constitution of the instrumentalist aesthetic are, in some senses, very different from those of the analytic aesthetic. As described previously, the analytic aesthetic strives to impose and maintain order by providing a stable, all-encompassing, objectivist frame. The instrumentalist aesthetic, by contrast, does not seek primarily to impose or maintain order, and thus it is not primarily oriented toward producing a stable frame.[71] Rather, the instrumentalist aesthetic seeks to produce "change," "reform," "progress," "progressive legal change," "transformative action." Accordingly, the constitutive metaphors and images of the instrumentalist aesthetic are, at least in their inception and ambition, much more *motion oriented* than *object framing*. The instrumentalist aesthetic creates a sense of progress by casting law in the metaphors and images of energy. It moves law through a series of motion-oriented metaphors and images organized in a source-path-goal schema.[72] Hence, law is cast in the image of energy, and the energy travels along this source-path-goal schema, assuming its usual forms along the way: various transformations of energy as state, force, and potential.[73]

As with the analytic aesthetic, the instrumentalist aesthetic casts "rights" in its own image. In the instrumentalist aesthetic, rights are prefigured as the sources, the instruments, or the ends of change—or all three at once. They are, in other words, prefigured as energy sources (as antecedents, motivations, starting points, spiritual origins, animated agencies, totems, and minor divinities), as trajectories (as paths, vehicles, connections, devices, relations, linkages, media),

71. Though, of course, ultimately, it does produce a frame—a frame consisting of its own stylized representations of (legitimate) sources, (permitted) pathways, and (desired) goals.

72. Much of what follows in this section, including the understanding of the instrumentalist aesthetic as energy source/trajectory channeling/end goal is inspired by Steven Winter's work on the metaphorical structuration of "law" and "rights." Winter, "Transcendental Nonsense," 1214, 1232.

73. The source-path-goal schema is coordinated in various, usually dramatically underspecified, ways, with the schema of energy as a function of potential/force/state.

as end goals (as prizes, trophies, conclusions), and as all three at once.

Law As an Energy Source

In the instrumentalist aesthetic, law is on a mission. Law is no longer the stabilized subpartitioned territorial space of the analytic aesthetic. It is no longer a "catalogue of rules or principles, each with its own dominion over some discrete theater of behavior."[74] Instead, law is cast, for instance, as an "interpretive enterprise" working itself pure, trying to become the best it can be.[75] Or it is cast as "efficiency"—a driving force that exercises its inexorable transaction-cost-reducing, market-replicating logic on one legal subject after another as each agent strives to maximize its rational self-interest.[76]

Now, in these descriptions, law is cast either as energy or as subject to energy.[77] But law cannot be just any kind of energy. Energy, without further specification of its identity or context, is extremely volatile. Unless the identity of the energy is further specified, law cannot serve its "mission"—whatever that mission might be. In the instrumentalist aesthetic, the identity of this energy can be specified through the metaphors typically used to describe energy—namely, state, force, and potential. And, as will be seen, this specification can occur at any phase of the source-path-goal schema.

Crudely reduced to a formula, the instrumentalist aesthetic would go roughly as follows: *law-as-energy grounds or shapes itself in proceeding through a constraining and directive trajectory to achieve its goals.* In other words, law as an energy source is described as a function of different specifications of transforming relations among energy as state, force, and potential. We can see some of these energy states at work in the thinking of Ronald Dworkin, who writes:

74. Ronald Dworkin, *Law's Empire* (Cambridge, Mass: Belknap Press, 1986), 413.
75. Ibid., 87–101, 228–32.
76. Richard Posner, *Economic Analysis of Law*, 4th ed. (Boston: Little, Brown, 1992). The metaphor and image of efficiency as traveling on a journey throughout the land of law—in short, the picaresque character of Posner's prodigious economic literature— was first identified by Arthur Leff: Arthur Leff, "Economic Analysis of Law: Some Realism About Nominalism," *Virginia Law Review* 60 (1974): 451.
77. One important "substantive" difference between identifying law as energy itself or as subject to energy is that in the former case, law can be autonomous, and in the latter case, it cannot.

> A full political theory of law . . . speaks both to the *grounds* [i.e., state] of law—circumstances in which particular propositions of law should be taken to be sound or true—and to the *force* of law—the relative power of any true proposition of law to justify coercion . . . *These two parts must be mutually supportive.*[78]

Similarly, Duncan Kennedy's description of the force fields of case law in terms of different field configurations—such as the "impacted field," the "contradictory field," and so on—draws on different variations in relations among the state, force, and potential of law as energy.[79] Likewise, when Robert Cover says that "To live in a legal world requires . . . the need to integrate, not only the 'is' and the 'ought' but the 'what might be,' " he is tracking the aesthetic representation of law as energy in terms of state (the "is"), force (the "ought"), and potential (the "might be").[80]

One of the ways in which the instrumentalist aesthetic directs energy is through a specification of *the identity* of the energy. In mid- to late-twentieth-century thought, law-as-energy is represented in a wide variety of ways at varying levels of abstraction. It is often identified as a kind of grand, overarching normative theory that produces and organizes lesser law such as doctrine, rules, and, most significantly here, rights.[81] This kind of vision is quite common. Consider, for instance, this description of normative theory as the generative source of legal rights:

> What is the foundation of rights? What goals or aims are institutions *which create* rights designed *to promote*? A foundational theory of institutional rights provides their normative basis. Among the possible foundational views are those which are

---

78. Dworkin, *Law's Empire,* 110 (emphasis added).

79. Duncan Kennedy, "Freedom and Constraint in Adjudication: A Critical Phenomenology," *Journal of Legal Education* 36 (1986): 538–42.

80. Robert Cover, "The Supreme Court 1982 Term—Foreword *Nomos* and Narrative," *Harvard Law Review* 97 (1983): 4, 10.

81. Ronald Dworkin, "The Forum of Principle," *New York University Law Review* 56 (1981): 469, 498 (arguing that the constitutional intentionalist must ultimately defend a conception of framer's intent in terms of a substantive political theory); Michael Perry, "Why Constitutional Theory Matters to Constitutional Practice (And Vice Versa)," *Const. Comm.* 6 (1989): 231 (arguing that normative theory is essential to the practice of constitutional law).

liberty-based and those which are in some sense, welfare-based. In these views, institutions *which create* rights *are designed either to promote* individual liberty or *to promote* welfare (individual, average, or general). Justificatory questions—for example, why confer upon individuals a right to freedom of speech, to a speedy and fair trial, or to private property—are answered by reference to the "foundational" theory. . . .

[T]he foundational theory *fuels* the complete theory of institutional rights. A commitment at the foundational level will suggest, though it will not strictly entail, certain views about the content and enforcement of rights. We should, therefore, expect that different foundational or normative theories will endorse different institutional arrangements, confer somewhat different institutional rights, and suggest different mechanisms for their enforcement.[82]

Sometimes, instead of "theory," the grand energy source is represented as "interpretive communities."[83] It is also represented as a systemic drive, such as the drive to wealth maximization.[84] The energy source can also be depicted as a value—such as justice, or self-realization, or human flourishing.[85] In less-exalted precincts, the foundational and organizing energy source can bear names like "society's needs" or "society's interests."[86] "Society's needs" and "society's interests" are typically transformed (quite quickly) into constrained trajectories—that is, into forces that go by the name of "principle" or "policy" or "public policy." Concrete instantiations

---

82. Jules L. Coleman and Jody Krauss, "Rethinking the Theory of Legal Rights," *Yale Law Journal* 95 (1986): 1335, 1340–41 (emphasis added).

83. Stanley Fish, *Doing What Comes Naturally* (Durham, N.C.: Duke University Press, 1989); Stanley Fish, *Is There a Text in This Class?* (Cambridge: Harvard University Press, 1980); Owen Fiss, "Objectivity and Interpretation," *Stanford Law Review* 34 (1982): 739, 744.

84. Posner, *Economic Analysis of Law*, 23 ("[M]any areas of the law, especially but not only the great common law fields of property, torts, crimes, and contracts bear the stamp of economic reasoning.").

85. See, for example, Michael Perry, *Morality, Politics and Law* (New York: Oxford University Press, 1988); Margaret Jane Radin, "The Liberal Conception of Property: Currents in the Jurisprudence of Takings," *Columbia Law Review* 88 (1988): 1667, 1687.

86. For a collection of commonplace legal academic specifications of "society's needs," see Robert Gordon, "Critical Legal Histories," *Stanford Law Review* 57 (1984): 57, 64–65.

include, for instance, "deterrence of risk-creating behavior" or "facilitation of consensual transactions."

In the most exalted realm of all, *Law's Empire*, the organizing energy source is accorded an almost mystical status: "Law's ambition for itself" is to work itself pure as it becomes the best it can be.[87] Or in Ronald Dworkin's own words, "Law's attitude is constructive: it aims, in the interpretive spirit, to lay principle over practice to show the best route to a better future, keeping the right faith with the past. . . . "[88] Even much of the early work associated with CLS seems to have been organized in terms of this instrumentalist aesthetic. Indeed, much of early CLS thought is cast in the aesthetic of an instrumentalist anti-instrumentalism—that is, as an instrumentalist attempt to break form with the instrumentalist aesthetic.[89] Much of CLS thought is cast in the form of seeking to transform law from a steady state so as to unleash forces that can achieve their true "transformative" or "liberatory" potential.[90]

87. Ronald Dworkin, "Law's Ambition for Itself," *Virginia Law Review* 71 (1985): 173.

88. Dworkin, *Law's Empire*, 413.

89. At first impression, CLS thought seems not to conform to the instrumentalist aesthetic. In its characteristic tendencies to upset any specification of the identity, trajectories, or goals of law—in short, in its affirmations of *the indeterminacy of law*—CLS thought at first appears not to partake in the instrumental aesthetic. But this is not so. Indeed, in its early forms, the aesthetic of CLS thought can be understood as instrumentally anti-instrumentalist. Like its more conventional counterparts, it, too, was on a "mission"—a mission to undo and eliminate the constrained, prescripted missions of conventional legal thought, a mission to activate the latent political character of law. Whereas more conventional thinkers sought to delimit the mission of law through an identification of the energy source of law, CLS thought inverted this vision. Hence, in CLS thought, the depiction of the originary energy as the unfolding of "the fundamental contradiction" (Duncan Kennedy), or "liberatory energy" (Peter Gabel), or "politics in the fullest sense" (Gary Peller) was designed to preclude the containment of this energy in a conventionally prescripted mission. Indeed, when the CLS accounts of the energy became hypostatized, when in Duncan Kennedy's words they were "turned into a cluster of pods," they were replaced with even more indeterminate identities designed to resist hypostatization—identities such as "making the kettle boil." Duncan Kennedy, "The Structure of Blackstone's Commentaries," *Buffalo Law Review* 28 (1979): 205; Gary Peller, "The Metaphysics of American Law," *California Law Review* 73 (1985): 1151, 1290; Duncan Kennedy and Peter Gabel, "Roll Over Beethoven," *Stanford Law Review* 36 (1984): 1, 4, 7, 37. For further discussion of CLS instantiation of the instrumentalist aesthetic, see note 100.

90. Peter Gabel aptly exemplifies the residual formative instrumentalism of this anti-instrumentalism when he writes:

[W]hen a movement manages to ricochet into existence through an unpredictable convergence of *"igniting" material* and cultural circumstances. . . . it produces *a*

Within this instrumentalist aesthetic, rights become radically subordinate to the foundational and organizing energy source. In grand
normative theory, rights thus become occasions to announce, vindicate, or celebrate this or that grand normative theory or value.[91] In law
and economics, rights become production factors.[92] In early CLS
thought, rights become intellectually failed attempts to mediate the
fundamental contradiction[93] or obstructions to authentic political action.[94] And in later CLS thinking, rights become useful political vehicles
for "energizing" the movement. As Peter Gabel put it:

In fact the struggle to increase the strength and *energy of a movement* can partially result from the acquisition of rights. The *struggle* to infuse *liberatory energy* into existing political discourse, like
that contained in legal reasoning, can at certain moments be
energizing.[95]

Channeling

As has been suggested, the more the identity of law's energy is specified, the more its possible trajectories have already been prefigured.
One way, then, of prescribing the possible trajectories of the energy
source is through the specification of its identity. But it is not the only
way. If the identity of the energy source is not sufficiently specified
relative to its "mission"—wealth maximization, the achievement of

---

disalienating energy that wants to challenge everything that is (capitalism, patriar-
chy, hierarchy, "the system") and a set of specific demands for change *that derive
from the movement's particular origins* and *that are inspired* consciously or uncon-
sciously, by its vision of *the larger end*.
Peter Gabel, "The Phenomenology of Rights-Consciousness and the Pact of the Withdrawn Selves," *Texas Law Review* 62 (1984): 1563, 1587–88 (emphasis added).
    91. Fiss, "Against Settlement," *Yale Law Journal* 93 (1984): 1073, 1085 ("Adjudica-
tion uses public resources, and employs not strangers chosen by the parties but public
officials chosen by a process in which the public participates. . . . Their job is not to
maximize the ends of private parties, nor simply to secure the peace, but to explicate
and give force to the values embodied in authoritative texts such as the Constitution
and statutes" [1085].)
    92. Coase, "Problem of Social Cost," 43–44.
    93. Kennedy, "Blackstone's Commentaries," 89.
    94. Gabel, "Phenomenology and Pact." For a sophisticated demonstration of the
residual idealism and objectivism in Peter Gabel's discussion of the state and rights, see
Winter, "Transcendental Nonsense," 1224–29.
    95. Kennedy and Gabel, "Roll Over Beethoven," 37 (emphasis added).

justice, human flourishing, and so on—direction can be supplied through a narrowing specification of the trajectory that the energy source must follow.

In Dworkin's world, this trajectory is specified through the metaphor of the "chain novel" and through the criteria of "fit" and "coherence."[96] In the jurisprudence of Owen Fiss, the trajectories that interpretive energy must follow are specified by "disciplining rules."[97] For Frank Michelman, the trajectories are specified through relentless reason giving: "The norm of justice to parties itself *commands* that no other norm *should ever* take a form that preempts questions or exempts from reason-giving. *Every* norm, *every* time, requires explanation and justification in context."[98]

In conventional doctrinal analysis, the trajectories are narrowed and specified in two prototypical ways. First, the possible consequences of any legal directives are typically cast in radically simplifying conceptions of linear causation: Hence, it is typically presumed that policies or principles yield rules or doctrines with incentives and deterrents that cause specified actors to engage in or to cease specified conduct. Typically, background is fixed. Agents are framed. Instrumentalities are identified and possible pathways severely limited. In this way, many controversial but limiting assumptions are made about the identity of human agents, how they respond to jural and other stimuli, what they value, how institutions, language, and reason perform. These controversial limiting assumptions are typically relegated to the background where they silently reduce the number of possible trajectories. Usually, there is nothing much for the legal thinker to do except to draw the vectors (the policies, the principles) and to remember where the boundaries should go, where to draw the lines. This last task is usually described elliptically as a matter of "good judgment" or "craft."

Much of the narrowing of the possible trajectories is also effectuated by continuing to honor what remains of the late-nineteenth-century analytical frame. The trajectories are narrowed and specified through the required showing of obeisance to traditional legal materials (case precedent, statutes, canons of construction). Hence, it is

---

96. Dworkin, *Law's Empire*.
97. Fiss, "Objectivity and Interpretation."
98. Frank Michelman, "The Supreme Court 1985 Term Foreword: Traces of Self-Government," *Harvard Law Review* 100 (1986): 4, 76 (emphasis added).

commonplace for those who conceptualize rights within the instrumentalist aesthetic to nonetheless deploy the remains of the nineteenth-century classifications (tort/contract, rights in rem/rights in personam, and so on) so as to ground, frame, and contain the instrumentalist aesthetic—indeed, not just the trajectory, but the energy source and the permissible end goals. All sorts of limits are thus introduced about the proper sources of law (e.g., text, authors' intent), proper trajectories (e.g., precedential and doctrinal reasoning), and proper goals (e.g., requirements of neutrality and generality). These limits function as a tacit background that frames the instrumentalist aesthetic and enables it to launch its projects.

Another strategy prevalent in mid- to late-twentieth-century American legal thought for narrowing the possible trajectories concerns the identity, character, and performance of law itself. Indeed, in mid- to late-twentieth-century legal thought, "law" is very often reduced to an ethereal, highly abstracted essentialization of all that might be called "law." Consider, for instance, that the most prominent jurisprudential book of the 1980s, boldly titled *Law's Empire*, nonetheless begins by reducing its ambitions to the study of "formal legal argument *from the judge's viewpoint* . . . because judicial argument about claims of law is a useful paradigm for exploring *the central, propositional aspect* of legal practice."[99] This background reduction and homogenization of law's jurisdiction greatly stylizes and greatly reduces the trajectories that law can take in producing its goals or effects. Interestingly, while conventional legal thought in the mid to late twentieth century preoccupied itself with trying to specify and channel trajectories, and to retire instabilities into the background, early CLS thought—true to its original destabilizing energy sources—engaged in exactly inverse strategies; hence it is that CLS thinkers often tried to break the form of constraining trajectories so as to "open up space to think and act in the world."[100]

---

99. Dworkin, *Law's Empire*, 13–14 (emphasis added).

100. James Boyle, "The Politics of Reason: Critical Legal Theory and Local Social Thought," *University of Pennsylvania Law Review* 133 (1986): 739 (quoting Gary Peller). In CLS thought, all these conventional attempts to preselect, specify, or constrain the trajectories (including rights and rights talk) were submitted to immediate critique. Given that in CLS thought, the organizing and foundational energy is so destabilizing, all the conventional attempts to channel the energy are obstructions that must be removed—as just so much false consciousness, ideological distortion, and the like. Not surprisingly, just as the favorite recurrent rhetorical move of conventional legal thinkers

Thus, in the attempts to specify trajectories or to specify the absence of trajectories, rights are subordinated to various jurisprudential projects. They are subordinated to projects seeking to specify and entrench various constraints on trajectories (e.g., "disciplining rules"[101]). Or they are subordinated to projects aimed at removing these constraints on trajectories (e.g., "trashing"[102]). Rights have even been subordinated to nostalgic projects aimed at simulating cherished trajectories of the past.[103]

End Goals

If the energy source is not "adequately" specified and if trajectories are not "sufficiently" constrained, it remains possible to direct the energy source by specification of the third moment: the end goals.[104] In consequentialist approaches—such as utilitarianism, law and economics, ad hoc policy analysis—as well as in many kinds of other utopian jurisprudence, the end goal plays a significant rhetorical role in specifying the character of the instrumentalist aesthetic.

In the instrumentalist aesthetic, not only are rights subordinated

---

in the mid- to late twentieth century was to reduce possible trajectories by retiring potentialities to the background, the favorite rhetorical move of the CLS thinkers was the infinite regress. The infinite regress is the inverse of backgrounding: it is the method through which the background is relentlessly brought to the foreground, where it is included in the (jurisprudential) action and thus submitted to the disruption of "fundamental contradictions" or "liberatory energy," or "politics in the fullest sense." Kennedy, "Blackstone's Commentaries"; Peller, "Metaphysics of American Law," 1290; Kennedy and Gabel, "Roll Over Beethoven," 37.

101. Fiss, "Objectivity and Interpretation."

102. Mark Kelman, "Trashing," *Stanford Law Review* 36 (1984): 293.

103. For elaboration, see Pierre Schlag, "The Problem of the Subject," *Texas Law Review* 69 (1991): 1627.

104. The question of where one phase ends and another begins is precisely the sort of objectivist question that is of no moment for the instrumentalist aesthetic. Each of these phases plays a greater or lesser constitutive role in various kinds of substantive visions. Hence, for instance, grand normative theory of the Dworkinian kind will tend to define itself in terms of the energy source and trajectory channeling, thus leaving specification of end goals as a largely derivative matter. Law and economics, by contrast, will tend to define itself in terms of end goals and trajectories, leaving the specification of the energy source as a largely derivative matter.

There is almost always some equivalence (and thus a rhetorical substitutability) between energy source and end goal. Equivalencies and substitutability are enabled by the possibility of relocating the energy source from the past to the future and vice versa. To give an example, efficiency maximization is most often cast as an end goal, but it is also cast as an imperative of the common law—that is, as an energy source.

to end goals, but indeed, they can themselves be cast as end goals. Acquiring rights, for instance, can be seen as the end goal or a subgoal of a particular legal or political project. In this sense, particular rights (for instance, "the ERA" or "gay rights") can become a focal point for the organization and direction of both the expenditure of effort (energy) and the identification of strategies and tactics (trajectories). Rights also become subgoals, marking incremental advancement along the path of progress. In this capacity, as subgoals, as markers, rights can have both enabling and disabling implications for movement.[105] As with the other defining moments of the instrumentalist aesthetic, the definition of rights in terms of end goals tends to instrumentalize rights themselves.

The Instrumentalization of Rights

We have already seen how the instrumentalist aesthetic fashions rights in its own image. One result of this instrumentalization is that rights are almost always on a mission. Rights are recognized and defined (both externally and internally) in terms that conduce to law's "mission"—namely, honoring this or that imperative, following this or that accepted trajectory, or reaching this or that objective. The result is that rights are subordinated to law's "mission"—whatever that mission might be.[106]

This increasing instrumentalization and subordination of rights is played out in the progression of the titles to Ronald Dworkin's three major books. Hercules, Dworkin's legendary judge, begins jurisprudential life by *Taking Rights Seriously*.[107] But soon he subordinates these

---

105. Peter Gabel articulated this point in writing about a "movement":
While a rights-victory can both strengthen the movement's confidence and awaken a feeling of possibility among a great many people, it can for these very reasons work to contain the movement and ultimately contribute to subduing its transformative potential. ("Phenomenology and Pact," 1590.)
106. As George Fletcher notes,
There is a good deal of talk about rights "trumping" utilitarian incursions against the interests of right-bearers. But the advocates of rights in contemporary jurisprudence typically concede that the rights themselves are "trumpable," or susceptible to being overridden in extreme cases.
George Fletcher, "The Right and the Reasonable," *Harvard Law Review* 98 (1985): 949, 978.
107. Dworkin, *Taking Rights Seriously*.

to *A Matter of Principle*.[108] And when last heard from, Hercules was trying to rule over *Law's Empire*.[109] Hence, it is that in the Dworkinian enterprise, rights feature as subordinates in the greater grander projects of law working itself pure as judges strive to show the "positive law in the best possible light."[110]

In the case of consequentialist approaches such as utilitarianism or ad hoc policy analysis, the instrumentalization of rights is even more acute and more obvious. Indeed, this openness of consequentialist theories to interests that can effectively constrict or preclude the recognition of rights is well known.[111] This subordination of rights to utils, consequences, or policies is, depending upon perspective— rights should pay their way or rights should trump everything— either an intrinsic strength[112] or an intrinsic weakness[113] in the consequentialist conceptualization and rationalization of rights. Either way, the result is that rights become subordinated to a greater grander consequentialist logic. This subordination of rights is achieved not just in theory, but in the ad hoc consequentialism of case law as well. Not only may rights be "overridden" or "balanced away" by paramount social interests, but even the "internal" structure of rights becomes defined in terms of social interests that will allow invocation or defeasance of the right. In the American constitutional case law of the late twentieth century, all manner of rights—rights of privacy, of equal protection, of free speech, of free exercise of religion, and so on—are protected, but only to the extent that the state cannot show that incursions on those interests are appropriately connected[114] to

108. Ronald Dworkin, *A Matter of Principle* (Cambridge: Harvard University Press, 1985).

109. Dworkin, *Law's Empire*.

110. Ronald Dworkin, "Law's Ambition for Itself," *Virginia Law Review* 71 (1985): 173, 176. The more elaborate version:

Judges who accept the interpretive ideal of integrity decide hard cases by trying to find, in some coherent set of principles about people's rights and duties, the best constructive interpretation of the political structure and legal doctrine of their community. They try to make that complex structure and record the best they can.

Dworkin, *Law's Empire*, 255.

111. See, for example, David Lyons, "Utility and Rights," reprinted in Jeremy Waldron, ed., *Theories of Rights* (New York: Oxford University Press, 1984), 110.

112. See, for example, T. M. Scanlon, "Rights, Goals and Fairness," reprinted in Jeremy Waldron, ed., *Theories of Rights* (New York: Oxford University Press, 1984), 137.

113. See Lyons, "Utility and Rights."

114. In technical terms, the appropriate connection is typically specified as: "rational relation," "intermediate scrutiny," "strict scrutiny," "sliding scale."

the advancement of a sufficiently important countervailing state interest. Similarly, in common law torts, contracts, or property, the scope,
content, and form of the rights recognized come to depend critically
on whether these rights are perceived to serve some important social
purpose or policy. The greater grander logic of consequentialism thus
is not simply something that "surrounds" a right on the "outside," as
it were. The greater grander logic of consequentialism defines rights
"inside" as well.[115]

The Coherence of the Instrumentalist Aesthetic

The constituting images and metaphors of the instrumentalist aesthetic
can be seen as rhetorically quite coherent (from a certain point of view).
In this aesthetic, law is represented as an energy source that travels
along specified trajectories toward specified end goals.[116] Each phase of
this aesthetic can be seen as leading to the next one. The instrumentalist aesthetic is an aesthetic of continual entailment. "Law" is at once
the entailment—the "progress," the "progressive legal change," the
"transformative action," "the working itself pure"—and, in passing

---

115. This consequentialist subordination of rights even occurs in somewhat surprising corners—such as Chicago school law and economics. In one sense, this might
seem counterintuitive. The Chicago law and economics school, with its idealization of
the "free market," its celebration of the "rational individual utility maximizer," and its
characteristic distrust of "government regulation," would seem to provide some intellectual defense of rights against subordination to the overriding logic of a greater grander
social interest. But aesthetically, this turns out not to be so. Law and economics is not so
much a resurrection of laissez-faire capitalism, as it is the attempt to simulate and
impose, through law, the kinds of transactions that would have occurred had market
transactions been possible. Most often, the law and economics prescriptions entail
replicating, through law, an approximation of what the market transactions would have
produced. As Posner puts it:

> What is fundamental is the distinction between settings of low transaction cost
> and of high transaction cost. In the former, the law should require the parties to
> transact in the market; it can do this by making the present owner's property right
> absolute (or nearly so), so that anyone who thinks the property is worth more has
> to negotiate with the owner. But in settings of high transaction cost people must
> be allowed to use the courts to shift resources to a more valuable use, because the
> market is by definition unable to perform this function in those settings.

Posner, *Economic Analysis of Law*, 57.

116. This aesthetic also has the coherence of what Winter, following Lakoff and
Johnson, elaborates as the conventional "Life is a Journey" metaphor. Winter, "Transcendental Nonsense," 1132–34, 1214.

through these phases, "Law" is each of these phases as well.[117] The same can be said of rights.

All of these "substantive" representations, in turn, are consonant with an aesthetic of legal thought whose form entails motion and change. Thus, the instrumentalist aesthetic coincides with the movement of the prototypical mid- to late-twentieth-century American law review article. Indeed, most of these articles are crafted in the image of a journey—a journey that typically progresses (often rather improbably) from . . .

problems to solutions
chaos to coherence
nonsense to good sense
inefficiency to efficiency
iniquity to goodness
oppression to liberation

and so on.[118] The moving tendency of the instrumentalist aesthetic is to *extend itself* in ways that reach all aspects of social life so as to enlist them in a great drive for juridically directed "change," "reform," "progress," "progressive legal change," "transformative action," and so on. All cultural resources, all intellectual achievements, even the most unlikely (i.e., deconstruction, poststructuralism, postmodernism) are tapped, transformed, and enlisted in the forced march of progress.

In mid- to late-twentieth-century American legal thought, the vitality of this instrumentalist aesthetic reached its most ambitious

---

117. These phases are:
source/path/goal
origin/process/end
premise/argument/conclusion
potential/force/state
motion/argument/decision
118. Particularly in the late 1980s and early 1990s, the law review articles exhibit a kind of desperate or frantic hyperinstrumentalist aesthetic—exhibiting an urgent passion to improve the law or advance the cause. The instrumentalist aesthetic of the mid- to late-twentieth-century legal text leads to imperial tendencies—tendencies to transform all social, political, or cultural forms into fit subjects for juridically defined instrumentalist projects. Pierre Schlag, "Normative and Nowhere To Go," *Stanford Law Review* 43 (1990): 167.

and grandiloquent expression in the closing pages of Ronald Dworkin's *Law's Empire*:

> Law's attitude is constructive: it aims, in the interpretive spirit, to lay principle over practice to show the best route to a better future, keeping the right faith with the past. It is, finally, a fraternal attitude, an expression of how we are united in community thought divided in project, interest and conviction. That is, anyway, what law is for us: for the people we want to be and the community we want to have.[119]

In this moving Dworkinian vision, law functions as the great moving mover that sweeps everything within its path. The progressive energy is working itself so pure that it is on the verge of working itself totally pure, that is to say, totally empty.

This seems to have been the high point in confident expressions of the instrumentalist aesthetic. Since that time, a number of commentators generally known for their bold and confident instantiations of the instrumentalist aesthetic have given voice to some strikingly humbled visions. In a book on jurisprudence, Judge Richard Posner, for instance, wrote:

> [T]here is no such thing as "legal reasoning" . . . . [T]he justification (akin to scientific verification) of legal decisions—the demonstration that a decision is correct—often is impossible. . . . [L]arge changes in law often come about as a result of a non-rational process akin to conversion. . . . No bounds can be fixed a priori on what shall be allowed to count as an argument in law. . . . [T]here are no overarching concepts of justice that our legal system can seize upon to give direction to the enterprise. . . . [120]

In such humbled statements, one can begin to discern the unraveling of the instrumentalist aesthetic. Expressions of faith in progress seem increasingly troubled, conflicted, perhaps even self-refuting. For instance, Margaret Jane Radin wrote in the concluding pages of an essay:

---

119. Dworkin, *Law's Empire*, 413.

120. Richard Posner, *The Problems of Jurisprudence* (Cambridge: Harvard University Press, 1990), 459–60.

> [E]ven in the midst of struggling with the complexities of these
> nonideal choices, we should not neglect the kind of visionary
> reconstruction that we hope will render them unnecessary. Yet
> though we cannot do without these visions and these hopes, we
> mislead ourselves if we try to cut them loose from *the nonideal*
> *circumstances that gave them birth* in order to set them up as a priori
> arbiters of social progress. We can reconceive our hopes and *recon-*
> *struct our world, lacking a transformative social theory.*[121]

In this "progressive" vision, there is still some faith in the instrumental
aesthetic, but it is an attenuated, a subdued faith—lacking confident
belief in its own rhetorical force, aesthetic state, or political potential.
While there is quite clearly still faith here, there is also the recognition
that our starting point, the source/state of law, is defined by "nonideal
circumstances," that law's goal/potential requires "reconstruction"
and that law's path/force is an aporia, a lack of "transformative social
theory."

What remains at century's end is a faith in an instrumentalist
aesthetic whose hold is dissipating. The aesthetic itself remains, but,
as with the analytic aesthetic, it remains like a shell—a shell, conceptual debris, and faith. With mostly faith as support—a faith that is
increasingly without a referent and very obviously in desperate
search of one[122]—the instrumentalist legal thought of the mid- to late
twentieth century is becoming acquainted with its own postmodern
condition. Sometimes this encounter is desired. Mostly it is not. The
advent of the postmodern condition seems to occur despite the
wishes of those who would rather not have anything to do with it.
The unwelcome advent of this postmodern condition yields some
bizarre admixtures of aesthetic styles. For instance, Robin West, a
leading proponent of progressive legal thought, writes

> All of these arguments, the positions they imply . . . are richly
> suggestive of the possibility of a progressive constitutional faith.
> As paradoxical as it may sound, it seems to me that further devel-
> opment of this tradition is, at one and the same time, utterly

---

121. Margaret Jane Radin, "Lacking a Transformative Social Theory: A Response," *Stanford Law Review* 45 (1993): 409, 424 (emphasis added).

122. Hence, in this condition much instrumentalist thought turns to the advocacy
of highly ethereal abstractions such as "law as integrity" or "transformative action."

futile, deeply utopian, absolutely necessary, terribly risky, and one of the most imaginative, fecund, and important shared enterprises presently going on in the legal academy.[123]

One senses a transition to the postmodern condition here.

Rights in the Postmodern Condition

When conceptualizations of rights are shaped by both the analytic and the instrumentalist aesthetic, two very different images of rights emerge. These different images provide the grounds for two very different kinds of celebrations as well as critiques of rights.

The analytic aesthetic establishes a conception of right where the "owner of the right" is left alone to exercise "dominion and control." This conception of right enables a particular kind of celebration as well as a particular kind of critique of rights. The analytic conception of right is typically celebrated for its authorization and protection of individualism, autonomy, self-direction, and so on. These virtues, of course, can easily be turned into vices. Hence, the analytical conception of right can be seen as creating anomie, allowing antisocial behavior, and dissolving the bonds of community. Indeed, the kind of right produced through the analytic aesthetic is precisely the kind of right found so wanting in Marx's critique "On the Jewish Question."[124]

The instrumentalist aesthetic, however, produces a significantly different conception of rights with significantly different potential virtues and vices. In the instrumentalist aesthetic, the character of rights and their legal and political roles are instrumentalized. This means that the character of the right is cast in terms of its ability to achieve law's "mission"—whatever that mission might be (efficiency, justice, and so on). Thus, the specification of what it is the rights bearer can do or have is highly specified and is subject to many highly specified conditions (ex ante or ex post) that will disallow or restrain the exercise of the right. The prototypical instrumentalist conception of right can thus be celebrated and criticized in very different ways from the analytical conception of right. The instrumentalist conception of

---

123. Robin West, "Constitutional Skepticism," *Boston University Law Review* 72 (1992): 765, 797–98.

124. Karl Marx, "On the Jewish Question," in *Early Writings*, trans. R. Livingstone and G. Benton (New York: Vintage Books, 1975).

rights can prompt a kind of celebration insofar as it appears to "socialize" and "rationalize" the exercise of rights in terms of law's collectively specified "mission". At the same time, instrumentalist rights can easily be criticized as the capture and subordination of all sorts of human endeavors and activities to a regimen of bureaucratic legal control.

Now, for much of the twentieth century, much of American legal thought has been organized, consciously or not, in terms of an opposition between the analytic and the instrumentalist aesthetic. Indeed, much of American legal thought in the mid- to late twentieth century can be understood as a kind of arrested, back-and-forth argumentation between instantiations of the analytic and the instrumentalist aesthetic at various levels of jurisprudential depth and self-awareness.[125]

In the postmodern condition, this oppositionalism loses its dominant significance. Instead, in the postmodern condition, the two aesthetics combine in ways that can easily seem dissonant. Thus, in the postmodern condition, the same right can appear at once as a legal protectorate of individualism, autonomy, and self-direction as well as the instrumentalized vehicle for delineating very specifically what that individualism, autonomy, and self-direction can do or be. In the postmodern condition, we have an intensification of both the analytic aesthetic's subpartitioning of rights as well as the instrumentalist aesthetic's instrumentalization of rights. Rights, and law generally, thus become analytically and instrumentally hypertrophied. Consonant with the analytic aesthetic and its subpartitioning, law becomes subdivided into an increasingly large number of compartmentalized rights. Rights themselves become subdivided into an increasing number of elements or multivariable factors and specifications. The analytic aesthetic produces an extraordinarily acute particularism.

Consonant with the instrumentalist aesthetic and its drive for progress, law expands its jurisdiction, its reach, and its ambitions so that all aspects of social life become the resource, the occasion, or the goal of legalicized notions of "change," "reform," "progress," "progressive legal change," "transformative action," and so on.

---

125. For a description of some of these conflicts, see Schlag, "Normativity and the Politics of Form," 814–28 (and authorities cited therein).

Ironically, then, both the analytic and the instrumentalist aesthetic combine in the postmodern condition to produce an extraordinarily intense legalicization of all aspects of life. The instrumentalist aesthetic *extends* its visions of "change," "reform," "progress," "progressive legal change," or "transformative action" to all aspects of life. This is the imperial colonizing tendency of the instrumentalist aesthetic at work. Meanwhile, the analytic aesthetic ensures that the new energy sources "captured" through the instrumentalist aesthetic are transformed into domains, which are then rigorously and meticulously charted and *subpartitioned* through an intense and seemingly endless analytical subdivision. This is the "dominion and control" enabled by the analytic aesthetic.

The result of this combined action is the production of endless increasingly intricate legalicized mazes—mazes that are inscribed not just in the casebook or the legal treatise, but in the organization of lawyers' practices, the practices of their clients, and in the organization of daily life. Ironically, this intense legalicization is imposed on and proceeds in the name of the very best rhetorics of western civilization. It is promoted in the name of *order* and in the name of *progress* and their respective versions of

freedom
fairness
justice
human flourishing
self-realization
liberation
reason

and so on. It is in this way that the rhetoric of order and the rhetoric of progress combine to produce an extraordinarily intense and florid bureaucratic legalism.[126]

It is an irony of the postmodern condition that this extraordinary internal and external proliferation of rights, this hypertrophic legalism, is occurring at precisely the moment that the aesthetics that shape this bureaucratic legalism are unraveling. Indeed, what can be noticed in the postmodern condition is precisely what has been de-

---

126. Pierre Schlag, "Clerks in the Maze," *Michigan Law Review* 91 (1993): 2053.

scribed throughout this chapter. The aesthetics that shape the legal conceptualization of "law" and "rights" are increasingly turning out to be intellectually incredible. Not to be credited. Not warranting faith.[127]

These points, of course, are not easy to accept. In part, that is because, even though these aesthetics may be lacking in intellectual credibility, they nonetheless remain sedimented at various levels of depth throughout much of American (legal) culture. Moreover, the rhetoric of order (for those who think they have control and dominion) and the rhetoric of progress (for those who think they can direct the movement and the energy of law) are at once soothing and flattering. Because these rhetorics are sedimented and because they are so gratifying, it is difficult to escape their hold.

It is particularly difficult for American legal thinkers to escape the hold of these rhetorics, inasmuch as it is these rhetorics that enable legal thinkers to believe that they always already "know" something valuable—the order of the law or path it will travel. And indeed, both rhetorics are helpful to the successful and pleasing presentation of the professional self of the legal thinker: the rhetoric of order enables the legal thinker to present himself or herself as the guardian of order. The rhetoric of progress allows the legal thinker to present herself or himself as the champion of change.

These self-images may seem appealing. But they will seem appealing only so long as the rhetorics upon which they depend, order and progress, remain credible, retain some hold on what is perceived as real. That is precisely what is disappearing. Order and progress may retain some normative appeal and fulfill some normative desires, but increasingly, these normative rhetorics fail to track with what is experienced as real. Accordingly, the great (and small) normative gestures of American legal thought now often seem tinny, without resonance—a kind of self-indulgent fakery.

---

127. Now, given the continued hold of the rhetoric of order and the continued force of the rhetoric of progress, it would be easy to misunderstand. The point is not that there can never be order in or progress through law. The point, rather, is that the a priori belief that law already imposes order or is already progressive or is already subject to or receptive to the demands of order or progress is a construction of certain aesthetics—aesthetics which, when revealed, appear unbelievable.

Similarly, the point is not that "rights" are worthless. The point is that an a priori belief that rights are worthwhile (or worthless) depends upon certain aesthetic constructions of rights—aesthetic constructions that can no longer be credited.

The aesthetics that have shaped the concepts and artifacts of American legal thought are unraveling. What happens to these concepts and artifacts, what happens to rights when these aesthetics unravel? It is difficult to tell. That is because there is no distinct aesthetic that would allow us in any determinate way to make sense (or nonsense) of rights. Once the aesthetics begin to unravel, we encounter all the other (ironic or paradoxical) problematics of the postmodern condition—the referent of "rights" disappearing or dropping out altogether; the signifier "rights" invoking multiple, sometimes dissonant, identities; the identities of "rights" performing simultaneously in many different modalities: representational, symbolic, causal, logical, rhetorical, affective, material, metaphysical, mythical, and so on; the shifts in perspectives and identities in observer and observed; the inability to stabilize the sign—in short, all the problematics articulated at the beginning of this chapter that have been elided in American legal thought through the operation of the analytic and the instrumental aesthetic.[128]

---

128. For a partial account of this clash among various versions of the analytic and the instrumental aesthetic, see Schlag, "Normativity and the Politics of Form," 814–28.

Contributors

Hadley Arkes is Edward Ney Professor of American Institutions at Amherst College.

William E. Cain is Mary Jewett Gaiser Professor of English at Wellesley College.

Thomas L. Haskell is Samuel McCann Professor of History at Rice University.

Morton J. Horwitz is Charles Warren Professor of the History of American Law at Harvard Law School.

Thomas R. Kearns is William Hastie Professor of Philosophy and Professor of Law, Jurisprudence, and Social Thought at Amherst College.

Annabel Patterson is Karl Young Professor of English at Yale University.

Michael J. Perry is Howard Trienens Professor of Law at Northwestern University.

Austin Sarat is William Nelson Cromwell Professor of Jurisprudence and Political Science and Professor of Law, Jurisprudence, and Social Thought at Amherst College.

Pierre Schlag is Professor of Law at the University of Colorado.

Jeremy Waldron is Professor of Law and Philosophy at the University of California, Berkeley.

Index

Experiential-determinist analysis, 22–23

Fairness, and treason trials, 7, 22–23
Fallibilism, 150, 152
Federalists, 191
Fetter, Frank, 123
Feudal system, 49, 50
Filmer, Robert, 108
Finnis, John, 245n.101
First Amendment: and academic freedom, 115, 126, 128, 160; and the difference between natural law and positive law, 191; and treason trials, 21–22, 34, 36–37
Fish, Stanley, 137–38, 141, 145, 151, 153–54, 157–58, 160–64
Fiss, Owen, 291
Flag-burning statutes, 160
Foner, Eric, 54
Foucault, Michel: and academic freedom, 120, 132, 162, 163n.82; power/knowledge in, 120, 132, 163n.82
Founding Fathers, 67, 74, 76, 80–81, 119, 186–87
Fourteenth Amendment: and civil rights, 178–80, 182, 185, 200; and the relation of rights to needs, 87–88; and treason trials, 18, 20–22, 36–37
Foxe, John, 31–32
Franklin, John Hope, 55–56
Fraser's, 72
Frederick Douglass's Monthly, 82
"Free soil" doctrine, 62, 64–66
Free-willed subject, 279–81
French Revolution, 47, 49, 50
Freud, Sigmund, 171
Friedman, Lawrence, 2n.13
Fuller, Lon, 46
Furner, Mary, 114

Gabel, Peter, 290, 294n.105
Garrison, William Lloyd, 63, 66–68, 70, 84

Gauthier, David, 246–48
Geertz, Clifford, 145
Gender, and disciplinary communities, 165
Genealogy of Morals, The (Nietzsche), 135
Gentile, Giovanni, 171
Gettysburg Address, 83–85
Gilman, Daniel C., 113–15, 116
Ginzburg, Carlo, 174
Glendon, Mary Ann, 88–89, 97–98, 101n.38
Glorious Revolution, 47–48
God, 27–28, 42–43, 89, 101, 176, 216–35, 261–62
Gold standard, 121
Goodell, William, 84
Good Samaritan, parable of, 221–22
Gospel: of John, 216–17; of Luke, 221–22; of Matthew, 216, 221n.40, 222–24, 254
Grammar, 106
Grant, Robert, 239
Gray, John Chipman, 280
Great Chain of Being (Lovejoy), 142
Greeley, Horace, 58–61, 66
Grey, Jane, 25–26
Griffin, James, 241

Habermas, Jürgen, 135, 146, 245n.101, 254–55, 288
Haiti, 56, 83
Hamilton, Thomas, 71
Harlan, John, 178–79
Hart, H. L. A., 46
Harvard University, 121, 124, 137
Haskell, Thomas L., 3–5, 9–10, 113–76
Heimat (film), 176
Henkin, Louis, 2–3
Henrician Treason Act, 28–29
Henry, Patrick, 75
Henry VIII (king), 28–29
Hermeneutics, 161
Heschel, Abraham, 211, 213n.19, 230–31